P9-DSW-499

Japan's Political Revolution under MacArthur

A Participant's Account

by

Justin Williams, Sr.

The University of Georgia Press
Athens

Copyright © 1979 by the University of Georgia Press
Athens 30602
All rights reserved
Published in Japan by University of Tokyo Press
UTP Number 3021–27121–5149
Set in 10 on 12 point Mergenthaler Times Roman type
Printed in the United States of America

Library of Congress Cataloging in Publication Data

Williams, Justin.
  Japan's political revolution under MacArthur.
  Bibliography.
  Includes index.
    1. Japan—Politics and government—1945– 2. Govern-
ment missions, American—Japan—History. 3. Japan
—History—Allied occupation, 1945–1952. I. Title.
JQ1626 1945.W54   940.53′144   78–5592
        ISBN 0–8203–0452–2

The publication of this book was supported in part by a
subsidy from the Japan Foundation. The University of
Georgia Press gratefully acknowledges this assistance.

To My Wife

Contents

Illustrations

Abbreviations

AFPAC, Armed Forces Pacific
ATIS, Allied Translator and Interpreter Section
CG, Commanding General
CIE, Civil Information and Education Section
CIS, Civil Intelligence Section
CLO, Central Liaison Office
CTS, Civil Transportation Section
DA, Department of the Army
DAC, Department of the Army Civilian
ESS, Economic and Scientific Section
FEAC, Far Eastern Advisory Commission
FEC, Far Eastern Commission
GHQ, Headquarters of SCAP and the Far East Command
JCS, Joint Chiefs of Staff
JG, Japanese Government
MG, Military Government
NPSL, National Public Service Law
NSC, National Security Council
POLAD, Political Adviser
PPD, Parliamentary and Political Division
SCAP, Supreme Commander for the Allied Powers,
    as a person or an organization
SCAPIN, SCAP instruction to the Japanese government
SWNCC, State-War-Navy Coordinating Committee

Preface

As a staff member of GHQ, SCAP throughout the occupation of Japan, I had in mind at the outset to write the story of the political side of the daring and ambitious experiment in social engineering. Employing the historian's techniques, I jotted down my impressions of passing events while accumulating a comprehensive file of official documents and articles from newspapers and periodicals.

Following the occupation, I spent ten months as international affairs adviser on the staff of Gen. Mark Clark, Commander-in-Chief, Far East Command, in Tokyo. Then for seven years I served as chief of the Korea Division, International Cooperation Administration, Department of State, in Washington, after which I completed a two-year tour in Paris as chief of ICA's Interregional Technical Cooperation Administration. While serving as assistant to the president, University of Maryland, for five years beginning in 1962, I was able to give some thought to the occupation story. Since scholarly interest at that time centered pretty largely in the origin of Japan's democratic constitution, I sought to clear up some of the confusion surrounding that subject in an article I contributed to the *American Political Science Review* (1965). I did another article for the *American Historical Review* (1968) to show that the neglected second half of the occupation was no less important than the first. I left the University of Maryland to participate as an international affairs specialist in a three-year global research project conducted by a Department of the Army "think tank." After retiring in 1971, I began writing this book.

To check my interpretation of occupation policy on political reform, I consulted freely with New York attorney Charles L. Kades and the late Maj. Gen. Courtney Whitney, my superiors in GHQ's Government Section. Information on specific items was obtained from former Government Section colleagues Frank Rizzo, Henry E. Robison, Alfred C. Oppler, Helen Loeb, and Maynard Shirven; from Col. Laurence E. Bunker, MacArthur's aide; and from Warren Hunsberger, former State Department official. Sidelights on certain aspects of the occupation were provided by Japanese politicians Miki Takeo, Kiuchi Shiro, and Chiba Saburo, former World Court Justice Tanaka Kotaro, former Japanese Supreme Court Justice Irie Toshio, retired House of Representatives Secretary General Oike Makoto, former Personnel Authority President

Sato Tatsuo, former Waseda University Professor Hasegawa Koichi, and Teramitsu Tadashi, formerly of the House of Peers secretariat. Professor Theodore McNelly of the University of Maryland, a keen student of the occupation, has liberally assisted me in many ways. Helpful to me in locating and duplicating many recently declassified radiograms between the Department of the Army and SCAP in the years 1948–1950 were Director Robert H. Alexander and his administrative assistant, Edward J. Boone, Jr., of the MacArthur Memorial Library in Norfolk, Virginia.

It was as a student and teacher of history and economics that I became an official of the occupation. I taught courses in American history and economics at the University of Wisconsin at River Falls from 1928 to 1942, the last twelve years as professor and head of the department of social science. The intellectual climate there was all that could be desired, and tenure in a progressive university system, particularly during the Great Depression, was not something to be despised. I took leave in 1942 to accept a commission as 1st lieutenant in the Army Air Corps.

With certificates of graduation from the Army's School of Military Government at the University of Virginia (1944) and the Civil Affairs Training School at Yale (1945), I was assigned to MacArthur's headquarters in Manila just as the Pacific War ended and the occupation of Japan began. Having to choose after two years in Tokyo between returning to teaching and continuing as an occupation official, I opted for the latter; the taste of power, influence, and status in a policymaking position rendered teaching a tame and less attractive substitute.

As an historian, I judged MacArthur by his performance in Japan, which I was in a position to appraise. If I had not witnessed his skillful reorientation of Japan's political system and his adroitness in preserving it from unwary cold war jockeying in Washington, I would not have believed that any living American, least of all a military man, could have successfully carried off such a next to impossible undertaking. Whatever his faults may have been, he demonstrated that he was a statesman of parts, an authentic liberal in many respects, and a sincere humanitarian who had the courage of his convictions.

More than a quarter century after Japan regained independence, American and Japanese scholars have done little research on how the democratization policy was framed in Washington and executed in Japan. While not ignoring the question of policy formulation in Washington, this book concentrates on policy implementation in Tokyo.

1

SCAP, Postwar Japan, and Occupation Policy

In mid-September 1945, after a brief stay in Manila, some 150 Military Government Section specialists attached to Gen. Douglas MacArthur's headquarters arrived in Tokyo. Having spent the previous fifteen months in the United States studying Japan and the Japanese language, they were still unprepared for what they initially observed. They were struck by the widespread destruction wrought by American B–29s, the eagerness of the Japanese to cooperate with the occupation forces, the range and variety of moves already taken by the United States military to effect the terms of surrender, General MacArthur's popularity with the Japanese masses, and the harshness of American occupation policy.

Japan was quite obviously in a state of complete physical exhaustion. Her once great industrial and commercial centers were little more than charred heaps of rubble. Many of her unemployed millions were living in shacks of plywood and corrugated iron; industrial raw materials and essential food supplies from foreign territories were cut off; the fishing fleets were badly crippled; and the stocks of fertilizer for domestic farming were woefully low. From every angle the outlook for the people was grim.

Nevertheless the Japanese viewed their sea of troubles philosophically. Vastly relieved that the war was over, and obedient to the emperor's command, they cheerfully cooperated with their government in carrying out the directives of the conquerors, offering no resistance whatever. If they disliked the galling punishment and sweeping reforms prescribed for them in Washington, they never showed it. During the first months of the occupation they viewed with complete equanimity the torrent of GHQ orders calling for a host of things, including quick demobilization of Japan's military forces, total destruction of her war equipment, complete closure of her war factories, arraignment of Gen. Tojo Hideki and other wartime leaders, arrest and trial of hundreds of war criminals, institution of a far-reaching purge in all walks of Japanese life, abolition of secret societies and the thought-control police, removal of all restrictions on civil liberties, release of Japanese political prisoners, the outlawing of a state-supported Shinto religion, the large-scale shake-up of the Japanese school system, free discussion of the emperor system, cleanup of the Japanese press, breakup of the large industrial and banking combinations, sale of large landholdings to Japanese peasants, legalization of labor unions and encouragement of collective bargaining, enfranchisement of women, liberalization of the election law, adoption of a democratic constitution, and a general election of members to the lower house of the Diet (Parliament). Indeed, as *Time* magazine noted in its 17 September 1945 issue, the Japanese had "quit as unanimously as they had fought."

In the beginning it was not easy for members of General MacArthur's staff to grasp what was taking place in occupied Japan. To understand the situation, they had, at the very least, to familiarize themselves with the organization and modus operandi of GHQ, the postwar Japanese psyche, and American occupation policy.

General MacArthur was appointed Supreme Commander for the Allied Powers (SCAP) on 15 August 1945. Initially his staff in Japan consisted of an advance echelon of General Headquarters, United States Army Forces, Pacific (GHQ, AFPAC), which included a contingent of seven Military Government Section officers. On 5 August a Military Government Section had been set up in Manila as a special staff section of GHQ, AFPAC to handle military government and civil affairs matters under invasion conditions. At that time, hundreds of experts in administration, law, finance, industry, commerce, public health, public safety, agriculture, labor, education, price control, and other fields—all holding certificates of graduation from the School of Military Government at the University of Virginia and from one of six Civil Affairs Training Schools at Yale, Harvard, Northwestern, Chicago, Michigan, and Stanford Universities—were stationed at the Civil Affairs Staging Area, Presidio of Monterey, California, awaiting orders for Far East duty. Despite the fact that Japan's surrender on 14 August automatically canceled "Olympic," the secret code name for the projected American invasion of Kyushu in November, during the week of 20 August, 297 of these officers, roughly a tenth of those trained for service in the Pacific theater, were rushed by air, under War Department orders, from California to Manila, for assignment. Brig. Gen. William E. Crist, GHQ, AFPAC's newly appointed Military Government Section chief, sent half of them to Sixth Army, Eighth Army, and XXIV Corps and retained half for his own staff.[1] Those of us who went to Tokyo as members of the Military Government Section assumed that General MacArthur would from the outset follow Washington's 29 August injunction to exercise his authority, to the extent feasible, through existing Japanese governmental machinery.[2] This assumption was not quite correct. The occupation formally began on V-J Day, 2 September, when the surrender terms were signed aboard the U.S.S. *Missouri*. Gen-

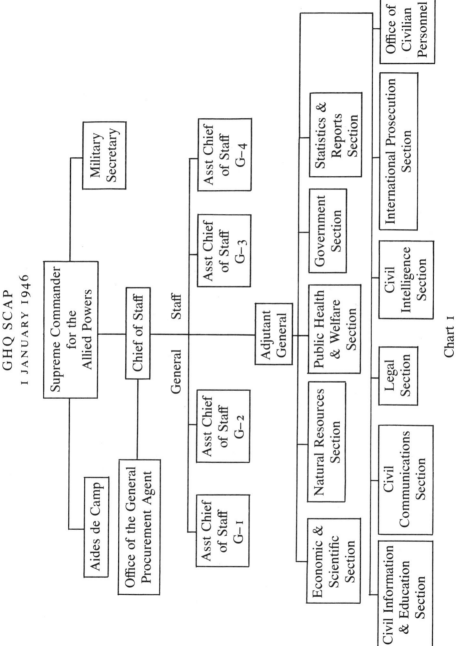

GHQ SCAP
1 JANUARY 1946

Supreme Commander for the Allied Powers

Aides de Camp

Military Secretary

Chief of Staff

Office of the General Procurement Agent

General Staff

Asst Chief of Staff G–1

Asst Chief of Staff G–2

Asst Chief of Staff G–3

Asst Chief of Staff G–4

Adjutant General

Economic & Scientific Section

Natural Resources Section

Public Health & Welfare Section

Government Section

Statistics & Reports Section

Civil Information & Education Section

Civil Communications Section

Legal Section

Civil Intelligence Section

International Prosecution Section

Office of Civilian Personnel

Chart 1

GHQ AFPAC
JANUARY 1946

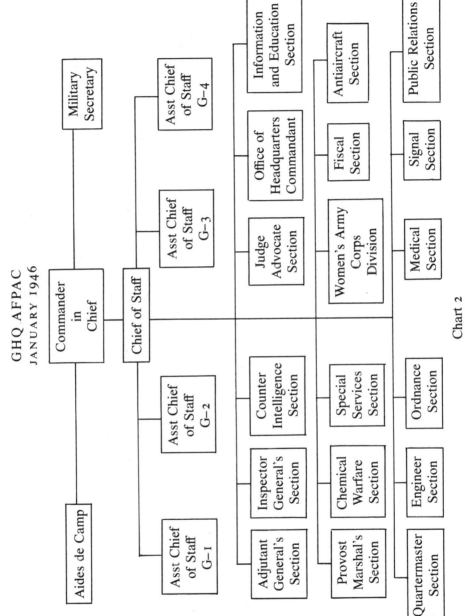

Chart 2

eral MacArthur's decision to use the Japanese government, however, was not made until 3 September. The day before, he definitely had planned to establish a military government, a fact attested to by the three proclamations to which he affixed his signature. Proclamation No. 1 placed Japan under military government, No. 2 fixed penalties for Japanese crimes and offenses against the occupation, and No. 3 made military currency legal tender in Japan. The proclamations were to have been posted by units of the Sixth and Eighth Armies as they took up positions in Japan.[3]

Getting wind of what was brewing, Foreign Minister Shigemitsu Mamoru rushed to Yokohama on the morning of 3 September for an emergency conference with General MacArthur and his chief of staff, Lt. Gen. Richard K. Sutherland. Mr. Shigemitsu warned the Supreme Commander to "think twice before instituting military government," since "it may well be that utter confusion will result, the responsibility for which will not be that of the Japanese Government."[4] MacArthur reversed himself then and there; until the Foreign Minister called, he had no way of knowing that the Japanese authorities were fully prepared and eager to do his bidding. Thenceforth in matters of occupation policy necessary directives were issued by GHQ, SCAP instead of by GHQ, AFPAC, thus charging the Japanese government with responsibility for executing occupation orders without compulsion. This highly significant move required replacement of the Military Government Section by a group of coordinate special staff sections—ultimately fourteen—constituting GHQ, SCAP, organized along functional lines to implement the nonmilitary aspects of the occupation. On 2 October 1945, GHQ, SCAP officially created eight of these special staff sections, the most important of which were Economic & Scientific (ESS), Civil Information & Education (CIE), and Government, all staffed at first mostly by Military Government Section personnel. The residue of the Military Government Section—eighteen officers, of whom I was one—formed GHQ, SCAP's Government Section, under General Crist. Charts 1 and 2 show the organization of GHQ, SCAP and GHQ, AFPAC as of 1 January 1946. AFPAC was later changed to FEC (Far East Command). As Commander-in-Chief of AFPAC, MacArthur had responsibility for American military affairs in the western area of the Pacific Ocean; as SCAP, his authority was limited to the four main islands of Japan. One mission of AFPAC was to support the occupation conducted by SCAP. MacArthur's chief of staff acted for both GHQ, AFPAC and GHQ, SCAP. So much for organization.

Learning how GHQ, SCAP operated was a more difficult task. There were no manuals to consult, no precedents to follow. Each staff section hammered out its own procedures for working with its counterpart in the

Japanese government. How the different sections made out in their relations with the Japanese offices was not reported in any official document; it was a matter for individual officers to pick up as best they could. Thanks to my roommate, Capt. Everett Sherbourne, a New Jersey banker, I got some glimpses of SCAP's ESS in action. In early October, with his section chief, Col. Raymond C. Kramer, a former New York department store executive, Sherbourne attended a dinner given by the governor of the Bank of Japan. The purpose of the event, according to Sherbourne, was to discuss reopening that powerful institution. When Colonel Kramer got around to asking for certain documents kept in one of the bank vaults, his host told him that that particular vault could not be opened until the next day, because the watchman had gone home with the keys. Refusing to believe that the only set of keys to the vault was entrusted overnight with a watchman who might be killed or kidnapped, Colonel Kramer, in Sherbourne's words, snapped: "Here I have inconvenienced myself to facilitate the early opening of your bank, and you have not shown the proper degree of cooperation. The bank will remain closed for some time to come, and when it is reopened it will be at my convenience, not yours. Goodnight."

Then there was the closing of the head offices in Japan of twenty-nine banks and other institutions with colonial functions. On 2 October, Sherbourne said, pursuant to a 30 September directive, our Military Police, without notifying the officials and employees in advance, descended on the banks and ordered their personnel to scram, allowing no time for them to clear their desks. The crowds of depositors that soon gathered around the banks were dispersed, and the sidewalks in front of the buildings were placed off-limits to Japanese pedestrians.

Another slant on ESS was furnished at this early stage by Mr. Charles F. Thomas, who had been prewar manager of National City Bank's Tokyo office. I entered his office just as Sherbourne, gesticulating vigorously, was saying: "Why, Mr. Thomas, we can't allow the Japanese financial structure to crumble without turning a hand. With low reserves, extensive loans, and many in default, Japan's banks are facing a crisis. To pay for the industrial losses with taxes, the national debt will have to be doubled, which means compensating the zaibatsu for what our B–29s smashed." To which Mr. Thomas calmly replied: "What you say is perfectly true, but your mispremise is that we give a damn what happens to Japanese banks." He went on to say that since the government had guaranteed deposits, there would be no banking crisis. Increasing the national debt to meet government obligations would be offset by a thirty percent capital levy then under consideration.

On one other occasion I came in contact with Mr. Thomas. As a Government Section administrative officer, I had the task of turning over to the appropriate GHQ agency a small wooden box, which had been addressed to "Military Government Section." In the box were 414 envelopes each containing about ¥100 confiscated from Japanese prisoners of war (POWs) on Wake Island. The GHQ fiscal director refused to take the box, because he could not enter Japanese currency in his books. The property custodian begged off, because he was not custodian of that kind of property. Sherbourne said that confiscated money was outside the jurisdiction of ESS's Public Finance Division. Mr. Thomas acknowledged that although he had written the policy for confiscating currency from POWs, it was not up to him to execute that policy. At that point, I plunked the box down hard on the desk of a former Military Government Section associate, Lt. Jim Smith of the Foreign Exchange Division, and insisted that he take it off my hands. He did.

Military Government Section acquaintances also provided some notion of how CIE was approaching educational reform. Navy Lt. Robert King Hall, with whom I had worked on research and planning at Presidio of Monterey, stopped by my room in the Nippon Yusen Kaisha Building (NYK) one evening to discuss a draft education directive he had prepared. A few days later I was reminded of his visit by this news item, which appeared in the 23 October 1945 *New York Herald Tribune*: "General Douglas MacArthur banned today the dissemination of militaristic and ultranationalistic ideologies, ordered discontinuance of all military education and drills, established a screening system for all teachers and officials, provided for the reinstatement of ousted liberal professors, and demanded that all textbooks be revised."

Before he transferred from the Higher Education Branch to the Religions Division of CIE and later wrote the SCAP directive abolishing state-supported Shinto, Navy Lt. W. Kenneth Bunce, who had been my Military Government Section branch chief in Manila, asked me to become chief of his curriculum unit. I would have accepted the offer had not Lt. Col. Henry E. Robison, Government Section executive officer, arranged with Col. Charles L. Kades, Public Administration Branch chief, for my transfer to the latter's policy-making unit.

In the first months of the occupation Government Section was weak and ineffective. This was admirably demonstrated by the treatment accorded a routine report I had prepared for inclusion in SCAP's daily cable to Washington. The report covered a conference between Comdr. Guy Swope and Capt. Frank Rizzo and a group of Diet members representing Tokyo, Osaka, Kyoto, and Gumma-ken. The parliamentarians had requested

SCAP authorization to advocate reform of Japan's political institutions. My report stated that Swope and Rizzo gave assurance that Government Section interposed no objection to their political reform efforts provided no SCAP directives were violated. This wording was approved by Colonel Kades and Lieutenant Colonel Robison. But General Crist, objecting to the inference that Government Section had given a green light to reform-minded politicians, had the report watered down. Robison's disgust with the section chief was plainly visible in his facial expression.

An October conference of working level officials, called by the Office of the Political Adviser (POLAD), defined the political responsibilities of certain SCAP staff sections. POLAD was represented by John K. Emmerson, Government Section by Swope and Rizzo, Civil Intelligence Section (CIS) by Dr. E. Herbert Norman, Capt. J. J. Ripley, Jr., and Lt. D. Pontius, and CIE by Capt. Arthur Behrstock. They agreed that it was the function of CIE to allot radio time to the different Japanese political factions; of CIS to compile and disseminate information about particular Japanese persons and organizations; of Government Section to keep abreast of Japanese legislation; and of POLAD to make studies of Japanese political movements, parties, actions, and opinions to determine whether they were in line with occupation objectives. Swope's memorandum on the conference contained nothing worth reporting to Washington, but it threw light on the occupation role POLAD intended to play. POLAD was in an anomalous position, however, in that it was not subject to SCAP orders. The matter was resolved a few months later by converting POLAD to SCAP's Diplomatic Section, with its responsibility limited to handling relations between foreign missions in Tokyo and the Japanese government. Henceforth it communicated officially with the State Department only through military channels, thus preserving the vital principle of unity of command.

On transferring to Kades's Public Administration Branch in December, I became involved immediately in occupation policy. Without any preliminaries whatever, I was assigned the task of conducting a five-month study that would be the basis for directing the Japanese government—in the words of Washington's Initial Post-Surrender Policy paper—to abrogate all laws and regulations that established discrimination on grounds of race, nationality, creed, or political opinion. This was the procedure by which Japan's political reformation was to be effected. After a week of interviews with Tokyo Imperial University professors and practicing Japanese lawyers, I learned only that a Mr. Paul de Gyarmathy of Kobe was probably the best authority in the country on most aspects of discrimination. Consequently I went to Kobe on 26 December to interview him.

Of Hungarian descent, Mr. Gyarmathy had resided in Japan for twenty-five years as a salesman of European-made machinery. In his possession was a 100-page booklet in galley form titled "Appeal to the Emperor," which was soon to be printed in Tokyo for distribution to appropriate SCAP staff sections. It contained detailed criticism of the Japanese governmental system and offered suggestions for revising the Imperial Constitution. Regarding my mission, he was certain that all Westerners were discriminated against and that he in particular had suffered innumerable abuses by Japanese officials; but offhand he was unable to cite any law or regulation that differentiated between foreign nationals and Japanese citizens. Since I had asked him especially about discrimination against the Eta (social outcasts), the Ainu (a small race of aborigines in Hokkaido), and Japanese women, he introduced me to an Inns of Court-trained Japanese lawyer, a Mr. Usami, for enlightenment on these subjects. I listened patiently to Mr. Usami's discourse on prostitution and the geisha institution.

Licensed prostitution, he said, would be very difficult to eliminate. It was a prime source of revenue for local governments, and its abolition would be strongly opposed by all government officials and most taxpayers, not to mention those who made their living by the trade. Two years ago a mother with five children asked him and his wife to take one of them, fourteen-year-old Sadako, as a servant girl. They took her into their home. She was efficient, loyal, and upright. For two years her allowance was fifteen yen a month.

Then the Americans came. He did not know exactly how Americans regarded their women, but he knew pretty well "how they regard ours." Many night clubs opened downtown. Girls were in great demand. By working fairly hard, each one brought in close to ¥1,000 daily for her manager. The usual charge was ¥100 per hour. Recently Sadako asked for her release; she had been offered ¥3,000 a week at the Starlight Club. She took it.

Mr. Usami switched to the subject of geisha. I had heard much about geisha, or singing girls, at Yale, but not from a Japanese lawyer who claimed his services were being sought by the emperor, as a prospective war criminal, and by others, including General Tojo. Trained from age six to dance, play musical instruments, sing, and arrange flowers, a geisha, he said, was not permitted to become an entertainer until she was seventeen or eighteen. When she did become an entertainer, she might have a wealthy patron who reserved her for himself only. When she outgrew her usefulness, she might operate her own house of entertainment, purchased for her by her patron. The life of the geisha was usually a happy one. The geisha was unhappy when the Salvation Army stepped in and secured her release from her contract.

Girls became obligated to owners of geisha houses in different ways. Sometimes a young girl was sold to a "guardian," but it was more common for her to become security for a loan made to her father. The average loan was about ¥3,000. When a girl saw fit to rebel against what some regarded as a form of slavery, the court always held in her favor. Such cases were rare.

Two weeks later (12 January 1946) Mr. Gyarmathy wrote to say that after consulting a cross section of Kobe businessmen, he was unable to cite specific instances of discrimination. Discrimination against him, he said, had been in the form of "a great number of petty acts and pinpricks which one could hardly adduce as evidence."

On the basis of the Kobe experience, it became clear that my study of discrimination could be completed in much less time than the five months allotted. Mercifully this approach to Japan's political reorientation was dropped at the beginning of February 1946, when all essential elements of political reform were worked into the model constitution that Government Section prepared for the guidance of the Shidehara Cabinet.

The Kobe trip gave me an opportunity to touch base with Military Government (MG) companies at Kobe, Osaka, Kyoto, and Nagoya. Although Eighth Army had jurisdiction over the forty-six prefectural and eight regional MG teams in Japan, Brig. Gen. Courtney Whitney, General Crist's successor as chief of Government Section, had expressed an interest in them. For this reason, Lieutenant Colonel Robison asked me to make a spot check on the part they were playing in Japan's democratization. The five MG team commanders interviewed had four gripes: lack of liaison between the MG companies and SCAP; absence of any clearly defined functions of MG units; slowness of SCAP directives in reaching them; and denial of authority to MG teams to compel local compliance with SCAP directives.

As a Government Section monitor of the 10 April 1946 general election for members of the House of Representatives, I learned still more about the way the occupation was conducted. This first election since 1942 was to test Japan's election law, revised in December 1945 to provide for woman suffrage, a lower voting age, larger election districts, and increased plural voting; to ascertain the effect of the January purge of many prominent politicians; and, above all, to gauge popular reaction to the Japanese government's project for revising the Imperial Constitution along lines laid down in the Government Section draft. I briefed four MG teams on how to oversee the election campaign and how to check the polls. Working closely with MG officers in northern Honshu on the day of the election, I backed up the effort of the Japanese regional governor to have 400 Yamagata-shi electors, whose names had been inadvertently omitted, added to the lists in time to vote. That evening at one of Sendai-shi's elementary schools, I observed 100 persons tediously but accurately counting 21,000 ballots. Of the small number of irregular ballots, some were left blank, some were cast for MacArthur and Tojo, and some carried such slogans as "Down with Communism," "Increase the rice ration," and "All candidates are no good."

While powerful Japanese ultranationalists mingled and maneuvered freely with our highest officers and diplomats, we company grade officers of GHQ, SCAP were on the lookout for opportunities to meet ordinary Japanese. After nearly a month of frustration, I accepted an invitation extended by Captain Sherbourne to accompany him on a visit to an important Japanese military installation. We were received at the dilapidated Peers School, the repository for the financial records of the Japanese General Staff, by Lt. Gen. Morita Chikazo and Brig. Gen. Endo Takekatsu. Through an interpreter we discussed the bombing of Tokyo, good restaurants, and our desire to meet some Japanese other than the waiters, maids, and common laborers at our billet. No business was brought up, but we gladly accepted their invitation to call again at the Peers School and to have dinner with them in Shimbashi. How our solicitous hosts expected to profit from their association with us, we could only guess, but we derived great pleasure from mixing with them.

On our second visit to the Peers School we met, in addition to the two generals previously mentioned, Lt. Col. Kumagai Takuji, Capt. Baba Masaji, and Lt. Kashiwaki Yusuke. A Japanese photographer snapped pictures of us with some Japanese girls who had been attracted to the area by our 1st Cavalry guards. Then we were served, in this order, beer, Lipton's tea, ginger ale, and Japanese green tea. We gave each officer a package of cigarettes, some chewing gum, and two bars of tropical chocolate. Lieutenant Kashiwaki presented to each of us a samurai sword fashioned in 1944 by "Yasuyoshi." We noted that General Endo was a handsome man in his late forties with a well-modulated voice, not unlike Charles Boyer's. Though not entirely at ease, he laughed jovially with us. We speculated afterward about how he might have behaved toward us had we been his prisoners in Manila. To the forthcoming dinner he asked Sherbourne to bring with him a certain ESS civilian employee who was familiar with Japanese Army finances. Realizing that our brief fling with the Japanese military had about run its course, we wanted to hold on only until after the Shimbashi dinner.

Twenty-eight-year-old Lieutenant Kashiwaki came for us at the NYK Building promptly at 5:00 P.M. on 21 October. Sherbourne being late, I had a good chat with the young officer. He preferred Dai Nippon beer and Manchurian cigarettes to Hamm's beer and American cigarettes. Having lived the first half of his life in New York, where his father managed a branch of the Yokohama Specie Bank, he spoke excellent English. He was anxious to have United States magazines, even old ones. When he volunteered that playing cards were much in demand by Japanese officers who had taken up bridge, I gave him the single pack I had brought from California. He mentioned a number of acts of destruction and pillaging by our troops soon after the occupation began, and he was bitter over the loss of family heirlooms which, he said, were forcibly taken from his home at Hayama by an American lieutenant colonel and four other officers of lesser rank. His monthly pay of eighty-five yen was equal to the cost of three packages of American cigarettes.

When Sherbourne arrived, we were driven to Hanaka-san's tearoom in the devastated and unlighted Shimbashi district. There we were joined by General Endo, Lieutenant Colonel Kumagai, and three other officers. Of the two geisha present, one was reputed to be an accomplished dancer, the other, Koume-san, a famous singer, known as Japan's "female Frank Sinatra." We were treated to "The Sakura" (cherry blossom dance) and to "Minami No Funa Uta" (Sailors' Song of the South Sea). The meal was an interesting part of our first exposure to a real *ryoriya*, the word we learned at Yale for restaurant. We were served pork chops, several kinds of fish (including raw octopus), fillets of uncooked chicken, sukiyaki, and rice, along with sake (rice wine), beer, and Japanese whisky. Sharply at 10:00 P.M. Hanaka-san indicated that the party had lasted long enough, and we were soon back at the NYK Building. In parting Lieutenant Kashiwaki reminded Sherbourne that someone in ESS was "raising hell" about certain financial records that had been missing since the Tokyo bombings six months earlier. Thus ended our first fraternization venture. We saw no more of the Japanese military. But as luck would have it, we soon established another and more appropriate relationship.

It happened this way. Cruising through Ueno Park one afternoon in an Army weapons carrier, Sherbourne and I became hopelessly lost. When I braked the vehicle to ask two Japanese girls of high school age, in my most polished Yale Japanese, for directions to Marunouchi, they were out of sight in a flash. At that instant a slender Japanese of around forty, Mr.

Tomura Heijiro, a commercial artist, asked politely in perfect English what was the trouble. After I explained, he provided the necessary directions and then asked us to have tea at his nearby home the next afternoon. We went, bearing a modest amount of PX items and food rations, which were gladly accepted after a perfunctory refusal by Tomura-san and his wife, Kimiko, to take gifts from strangers. We stayed for supper. On subsequent visits they introduced us to a few of their neighbors, who were professional people and artisans. This association gave a few Japanese an inkling of what we Americans were up to, and gave us insights into Japanese culture beyond those discussed by our Yale lecturers and by Ruth Benedict in her 1946 masterpiece of cultural anthropology.[5]

In December 1945 Tomura-san arranged for me to have dinner at the modest home of Mr. Akiyama Tokuzo, Paris-trained chef to Emperor Hirohito. Besides Tomura, the Japanese guests were his neighbor, Mr. Oishi Miyoshi, and Mr. Shishikui Seiichi, secretary to the Minister of the Imperial Household. The main course was wild goose, cooked by Mr. Akiyama. Of course, there was the ever-filled sake cup. Mr. Akiyama's daughter gave a demonstration of the tea ceremony. Every time mention was made of his deceased first wife, Mr. Akiyama, fifty-seven, broke down and cried profusely. Mrs. Akiyama, his second wife of eight years, did not seem to be moved by talk of her deceased first husband. Mr. Akiyama proudly displayed an autographed picture of Colonel Kramer, who had just resigned as chief of ESS. The only reference to politics was made by myself. Having in mind a recent *New York Times* blast at MacArthur for permitting Prince Konoye Fumimaro, prewar prime minister, to undertake a project for revising the Imperial Constitution, I asked if they considered Prince Konoye a militant ultranationalist. Their reply was an emphatic yes, and Mr. Shishikui added that a lot of field-grade officers as well should be rounded up and convicted. There was bitterness toward the war crowd, both military and civilian, but not toward the emperor, who had been "misled." Just after 10 P.M. I was driven to the Yuraku Building (billet for company-grade officers from November 1945) in Mr. Shishikui's black Packard, better aware of the reaction of some Japanese to current developments.

Through Tomura-san I also became acquainted with the headmaster of a boys reform school near Tokyo. At the start of the occupation he gave his Leica camera to the first American soldier he encountered, "out of gratitude for not having been shot." He would just as gladly have given him his home, he added.

Little did I suspect that a routine visit to the home of the Tomuras in the spring of 1946 would open my eyes to unsuspected facets of Japanese society, the operations of our Counter Intelligence personnel, and the foreign press corps. Present at the Tomuras that evening were their friends, Mr. and Mrs. Oishi, whom I had met before. The general atmosphere was depressing. Mr. Oishi, a frail man of about fifty-five, could not conceal behind his usual buoyant mien a flushed and badly swollen face. When I asked what had happened, the two wives began to cry, and Mr. Oishi hung his head. But Tomura-san, the only one who spoke English, said simply that Mr. Oishi had been tortured for seven hours that day by agents of our Counter Intelligence Corps. As Mr. Oishi told it, he was ordered by two agents, one a nisei, to tell what he knew about Ando Akira, transportation magnate, night-club operator, and friend of high-ranking occupation officials, who had been convicted by an Army military court for possessing a few black-market items of American origin. Oishi's patron and protector, or *oyabun,* Ando had once been on intimate terms with the likes of Kunitoshi Tsukumo, Tokyo's wartime political boss, Tomita Kenji, Chief Secretary of Konoye's second and third cabinets, and Narahashi Wataru, Chief Secretary of the current Shidehara Cabinet.

For his inability to supply information regarding Ando's connection with a company allegedly engaged in smuggling with China, or with an unspecified dangerous underground movement in Japan, Mr. Oishi was subjected to third degree treatment such, he said, as the Japanese police would never have employed against a witness. He was struck sharply on the face fifteen to twenty times with a rubber hose, causing the swelling that remained after ice packs had been applied for over two hours. While held on the tatami (straw mats) stripped of all clothing except his shorts, his already badly crippled arthritic hands and feet were walked on and his body was repeatedly kicked. A threat was made to pour acid on his naked stomach, and sharp-pointed pencils were thrust under his finger nails, causing extreme pain but drawing no blood, at the same time an agent's thumbs pressed hard under his ears. The following day I related these facts to Mark Gayn, liberal *Chicago Sun* correspondent, who, after making a check, advised me to forget it, as Oishi was "in cahoots with ultranationalists." (Before the war, Oishi had been secretary to Minister of Justice Iwamura Michiya.)

Infinitely more difficult to master than the ways of SCAP and the thinking of the Japanese was the true nature of American occupation policy. One thing soon became clear: the objective of the occupation was draconian in intent. Not only were Japan's military machine, military caste, and military system to be permanently eradicated, but as Under Secretary of

State-Designate Dean Acheson told a Senate committee in September 1945, "the present economic and social system in Japan which makes for a will to war will be changed so that that will to war will not continue." [6] Reflecting this determination, Washington's two major policy directives of September and November 1945 instructed MacArthur to root out the cult of militarism by abolishing military organizations, destroying the industrial war potential, dissolving the large industrial and banking combinations, punishing the ultranationalists, and eliminating state-supported Shinto. In addition, he was to strengthen democratic tendencies, encourage a desire for civil rights, establish a responsible government, foster local autonomy, support labor unions, promote an equitable distribution of income and ownership, and reform the school system. Up to this point, SCAP and the architects of American occupation policy appeared to be in complete accord.

But regarding other and possibly more important steps for achieving the goal so pithily spelled out by Mr. Acheson, sharp differences between the framers and executors of policy were detected. The principal differences were over disposition of the Japanese throne, the fate of the emperor, and maintenance of the balance of power in the Far East. Identifiable policy adversaries were the "Japan Crowd," the "China Crowd," and the Pentagon in Washington and SCAP in Tokyo.

The Japan Crowd, led by Under Secretary of State Joseph C. Grew, prevented the United States government from making a commitment in the heat of war to eliminate the throne and establish a republic, or to try the emperor as a major war criminal and possibly execute him. Their major contribution to policy was to persuade President Truman, over the opposition of men like Office of War Information director Elmer Davis, columnist Drew Pearson, and Assistant Secretary of State Acheson, to leave the emperor system to the judgment of the Japanese. The President's decision in the matter was relayed to the Japanese government as Article 12 of the 26 July 1945 Potsdam Declaration, which stipulated that the Allied troops would be withdrawn from occupied Japan once "there has been established in accordance with the freely expressed will of the Japanese people a peacefully inclined and responsible government."

It should be pointed out here that postwar American and Japanese scholars have interpreted Article 12 to mean that no form of government was to be imposed against the will of the Japanese. From this interpretation they draw the conclusion that MacArthur transgressed his authority by secretly preparing a model constitution and pressuring the Shidehara Cabinet to accept it; that he thereby reneged on the Allied guarantee to let the Japanese people freely choose their own form of government. The history of Article 12 does not support such a conclusion. To be correctly understood, it should be read without the phrase, "in accordance with the freely expressed will of the Japanese people." Thus shortened, the article reflects the true intent of the United States, which was to establish "a peacefully inclined and responsible government," regardless of Japanese sentiment to the contrary. The "freely expressed will" phrase was inserted solely as a psychological warfare stratagem for terminating the conflict by Japanese surrender, if possible; its purpose was to signal the Suzuki Cabinet that the Imperial institution was no stumbling block to negotiations, since the Allies would let the Japanese people resolve that issue. As ex-Prime Minister Yoshida Shigeru wrote years later about Article 12: "the Americans declared it to be their policy to respect the will of the Japanese people in regard to the status and position of the Emperor." [7] Mindful of the double entendre of the language used in the article, SCAP undertook conscientiously to establish a responsible government with popular if not voluntary cabinet approval, and to do so without exceeding his authority. As to the outcome of the delicate operation, no less an authority than Edwin O. Reischauer says: "the new Constitution . . . was welcomed and supported by a large proportion of the Japanese, even though, strictly speaking, they had not been entirely free to shape it as they desired." [8] This subject is fully explored in subsequent chapters.

It was axiomatic with the China Crowd, as with troubled liberals generally, that the Emperor system must go. Their thinking was reflected in the writings of Johns Hopkins University professor Owen Lattimore, Moscow-trained Japanese Communist Nozaka Sanzo, and Navy Lt. Andrew Roth. Lattimore postulated that all Asiatic peoples were more interested in "actual democratic practices, such as the ones they can see in action across the Russian border," than they were in the fine theories of Western democracies, "which come coupled with ruthless imperialism." He agreed with those who held that the only real democracy in China "is found in Communist areas." He assumed that postwar Japan would become a republic, launched with the help of the United States, and advocated that Emperor Hirohito be interned in China and his estates be divided among the landless peasants. [9]

Carbons of Nozaka's 8 September 1944 "Program of the Japanese Communist Party" were passed unofficially to Government Section by POLAD. POLAD's staff included, among others, Minister George Atcheson, Jr., John S. Service, executive officer, and John K. Emmerson, political liaison officer, former members of the American Embassy staff at Chungking, China, who were contemptuous of Chiang Kai-Shek's Kuomintang and favorably disposed toward Mao Tse-tung's Communist regime. In the summer of 1944, a United States Army Observer Group, to which Mr. Service was attached, and several American newspapermen paid an extended visit to Yenan, the Communist capital, where they conferred not only with Chinese leaders but also with Nozaka, who impressed them by his thoughts on a Japanese peace settlement. Incorporated in Washington's policy directives to SCAP were most of the following Nozaka points: purge the militarists, punish the militarists and the politicians who were responsible for the war, rid Japan of militarism, break the power and influence of the big capitalists, place large-scale monopoly capital under government control, democratize the government, give the people freedom of speech, thought, expression, person, and assembly, set up a "People's Democratic Government," institute universal suffrage, place the governing power in the Diet, make land belonging to absentee landlords available to land-poor peasants on easy terms, recognize unions, and give workers the right to strike and to bargain collectively.

Nozaka had no use for the emperor. As a matter of expediency he did not favor immediate abolition of the Imperial institution, but would force Emperor Hirohito to abdicate and reduce the constitutional powers of his successor, should there be one. He recommended that the emperor be tried as a war criminal. He believed that any attempt by the Allied Powers to utilize the emperor for any purpose would set a dangerous example, which might be employed by groups "working against our interests."

Also available to the Washington framers of occupation policy was Andrew Roth's 1945 book, *Dilemma in Japan*. Making the most persuasive case of all for abolition of the Japanese throne, Roth enthusiastically endorsed Nozaka's program of political, economic, and social reform. As Roth saw it, the greatest single political obstacle to democracy was the future role of the Emperor institution. It must be demolished completely, he wrote, foundations and all, and the emperor should be tried as a war criminal. He advocated transferring political power to "a core of conscious democrats" found in four groups: small businessmen, professionals, industrial workers, and peasants.[10] Washington's basic directive advised SCAP to look the other way should these groups resort to force to modify the feudal and authoritarian tendencies of the government.

The Pentagon's voice in policy formulation was much stronger than that of the State Department. With the impressive list of military personalities exerting pressure on foreign policy, it could hardly have been otherwise. Admiral of the Fleet William D. Leahy was President Truman's chief of staff. General of the Army George C. Marshall carried great weight at the top levels of government. General of the Army MacArthur was flanked in the military hierarchy by Maj. Gen. Frank R. McCoy, United States representative on the Far Eastern Commission. Military figures were able to hedge by countless minute reservations the foreign policy commitments made by civilian policymakers. After V-J Day, the State-War-Navy Coordinating Committee (swNCC), which had shaped wartime policy, became a peacetime mechanism by which the armed services intruded deeply into the precincts of the State Department.

The chief concern of the military was to safeguard Japan's industrial potential against Russian designs. The War Department, therefore, objected bitterly to the State Department's advocacy of a plan for a Far Eastern Advisory Commission to work with SCAP. While the State Department contended that there could be no peace in the Pacific except a peace based on the consent of all interested parties, which the new

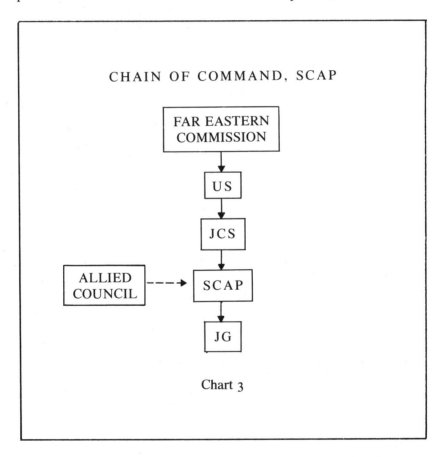

CHAIN OF COMMAND, SCAP

FAR EASTERN COMMISSION

US

JCS

ALLIED COUNCIL ----> SCAP

JG

Chart 3

machinery was designed to secure, the War Department insisted on unilateral American direction of Japanese affairs. In the end the Pentagon showed a willingness to compromise by approving this sentence in Washington's 6 September 1945 directive to SCAP: "Although every effort will be made . . . to establish policies for the conduct of the occupation . . . which will satisfy the principal Allied powers, in the event of any differences of opinion among them, the policies of the United States will govern." At Moscow in December 1945 Secretary of State James F. Byrnes yielded to Russian demands for a Far Eastern Commission (FEC) to make occupation policy and an Allied Council to advise SCAP (Chart 3).

Nevertheless, by means of seemingly innocuous provisions tucked away in the 3 November basic directive to SCAP, the Pentagon ensured ultimate military control of the occupation. By preventing civilian agencies from functioning independently in Japan, except with SCAP approval, and placing all Allied operatives under SCAP control, the State Department and POLAD, its arm in Japan, were effectively curbed. By requiring Joint Chiefs of Staff approval of directives sent to SCAP, not only was the State Department further weakened but dispatch of undesirable FEC directives to SCAP was precluded, even in the unlikely event an unacceptable proposal in that international body got past General McCoy, its chairman.

General MacArthur was as much policymaker as policy implementer. He was authorized to run the occupation much as he pleased. To compensate for inevitable shortcomings in Washington's directives, President Truman instructed him to exercise his authority as he deemed proper to carry out his mission.[11] The 3 November directive gave him not only the conventional powers of a military occupant of enemy territory but also the power to take any steps he thought "advisable and proper" to carry out the surrender terms and the provisions of the Potsdam Declaration. With this virtually unlimited grant of power, General MacArthur reshaped and amended Washington's occupation policy without disobeying his orders.

For example, he unilaterally decided to dispense with military government on 3 September 1945. And some two weeks later he announced that United States troop strength in Japan would be reduced to 200,000 within six months. For making this announcement he was rebuked by Secretary of State-Designate Acheson, but repetition by him of exactly the same statement evoked no further complaint from the State Department (*Baltimore Sun,* 29 October 1945). Then he used his power to put a stop to public utterances on occupation policy by SWNCC spokesmen in Washington. He had been embarrassed by diplomat John Carter Vincent's explosive assertions on a radio program that the Emperor institution—"if the Japanese do not choose to get rid of it"—would have to be radically modified, and that state-supported Shinto would have to go (*Chicago Sun,* 14 October 1945). Another instance of MacArthur's exercise of the power given him was his decision to build up Emperor Hirohito as the main stabilizing factor in Japan. Hirohito's New Year 1946 rescript denying his divinity and MacArthur's public statement that the emperor had thereby taken a stand along liberal lines indicated that there had been a meeting of minds between the Supreme Commander and the emperor.[12] To mention one more example, drafting a model constitution for Japan and inserting in it a no-war clause was a decision that was not beyond MacArthur's authority to make. Thus, in important particulars he made occupation policy. Without knowledge of this and the other policy inputs, as well as knowledge of SCAP's methods and of the postwar Japanese mentality, the political revolution in Japan would have been beyond the understanding even of the Americans who participated in it.

2

Establishing SCAP–Diet Relations

More than six months of the occupation had passed before SCAP's Government Section paid any attention to the Japanese national legislature (Diet). This lack of concern reflected in part the high priority SCAP assigned at first to demilitarization; but even more, it reflected the section's confusion over the dimensions of its role in the occupation. As late as mid-December 1945 Government Section was still uncertain about how to proceed with Japan's political reorientation. Its Public Administration Branch, composed of fourteen former Military Government Section officers, had just been organized into three working units: Planning, Legislative, and Foreign Affairs. Several days later the branch was reorganized and divided into two major groups, one for operations and one for planning. The operations group, consisting of the officer component, was split into three units: Internal Affairs, External Affairs, and Judicial Affairs. Their function was to discharge the responsibilities assigned to Government Section under Washington's 3 November 1945 basic directive to SCAP by formulating policies and preparing directives relating to Japanese governmental affairs. The principal subdivision, the Internal Affairs Unit, was responsible for matters pertaining to the national government, local governments, political parties, and national elections. The Diet was not specifically mentioned. It was the function of the External Affairs Unit to sever Japan's control over areas outside the jurisdiction of SCAP, and to assume control of Japanese foreign affairs. The Judicial Affairs Unit was responsible for controlling Japanese civil and criminal courts, removing and excluding from office militant nationalists, dissolving secret societies, and reviewing proposed directives to the Japanese government.[1]

The planning group, assigned office space in the Mitsui Building, on the Ginza, where POLAD's staff was located, was composed of two officers and sixteen civilian experts who were expected to arrive momentarily from Washington. The function of the planning group was to make studies and recommendations on demilitarization and decentralization of government, elimination of feudal and totalitarian practices, and strengthening of democratic tendencies in political, economic, and social institutions. The miscellany of civilians hastily recruited by the War Department's Civil Affairs Division would bear the brunt of drafting a detailed blueprint of revolution for implementation by the operations group.

Soon after this reorganization was effected, I was transferred from the operations group to the planning group and dispatched to Kobe to consult Mr. Paul de Gyarmathy on discriminatory practices in Japan (see Chap. 1). Brig. Gen. Courtney Whitney, who replaced General Crist as chief of Government Section two weeks earlier, was already beginning to voice the doctrine of rule by SCAP pressure rather than by SCAP directive, a corollary of General MacArthur's sudden 3 September decision to dispense with military government and let the Japanese do his will. A member of the MacArthur coterie, General Whitney was in no hurry to discard Crist's cumbersome system in favor of a simpler and more direct method of political reform. He realized that his Government Section associates were operating on a different wavelength from that of General MacArthur. They were skeptical about SCAP's recently announced decision to issue no more directives, save one, to effect Japan's democratization. They were not conditioned to believe SCAP's press release saying that, with the establishment by directive of freedom of press, religion, speech, and of the abolition of state-supported Shinto, the framework of Japanese democracy had been constructed, and that the job was now to prod the Japanese into action implementing the directives. The single remaining directive would define who could and could not hold public office in the new Japan.[2]

It was in late January 1946 when General Whitney scrapped the infeasible planning-operations approach to political change and recalled the planning group from the Mitsui Building. Events had outrun the need for long-range planning and protracted research, he told his reunited staff, and Government Section would henceforth have its hands full coaxing the Japanese government to implement the directives already issued.

This move by Whitney made mandatory still another reorganization of Government Section's policy body. Accordingly on 1 February, upgraded to division status and enlarged by the addition of ten civilian experts from Washington, it was divided into six branches: Legislative and Liaison, Political Parties, Governmental Powers, Local Government, Opinions, and Review and Reports. Of the four substantive branches, the responsibilities of two of them, Political Parties and Local Government, were self-explanatory. The duties of the Governmental Powers Branch were to reform the Japanese governmental system, abrogate laws prejudicial to occupation policies, examine proposals relating to Imperial institutions, and supervise criminal and civil courts. No reference was made to revision of the Imperial Constitution which, even then, was in the process of becoming Government Section's biggest undertaking of the occupation. The Legislative and Liaison Branch, headed by Comdr. Guy J. Swope, a former congressman from Pennsylvania, was given responsibility for maintaining liaison with the Cabinet Legal Bureau, keeping SCAP staff sections informed of legislation pending in the Diet, monitoring election campaigns, eliminating corrupt practices, and maintaining liaison with the Allied Council for Japan and the Far Eastern Commission. This branch would become Government Section's Legislative Division. Commander Swope, my supervisor from February to July 1946, gave me responsibility for preparing a manual on Diet rules and procedures, developing a system for maintaining SCAP surveillance over the Diet, and devising a method of reporting within SCAP the activities of the Ninetieth Imperial Diet.

Not until after the Shidehara Cabinet agreed to sponsor a democratic constitution did Government Section make direct contact with the Imperial Diet. The result of Government Section's October 1945 memorandum instructing the Japanese government to establish a procedure for keeping SCAP informed of the progress of legislation was only the delivery to SCAP of bills deliberated by the brief Eighty-ninth Diet (25 November to 18 December).[3] There was no SCAP coverage of Diet debates, no supervision of the legislative process, no official dealing with the presiding officers of the two chambers. The still-sitting wartime House of Representatives was regarded as a hotbed of ultranationalism, not to be approached until it had undergone the cleansing effect of a purge and a national election. When contact was made with the Diet, it was in response to three developments: the January purge from political life of 381 members of the 466-member lower house who had been elected in 1942 on the recommendation of the Tojo government; the March decision of the Shidehara Cabinet to sponsor a constitution patterned after the Government Section model; and fixing the date of a general election to choose a new House of Representatives, whose main task would be to deliberate the proposed democratic constitution. On the strength of these events, Commander Swope and his two assistants were prepared to do business with the Diet as the prospective "chief organ of state power."

While Swope and 1st Lt. Milton J. Esman were concerned with corruption in the current election campaign and with improvement of the Japanese civil service, I undertook to learn how the oldest parliament in the Orient worked. The first order of business was to examine the "Law of the Houses of the Diet," the "Rules of the House of Representatives," and the "Rules of the House of Peers." Then followed the initial SCAP contact with the secretariat of the House of Peers. For three hours on 27 March, I questioned Chief Secretary Kobayashi Jiro and Assistant Secretary

Kondo Hideaki on the organization and operation of the upper chamber. A few days later, a similar discussion was carried on with House of Representatives Chief Secretary Oike Makoto and members of his staff. Then I prepared a handbook titled "The Japanese Diet: Manual of Organization and Procedure." It covered ten subjects: convocation, election of officers, organization, committees, daily sessions, passage of bills, record of proceedings, representations and petitions, discipline, and relations with the people. There was a glossary of terms, which defined in English and Japanese over fifty legislative expressions, such as agenda, debate, prorogue, quorum, and voting.

Although the rules of both Houses of the Diet were strikingly similar to those of any national legislature, a few were peculiar to Japan. For example, the emperor read the rescript of convocation to members of both Houses meeting in the chamber of the House of Peers, with the president of that body presiding; the Speaker of the lower house was elected by its members, while the president of the House of Peers was nominated by the prime minister and appointed by the emperor for a seven-year term; the prime minister also nominated the chief secretary of each House; in the House of Peers members of the Imperial family occupied the front rows, followed in order by princes and marquises, counts, viscounts, barons, Imperial nominees, and finally highest taxpayers; Diet members were forbidden to wear clothes other than *haori* (Japanese coat) and *hakama* (shirt formerly worn by samurai), or trousers and frock or morning coat; neither House was permitted to take testimony from the people; business in the rules committee of each House was decided only by unanimous decision reached through negotiation. Knowledge of how the Diet functioned was necessary to understand the Japanese lawmaking process. The next step was to bring that process under SCAP surveillance.

1946. In early June Commander Swope and his aides met with Speaker Higai Senzo and Chief Secretary Oike to talk about revising and liberalizing the rules and procedures of the House of Representatives. Swope's first question was whether it would be practical to set up a House committee for this purpose. It could be done, Mr. Higai said, but he favored having the Cabinet Legal Bureau make the study—to avoid the evil of filibustering by a parliamentary committee. In response to Swope's recommendation of permanent committees as instruments for training members to become experts in banking and finance, appropriations, health and welfare, agriculture, commerce, and the like, Mr. Oike recalled his attendance at an international parliamentary conference in the United States sixteen years before, following which he recommended a standing committee for each ministry and an office building for Diet members, projects twice approved by the lower house and twice rejected by the House of Peers. But, he added, the efforts of the House of Representatives at that time to elevate the status of the national parliament led to construction of the handsome new Diet Building, which was completed in 1936. At the conclusion of the discussion, Messrs. Higai and Oike invited Government Section to help the Diet "regain favor with the people," and Commander Swope proposed that another meeting be held in the near future.

When the next meeting convened four days later at the Speaker's official residence, Mr. Higai was rigidly set against the idea of establishing a rules revision committee. But his opinion was not voiced until his Government Section guests and officials of the House secretariat had been treated to a delicious dinner. He objected that the House would be too busy during the forty-day session deliberating some seventy government bills to take on the added burden of rules revision. Besides, he repeated, the Japanese way was to have the secretariat or the Cabinet Legal Bureau draw up the rules and present them to the House for its approval; a House committee, he said, would merely draw up different sets of rules along party lines and submit conflicting reports. By now it appeared to the Swope party that without some form of persuasion the Speaker could not be moved from the rigid position he had taken. A day later, 11 June, in a memorandum to General Whitney, Swope reported that the new Speaker was "tragically unfit" for the job. For one thing, as a career bureaucrat, he regarded legislation as a subordinate function of government and looked on members of the House of Representatives as "half-educated, incompetent boors and ignoramuses."[4] Moreover, he stubbornly refused to establish a select House committee on rules as recommended by the Legislative Liaison Branch, offering the flimsy excuse of inadequate funds and a heavy legislative workload.

Informed indirectly by Swope that "responsible government" required a strengthened Diet, the Speaker saw the light and became more cooperative. Following discussions with various political party leaders, he decided after all to appoint a special rules revision committee. The progress of the committee during the summer of 1946 was recorded in a series of Government Section Diet reports, the nature of which is explained below. The report of 27 June stated that the committee would be composed of twenty members; by 4 July, the committee had become an unofficial research body prepared to revise the repressive 1890 Law of the Houses as well as the rules of the House. The committee's membership consisted of such powerful party leaders as Liberals Okubo Tomejiro, Ashida Hitoshi, Bando Kotaro, Ono Bamboku, and Hanashi Shingoro; Progressives Inukai Ken, Tanaka Manitsu, and Inoue Tomoharu; Socialists Nakamura Takaichi, Mizutani Chosaburo, and Satake Haruki; Cooperatives Uda Kunie and Matsumoto Takizo; and Communist Tokuda Kyuichi. The 1 September report noted that the committee, inspired by the trend of the times, had decided on its own initiative to replace the Law of the Houses with a new Diet Law. On 7 September attention was called to the fact that the Cabinet's Special Provisional Investigation Committee was rewriting the Law of the Houses in competition with the House of Representatives committee, which had no legal basis for even "studying" that law, let alone revising it. As the 11 September report pointed out, House leaders felt that it would be beneath the dignity of that body under the revised constitution to have a Diet Law other than their own. In the end, according to the Diet report of 15 September, the Cabinet Investigation Committee yielded to the House of Representatives.

The full story of the Diet Law, which was a major step in effecting Japan's political reorientation, is told in Chapter 8. It is brought to the reader's attention here to show the initial efforts of SCAP officials and Diet members to strengthen the Diet. Shortly after the House decided to establish the rules revision committee, Commander Swope returned to the United States, and I succeeded him as branch chief.

The arrangement by which Government Section maintained oversight of the legislative process was worked out in May and June 1946. Basic to the arrangement was the above-mentioned October memorandum directing the Japanese government to keep SCAP informed of the progress of proposed legislation. During the Eighty-ninth Diet session the Japanese side merely provided Government Section with copies of government-sponsored bills and Diet-proposed amendments to them. Although these bills were drafted to implement SCAP directives, the SCAP sections concerned lost sight of them once they passed from the ministries to the Cabinet Legal Bureau and thence to the Diet. Lacking was a procedure by which any SCAP section could propose amendments to bills in the Diet or to offer objections to Diet-proposed amendments. The Diet, it must be remembered—answerable to the electorate and slated to become, in the words of the Potsdam Declaration, the cornerstone of "a peacefully inclined and responsible government"—could not be ordered around by either the Supreme Commander or the Japanese prime minister. But deferential regard for the people's representatives did not preclude finding a suitable way for the Diet to cooperate in effecting the terms of surrender, a quest Government Section's Legislative Branch hoped to complete *i.e. institute changes quickly, before the new institution can control them excessively*

before Diet deliberations on the new constitution revision bill began in June 1946.

In this endeavor, my contact was with the Japanese Central Liaison Office (CLO). Staffed by Foreign Ministry officials, CLO had the function of translating SCAP demands into action; it was the "go-between" for SCAP and the Japanese government. Developing a procedure for keeping Government Section fully informed of the whole lawmaking process involved, in addition to CLO, the Cabinet Legal Bureau and the Diet secretariats, all of whom were jealous of their traditional rights and suspicious of proposed innovations. This made it difficult for them to reconcile their welfare and security with the unusual demand of SCAP's Government Section. Bearing up none too well under the strain of his thankless assignment, the CLO representative, Mr. Uyama, could not conceal his impatience with both his American and Japanese tormentors. Nevertheless he succeeded in producing a two-point plan for reporting Diet proceedings designed, hopefully, to satisfy the requirements of SCAP. Regarding bills, his plan provided that synopses of projected cabinet proposals would be made available to Government Section the same day they were referred to appropriate ministries for elaboration, study, and drafting. When the cabinet submitted the final draft of a bill to either House, a copy would be simultaneously transmitted to Government Section. Changes proposed in either House would be reported to Government Section in a daily CLO report on Diet proceedings. Regarding the daily CLO report, each morning it would be submitted to Government Section, in English, summarizing the previous day's proceedings in the two Houses. The one- or two-page summary would give the names of the main speakers, the substance of their remarks, and the text of any amendments offered on the floor. The agenda for each succeeding daily session would also be furnished.

A question immediately arose over the soundness of the CLO reporting system. *Nippon Times* of 7 June stated that seventy legislative bills were being drafted by the different ministries for presentation to the Diet. This information did not tally with CLO's report to Government Section that only forty bills were under preparation. Then, *Nippon Times* printed many details of the Law Reform bill, a measure about which Government Section had not been informed. About the same time, Government Section received from the Adjutant General's Office a single copy of the bill to Abrogate Wartime Exceptions to the Industrial Property Law, which CLO had addressed to GHQ without identifying the originating ministry or the SCAP section for which it was intended. Obviously the 11 May agreement was not being observed, and I so informed my CLO contact. In no time the misunderstandings were cleared up, and thereafter the working relationship with CLO was smooth and harmonious.

Just before the opening of the Ninetieth Diet, General Whitney notified all SCAP sections by memorandum of the service Government Section was prepared to render in connection with the Japanese legislative process. Government Section, he said, maintained liaison with the cabinet, the ministries, and the Diet secretariats on all matters pertaining to legislation. As soon as any ministry announced the title of a bill to be drafted, Government Section was informed. When the main features of a bill had been agreed on by the ministries concerned and approved by the cabinet, a synopsis of it was sent to Government Section. The final draft reached Government Section three to five days before its introduction in either House. Actions on bills in committee and on the floor were reported to Government Section daily. Although most bills originated in the ministries, Diet members could present bills of their own; such bills were made available to Government Section two or three days before they were introduced. Thus, Government Section was in a position to provide accurate information on the status of any bill in the Diet. The following seven staff sections designated representatives to maintain liaison with Government Section on legislation: ESS, Natural Resources, Public Health & Welfare, Civil Communications, Statistics & Reports, G–2, and G–4.

Anticipating the 20 June 1946 opening of the Ninetieth Diet, General Whitney directed the Legislative Branch to prepare for internal SCAP use a daily report on important doings in the Diet. Commander Swope named me to perform this chore. The kinds of information the general wanted or expected and the format, length, and distribution of the reports were items left to my discretion. On the second day of the Diet session, two reports were submitted to General Whitney, each a page or so in length. Meant to be timely, the first few lines of the initial report, which was unclassified and uncensored, are reproduced here.

THE DIET

No. 1   21 June 1946

DIET PROGRAM TO BE OUTLINED BY PRIME MINISTER IN TODAY'S ADDRESSES

Prime Minister Yoshida will address the House of Peers at 10 A.M. today and the House of Representatives at 1 P.M. Highlights of the address:

Constitution: "At the outset of the present session of the Diet the draft of a revised Constitution, which is to form the foundation for the construction of a new-born Japan, has been submitted by Imperial order."

Education: " . . . the government is proceeding with a radical renovation in all lines of the educational policy and system with a view to eradicating every vestige of militarism and ultranationalism and to prevent their resurgence in the future."

The report went on to summarize the prime minister's position on law and order, food, agricultural reform, inflation, labor unrest, small industries, unemployment, and reconstruction. Except for minor changes, this format remained the same throughout the occupation.

The aim of the second report was to acquaint General Whitney, Colonel Kades, and Government Section's division chiefs with the way Japan's political parties managed the House of Representatives. Their instrumentality for the purpose, the report stated, was the Negotiating Conference, or steering committee. Only parties and clubs with twenty-five or more members were entitled to representation on the committee. All decisions had to be unanimous. The committee decided the procedure for deliberating the draft constitution. It established a special committee to revise the rules and procedures of the House. The report called attention to the earlier conferences Swope and his assistants had with House Speaker Higai, who was reluctant to appoint such a committee because of funding difficulties and a break with tradition. Just as the Speaker and the Negotiating Conference had second thoughts about setting up a rules committee, the report continued, so did they relax the rule denying speaking privileges to members of parties and groups with less than twenty-five members. Henceforth the list of speakers would be decided on each occasion; that is, the Communists, if insistent enough, would be permitted to speak in the House.

Beginning with the sixth Diet report, distribution was widened to include the designated legislative liaison representatives of other staff sections. Of the 102 reports prepared during the Ninetieth Diet session (20 June to 9 October), eighty-five were thus distributed, and only fifteen were restricted to Government Section. As might be expected, many of the reports dealt with Diet deliberations on the draft constitution. The purport of one of them, the fifteenth, titled "Position of Emperor Main Point in Discussion on Draft Constitution," was that a number of eminent constitutional scholars in the House of Peers proposed to substitute "Sovereign" for "symbol" in Article 1 of the draft, which read: "The Emperor shall be the symbol of the state." General Whitney's copy, which he left with General MacArthur, carried the notation, "This will be closely watched—CW." Not long after this, General Whitney instructed me to deliver the original of each report to the office of the Supreme Commander and only then to leave a carbon with him. He did not explain the logic of this procedure, which would have been novel in any organization, and particularly so in a military headquarters. Perhaps General Whitney wanted to underline the fact that the reports were not censored by him, that they were entirely free to tell not what General MacArthur might like to read but what he needed to know.

Only once did General Whitney take exception to the wording of a report. On reading Diet Report No. 43, he recalled the original from General MacArthur's office, and asked that it be rephrased. The report referred to views expressed to me by Dr. Ashida Hitoshi, chairman of the lower house Constitution Committee, involving a disagreement between the Yoshida Cabinet and SCAP over Article 84 dealing with the imperial estates. General Whitney cautioned that mention of a Government Section official's participation in the discussion might infer SCAP interference with Diet deliberations on the constitution, and thus raise questions as to whether a responsible government, in the meaning of the Potsdam Declaration, was being established in accordance with the freely expressed will of the Japanese people. After that, the doctrine of noninterference was scrupulously observed in the reports. *but in practice?*

Shortly before leaving Japan, Swope, assisted by Esman, wrote a memorandum recommending nine Diet reforms, which was approved by Colonel Kades and General Whitney. The document called for permanent standing committees, more time for deliberation of the annual budget, protection of the rights of minority parties and groups, free discussion, increased pay for members, Diet determination of length of sessions, secretarial assistance for each member, a legislative reference service, and power to subpoena witnesses.[5] Some three weeks after Swope's departure, Esman and I met with Mr. Sakata Ishino of the Finance Ministry's Bureau of Pay and Allowances to discuss the only one of the nine reforms immediately achievable, that of increasing the annual stipend for Diet members. By a temporary measure, Mr. Sakata told us, all government people, including Diet members, had already received postwar pay boosts. The pay level of Diet members, he said, traditionally set by the Minister of Finance in consultation with the chief of the Cabinet Legal Bureau and the leaders of the principal political parties, placed them in the category of third rank, or *sonnin*, officials. To add to the prestige of Diet members, he was told, their pay should be no lower than that of second rank, or *chokunin*, officials (i.e., of vice-ministers and bureau chiefs).

Three days later the matter was resolved to our satisfaction when Mr. Sakata informed us that Finance Minister Ishibashi Tanzan, with the concurrence of Cabinet Legal Bureau Chief Hayashi Joji and House of Representatives Chief Secretary Oike, had changed the pay scale to give Diet members a fraction more than the pay of a vice-minister.

With the pay issue settled, I resumed the interviews Commander Swope had begun with the respective political party delegations of the

House rules revision committee. My first interview was with Liberal Party members Ashida Hitoshi, Okubo Tomejiro, Hanashi Shingoro, and Bando Kotaro, all eminent political figures. They showed no disposition to take advantage of my newness to the job. If they had no ideas on political reform more advanced than those previously expressed by Speaker Higai, they were at least committed to a radically revised Law of the Houses, which the Cabinet Legal Bureau had prepared for them. It seemed to be an encouraging sign that they had begun to think in terms of a new National Diet Law rather than a mere rules revision.

A week later I met with representatives of six minority parties, including, among others, thoroughly Americanized Matsumoto Takizo of the Cooperative party and Tokuda Kyuichi, secretary general of the Communist party. Like the Liberal party members mentioned above, they favored establishing a House legal bureau but, unlike their conservative colleagues on the rules committee, they believed that a system of permanent committees was the Diet's greatest need.

Next I sat down with Socialist Suzuki Yoshio, former Tohoku University professor and an authority on the Imperial Constitution. In addition to expressing support for a stronger and more democratic Diet, he freely shared his views on the Socialist party and Diet members generally. His party, he said, under the leadership of Katayama Tetsu, Nishio Suehiro, and Suzuki Mosaburo, was governed by a committee of fifteen, elected by the party's membership. Committee decisions had to be followed by every member, on pain of expulsion from the party. He rated the newly elected House of Representatives superior to that of 1942 and those of the 1930s. Because of inflated prices of paper, printing, gasoline, and food, the 1946 election, he believed, set a record for expenditure of money, but graft and corruption were less marked than before.

Then I interviewed Mr. Katayama Tetsu, Socialist party president. In his opinion, conservative leaders like Baron Shidehara Kijuro, representing the prewar Minseito and Seiyukai political groups, spearheaded the financial interests that wanted to preserve the old order. They clung to the skirts of the emperor who, though opposed to them, could not free himself. Such interviews were helpful to an outsider in getting acquainted with the thinking of Japanese politicians. They would not, it seemed, be averse to upgrading the legislative branch under the proposed democratic constitution.

The SCAP-Diet relationship encompassed more than Diet procedural changes, SCAP oversight of the legislative process, reporting of Diet activities, and upgrading the Diet. There were also common peripheral functions to be performed by SCAP and Japanese officials. One of these was to accommodate visiting American dignitaries by arranging conferences for them in the Diet Building with Japanese political leaders. Another was to sit in on some of the meetings between General MacArthur and Diet leaders, and to join foreign parliamentary delegations at their audiences with the emperor. Still another and more frequent function was to intervene when GHQ officials became excessively bureaucratic where the Diet was concerned. There was, for instance, the case of the Finance Ministry request for release by GHQ of silver and gold to make 1,500 souvenir cups for distribution at the Diet ceremony commemorating the promulgation of the new constitution. SCAP's Civilian Property Custodian rejected the request and advised the Japanese government to make the ceremonial cups out of wood and lacquer. The CLO representative in the lower house of the Diet routinely reported this incident to Government Section's legislative officer, who included it in a Diet report for limited distribution within SCAP. A few hours later, on orders from General MacArthur, the Civilian Property Custodian released silver and gold in the amounts requested by the Finance Ministry. Numerous other cases of friction involved the Diet.

The foregoing is sufficient to show the nature of the SCAP-Diet relationship, which was fundamental to the execution of the political reform program. The next three chapters are devoted to the individuals in Government Section who played important roles in effecting Japan's political reorientation.

3

Charles L. Kades: Dynamic Libertarian

Although General MacArthur deserves great credit for turning a potential American diplomatic fiasco into a notable diplomatic success, he did not act alone in administering the Allied occupation of Japan. He relied heavily on his Government Section to translate Washington's rudimentary policy directives into a balanced and workable plan for democratizing a once powerful authoritarian state. Too little notice has been taken of the individuals who staffed Government Section. This chapter and the following two are therefore concerned with the principal officials of that section and their roles in Japan's political reorientation.

Government Section's professional group initially included only the small band of military government-trained officers bequeathed to General Whitney by his predecessor. Members of this team who remained in Japan long enough to make their influence felt were Col. Charles L. Kades, Comdrs. A. Rodman Hussey and Guy J. Swope, Lt. Cols. Milo E. Rowell, Pieter K. Roest, Cecil G. Tilton, and Frank E. Hays, Maj. Frank Rizzo, 1st Lt. Milton J. Esman, Navy Lt. Osborne I. Hauge, and myself, an Army Air Corps captain—all holding temporary or reserve commissions. Beginning in January 1946, this officer contingent was augmented by a number of civilian specialists recruited through the War Department's Civil Affairs Division. Of these, comprising more than forty by the end of 1947, Alfred C. Oppler and Blaine Hoover were the most important. A few others are identified in these pages, but the constructive work of the section during the first three years of the occupation was channeled through the fourteen persons just mentioned. All but two—Rowell and Esman—had a hand in writing Government Section's comprehensive report on the first three years of the occupation, *Political Reorientation of Japan*.

Accurate and surprisingly revealing, this contemporary state paper was reviewed in 1951 by Sir George Sansom, eminent British authority on Japan's history and culture, United Kingdom representative on the Far Eastern Commission (FEC), and an instructor in the Civil Affairs Training School at Yale in 1944–1945. Whether one agreed or disagreed with the basic assumptions of the Government Section chronicle, he wrote, one had to admire the single-minded devotion with which the Supreme Commander and the Government Section staff performed an undertaking "calculated to appall the sceptical or the faint-hearted." He thought that General MacArthur's brief introductory message displayed his "characteristically confident attitude in the face of difficulties." General Whitney's five-page foreword, he said, was lacking in modesty. He complimented that part of Colonel Kades's introduction entitled "On Balance," which, if expanded, would have been interesting and useful. Having conferred personally with Kades at a Government Section briefing of an FEC delegation in January 1946, Sir George depicted him as an able man who, out of the knowledge and experience gained during his "difficult work," might have given a valuable appraisal of the situation in Japan as it appeared to him at the end of 1948.[1]

In his essay, Kades did in fact venture a prophetic opinion on the prospects of democracy in postoccupation Japan. The skeptics who foresaw the return of the old order after the occupation ended, on the theory that the revolution was of external origin and therefore transient, were wrong, he said, because they failed to recognize that the Japanese people were left wide discretion in the reformation of their institutions. The changes were timed and tempered to avoid violent conflict with the people's legitimate longings. Such changes as were made with the approval and assistance of the Japanese have endured, and those that were imposed did not last long after Japan's independence was restored.[2]

Some Japanese of a later generation are persuaded that the occupation had little permanent impact on their society, that such changes as did occur were only temporary. They seem to be hardly aware, as Kades wrote, that every step taken toward democracy during the occupation was met by wails that the consequence would be chaos, anarchy, and communism. These arguments were used against elimination of thought control, granting of basic civil liberties, the purge, popular election of prefectural governors and assemblies and municipal mayors and councils, decentralization of police control, repeal of the lese majesty provisions of the penal laws, establishment of a modern civil service system based on merit, and so on.[3]

Kades was acutely conscious of the fact that the SWNCC policymakers in Washington, preoccupied as they were with destruction of the old system in Japan, had only the vaguest notion of what should replace it. The specific course to be taken by the Allied powers, he said, was none too clear. American policy as spelled out in the basic 3 November 1945 directive was a hodgepodge of inputs hastily prepared by an assortment of government experts on politics, labor, economics, and finance, few of whom were identified in Hugh Borton's helpful 1967 article on this subject.[4] Kades perceived that on the question of a capitalistic versus a socialistic democracy, Washington policy was ambivalent; on Western ways the Japanese could be expected to welcome and cherish, it was superficial; on United States national security requirements, it was short-sighted; and on the inevitability of unacceptably high occupation costs and rapidly declining American public interest, it was insensitive. But the ultimate objective, he said, being to secure a peacefully inclined and responsible government, elimination of the existing system was unquestioned.[5] Kades saw, in short, that Washington relied heavily on the initiative and discretion of SCAP, who in turn had to rely on Government Section. As to political reform, Government Section was MacArthur's main source of ideas, stimulation, and guidance.

Whereas MacArthur professed to take a neutral stance toward Japanese political parties, Kades made no effort to conceal his preference for the Socialist party. The minor Communist party, he felt, merely endeavored to shape its policy in harmony with the party line abroad. In his view, the Japanese bureaucratic clique was the greatest danger to representative government. Top officials, he declared, generally sided with the reactionary elements and rejected republican ideals as inconsistent with the national character.[6]

How Kades escaped the notice of contemporary writers and observers is hard to understand. Only a few appreciated the key role he played. Whitney remembered him as "my deputy, a brilliant officer." MacArthur lumped together Whitney, Marquat, Willoughby, Sams, Dodge, Moss, Schenk, Shoup, Kades, "and many others [as men without whose] . . . special talents and skill, little could have been accomplished." Maj. Gen. Charles A. Willoughby referred to him as one of Whitney's "clever and able assistants." To W. Macmahon Ball of Australia, representing several states of the British Commonwealth on the Allied Council in Tokyo, he was the occupation official who tried "to arouse public opinion against the oyabun-kobun system." Mark Gayn's *Japan Diary* mentioned his name in connection with constitutional revision, the 1946 general election, land reform, the legal rights of a Communist printer, and the purge of Mr. Hatoyama Ichiro. John Gunther cited him, imprecisely, as "the author (for the most part) of the organic law ruling 83,000,000 people."[7] But American newspapermen by and large overlooked him. They failed to sense that he was the second most important SCAP official, ranking just below General Whitney. They were three disparate characters all working in near perfect harmony: MacArthur, the worldly-wise conservative; Whitney, his shrewd alter ego; and Kades, the brainy New Dealer. Only once did MacArthur overrule Kades—to exempt a particular cabinet minister from the purge. And only once did Whitney criticize him—for requesting the provost marshal to investigate a three-million-yen bribe charge, which Whitney thought too ridiculous to warrant an investigation.

In his January 1946 biographical sketch for internal Government Section use, Kades listed these facts: age forty; graduate of Cornell University and Harvard Law School; member of the New York law firm of Hawkins, Delafield, and Longfellow; Assistant General Counsel to the Federal Public Works Administrator from 1933 to 1937; Assistant General Counsel for the United States Treasury from 1937 to 1942, when he entered on active duty as a 1st lieutenant; graduate of the Infantry School and the Command and General Staff School before being assigned to the War Department's Civil Affairs Division; assistant G–5 of Seventh Army and 1st Airborne Task Force in the invasion of southern France and during the Alpine and Rhineland campaigns.

Charles Kades, or Chuck as he was usually called, was popular with Government Section's lawyers, federal and state officials, professors, writers, press agents, and secretaries. Always accessible, he welcomed ideas and enjoyed debate. Where General Whitney, though courteous to a fault, was withdrawn, Kades was gregarious and had a friendly smile for everyone in the section. He was game but not brash. He probably had the quickest intellect in GHQ. His capacity to grasp quickly all angles of a problem and to develop lines of action was unequaled. When he lost an argument, he did so with good grace, never blaming his disappointments or failures on others. Though decisive, he did not bark out orders; he could say no without offense.

Kades did not shrink from using power. With determination and confidence, he executed Washington's directives to bring Western democracy to Japan. Playing the game to win, he demonstrated time after time that the ability to prepare a good brief was an effective form of power. Sitting ducks for the shafts of his keen logic and sound reasoning were the blustery checksheets of G–2 and ESS, whose top people could never quite fathom, or accept, Washington's democratization policy.

Kades was associated with the reform period of the occupation. During the first three years, his word carried weight. His objectives were those of the Potsdam Declaration and Washington's September and November 1945 policy papers on Japan: purge ultranationalists, stamp out feudal leftovers, encourage democratic tendencies. He took the part of the Japanese underdog against the combined might of the aristocracy, the family monopolies, and the bureaucracy. Had MacArthur not declared SCAP's neutrality, Kades would have thrown his weight against the conservative Yoshida Cabinet's successful move to revise the election law in

1947 (but he supported the National Public Service Law Revision bill of 1948 banning strikes of government employees). He consistently struck blows for the common people by espousing such causes as repeal of the lese majesty provisions of the Criminal Code, Diet investigation of illegally hoarded goods, local autonomy, recision of the Rescript on Education, and elimination of bossism and corruption in politics. Without his initiative and drive, these reforms might not have been undertaken.

Kades had no base in the MacArthur inner circle. To play an important part in SCAP policymaking, therefore, he required a close tie-in with an influential MacArthur lieutenant, like General Whitney. He and Whitney, his senior by nine years, complemented each other. Whitney gladly entrusted the operation of the section to a man whom he recognized as having the necessary credentials for the job: loyalty, familiarity with the official climate of Washington, a sharp mind and level head, devotion to duty, imagination, and the attributes of leadership. From the outset Whitney appreciated the fact that Kades was an Ivy Leaguer without an old-school-tie complex, and drove everyone, himself in particular, to the limit of his endurance. When Kades was offered the position of Assistant Secretary of State for Occupied Areas in 1947, Whitney had him discuss the matter with General MacArthur (their first meeting even though their offices were separated by no more than thirty steps). MacArthur persuaded the New York lawyer that he could be more useful in Tokyo than in Washington. After MacArthur and Whitney retired from the Army in 1951, both retained Kades as their legal counsel.

Kades was the indispensable man in SCAP's reformation of Japan's political system. It is highly doubtful that Government Section would have taken on the task of drafting a model constitution for Japanese use if Kades had not been on hand. Without Kades, Whitney would have been less confident of Government Section's capacity to perform such a grave and delicate operation. Viewing the occupation through a SWNCC prism, which reflected Washington's diligent attention to demilitarization, punishment, and radical democratization, Kades was not fazed by the almost immovable obstacles to accomplishing the job. Without hesitation he took the offensive against the old order on all fronts. If he failed to drive the conservative Japanese from the field, it was because he underestimated the vitality of their culture and tradition and misreckoned the limitations of SCAP's power. But he knew how to beat a hasty retreat from an exposed position and to regroup. He made no effort to ingratiate himself with Japanese politicians and high government officials, and he contrived, deliberately it seemed, to alienate Japanese conservatives in and out of government. He was at his best keeping the conservative forces off balance and on the defensive, continually unnerving them with Diet investigations, Government Section press conferences, and political maneuvers. Early in the occupation his name became closely identified with the purge.

Kades had primary responsibility for eliminating the authority and influence of active exponents of militant nationalism and agression. During October and November 1945, Comdr, Dever S. Byard, onetime assistant corporation counsel of New York City, toiled quietly in a remote corner of the Dai Ichi Building ballroom, under Kades's constant supervision, at what was to become the 4 January 1946 twin directives for abolishing ultranationalistic organizations and excluding undesirable persons from positions of leadership.[8] A split developed within GHQ over the Byard-Kades draft purge directive between those who believed that Japan should be reshaped drastically and those who believed that a slight face lifting would suffice. Opposition to the purge included a solid phalanx of the four military staff sections, spearheaded by spokesmen for Military Intelligence. Maj. Gen. Charles A. Willoughby, assistant chief of staff, G–2, prepared a long memorandum on the subject. Kades promptly issued a sharp rejoinder. The matter was referred to General MacArthur, who sided with Government Section against G–2.[9]

Throughout his stay in Japan, Kades made certain that every reform he championed was consistent with the letter of Washington's directives. If MacArthur did not accede fully to Kades's recommendation for a clean sweep of all persons who had been active ultranationalists, neither did he accept G–2's recommendation to purge only war criminals. G–2 was guided by balance of power considerations in the Far East while Kades followed the policy laid down by SWNCC in Washington. SWNCC purge policy reflected the will of the president, of Congress, and of the American people in general. In this atmosphere plans for the second and third phases of the purge took shape, and tempers flared again. At a May 1946 conference in the Forestry Building, those in attendance promptly divided into two irreconcilable camps. The general staff officers, with help from Diplomatic Section's Max Bishop, were ranged against representatives of ESS, CIE, and Government Section. Bishop questioned the validity of the Potsdam Declaration, underscoring the point that it was not an inviolable document. G–2's Col. H.I.T. Creswell held that the purge would remove all experienced personnel from industry and finance.[10] Kades carried the day for the SCAP representatives. MacArthur designated Government Section to assume responsibility for all matters relating to removal and exclusion of Japanese personnel from national and local elective and appointive posts and influential political and economic positions. By the summer of 1946, under the first phase of the purge, some 1,100 officeholders or candidates for important government offices had been removed or barred, including most members of the 1945 Diet. The second and third phases of the purge, implemented in 1947, saw the removal of about 7,000 persons from positions of leadership in prefectural, city, and village governments, and approximately 420 top people from economic and public information posts. In addition to those removed or barred from specific positions, many more were found subject to exclusion. In all, a total of 210,288 persons were designated as purgees, including 167,035 military personnel, 1,809 bureaucrats, 34,892 politicians, 3,438 ultranationalists, 1,898 business leaders, and 1,216 information media people.[11]

In retrospect, both General MacArthur and General Whitney played down the purge. They were not proud of their part in it, even though they conceded that it would have been the height of folly to entrust the operation of the new democratic machinery to persons who would try to sabotage it. The Allied Council's W. Macmahon Ball took the position that in Japan it was not possible to separate the innocent followers from the wicked leaders, that a whole nation could not be purged.[12] But Kades did not share the qualms of MacArthur, Whitney, and Ball. Duty bound to carry out the unambiguous and unequivocal language of the Washington directive, he knew that MacArthur would leave himself open to charges of dereliction if the purge order was not rigidly enforced. In contrast to the few dozen words Whitney and MacArthur used in their postoccupation books to dispose of the subject of the purge, Kades sanctioned the use of seventy-three double-columned pages in Government Section's *Political Reorientation of Japan* to describe and defend every aspect of the program, which was twice the space devoted to the new constitution. Consistent with his support of the Potsdam Declaration clause removing ultranationalists "for all time," he was party to General Whitney's 22 June 1948 press release, which stated that "final action taken under the purge program is regarded to be of a permanent nature for which the Allied Powers will unquestionably hold future Japanese governments fully responsible."[13] Although Washington decided to reverse the purge policy in 1948, General MacArthur successfully resisted the pressure from that quarter and pursued the original purge policy until he was relieved of his command in April 1951.

For eight months beginning with February 1946, Government Section's first order of business was revision of the Meiji Constitution, a project in which Kades had the leading part. Early in the occupation, on the strength

of recommendations made by the State Department, MacArthur had
stressed to both Prime Minister Higashi-kuni Naruhiko and his successor,
Baron Shidehara Kijuro, the importance of constitutional reform; and by
the time Japan's disarmament was completed, the purge program successfully launched, and a date set for the first postwar election, he was ready to
address himself to that sine qua non of the occupation. After much
prodding, the Cabinet Constitution Investigation Committee, appointed
by Prime Minister Shidehara in October, finally submitted to SCAP on 1
February 1946 its revised draft of the Meiji Constitution. In a matter of
hours, Government Section's A. R. Hussey, Milo Rowell, and Cyrus
Peake, under Kades's oversight, prepared a detailed memorandum de-
precating the Japanese revision. MacArthur and Whitney interpreted the
Japanese document to mean that the cabinet had no intention of revising
the Meiji Constitution under SCAP supervision, preferring instead to take
its chances with the soon-to-be activated FEC, an eleven-member body
sitting in Washington, which would presumably quibble much and decide
little. How different the occupation might have been had the Constitution
Revision Committee been advised by the cabinet to propose a few substantive changes in Japan's basic charter! Forced to intercede, MacArthur
decided to put a stop to the "shilly-shallying"—to borrow General Whitney's expression—by having drafted in his own headquarters a democratic model for the confused, and possibly defiant, Japanese cabinet to
follow. This crucial step was almost certainly taken on the recommendation of General Whitney. Knowing the caliber of his Government Section
staff, he probably convinced General MacArthur that the necessary talent
was available to spell out for the filibustering Japanese conservatives
precisely how to convert their absolute monarchy to a constitutional
monarchy.[14] MacArthur withheld his decision just long enough to check
on his power to act. He looked to Whitney for an answer, and Whitney
turned to Kades, SCAP's leading authority on Washington's occupation
policy.

General Whitney's memorandum on the subject, which erased all doubt
of MacArthur's authority to initiate constitutional reform, bore the Kades
stamp of thorough familiarity with the documentary sources bearing on
the subject. In the absence of any policy decision by the FEC, Whitney's
memorandum read, "you have the same authority with reference to
constitutional reform as you have with reference to any other matter of
substance in the occupation and control of Japan." That is to say, he had
ample authority to make policy decisions on constitutional reform until
the FEC, to be activated 26 February 1946, promulgated its own policy
decisions on the subject. Without the presence of Kades, Whitney's
clinching argument, that his memorandum was backed by all officers in his

section who had examined the question, would have carried less weight.[15] Assured that he was not yet obliged to leave constitutional reform to the nations comprising the FEC, four of which could veto any proposal, MacArthur decided to entrust the job to Government Section.

This decision brought welcome relief to Kades, who had counted on a Government Section planning group to make studies and recommendations designed to attain the occupation's long-range objectives in the field of government and politics. As he explained to the FEC visitors in mid-January 1946, the Government Section planning group of four officers was being strengthened by the addition of twenty civilian experts from Washington. Pointing to the civil liberties directive of 4 October and the purge directives of 4 January, Kades prophesied that the forthcoming Diet election would be a long step toward establishing the peacefully inclined and responsible government contemplated by the signers of the Potsdam Declaration. Prompted by the recent MacArthur press release stating that Japanese reform by SCAP was virtually at an end, Kades told the FEC members that Government Section was making every effort to encourage the Japanese to correct defects in their governmental system through their own administrative reforms. This did not mean, however, that Kades ruled out formal changes in the Meiji Constitution by the Cabinet Constitution Investigation Committee, whose recommendations SCAP even then eagerly awaited. It meant only that neither he nor Whitney nor MacArthur had seriously considered the prospect of having Japan's constitution revised by the FEC in Washington. Kades welcomed, therefore, the opportunity to help establish the Supreme Commander's legal right to initiate constitutional reform in Japan before the FEC became operative.

Informed by Whitney on 3 February, a Sunday, of MacArthur's decision, Kades, Hussey, and Rowell met that evening to sketch the broad outline of the model constitution to be drafted and to decide the ground rules for Government Section's staff to follow. At the staff meeting the next morning, Whitney announced the appointment of these three men to a Steering Committee, with Kades as chairman, a position that permitted him to exert a preponderant influence on the outcome of the subsequent proceedings. Because of preconditions set by MacArthur—limited monarchy, renunciation of war, abolition of the feudal system—and of important contributions made by a number of staff members, no single individual of Government Section could truthfully claim the finished draft as an extension of his own shadow, but the Kades influence was the most pervasive. If MacArthur and Whitney between them made the "big" decisions, Kades by dint of knowledge and prestige contrived to make most of the "little" ones. In Government Section's official minutes of the constitutional debates, Kades is mentioned forty-six times. That is, in connection with each part of the draft constitution—executive, legislative, judicial, budget, civil rights, social welfare, local government—he "suggested," "emphasized," "objected," "recommended," "protested," "questioned," "believed," "stated," or "granted" something or other. Hussey and Rowell are mentioned twenty-three and twenty times, respectively. The only other staff members singled out more than five times each are General Whitney and Pieter Roest. However numerous and serious the defects of the Government Section draft, they would have been more numerous and more serious without the steadying hand of the Wall Street lawyer.

Kades personally drafted the Macarthur-dictated no-war clause of the model constitution, and though he never laid claim to any such distinction, he may possibly have had a hand in its origin. MacArthur, it will be recalled, credited Prime Minister Shidehara with suggesting renunciation of war at a meeting between the two men in MacArthur's office on 24 January 1946. Some ten days before, Whitney and Kades had called on the prime minister to explain the several categories of the 4 January purge directive. In the course of the ride to the prime minister's official residence, Kades, thinking of the recent New Year rescript renouncing the emperor's divinity, and perhaps inspired by his warm espousal while in law school of the Kellog-Briand Peace Pact (1928), wondered out loud whether the Japanese leaders might be willing to consider renouncing war by rescript. Whitney made no comment. As they were leaving the official residence, Whitney took the liberty to tell Mr. Shidehara that the emperor's renunciation of his divinity a short time before had been well received throughout the world. Mr. Shidehara, himself a participant in the discussions that led to the Kellog-Briand Peace Pact, reacted favorably to the remark, whereupon General Whitney asked offhandedly whether Japan might consider renouncing war by rescript. Mr. Shidehara made no response. May not a random question posed by Kades and repeated by Whitney have generated, or fortified, a chain of thought in the mind of the veteran diplomat and head of state that led to a remark several days later, which MacArthur interpreted as a suggestion to outlaw war?[16] Stranger things have happened.

Kades's decisive if limited part in revising the Criminal Code under the new constitution typified his whole approach to the occupation's main task of removing obstacles to the revival and strengthening of democratic tendencies among the Japanese people. Alfred C. Oppler and a group of Government Section lawyers under his supervision had responsibility for helping Japanese legal experts revise the civil, criminal, and procedural laws, but Kades intervened personally to settle a knotty problem growing out of Articles 73 and 75 of the Criminal Code relating to lese majesty; for example, acts of violence against the person of the emperor. The problem arose when Prime Minister Yoshida Shigeru appealed to General MacArthur by letter on 27 December 1946 to overrule General Whitney's oral instruction to delete the two articles from the revised law. In his erudite reply of February 1947 rejecting the request, prepared mainly by Kades, General MacArthur drew on principles underlying the new democratic constitution and on statutory provisions in British and American law.[17] Later in the year, when the Diet was deliberating the Criminal Code Amendment bill, the conservative forces, as if unaware of the MacArthur letter, made a desperate final effort to gain, at the very least, political credit for trying to give the emperor greater legal protection than the ordinary citizen enjoyed. Kades strongly opposed this tactic. He had me inform the chairman of the House of Councillors Judicial Affairs Committee that the cabinet had been instructed by SCAP to effect the immediate repeal of the lese majesty provisions of the Criminal Code, and that any further attempts by his committee to win concessions from SCAP on that subject would be futile. The same message was conveyed to House of Representatives Speaker Matsuoka Komakichi and Secretary General Oike.

But there was no procedure by which SCAP could prevent an opposition political party from proposing amendments to bills under deliberation in the Diet. Aware of this fact, the Liberal party had in mind offering an amendment to the Criminal Code bill providing imprisonment of from three months to five years for anyone found guilty of insulting the emperor. Though certain of defeat, the proposal would place the party on record as expressing the sentiment of the majority of the people for the emperor. To further the project, Liberal party president Yoshida sent a messenger to Kades to inquire whether it would be in order for his party to offer such an amendment. Kades instructed the messenger to tell Mr. Yoshida that his question was an affront to the Supreme Commander, and that if he wanted to know SCAP's attitude he should ask the prime minister. Please tell him further, Kades added, that his position was "untenable, ill-advised, and wholly outrageous." After a Liberal party caucus voted to leave the lese majesty issue entirely to the discretion of Mr. Yoshida, the project to amend the bill was dropped. A week later the Diet passed the Criminal Code bill as approved by SCAP. Kades was now free to turn his attention to an even more heated contest over police decentralization.

Whitney and MacArthur in their postoccupation books devoted only a few hundred words to decentralization of Japan's police system. By contrast, Government Section's *Political Reorientation of Japan* under Kades's watchful eye devoted 8,000 words to the subject.[18] He successfully put through a reorganization plan that was fought viciously by both the Japanese government and SCAP's Civil Intelligence Section (CIS). To Prime Minister Yoshida, viewing the affair in retrospect, it was a contest between the veteran soldiers who had participated in MacArthur's military campaigns and idealists—"lawyers, salesmen in department stores, editors of provincial newspapers and so on"—who had been sent from the United States for the express purpose of putting into effect a plan that had been conceived before Japan's surrender. The latter, he said, insisted that the police reorganization plan be followed to the letter, "and were comparatively uninterested whether the measures they proposed were sound in their relation to the actual conditions existing in Japan." They were the men of Government Section. "Those who supported us . . . were the men in the Public Safety Department [of CIS]." But Mr. Yoshida acknowledged that it was with Government Section that he had to deal.[19]

As for choosing between the CIS plan for police reform and Washington's dictum to encourage "local responsibility for the local enforcement of national policy," Kades, of course, obeyed Washington. Contemptuous of Washington's order to decentralize the national police organization, a Public Safety Division officer argued that the course proposed by Government Section would enable the Communists to topple a weakened Japanese government. General MacArthur, he feared, was having the wool pulled over his eyes by the Government Section men "just down the hall."

Objecting to a February 1947 Yoshida Cabinet police system reform plan recommended by Lewis J. Valentine of New York and Oscar G. Olander of Michigan, public safety experts recruited by the Public Safety Division, Kades made the case for total and immediate police decentralization on the basis of SWNCC and FEC directives. Encouragement of local responsibility was plainly spelled out in the 1945 basic directive to SCAP, he wrote in a 4,000-word brief. Continued minute regimentation from Tokyo, he said, was the only interpretation that could be made of the Japanese government's plan, as outlined in its February 1947 memorandum to SCAP, which urged that the police system "be decentralized as far as possible" and that police administration "be entrusted in principle" to the local public bodies. As long as the police force remained centralized, he argued, there would be serious doubts as to the intent of the Supreme Commander to encourage the full and spontaneous democratization of Japan or to adhere to the terms of the Potsdam Declaration. Moreover, critics would imply that the central police force was retained as the principal instrument of postoccupation American control of Japan. The Whitney-approved Kades memorandum served notice that Government Section would not concur in any SCAP police proposal failing to recognize that decentralization must come without delay and must be full and final.[20] General MacArthur put an end to the debate by deciding in favor of Government Section.

The Police Law was enacted in December 1947 and became effective in March 1948. Mainly because of Communist-inspired disturbances throughout the country, the law was amended in 1950, with SCAP approval, to permit closer relations between the national police force and local police forces. Soon after Japan regained independence, a law was passed by the Diet abolishing the local autonomous police units and replacing them with a separate police force in each prefecture coordinated by the national police. But there was no return to the one monolithic police organization under autocratic control that existed before the occupation.[21]

Apart from specific Washington policy guidelines, Kades undertook on his own to remove obstacles to the development of democracy in Japan. Noteworthy in this respect were two evils of postwar Japanese society that became targets for his crusading zeal. One of these was the political corruption resulting from illegal disposition of Japanese military stockpiles, and the other was the widespread gangster activity reaching into the sacrosanct precincts of law enforcement, labor, business, and politics. The first evil became known as the "great hoarded goods scandal," the second as the "*oyabun-kobun* menace." Government Section's *Political Reorientation of Japan* devoted 5,000 words to the hoarded goods investigation by Japanese agencies without so much as mentioning the *oyabun-kobun* evil.[22] The *oyabun-kobun* crusade did not have General MacArthur's support. He regarded it as unwarranted tinkering with a deeply ingrained Japanese cultural trait. But he did not interfere with Kades's probing efforts. To Kades it was a matter of eliminating feudal and totalitarian practices that tended to prevent government by the people. He used the hoarded goods and racketeering disclosures to instruct procurators, Diet members, and voters in the ways of democracy under the new constitution. If it was in order for SCAP to change Japan's historic national polity by transferring sovereignty from the emperor to the people, a revolutionary and most traumatic change, he wondered why it was not equally in order to seize the unparalleled opportunities to relate the new democratic principles to actual political, social, and economic conditions.

Kades became interested in the hoarded goods issue when Liberal party Diet member Seko Koichi, onetime vice-chairman of the Economic Stabilization Board, charged openly in July 1947 that billions of yen in hoarded goods were concealed throughout Japan. The reference was to military supplies of industrial raw materials and consumer goods distributed hastily to prefectural officers, control associations, and private companies at the end of the war, in violation of GHQ's General Order No. 1 designating goods of this sort as Allied property. ESS was concerned with the allegation that the hoarded goods had nourished the black-market. Kades sensed that large sums derived from the sale of such supplies were being used to corrupt political parties and to bribe public officials. Because of the threat posed to the entire program of political reform SCAP had undertaken, Government Section proposed to the Procurator General of Japan that an investigation of hoarded and illegally handled ex-military goods be undertaken. With full Government Section and ESS backing, the procuratorial staff, enlarged to 157 second-class procurators and 1,399 assistant procurators, sought to bring to justice those who dealt in and profited from hoarded goods. Kades claimed for the ensuing investigations, carried on by a special Diet committee, only that they made commendable progress in recovering substantial misappropriated public properties and in bringing about the indictment of a number of important and powerful political figures responsible for the fraud.[23]

While the hoarded goods scandal made headlines for one and a half years from July 1947, the companion antiracketeering drive petered out the second month after it began with a Kades press conference in September 1947. On that occasion he charged that there were mobs, gangs, and racketeers seeking to pressure and intimidate public officials. The root of the evil was thought to be the *oyabun-kobun* system. Deeply rooted in Japan's past, the system, in occupation parlance, suggested a boss–henchman relationship. Makoto Matsukata, Government Section research analyst (a grandson of Prince Matsukata Masayoshi of Satsuma, prominent statesman of the Meiji era), informed Kades, in an interim report on the subject, that an attempt to outlaw personal relationships between *oyabun* and *kobun* would be almost impossible. Nevertheless, there was set up a twenty-four-member SCAP *Oyabun-Kobun* Committee, representing Government Section, G–2, Natural Resources Section, Legal Section, CIE, Eighth Army, General Procurement Agency, and ESS. The committee was able to propose little more than a vigorous SCAP publicity program to expose a hidden *kuromaku* (black curtain) government operating in Japan and the street stall (*tekiya*) and gangster (*gurentai*) associations. International News Service Far East Bureau chief Howard Handleman's long article in *Nippon Times* (27 November 1947) describing SCAP's concern over the *oyabun-kobun* problem was the high point of Kades's drive against government by underground organizations. After the article appeared, Prime Minister Katayama acknowledged that vestiges of feudalism did exist, but categorically denied the existence of underground organizations in Japan. Henceforth the crusade against *oyabun-kobun* diminished in intensity.

In a December 1947 memorandum Kades gave notice to Government Section's division chiefs that SCAP's political reform program was drawing to a close. Of the eleven bills still to be acted on by the Diet, he said, all except the Code of Criminal Procedure bill would be enacted within a month or so. The Code of Criminal Procedure bill would be ready for introduction in the Diet by the middle of March. No other bills would be sponsored by the section in the absence of a command decision by the Supreme Commander. This marked the completion of the section's legislative program to achieve the objectives of the occupation. SCAP's political assignment under the basic directive was all but finished.

But since the Allies were unable to agree on the terms of a treaty for restoring Japan's independence, the occupation would continue for an indefinite period. To prepare for this contingency, Government Section liquidated or transferred to other agencies during the first half of 1948 all but three of its ten functional divisions. Theoretically restricted to observing and advising the Japanese government, Kades now had more time for consultation on a wide range of questions. When asked by CIE, for example, to concur in a Ministry of Education request to postpone local school board elections until the School Board Law could be amended to bar members of the leftist Japan Teachers Union from standing for election, he examined the proposal carefully, and vetoed it. In a lighter vein, when his opinion was sought on a formal invitation extended to Prime Minister Katayama to represent Japan at an annual convention of a world federation movement in Luxembourg, he penciled this note on the letter of invitation: "Please advise P. M. to file in his deep freeze." And so on.

Three of the many actions taken by Kades in 1948 will suffice to show the character of the blows he struck for democracy midway in the occupation. One of these involved the Akasaka Detached Palace, another the Imperial Rescript on Education, and the third an effort to name a prime minister.

A conspicuous target of opportunity for Kades was the elegant Akasaka Palace of more than 300 rooms in the vicinity of the Diet Building. Modeled after the French palace at Versailles and built between 1899 and

1909, this structure, some Japanese had speculated, would become General MacArthur's occupation headquarters. Early in the war the building housed Manchukuo's ruler, Henry Pu Yi, after which it was occupied by the crown prince until American fire bombs landed on its roof in May 1945. The last impressive function held there was the October 1947 farewell party given by the emperor for the former members of the Imperial family, who became commoners under the new constitution. General Whitney had suggested to the cabinet that the edifice might be occupied by the National Public Service Authority, the Supreme Court, and the Attorney General's Office, but these agencies were reluctant to move there. So Kades called a conference of the parties concerned in February 1948.

Present were spokesmen for the cabinet, the Finance Ministry, the Imperial Household, the House of Representatives, and the House of Councillors. Stuart Baron represented ESS, and I sat in for Government Section. Kades urged that the palace be dedicated to the fullest possible use of the people. A realistic plan, he said, would be for agencies of the three branches of government to occupy it. To Councillor Kiuchi Shiro's inquiry whether use of the building for the National Diet Library would be sufficient, Kades said no, because the library could not utilize the entire space available. To Mr. Ikeda Hayato's observation that jurisdiction over the palace had been transferred from the Finance Ministry to the Imperial Household, Baron, quoting the chief of the State Property Bureau, said that it was state property and therefore no longer subject to Imperial Household control. Kades requested that steps be taken immediately to transfer custody of the property back to the Finance Ministry. He took no exception to the proposal of Asanuma Inejiro, chairman of the powerful Negotiating Conference of the lower house, that the greatly strengthened Diet, with its forty-two standing committees, take over the whole building. But the next day the cabinet decided that the palace would be used jointly by the Diet, the cabinet, and the Attorney General's Office.

In anticipation of the spring 1946 arrival in Japan of the American Educational Mission, *Nippon Times* (3 March 1946) predicted that the Imperial Rescript on Education would remain a classic expression of the basic principles of the nation's educational ideal. A few months later, the testimony of Education Minister Tanaka Kotaro before the Constitutional Committee of the House of Representatives caught the attention of SCAP's CIS. Former law professor at Tokyo Imperial University and later to become Chief Justice of the Supreme Court, Dr. Tanaka took the position that the rescript should constitute one of the bases of Japanese education. Seizing on this statement, CIS warned other SCAP sections that the Imperial Rescript on Education had to be rescinded if the occupation was to achieve its long-range objectives. To support its stand, CIS quoted from William C. Johnstone's 1945 book, *The Future of Japan*, which said that, through interpretation, the rescript was a document fully as important as the Imperial Constitution, and had been made the source and sanction of "a nationalistic, regimented educational system."

This was enough for Kades. In May 1948 he asked me whether the rescript might be rescinded by the Diet—and thus avoid raising any question of jurisdiction between Government Section and CIE. I discussed the matter with Dr. Tanaka, now chairman of the Education Committee of the House of Councillors, and he did the rest—with considerable gusto, I thought.[24] In order to make a clean sweep of the several rescripts pertaining to education, both Houses of the Diet resolved in June 1948 that all copies of the Imperial Rescript on Education, the Imperial Rescript to the Army and Navy, and the Imperial Rescript to Students, having lost their validity, should be withdrawn from universities and schools; to be stressed henceforth were the new educational concepts manifested in the new Basic Law of Education.

In the political arena, Kades identified himself with the coalition government of Socialists, Democrats, and People's Cooperatives, which came to power simultaneously with the enforcement of the new constitution in 1947. It was reasonable for him to assume that this coalition would remain in power for the full four years permitted by the constitution or until Japan regained her independence, whichever came first. Committed to democratic principles, the Katayama coalition government, in contrast to previous conservative governments, cooperated willingly with Government Section.

But that unprecedented and "unnatural" coalition—weak, inexperienced, and divided—was not destined to last long. It very nearly fell apart trying to nationalize the nation's coal mines, and Katayama stepped down after some eight months when the extremists and moderates of his own Socialist party failed to reconcile their differences over the annual budget, which was dictated by SCAP's ESS. Dr. Ashida Hitoshi of the Democratic party took over as prime minister, and the coalition regime remained in power. The ensuing storm of Japanese press protest was such as the occupation had not witnessed before. Disapproval of Ashida's election by a vote of 216 to 180 in the House of Representatives was voiced by all metropolitan editors, who unanimously condemned the three government parties for shady but successful maneuvers to stay in power (*Nippon Times*, 29 February 1948). Kades rushed immediately to Ashida's defense through a press conference held by former congressman and ex-Comdr.

Guy Swope. Vowing to make a "frank examination . . . of the propaganda and publicity which were released during the period from the resignation of Prime Minister Katayama to the election of Prime Minister Ashida," Swope said emphatically in his 24 February 1948 statement that "what has just happened in the Diet is thoroughly democratic and in complete harmony with . . . Article 67 [of the constitution which reads]: 'The Prime Minister shall be designated from among the members of the Diet by a resolution of the Diet.'" He scoffed at demands that had been made for a new election just because certain elements had become dissatisfied with the manner in which public affairs were conducted. The election process, he said, was costly and disturbing to the social and economic life of the country. Of course an election had to be called when the Diet and the government were in an irreconcilable position and the Diet could find no other way out (*Nippon Times*, 25 February 1948). Liberal party leaders jeered at this statement, terming it "Swope's love letter to the Democrats."

When the Showa Denko bribery scandal hit the front page of every Japanese newspaper, the Ashida Cabinet, following the example of the Katayama Cabinet, resigned. It was now October 1948. Kades, taking his cue from press speculation, conceived of prolonging the power of the coalition parties once more by having them elect as prime minister former House Speaker, Yamazaki Takeshi, secretary general of the opposition Democratic-Liberal party. As "go-between" in this scheme, I received Yamazaki's assurance that he would serve if elected and Dr. Ashida's assurance that the three coalition parties would vote for the popular Democratic-Liberal politician. This deal fell through when Mr. Yamazaki decided to extract himself from an awkward and illogical situation by resigning his Diet seat, thus rendering himself ineligible under the constitution to become prime minister. At this point Mr. Miki Takeo, president of the small People's Cooperative party, a member of the coalition, was asked personally by General MacArthur why it would not be in order for him, Miki, to succeed Ashida. He answered by telling the Supreme Commander that the only solution under the circumstances was for the Diet to elect Democratic-Liberal party president Yoshida Shigeru.[25] This was done on 15 October. After one and a half years on the sidelines, the conservatives were back in power.

Kades's reaction to this turn of events was expressed by the *New York Herald Tribune* (17 October 1948), which said about Mr. Yoshida: "He is not desirable to Americans who have been striving to create a basis for democracy in Japan." Exactly one month after Mr. Yoshida became prime minister for the second time, Kades, at his own request, was placed on temporary duty in Washington. Then he tendered his resignation. The return to power of the Japanese conservatives, together with the decision of the United States government to switch occupation policy from political and social reform to economic recovery and security, effectively ended his usefulness as a SCAP official. Although the occupation still had three years to run, there would have been no more situations requiring his special talents. Having participated in the entire constructive phase of the occupation, he played the leading role in removing obstacles to the revival and strengthening of democratic tendencies among the Japanese people.

4

Government Section: Profiles of Key Officials

On 2 April 1946, less than a month after the Japanese cabinet accepted and embraced as its own the democratic constitution framed in Government Section, I stopped at the Mitsui Building for a chat with a former military government associate, Dr. K. C. Leebrick, ex-president of Kent State University in Ohio and now a special assistant to POLAD. Without any preliminaries he asked if I were the author of the new basic charter about which everyone was talking. Before I could deny authorship by reason of having been hospitalized with lacquer poisoning at the time of that historic undertaking, he began to reconstruct the story of what General Whitney called the best kept secret of the occupation. MacArthur, he ventured, disapproved of the revision of the Meiji Constitution submitted by Dr. Matsumoto Joji, chairman of the Constitutional Problem Investigation Committee, and decided to have a model prepared for the Japanese to follow. The result was Government Section's feverish fabrication of a democratic constitution, which MacArthur and the emperor pressured the cabinet into accepting. Who actually wrote the document? According to Dr. Leebrick, Lt. Col. Milo Rowell, a Californian, laid claim to being the main composer, and so did Comdr. A. R. (Rod) Hussey, Jr., a New Englander. Were they little fishes talking like big whales, or were they, between them, the architects of a new constitution for Japan?

As a matter of fact, Rowell and Hussey, together with Kades, were the chief drafters of the Government Section model. As members of the section's Steering Committee, they, individually and collectively, wrote many of the provisions of the draft and rewrote, revised, or vetoed most of the provisions drawn up by their colleagues on the legislative, exectuive, judiciary, civil rights, local government, and finance committees into which the staff was divided. At Civil Affairs Training Schools Rowell and Hussey had been exposed to the despotic character of the Imperial Japanese regime, and in Government Section they had made studies of minimal constitutional changes that would be required to bring about "a peacefully inclined and responsible government." Hussey concentrated on changes needed in the executive branch, Rowell on those needed in the judicial branch. In Government Section's December 1945 paper for briefing Maj. Gen. Frank McCoy, United States member of the FEC, neither Rowell nor Hussey was listed among the "outstanding personnel." In subsequent listings for distribution to distinguished visitors, both were included. A member of the Judicial Affairs Unit, the forty-two-year old Rowell from Fresno, California, received his B.A. from Stanford University, attended Harvard Law School, completing his law degree back at Stanford. From 1926 to 1943, when he entered the service, he specialized in representing business associations before various agencies of government. At one time or another he was assistant United States attorney in Los Angeles, director and president of the Fresno County Taxpayers Association, and active in several state and local organizations. His military service included completion of courses at the Provost Marshal General's School, the School of Military Government at Charlottesville, and the University of Chicago Civil Affairs Training School, after which he saw active duty as a commander of a Philippine Civil Affairs unit following the Battle of Leyte.

A conservative Republican, Rowell was held in high esteem by General Whitney, who persuaded him to postpone resumption of his law practice in Fresno long enough to participate in Government Section's project for drafting a model constitution. In that undertaking, Rowell exerted considerable influence. He pressed in particular for an independent and effective judiciary, extensive home rule, short election campaigns, delimitation of the emperor's powers, Diet control of Imperial Household properties (except the hereditary estates), Diet supremacy over the cabinet, and Diet approval of all treaties.

Two years senior to Rowell, Hussey, of Plymouth, Massachusetts, graduated from Harvard University and obtained his law degree from the University of Virginia. As a practicing lawyer from 1930 until he entered on active duty in 1942, he had been auditor and special mastery in chancery for the Massachusetts Superior Court while holding a number of local elective and appointive public offices. His military service included duty with the Amphibious Training Command, Pacific, as maintenance, transportation, and legal officer, and attendance at the Princeton School of Military Government and the Harvard Civil Affairs Training School.

Rod Hussey, his Government Section colleagues thought, was a bit humorless and inclined to be puritanical, evangelical, conceited, and arbitrary. He aligned himself closely with Dr. Ashida Hitoshi, a Democrat, and campaigned actively for the depurge of the flashy Democratic politician, Narahashi Wataru. Dedicated to the lofty principles and ideals of the Declaration of Independence, the Four Freedoms, and the United

Nations Charter, he called press conferences in 1947- 1948 to lecture the Japanese on civil liberties, the individual under the new constitution, and other aspects of Western democracy. He insisted on incorporating into the preamble of the new constitution a universal law of morality. Similarly, his tenacity was a major factor in giving the Supreme Court absolute power to interpret the constitution, appointing rather than electing judges, establishing Diet supremacy, separating church and state, differentiating between statutory regulation and constitutional law, and vesting power in the cabinet rather than in the prime minister or the emperor.

Hussey produced no notable background papers on the constitutional issue, but he wrote the thirty-six-page section on "The New Constitution of Japan" and most of the twenty-three-page section on "The National Executive" in Government Section's *Political Reorientation*. Sir George Sansom rated the section on the constitution as "probably the most important and certainly the most interesting part of the Report." As the United Kingdom member of the FEC, he observed that SCAP's statement of principles deemed basic to political reform "took the form of a draft constitution prepared behind closed doors," and that the Japanese side was under no compulsion to accept those principles, but, "failing action by the Cabinet, General MacArthur was prepared to lay the issue before the people himself." [1]

The section on the executive branch, Sir George pointed out, described changes that had taken place either as a direct result of action by SCAP or on Japanese initiative with the advice and guidance of SCAP. Many of the changes flowed naturally from the adoption of the new constitution. Thus, whereas the Ministries of War and Navy were abolished and the Home Ministry was reorganized by order so as to meet specific requirements of occupation policy, a Labor Ministry was created in order to implement basic rights secured by the constitution. Similarly the Ministry of Justice was replaced by an Attorney General's Office. "This section is clearly written," he said, "and . . . repays careful study." [2]

Comdr. Guy J. Swope, the one-term New Deal congressman, was totally devoid of any egghead pretensions. He boasted of being a self-made man, having no more than an elementary school education. In civilian life he had been a department-store controller, a public accountant and tax specialist, banker, budget secretary in the governor of Pennsylvania's cabinet, governor of Puerto Rico, and director of United States territories, Department of the Interior. Commissioned in the Naval Reserve in 1943, he graduated from the Navy School of Military Government, Columbia University, served as executive officer in the Military Government of

Saipan, and gave special lectures at the Navy School of Military Government, Princeton University.

Swope had a number of distinctions. He was the oldest member of Government Section's Public Administration Branch. He was the only ex-congressman and ex-territorial governor in the section, and had the most business experience. Like a majority of his colleagues he was an ardent New Dealer, but unlike any of them he had the broad shoulders, facial features, lung power, and broad smile of Franklin D. Roosevelt—a remarkable resemblance. He was the first Democrat sent to Congress from the Harrisburg district since the Civil War, and the only staff member to head three separate Government Section divisions at different times in the period 1945–1948.

Guy Swope was my first supervisor in the Public Administration Branch, and I thought highly of him. Politically astute and endowed with a lot of common sense, he made the big decisions for the Legislative Unit, relying on Milton Esman and me to make the necessary studies and write the necessary staff papers. When he quit his Government Section post in July 1946, I was chosen to replace him; and when he returned to Tokyo several months later, he was named chief of the National Government Division, created expressly to accommodate him. In the fall of 1947 he became chief of the Political Affairs Division, trading jobs with Carlos Marcum. When Swope left Tokyo for the second and last time in February 1948, the remaining functions of his Political Affairs Division were assigned to my Legislative Division (which then became the Parliamentary and Political Division).

While Swope's impact on Japan's political reorientation was not profound, neither was it insignificant. He played a minor role in the making of the model constitution, his name being mentioned only twice in the minutes of the Government Section debates. In two other respects, however, he made a contribution to the work of the section. In the spring of 1946, when he was chief of the Legislative Branch, he established the first contact between SCAP and the Speaker of the House of Representatives, thus laying the foundation for strengthening the weak legislative branch and for maintaining effective SCAP surveillance over Diet activities. Then, as chief of the Political Affairs Division, he undertook in the winter of 1947–1948 to stop what he, and Kades, considered reckless exploitation of the self-governing prefectures and cities by the Imperial Household Ministry in its efforts to humanize the emperor.

Swope's attention was first drawn to the matter by a monthly report of the military government unit of Nagano prefecture describing a recent visit there of the emperor. What impressed him was the huge sum of money appropriated by the prefectural assembly, which had caused more than a little public criticism. Swope reacted by directing an official of the Imperial Household Ministry to provide detailed accounts of all expenses incurred by prefectures in connection with the emperor's recent visits. When the official begged off with the excuse that the Local Autonomy Law made it impossible for any central government agency to exercise control over local government accounts, Swope requested that he produce the desired information or risk dismissal from his position. The report on Nagano prefecture was promptly submitted and a schedule agreed on for submission of the remaining reports.

Concluding from these reports that the campaign to popularize the emperor was financially devastating to the areas visited, Swope arranged to have a Government Section official, Makoto Matsukata, trail the imperial jaunts. Telegraphic messages from Matsukata disclosed that Shimonoseki, to mention but one city, had appropriated 300,000 yen to defray the costs of the emperor's brief stopover there, and that two corporations in Mihara had donated more than a million yen of company funds for the same purpose. Imperial Household Ministry reports filed with Government Section showed that eighteen prefectures had spent a total of 24 million yen on the emperor's visits, an outlay which, combined with estimated expenditures by the national government, cities, and private corporations, probably doubled the cost. If the same ratio were maintained for a visit to all forty-six prefectures, Swope figured, the bill would add up to 140 million yen, nearly three times the amount recently divided among the princely houses when their members became commoners. Were the lavish expenditures for the emperor's travels a plot to by-pass the new constitution? Swope charged that the Imperial Household Ministry was circumventing scap's intention to bring the emperor's budget under public control simply by permitting local government entities and private corporations to supply the funds no longer made available through Diet appropriations.[3] Swope's efforts marked the end of the Imperial Household Ministry's program to popularize the emperor at the expense of local governments and private businesses.

Swope was unhappy over the 1948 liquidation of several Government Section units, including his own Political Affairs Division. But he was pleased that in his forty-five-minute parting interview, General MacArthur "told me to let *him* know if I wanted to come back." Making the rounds of the upper levels of different government agencies in Washington, particularly the Defense Department under Secretary Louis Johnson, he had "one helluva time." The trouble, he said, stemmed from the fact that he had been lumped with "the small group of longhaired boys . . .

who have helped Gen. MacArthur put over his socialistic schemes. . . . Powerful American interests are plenty sore at the Big Chief for what they consider his unnecessarily enthusiastic and drastic implementation of the Economic Directives under which he operates."[4] Ultimately Swope was appointed to a top position in the Office of the High Commissioner in the American Zone of occupied Germany.

One of my final acts as an occupation official was to write a recommendation for Dr. Milton J. Esman, applicant for a government-financed Johns Hopkins University research position. A member of the Government Section staff during the first year of the occupation, I wrote, he participated in the making of the model constitution, drafted the initial report for reconstructing the legislative branch, and started the movement for bringing a civil service mission to Japan. Of the fifty or sixty professionals who saw service with Government Section, I said, Esman was one of the four or five top-notchers.[5] A native of Pittsburgh, the twenty-seven-year old 1st lieutenant took his B.A. from Cornell and his doctorate from Princeton in politics and public administration before joining the United States Civil Service Commission as an administrative analyst. His military service, dating from 1942, included duty as an information and education officer at New Orleans Staging Area and attendance at the University of Virginia School of Military Government and the Harvard Civil Affairs Training School. His last official action in Government Section was an August 1946 study of local autonomy sentiment in Toyama and Ishikawa prefectures. At that early date he found strong sentiment for breaking the power of the Home Ministry in prefectures and cities, for popular election of local officials, local control of teachers but not of school curricula, local control of administrative policy but not of the national criminal police, and for much broader local taxing authority. He had a standing offer to return to Government Section in a civilian status. He became a professor of political science at Cornell.

From the fall of 1945 until he left Government Section in the spring of 1947 to return to the Department of Agriculture, Lt. Col. Pieter Roest was chief of the Political Parties Division, with responsibility for promoting democratic political parties, developing democratic election laws, and preventing formation of antidemocratic organizations. Calling San Francisco home, the forty-seven-year-old Roest was a medical alumnus of Leyden University (Holland), a Ph.D. in anthropology and sociology, University of Chicago, and a postgraduate student of international relations, law, and economics at the University of Southern California. His civilian experience included lecturing at a small college in Madras, India, studying Australian nationalism, conducting research in racecrossing in Java, chairing the social science department at the University of Toledo (Ohio) and at Reed College (Oregon), and serving as a marketing specialist in the United States Department of Agriculture. Commissioned a major in 1942, he later graduated from the School of Military Government at the University of Virginia and the Civil Affairs Training School at Yale.

Roest's tenure in Government Section was about as variegated as his preoccupation experience had been. He was something of a visionary. During the section's deliberations on the model constitution, he had responsibility for drawing up the section on civil rights. The Kades-Rowell-Hussey Steering Committee found much in the civil rights section to be irrelevant, fuzzy, and impractical and as a consequence rewrote most of its provisions.

Roest's name and that of his successor, Lt. Col. Carlos Marcum, who transferred from CIS to assist Kades with the purge, were linked to an ambitious effort to have the Diet enact a political parties law designed to eliminate splinter parties and to require a printed ballot. In his angry book on the occupation, *Typhoon in Tokyo*, showing how his and MacArthur's views differed about Japan's political reorientation, Dr. Harry Emerson Wildes said about Roest, without mentioning his name: "To cure obvious evils whose cause and probable implications he did not comprehend, a wholly incompetent Occupationnaire embarked upon a dangerous experiment." And regarding Marcum, without mentioning his name either, he wrote: "Soon afterwards, a successor, equally unqualified by education or experience, drafted another scheme designed to eliminate independents and small parties from campaigning."[6] Temperamentally unsuited to work under Roest, or subsequently under Osborne Hauge, chief of the Public Affairs Division, the scholarly but frustrated and grumpy Wildes soon drifted away from Government Section and in time was employed by SCAP's Civil Historical Section, where he was equally unhappy. As for the political parties bill, which MacArthur personally decreed the Diet could take or leave, it was finally denounced by the Japanese press and then permanently shelved by the House of Representatives.

Roest was partially responsible for the establishment in February 1948 of the Special Investigation Bureau in the Attorney General's Office. The special mission of this organization was "to insure that ultranationalistic societies . . . do not attempt to resume their proscribed activities" and to "maintain a check on former leaders of dissolved organizations." As the Government Section official charged with preventing the formation of antidemocratic societies, Roest had complained frequently of the frustrations he experienced in trying to obtain information requested by his superiors to perform this task. Finally, in desperation, he dashed off a memorandum to Kades calling attention to the absence of a Japanese government investigative agency. Yet, he said, "you have expected complete and up-to-the-minute information on any organization or person 'breaking' the newspapers. Obviously this is asking the impossible. Either we must allow the Japanese Government an adequate equivalent of our FBI, or we must rely on our own investigative agency, the C[ounter] I[ntelligence] C[orps]." [7] In the end, though in absentia, Roest had his way.

Government Sections's most publicized official during the first year or so of the occupation was Lt. Col. Cecil G. Tilton. He was mentioned prominently in Richard Tregaskis's September–October 1945 *Saturday Evening Post* articles on military government,[8] and he was singled out by Noel Busch in a 1946 *Life* magazine article, which said:

> Tilton with the help of two assistants has been effecting a complete renovation of local government throughout Japan.
> Governors of Japan's 46 prefectures used to be appointed by the national government in Tokyo. Henceforth governors, as well as town and village mayors, who used to be approved by the governors and elected by local councils, will be elected by direct popular vote. Municipal and prefectural assemblies will be reformed and methods of electing their members improved. Net result of all this will be to take the whole provincial government out of the hands of the national government . . . and put it in the hands of the people. Japanese political leaders in future should come up from the ranks of local politics and not from the elite of Tokyo's governing bureaucracy.[9]

From Prescott, Arizona, the forty-four-year-old Tilton took his B.S. and M.S. degrees from the University of California at Berkeley and his M.B.A. from the Harvard Graduate School of Business Administration. In civilian life, he had been a faculty member at the University of Hawaii and the University of Connecticut, a lecturer-consultant at United Aircraft's Pratt and Whitney Division, and a special administrator of the Office of Price Administration. He conducted extensive economic and political research on the Far East in the University of Chicago Civil Affairs Training School, and wrote the Army Service Forces's Manual M354–2, *Government and Administration of Japan* (United States Government Printing Office, January 1945). He graduated from the Provost Marshal General's School and the School of Military Government.

A conservative in politics, Tilton was a diligent worker for local government in Japan. That it was impossible to transplant to Japan the principles and practices of local autonomy as they evolved from the experiences of American frontiersmen was not his fault; he had no choice but to carry out as best he could the basic directive's irresolute injunction that "local responsibility for the local enforcement of national policy will be encouraged." The detailed section on local government drawn up by Tilton's committee for inclusion in Government Section's model constitution was discarded as inadequate and rewritten by the Steering Committee to guarantee limited local autonomy to prefectures and municipalities having the power to tax. These local entities were privileged to manage their own affairs and frame their own charters within limits defined by the Diet. The chapter on local government was a reconciliation of opposing views represented by Rowell, a strong home-rule man, and Kades, a central government man. Under the broad terms of the new constitution, Tilton's group, with the help of countless Japanese, put together, in the face of strong opposition from at least six SCAP staff sections, the provisions of the Law Concerning Local Autonomy, which was enacted by the Diet in April 1947.

In his review of Government Section's *Political Reorientation,* Sansom had this to say about the section on local government:

[It] contains an interesting analysis of the prewar structure and organization of local government . . . which was so authoritarian in character that in practice it allowed little real autonomy to local bodies. . . . The Government Section appears to have made a most careful and thorough investigation, an interesting piece of sociological research, in the course of which it discovered untapped resources of talent and strong currents of local opinion. . . . After the passage of the Law [Concerning Local Autonomy], some of the agencies of the central government attempted to diminish its effect, but they evoked strong reactions among local authorities and assemblies . . . it is unlikely that local bodies will surrender their new powers without a struggle.[10]

Tilton and the other members of the Local Government Division were transferred in mid-1948 to the Eighth Army, an arrangement that permitted them to carry on directly with military government teams and local government entities throughout Japan. Regarding the results of the experiment in local autonomy, the perceptive scholar Kazuo Kawai wrote in 1960:

On balance it can probably be said that local autonomy is proving to be more of a success than otherwise. It did not result automatically in the invigoration of a grass-roots democracy as the Occupation had apparently hoped for, and in some respects it even served to hamper the process of democratization. On the other hand, despite some serious defects and abuses, local autonomy has increased the opportunities for popular participation in government, and there can be little doubt that its long-range effects will be to bring responsibility for good government closer home to the people.[11]

On his return to the United States toward the end of the occupation, Tilton made a lecture tour of the country warning of the Communist threat in the Far East.

Born in 1903, Maj. Frank Rizzo grew up in New York City. After obtaining a degree in electrical engineering at Cornell, he completed three years of graduate work in economics, finance, and international relations at New York University and George Washington University. In civilian life he was an industrial economist and managing partner of Clinton Gilbert and Company, New York investment bankers. Prior to entering the service in September 1942, he was chief economist and technical expert for the National Association of Securities Dealers, the regulatory body for the investment banking business. His military service included duty as cost control officer, New Orleans Port of Embarkation; preparation of civil affairs studies in the Military Government Division, Provost Marshal General's Office; and organizer of the flow of information in the War Department's Civil Affairs Division. He graduated from the Infantry School, the Military Government Fiscal Officers' Course at Duke University, and the Provost Marshal General's School, and attended the Civil Affairs Training School at Yale.

When the financial and economic experts of General Crist's Military Government Section were transferred to the new Economic and Scientific Section in September 1945, Rizzo alone remained behind—thanks to the persuasiveness of Kades. Not a publicity seeker, the modest, industrious, and mentally poised Rizzo developed eventually, in some important respects, the kind of working relationship with Whitney that Whitney had with MacArthur. While Whitney wrote messages and letters for MacArthur's signature, Rizzo conducted research and wrote memorandums for Whitney's signature. Rizzo could write clear, understandable English. He contributed the chapter on finance in Government Section's democratic constitution. John Gunther called him "a remarkably able civilian."[12] Government Section's two-volume *Political Reorientation,* published in 1949, was coordinated, revised, and edited in the Pentagon under his personal supervision. Whitney referred to him as "an extraordinarily able engineer-turned-economist."[13] He became deputy chief of the section when Kades resigned in 1949 and section chief in April 1951 when Whitney accompanied MacArthur into retirement. As chief of Government Section during the final year of the occupation, he advised Gen. Matthew

Ridgway on progressive relaxation of controls to prepare the Japanese for resumption of sovereign responsibility. In 1952 he received a Presidential Letter of Commendation for outstanding contributions to the Occupation of Japan. After the occupation ended, he remained in Japan to manage and later head the International Inspection and Testing Corporation. At one time or another during his postoccupation residency in Japan he has been president of the Tokyo American Club and governor of the American Chamber of Commerce.[14] In November 1973, "in recognition of . . . [his] outstanding contributions . . . to the cause of the postwar rehabilitation of Japan, and . . . the promotion of Japan-U.S. friendly relations, His Majesty the Emperor was graciously pleased to confer upon [him] the First Class Order of the Sacred Treasure."[15]

From February 1946 to June 1951, Government Section had a separate division that engaged in a number of reporting and publicity activities. Named at one time or another the Review and Reports Branch, Information and Management Division, Special Projects Division, and Public Affairs Division, it reported Government Section doings to SCAP and the Pentagon, published news summaries of governmental affairs for distribution to military government teams in Japan, and assisted CIE in preparing domestic publicity programs on democracy, including press conferences held by Government Section officials. The director of this operation was Navy Lt. Osborne I. Hauge. Thirty-two years old, he graduated from St. Olaf College, Northfield, Minnesota, edited a Midwestern weekly newspaper from 1935 to 1937, directed publicity and promotion for the National Lutheran Council in New York from 1937 to 1942 when he joined the staff of the Norwegian Embassy in Washington, D.C. He served there until he was commissioned by the Navy in 1944. He received certificates of graduation from the Princeton School of Military Government and the Stanford Civil Affairs Training School.

Hauge was a member of Lt. Col. Frank Hays's Legislative Committee during the preparation of Government Section's draft constitution. The chapter he wrote for Government Section's *Political Reorientation* was, Sansom said, "an account of the progress of political education undertaken either directly by SCAP or by Japanese official and private organs."[16] A member of Hauge's division, Marcel Grilli, from Los Angeles, wrote the section on elections for the Government Section publication and also "Political Reorientation of Japan from 1949 to 1951." Hauge left Government Section in 1950 to join the Department of the Army's Civil Affairs Division. Later he was an official of the Bureau of the Budget and the Agency for International Development.

Whitney was indispensable to MacArthur and Kades was indispensable to Whitney, but every other member of the Government Section might have been replaced without untoward consequences. Except possibly Alfred C. Oppler. Another individual with Oppler's unique legal background, keen mind, and judicious temperament would not have been easily found. And lacking these qualities, no SCAP legal officer could have persuaded the Japanese legal community, as Oppler did, to participate meaningfully in setting up the kind of court system and writing the kinds of basic codes called for by the democratic constitution.

The fifty-three-year old Oppler joined Government Section in February 1946, just days too late to participate in the making of the model constitution. He had studied law at the Universities of Munich, Freiburg, Berlin, and Strasbourg and passed the two rigid law examinations required for the bar and judicial duty. His law career was interrupted by four years of military service on the Western Front (during World War I) where he took part in the fighting around Ypres and Verdun, first as a private and later as a lieutenant of artillery. Following the Armistice, he resumed the practice of law, becoming, by the age of thirty-eight, an associate justice of the Prussian Supreme Administrative Court and vice-president of the Prussian Supreme Disciplinary Court, both in Berlin. Treated as an outcast—because of Jewish grandparents—under the Nuremberg Laws (1935), he made his way to the United States in 1939, with no knowledge whatever of English. For two years or so of the war he delivered lectures and conducted research on German political, legal, and cultural institutions at Harvard University. In 1944 he was employed by the Foreign Economic Administration to prepare handbooks and other materials for use in the occupation of Germany. The next year he was approached by the Pentagon to assist SCAP in Japan.[17]

Oppler's first important contribution to the work of Government Section was a scholarly four-thousand-word brief making the case for the democratic constitution, then under debate in the Diet, as a legitimate successor of the Meiji Constitution. His masterly discourse, "Powers of the Diet with Regard to Constitutional Amendments under the Meiji Constitution," provided, as intended, "a safeguard against attempts to invalidate the new Constitution on the basis of legalistic arguments."[18] Of the many studies made by different Government Section lawyers on constitutional reform in Japan, only this one by Oppler was considered weighty enough to warrant publication in Government Section's voluminous *Political Reorientation*.

Inside SCAP, Oppler became a tower of strength. He advised SCAP staff sections on legal aspects of proposed directives and proposed Japanese reform legislation. He was turned to for counsel in matters involving Continental law. For instance, in MacArthur's February 1947 letter on lese majesty to the prime minister, most of which Kades wrote, Oppler conducted the research for the paragraph relative to violence against the person of the British king.

As Milo Rowell's replacement in the Governmental Powers Division, Oppler was bound sooner or later to have differences with the self-assured Rod Hussey, his supervisor. He regarded Hussey as an excellent American legal light, but not as a student of the Japanese legal system, which was German in origin. And he thought Hussey dealt with Japanese officials in an entirely uncalled for high-handed manner. But what brought the two to a parting of the ways was Hussey's brusque treatment of Tom Blakemore, Oppler's only assistant at the time. This brilliant Oklahoman, who had studied law in Japan before the war (and was to become the West's most prominent lawyer in postoccupation Japan), was invaluable to Government Section because of his linguistic abilities and extensive knowledge of Japanese law. If he was a bit stubborn and inclined to the Japanese point of view, he served as a necessary counterbalance to those Government Section lawyers who knew only the American way. Forced to choose between Blakemore and Hussey, Oppler quite naturally opted for his assistant. Kades eased the tension by giving Oppler quasi-independent status in the Governmental Powers Division, and subsequently resolved the issue by creating the Courts and Law Division and naming Oppler to head it. Ironically, when Hussey's Governmental Powers Division was abolished in 1948, its residual functions were transferred to Oppler's division upon its move to the Legal Section. Among the first-rate lawyers assisting Oppler were, in addition to Blakemore, Howard Myers, who would later reach the top rung of the ladder in the State Department; Richard B. Appleton, an able and indefatigable worker; the conservative and reliable Walter Monagan; and Dr. Kurt Steiner, a refugee from Nazi Austria, who, in time, became a political science professor at Stanford University.

Oppler will long be remembered for his revision of the Japanese codes of law along democratic lines. It was he who brought about the sweeping reforms of the Civil, Criminal, and Procedural Codes and the enactment of the Court Organization Law, innovations that breathed life into the new constitution. He saw to it that the best features of the Continental and Anglo-Saxon legal systems were adopted without imposing by fiat unsuitable American legal practices; and in the process of modernizing and humanizing the revised statutes, he stressed the rule of law and individual rights as opposed to the power of the government. To help insure acceptance of the radical changes, he divided his staff into standing committees in which all points were freely and fully discussed between American and Japanese jurists until a meeting of minds was reached. This practice of democracy won for him the respect and gratitude of Japanese legalists.

Judge Oppler remained in Japan after the occupation ended to advise the Commander-in-Chief, United States Forces, Far East, on legal and political matters. He tells all this in his excellent 1976 book, *Legal Reform in Occupied Japan: A Participant Looks Back.*[19]

American policy makers believed that the main obstacles to the growth of democracy in Japan were the military, the family monopolies, and the bureaucracy. Washington directed MacArthur to destroy the military and dissolve the monopolies, but was strangely silent on what he should do about the bureaucracy. Consequently SCAP developed its own policy. On the basis of Esman's recommendation that civil service reform should remain a major priority of Government Section, Kades put in a request to the War Department for a civil service mission to reform the Japanese bureaucracy.[20] The War Department responded by dispatching to Japan a team of civil service experts (W. Pierce MacCoy, State Department director of personnel, and Civil Service Commission experts Robert S. Hare and Manlio F. DeAngelis), headed by Blaine Hoover. Their function was to effect improvement in the overall personnel administration of the Japanese government.

At age fifty-three, Blaine Hoover of Evanston, Illinois, had the best of credentials for his assigned task in Japan. He had studied three years at Beloit College and one year at the University of Chicago, after which he spent twenty years or so in business corporations and on public commissions as a personnel and management expert. Since 1937 he had been superintendent of employment and secretary and member of the Civil Service Board of the Chicago Park District. In addition to his Chicago Park District duties, he was, in 1946, a consultant of the United States Civil Service Commission, a member of the Council of the National Civil Service League of the United States, and president of the Civil Service Assembly of the United States and Canada.

Civil service reform made considerable headway between the fall of 1946, when Hoover first went to Japan, and the fall of 1948, when he presided over the annual meeting of the Civil Service Assembly of the United States and Canada. Before the Assembly for decision was a resolution opposing the employment of Communists in the public service at any level, the subject to which Hoover, as the principal speaker, addressed himself. He began by referring to Japan's upper bureaucracy which, in the name of civil service, had constituted a self-perpetuating and all but closed fraternity of men in the controlling positions of government, and to the labor boss system under which certain men hired government employees at any rate for which they would work, collected a standard wage from the government, and pocketed the difference.[21]

Then he got down to the nitty-gritty of his two-year ordeal in Japan, making these points:

To understand what happened in Japan, we must understand . . . the pattern of labor relations in the Government. . . . In the early days of the occupation . . . the [SCAP] men responsible for labor policy were largely experienced in the field of private enterprise. . . . Of 30,000,000 persons gainfully employed . . . about 2,500,000 are in the Public Service. Out of the approximate 8% of the gainfully employed who were in the government service, these labor advisers developed almost 40% of the organized labor of the country. . . . [With minor exceptions] these men applied in government the same pattern of labor relations which they had applied to private enterprise. This included the right to bargain collectively and the right to strike against the government. . . . [As a consequence there were] ministries with thousands of their employees on government pay giving full time to the work of their unions . . . union meetings during business hours . . . tax collectors who wouldn't collect taxes because their union did not approve of the legislative policy on which the taxes were based . . . railroad employees who refused to operate trains on government railroads because the union's approval of time schedules had not been secured . . . inefficiency, destandardization, collapse of discipline, all produced by a program of "strike, struggle and sabotage."[22]

Some observers saw in the Japanese labor situation of 1948 the long-awaited opportunity to effect "changes in the direction of modifying the feudal and authoritarian tendencies of the government . . . [by] the use of force," which, according to Washington's basic directive, the Supreme Commander was to permit and favor. Hoover objected to this Washington dictum.

The Communists [he told his Ottawa audience] . . . came into control of some of the largest unions in the government. They were then in a position to dictate to the government in many critical areas of operation—and did. . . . this Communist command had maintained close contact with our labor advisers, seeming to seek their advice and cooperation. . . . as their program of strike, struggle and sabotage gained momentum, and they became increasingly secure in their positions, they became less and less regardful of these very labor advisers on whose shoulders they had hoisted themselves to eminence. Finally . . . they all but ignored their advisers. . . . April, 1947, the Personnel Advisory Mission had recommended legislative and operative programs designed to correct the conditions of malad-ministration existing in the public service. In our absence from Japan during the latter part of last year, the civil service law was passed. However, the combined machinations of the feudal bureaucrats and these gentlemen who were operating in the name of labor had made the law a feeble instrument.

As the new civil service commission came into authority on July 1, 1948, a crisis was shaping up. . . . government business was, in some areas, practically suspended while government employees loafed, held union meetings, and even conducted parades. The Japanese public . . . was viewing this strange spectacle, enacted in the name of democracy, with a contempt which almost equalled the dislike they had previously entertained for their feudal bureaucracy. . . . there was set up a program of strikes to begin in August, which whould have had many of the effects of a general strike. . . . What a scene in history—80,000,000 persons . . . helpless in the hands of a few radicals who commanded a bureaucracy possessed of . . . the right of collective bargaining . . . supported by the right to strike.[23]

Completing his description of the chaotic labor scene, Hoover then proceeded to explain the steps taken in Japan to establish an effective civil service system.

Of course [he said], action was taken by the Occupation authorities. On July 22nd, General Douglas MacArthur addressed a letter to the Prime Minister . . . in which he indicated accord with proposed revisions to the National Public Service Law necessary to give it much of the character and force recommended by the . . . Advisory Mission. . . . he quoted . . . Franklin D. Roosevelt . . . to the effect that "all government employees should realize that the process of collective bargaining . . . cannot be transplanted into the Public Service. . . . a strike of public employees . . . looking toward the paralysis of government by those who have sworn to support it, is unthinkable and intolerable."

General MacArthur then stated his own position . . . as follows: "No person holding a position in the public service of Japan . . . should resort to strike or engage in delaying or other dispute tactics which tend to impair the efficiency of government operations."

The effect of this communication was tremendous. The Cabinet . . . under the Potsdam arrangements . . . almost immediately gave it force of law pending passage of implementing laws. A special session of the Diet was called. . . . Many strikes called for August were cancelled. . . . At one stroke, General MacArthur had decapitated the creature which . . . had been gaining strength and was, even then, twining itself around the throat of the young Japanese democracy. . . . On August 11th, the Russian General Kislenko wrote General MacArthur protesting the policy. . . . The Diet will convene this month and we anticipate sound revision of the Civil Service Law. . . . the new civil service commission will see that government employees are properly compensated.[24]

I associate Blaine Hoover with two events in 1948. One of these involved Jim Killen, chief of the ESS Labor Division, and the other involved Frayne Baker, acting as agent for the ESS Finance Division. When it became clear in mid-1948 that Hoover and Killen, on leave from an American Federation of Labor post, could not reconcile their differences over the scope of the coverage of the National Public Service Law, the meaning of collective bargaining as applied to government workers, and the use of strikes or dispute tactics against the government, the points at issue were laid before MacArthur for resolution. A date was set for the disputants to present oral arguments in support of their respective positions.[25] Each announced in advance that he would resign if the decision went against him. "I'll beat him," Hoover told me, "for two reasons. First, my position accords more nearly with American philosophy and practice. Second, even if our arguments were equally sound, my dignified bearing and impeccable attire contrasted with his cloddish manner and tawdry appearance will prejudice MacArthur against him." MacArthur upheld Hoover, and Killen resigned. (For MacArthur's slant, see Chapter 14.)

When the Temporary National Personnel Commission recommended in October 1948 an increase in the average wage for government employees from ¥3,800 to ¥6,307, the Finance Ministry and the ESS Finance Division were dumbfounded. The Finance Ministry resented the unprecedented interference by the Personnel Commission with its control of the budget, and the ESS Finance Division uttered unprintable imprecations at Government Section's disruption of SCAP's economic stabilization plan. The Yoshida Government's budget bill, which was scheduled for passage by the House of Representatives the evening of 13 December, provided for a wage scale of ¥5,330. The opposition parties in the House, which outnumbered the minority government party, planned to offer an amendment boosting the level to ¥6,307. Throughout the evening and until the wee hours of the next morning, ex-Brigadier General Baker repeatedly conveyed orders to Speaker Matsuoka Komakichi, in the name of SCAP, to uphold the ¥5,330 figure; while Hoover from another quarter conveyed countermanding orders, also in the name of SCAP, demanding that the ¥6,307 amendment be adopted.[26] Because of the uproar that very evening over Finance Minister Izumiyama Sanroku's becoming "dead drunk" in the Diet Building, making it impossible for him to answer interpellations in the lower house chamber, followed by his forced resignation from the cabinet two hours past midnight, the House vote on the matter was postponed. When the budget bill finally received Diet approval on 21 December, it contained the ¥6,307 provision recommended by the National Personnel Commission.[27]

Unlike Alfred Oppler, who solicited the views of Japanese officials and legislators, Blaine Hoover turned a deaf ear to their counsel and compelled them to accept his civil service reform plan exactly as he drafted it. Only with MacArthur's strong backing, therefore, was he able to accomplish the dual mission of amending previously enacted labor legislation to prevent strikes by government officials and public enterprise employees, and of writing into law a new civil service code to help adapt the bureaucracy to an uncustomary subordinate role. Hoover's aim was to establish a democratic and efficient public service system encompassing such things as position classification, entrance examinations, evaluation of performance, training programs, pay scales, transfer, tenure, retirement, and pensions. Whether he provided Japan with the most up-to-date system, and whether his rejection of Japanese advice hurt the cause for which he labored, are points that might be raised about many other occupation changes, including the democratic constitution. To SCAP, the pertinent questions were: Did the bureaucracy get a thorough shaking-up? Did the Diet and the people become well-informed of the place of the bureaucracy in a democratic society? As with other occupation reforms, the Japanese have retained that part of the civil service program which served their purpose and discarded that which they found unacceptable. In any event, John M. Maki wrote ten years after the occupation ended that the

new and detailed civil service law . . . broke down the exclusive character of the old system. Wider eligibility for entrance examinations, new standards for promotion, and more emphasis on technical knowledge and training in nonadministrative matters have operated to provide officialdom with a broader base in society. . . . the bureaucracy is still strong, but its old power of direct control over the daily lives of the people seems safely eliminated.[28]

When Hoover died in September 1950, he was succeeded by Maynard Shirven, examination specialist on leave from the Civil Service Commission, who helped to write, and to expedite Diet passage of, the Local Public Service Law of 9 December 1950.

Note should be made here of four additional members of the professional staff of Government Section: Frank E. Hays, Cyrus H. Peake, T. A. Bisson, and Eleanor Hadley.

About forty years of age, Lieutenant Colonel Hays, from Lander, Wyoming, was Deputy Chief Kades's right-hand man for more than two years. At the University of Chicago Civil Affairs Training School he had prepared a scholarly forty-six-page paper titled "Forces Influencing the Japanese Cabinet, 1885–1945." Coolheaded and even-tempered, he kept the store while Kades ranged far and wide. General Whitney singled him out as "an able lawyer of long practice [who] worked out the section on the Diet [in the draft constitution]."[29] He wrote Section 9, "Governmental Aspects of Law Enforcement," for the Government Section's *Political Reorien.ation*. In 1948 he resumed the practice of law in Wyoming.

Dr. Peake was a Government Section stalwart for twenty months or so beginning in January 1946. One of twenty civilian experts hired in Washington for the section's original planning group, he made a major contribution both to the writing of the model constitution and to the revision of many important laws implementing the new constitution. Born in Minnesota in 1900, he graduated from Northwestern University and obtained his M.A. and Ph.D. from Columbia University. Following two years of teaching in Japan, he settled down at Columbia University as instructor, lecturer, assistant professor, and managing editor and co-editor of the *Far Eastern Quarterly*. In 1942–1943 he was an official of the Foreign Economic Administration. On separating from Government Section in the fall of 1947 he joined the State Department to become chief of the Northeast Asia Political Branch, Division for the Far East.

Ex-Prime Minister Yoshida referred in his *Memoirs* to only four members of the Government Section staff. Two of these were Whitney and Kades, mentioned in the preceding chapter. The other two "had played particularly important roles in the drafting of the [economic] purge plan, a Mr. Thomas Arthur Bisson, who had been in Japan before and was an enthusiastic New Dealer with advanced views regarding ways and means of democratising our financial world, and a Miss Eleanor Hadley . . . known for her researches into our financial concerns."[30] Born in New York in 1900, Art Bisson took his B.A. from Rutgers and his M.A. from Teachers College, Columbia University. After a four-year stint as a missionary teacher in Anhwei and Peiping, China, he became a member of the research staff of the Foreign Policy Association in 1929, concentrating on the Far East. A year's leave of absence in 1937 on a fellowship from the Rockefeller Foundation afforded him an opportunity to explore the Far East, including a visit in company with Philip Jaffe and Owen Lattimore to the Communist outpost of Yenan, China. He was principal economist for the Board of Economic Warfare in 1942–1943, a member of the international secretariat of the Institute of Pacific Relations in 1943–1945, and a member of the United States Strategic Bombing Survey in 1945–1946, before becoming economic adviser to the chief of SCAP's Government Section, in 1946–1947. His books included *Japan in China* (1938), *America's Far Eastern Policy* (1945), *Japan's War Economy* (1945), *Prospects for Democracy in Japan* (1949), and *Zaibatsu Dissolution in Japan* (1954). He contributed articles to *Pacific Affairs, Amerasia, American Political Science Review, New Republic, Saturday Review of Literature, Annals of the American Academy,* and others.[31] It was his belief that "destruction of the great *Zaibatsu* combines is indispensable to clearing the path for a healthy growth of the small industrialists and merchants. This group, linked with the workers and farmers as victims of the oligarchy's greed, will offer an additional support to the development of a stable Japanese democracy." He believed further that the 1889 Constitution, the old bureaucracy, and the Emperor system must be eliminated and that a constitutional assembly, freely elected by the Japanese people, be enabled to establish the foundations of a new democratic regime. Only such a regime, he felt, could be expected "to elaborate and enforce the genuine nationalization measures for large-scale industry which will shake loose the grip of the *Zaibatsu* and thus permit the development of a Japan that can enter into normal and peaceful relations with the other members of the world community." [32] Harry Wildes wrote: "A strong contingent, headed by John Carter Vincent . . . Thomas A. Bisson . . . and Andrew Roth of Naval Intelligence, vigorously argued that to punish Hirohito as a war criminal would convince Japanese of the enormity of Japan's offenses. These men, although more familiar with Chinese than with Japanese affairs, carried great weight because of their access to periodicals. Their thesis had strong support in Australia, Canada, China, the Philippines, Russia, and, less notably, Great Britain." [33]

Though Bisson may have exerted considerable influence on the framers of Washington's basic occupation directive, he had no impact on the course of the occupation. He followed Kades's instructions in helping to implement the Washington-ordered economic purge, and he tried, on his own initiative, to obtain SCAP backing for the general strike scheduled for 1 February 1947. As Theodore Cohen, then chief of the ESS Labor Division, recalled years later, "Bisson was one of the pople who argued in favor of permitting the general strike, but Bisson had nothing to do with the decision. . . . Nobody ever asked him and he was wholly outside of the decision. I had a 'friendly' discussion with Bisson in December, 1946 in which I told him he was crazy. It was impossible to have a general strike and still have a continuing government . . . in my opinion . . . he was pro-Stalinist. . . . He never made any labor policy. . . . He was out of it." [34]

Art Bisson was intellectually honest; he made no bones about laying his pro-China beliefs on the line. He was a fellow traveler of Mao Tse-tung but he was not a party card holder. After leaving Japan in 1947, he finished writing his book, *Prospects for Democracy in Japan,* and then became a teacher at the University of California, Berkeley.

Like Bisson, Eleanor Hadley of Seattle, Washington, a Mills College graduate, was, as Mr. Yoshida pointed out, concerned with breaking up the great industrial combines, the zaibatsu. An employee of the State Department from 1944 to 1946, she helped draft United States economic policy for occupied Japan. Recruited to assist Government Section in developing recommendations for eliminating "those relationships between government and business which tended to continue the Japanese war potential," she advised Kades on the economic purge and also completed a study for him showing that some eight to ten families controlled approximately eighty-five percent of the Japanese economy. But she worked mostly with the ESS Antitrust and Cartels Division. The title of her 1949 dissertation for the doctorate at Radcliffe College was "Concentrated Business Power in Japan." In 1970 the Princeton University Press published her thoroughly researched and highly authoritative work, *Antitrust in Japan*. In this book she shows that "Delay, bureaucracy and American ignorance of Japanese commerce operated against the Occupation reformers." She concluded that "the antitrust program accomplished little that would not quickly be undone." [35] She left her teaching position at Smith College to become an economist with the United States Tariff Commission. Later she switched to the General Accounting Office.

Responsible for the smooth administration of Government Section during its busiest and most fruitful years were Col. Henry E. Robison, my supervisor at the start of the occupation, and his successor, Lt. Col. Carl Darnell, Jr. Robison, just past thirty, was in the sugar business in Manila before the war. A graduate of Stanford University and of the School of Military Government, and wartime executive of the Military Government Division, Office of the Provost Marshal General, he was persuaded by General Crist in August 1945 to serve with the Military Government Section of GHQ, AFPAC, in Japan. Both Crist and Whitney highly praised Robison for his administrative skill, intense loyalty, and overall performance in a difficult position. Some time after leaving Government Section in the late summer of 1946, he became executive vice-president of Stanford Research Institute, famed international economic development center of Menlo Park, California.

Darnell was equally successful during the next two years in smoothing the skids for the section chief and ministering to the needs of the civilian staff. A genial West Pointer (who would retire from military service twenty years later as a major general), he demonstrated his versatility by the manner in which he cautioned his nonmilitary associates to respect sacrosanct Army regulations. Instead of attacking the problem frontally, in true military fashion, he posted the following message on the bulletin board for all staff members to read and take to heart:

Impulsiveness struck the Government Section a telling blow! In his zeal to acquire a concurrence from another section, one of our bright young men failed to obtain it in writing. Even more horrible, he couldn't remember the name of the person who concurred. Result: confusion and red faces. So be guided by this sad example and obtain concurrences in writing.

Furthermore, concurrences given by this section must be of a formal nature. Beware of the curb-stone opinion. Only the Chief can give concurrences.
Happy New Year, and don't forget the Memorandum for the Record.[36]

With Mr. Shirasu Jiro, a bilingual Japanese who made frequent visits to Government Section in the capacity of a Central Liaison Office emissary, Darnell was not so patient. When Mr. Shirasu's insatiable curiosity about the notices posted on the Government Section bulletin board get beyond his control, Darnell placed the entire section off-limits to him.

Maj. Jack Napier, a career Army officer, succeeded Darnell and carried on until the end of the MacArthur regime. He ultimately retired as a colonel.

Maj. William C. Curtis, Jr., filled the post during the final year of the occupation under Frank Rizzo.

Courtney Whitney: SCAP Strong Man

Veteran diplomat and distinguished historian George F. Kennan has made two perceptive comments on the American occupations of Germany and Japan following World War II. For one thing, he said, the Washington directives by which the occupational establishments were supposedly governed "reflected at many points the love for pretentious generality, the evangelical liberalism, the self-righteous punitive enthusiasm, the pro-Soviet illusions, and the unreal hopes for great-power collaboration in the postwar period which . . . had pervaded the wartime policies of the Allied powers." In the second place, regarding the administrations of General Clay and General MacArthur, he observed that "any great military-occupational government at once takes on certain of the aspects of a sovereign government and is in a position to require that it be treated accordingly, even by the government it purports to represent." [1] In these two statements, Kennan pinpoints what a number of SCAP personnel were groping for in the first months of the occupation of Japan: Washington's aims and how MacArthur planned to achieve them. Quite obviously in the basic directive to SCAP there was a preponderance of the philosophy of Owen Lattimore, Andrew Roth, Nozaka Sanzo, and the China Crowd in the State Department, but it was difficult to single out the individuals in GHQ who were doing MacArthur's planning. Government Section officers had concluded only that General Crist, their chief, was not one of them. And then a totally unanticipated event took place.

On 13 December 1945 Crist gave up his post and was succeeded two days later by Brig. Gen. Courtney Whitney, a well-to-do Manila attorney who was purported to have known MacArthur before the war. He had been MacArthur's deputy for civil affairs during and after the 1944–1945 Philippine military campaign, and it was said that he had the Supreme Commander's ear at all times.

Not until 24 December, his tenth day in office, did the new chief of Government Section assemble his full staff. A saturnine and soft-spoken man in his upper forties, he said solemnly: "General MacArthur views the occupation as one of the greatest events in the history of American foreign policy and considers Government Section the backbone of the occupation. What this section does or fails to do, he told me a few evenings ago, will be of tremendous significance to the United States, and to Japan, for generations to come. This means that we have a grave responsibility which we must shoulder together. We must work as a team. I need your help. The door of my office is open to you. Drop in any time, even for a chat." Unlike his predecessor, he made no mention of secrecy or security. He seemed to have MacArthur's confidence. He was not afraid of his shadow. He had something on the ball.

Exactly a week later, on the last day of the year, he called us together again. "This will be a regular affair," he said. "I want all of you to be conversant with what goes on. I want your reaction to every proposed directive to the Japanese government prepared in this section. The junior officers are as well if not better qualified to pass judgment on our moves as the higher ranking ones, including myself. I mean exactly what I say. And I look forward to the time when a lieutenant will barge into my office, bang my desk, and say: 'Goddammit, general, such-and-such a proposed directive is preposterous, and you would be out of your mind to ask General MacArthur to approve it.' " Then he divulged what he was driving at. "Take the Japanese election law," he said, "as amended earlier this month by the Imperial Diet. Our expert on politics, Major Roest, believes that we should not meddle with it, that a fair election can be held under it as is. He may be right, but I want a section hearing on the matter anyway. Accordingly I have asked Colonel Kades to appoint a staff member to marshal all the opposition he can to Roest's position."

Two days later, on 2 January 1946, twenty-one Government Section officers gathered to hear Major Roest and Major Rowell argue the merits and demerits of Japan's election law. Also present were representatives of CIE, ESS, G–2, and POLAD. Each speaker had twenty minutes to make his case. Roest, defending the law, emphasized that all leaders of the several Japanese political parties—Liberal, Progressive, Socialist, People's Cooperative, Communist—approved it in its present form. Admittedly, he said, to many Americans Japanese election procedures were narrow, quaint, and undemocratic. There was no printed ballot, candidates were not permitted to make house-to-house canvasses, newspapers were forbidden to support or oppose individual candidates, and electors could vote for only two or three of all candidates contesting the ten to fourteen seats at stake in each of the country's forty-six election districts. Yet no Japanese claimed that the law was partial to any party, group, or faction. No press or radio commentator maintained that a democratic election could not be held under it.

Taking issue with Roest, Rowell contended that the Supreme Commander should direct the Japanese government to conduct the forthcoming election for members of the House of Representatives in conformity with American election practices. To guarantee a democratic election, he concluded, the printed ballot must be used, house-to-house visits permitted, newspaper support for individual candidates authorized, restrictions on the use of posters and postcards removed, and the proportional representation voting formula eliminated. "Otherwise," he warned, "the Imperial Rule Assistance Association, the fascist organization, will be returned to power."

After a five-minute rebuttal by Roest, Colonel Kades invited questions and comment from the audience. Guy Swope, the former congressman and territorial governor, upheld Roest's proposition by citing dangers inherent in Occidentals tinkering with the subtle and complicated election practices of an Oriental country. Old Japan hand Max Bishop, speaking for POLAD, vouched that the main features of the existing Japanese election law, which had been on the books since 1925, were ideally suited to the character and temperament of Japanese voters. But G–2's Col. F. P. Munson thought it undemocratic for electors of a district to be permitted to vote for only two or three candidates when there were ten to fourteen seats to be filled. Others were critical of blank ballots, restrictions on electioneering, too few voting booths, the role of the police, and the like. It appeared to me, and I said so, that the real question was whether we wanted an American election or a Japanese election. A Japanese election, regardless of the outcome, would be in effect a Japanese poll on occupation reforms and the wartime Diet. On the other hand, an American-type election would provide a tailor-made platform for Japan's ultranationalists following our withdrawal. We had nothing to gain by rigging the election in our favor. But by needless interference with Japan's time-honored voting system, we stood to lose the goodwill we had gained. Throughout the discussion General Whitney sat in silence with his head tilted back against the wall, his eyes fixed on the ceiling, and his face devoid of expression.

At the conclusion of the proceedings a vote was taken on the question: "Will this law as it stands make for a democratic election?" Printed on the ballots were eighteen separate provisions of the law, all of which were at odds with American practices and therefore easy to adjudge undemocratic. Omitted were any favorable points, such as support for the existing statute by leaders of all Japanese political parties. Not surprisingly, therefore, the vote was twenty for changing the law by GHQ directive and seven for leaving it alone.

Apparently displeased with the result, which might have been unduly influenced by the outsiders present and voting, General Whitney took the unusual step of requesting that members of his own staff reflect further and be prepared two days later to cast a record vote on the same question. Roest and Rowell circulated separate papers summarizing their respective arguments and providing space for the signatures of like-minded colleagues. Fifteen officers signed Rowell's paper, and four—Swope, Tilton, Hauge, and myself—signed Roest's, a lopsided majority of nearly four to one in favor of changing the election law by SCAP directive.

Elated with their smashing victory, the Government Section majority—including among others Kades, Hussey, Hays, Rizzo, and Esman—naturally assumed that General Whitney, a newcomer, would as a matter of military routine uphold their position. So did the minority. Seeing my name at the top of Roest's list of supporters, Colonel Kades zestfully badgered me by asking how in good conscience I could defend a law that was so patently undemocratic. When I answered by restating my objection to an American-type election, he twitted me with the comment: "Ah, nuts, you're evading the issue. The Potsdam Declaration calls for establishment of democratic institutions, and this election law is certainly undemocratic."

Relaxing the following week at the Fujiya in Miyanoshita, an Army rest hotel, I forgot all about the Roest-Rowell debate and its outcome, assuming that SCAP would order an American-type election. It never occurred to me that the new section chief would be so bold as to rule against his staff so early in the game. When I returned to Tokyo in mid-January I was unprepared for the biggest surprise of my three and a half years in uniform, General Whitney's rejection of the majority recommendation. Routinely thumbing through the Government Section file, I came across his two-page memorandum of 7 January to General MacArthur on the subject, in which he concluded that a democratic election could be held under the existing law and recommended that no action be taken to change it. I noted his reference to the inefficacy of a SCAP election and the advantages of a true Japanese election.

Checking with Colonel Robison, the executive officer, I was told that General Whitney, before personally delivering the memorandum to General MacArthur, had read it to his staff. By the time he finished, a number of faces were scarlet and a hushed silence hung over the room for a long second, until Colonel Kades relieved the tension by declaring amiably that his head was "awfully bloody but not bowed." Everybody laughed. Then, according to Robison, General Whitney "marched down the hall and read the memorandum to General MacArthur, who approved it without reservation. How different from the past," Robison said, "when every memorandum prepared in this section got bogged down in GHQ red tape. Hell," he continued, "with a bellyful of that by early November, I wrote my former boss, Maj. Gen. Archer Lerch, Provost Marshall General in Washington, and asked him to bail me out of this mess. When he passed through Tokyo last month enroute to South Korea to become the military governor there, he invited me to accompany him. I declined, however, for by that time General Whitney had taken over here and there was reason to believe, on the basis of his close ties with MacArthur, that he would be able to do something with the section. I'm glad I stayed on."

Everybody rejoiced at having a boss who could and would throw his weight around. But whether General Whitney meant it when he said that all important directives would be thrashed out by the entire staff, there were doubts. For on 4 January, while the election law hassle was in progress, SCAP sent to the Japanese government the sensational twin directives for purging ultranationalists and abolishing ultranationalistic societies. Though prepared in Government Section, these instructions had not been seen, let alone debated, by members of the Public Administration Branch. This led to the belief that General Whitney may have staged the election law debate for ulterior purposes. It was surmised that he desired, for one thing, to familiarize himself with the caliber and character of the staff he inherited. More important, he may have had in mind thwarting by majority vote of the civilian soldiers under him Colonel Kades's known intent to "democratize" the election law by GHQ directive. How else could he avert the painful necessity of overruling his brilliant and indispensable senior officer? If so, the ploy backfired and he had to overrule Kades anyway. The unproductive debate technique would not be used again.

The significance of the one and only "great debate" did not escape Government Section personnel. We learned from it that our new chief was an aggressive, resourceful, and influential man, the man MacArthur heavily relied upon to modify and temper the half-baked, draconian Washington occupation policy directive. It also made us aware for the first time of MacArthur's preponderant interest in Government Section and of his deferential regard for the Japanese way of life. Above all, it made us realize that Government Section had moved up overnight to an indisputable position of primacy within GHQ, freed from much of the debilitating friction and frustrating bureaucratic inaction at the highest echelons of the headquarters, and assured us that it would not be hamstrung by divisive tactics of other staff sections assisted by artful Japanese lobbyists. In short, we appreciated that Whitney had placed us in the driver's seat.

How General Whitney himself viewed the election law exercise was something else. None of us knew his slant until he wrote the Foreword for the Government Section's *Political Reorientation,* in which he had only this to say:

When the Japanese Government caused legislation to be enacted early in the occupation to democratize the election law, as a prelude to the first general election, the law was found by the Government Section to be entirely within the framework of democratic principles, practice, and precedent, but various loopholes were discerned which might well have given rise to corrupt electoral practices. MacArthur studied the points involved and decided that he would prefer to let the imperfections stand rather than require amendments which while perfecting the law would vitiate its character as a Japanese instrument. This principle has guided all subsequent action taken by the Government Section on Japanese legislation.[2]

Writing in 1955 on the same subject but from the standpoint of MacArthur rather than Government Section, he amplified his earlier statement a bit.

It was at this point that MacArthur made one of the fundamental decisions of the occupation. . . . The election law, he pointed out, was basically sound and democratic. . . . he said ". . . should we require a change, however slight, it will assume the attaint of Allied force and become marked for possible repeal once that force is lifted."[3]

There was no mention in either account of the Government Section debate on the election law, of the countrary position taken by the Government Section majority, or of his memorandum to MacArthur on the subject.

More light was thrown on General Whitney's unique place in SCAP at a long session of the Public Administration Division on 25 April 1946. Obviously still smarting from the storm of criticism that followed his "filibuster" in the four-member Allied Council the previous week, he took pains to justify his performance on that occasion. The surface issue was SCAP's administration of the 4 January purge directives, but the underlying issue was the very existence of the council itself. In the words of AP correspondent Russell Brines,

The council was reduced to virtual sterility by a calculated SCAP program. General MacArthur and his spokesmen used ridicule, sarcasm, bluster and disdain in summarily rejecting most of what was said before the organization. Soviet representatives used the same tactics in veiled propaganda speeches and raw attacks on the occupation. . . . But they lost the chance to influence policy, the evident aim of Moscow's insistence upon setting up the organization. So did the British and Chinese members. As a result, the American base of the occupation was broadened.[4]

Chicago Sun correspondent Mark Gayn, no Whitney admirer, gave this eyewitness account of the 17 April Council meeting:

For two days now the Allied Council has been engaged in wrangling. . . . The wrangle began . . . with Headquarters' reply to General Derevyanko's request for information on the reported Japanese failure to comply with the purge directives. The answer was given by General Whitney. He spoke in a peremptory manner, which, one witness said, "skillfully borders on the line between the permissible insult and the point where you get punched on the nose." Whitney asserted that Derevyanko's question endangered the progress of the Occupation. . . . Whitney now embarked on an old-fashioned filibuster. . . . He read an entire three-month-old 10,000-word directive, already familiar to everyone in the room. . . . it was a juvenile, small-time performance. . . . it made it plain, in the most discourteous manner, that we did not intend to cooperate with the other Council members.[5]

For the light it throws on Whitney as the agent of MacArthur, the attitude expressed by British Commonwealth Council member W. Macmahon Ball, former head of the political science department at the University of Melbourne, is worth noting.

General Whitney [he wrote] behaved in an unusual way. . . . He . . . delivered an address lasting for about three hours . . . reading slowly long lists of political organizations that had been banned by S.C.A.P. . . . he said in an aside: "There are 30,000 members of these organizations, and I must apologize to the Council for not having the names with me. . . . General Whitney's performance was a gross and ill-mannered affront to every Member of the Council. . . .
This second meeting . . . decided the Council's fate. . . . General Whitney, speaking on behalf of General MacArthur, insisted that "the Council is not set up for the purpose of prying into S.C.A.P. affairs, attempting to find weak points in S.C.A.P. armour, probing for something by which to create national sensationalism."[6]

General Whitney was, of course, aware that the members of his Public Administration Division were familiar with the unfavorable press reaction to his behavior at the council meeting. He began, therefore, by pointing to previous provocative steps taken by the Russians to embarrass the Supreme Commander. An example of this, he said, was the request by the Soviet member that MacArthur withhold appraisal of the 10 April general election until the council could examine the SCAP analysis; to which he replied: "General MacArthur will comment on any aspect of the occupation without consulting the Council." There was no doubt, he went on, that the Soviet Union intended to use the council as a sounding board for its propaganda to discredit the occupation. As he had observed in his prepared statement to the council, he told us, the available information on the purge to which General Derevyanko referred was not obtained from General Headquarters, nor had any attempt been made from that source to verify its accuracy. To counter the Soviet strategy, General MacArthur decided to retaliate in kind. "If the Russians wanted a knock-down-dragout, we would play that game; if they insisted on long speeches, so would we; if they read long reports, we would read long reports." (This anticipated by more than a year George F. Kennan's "X-Article" in *Foreign Affairs* suggesting "confronting the Russians with unalterable counterforce 'at every point where they show signs of encroaching upon the interests of a peaceful world.'")[7] "And," General Whitney added, "Washington has been informed of the decision." General Whitney's esteem for Mr. Ball was little if any higher than for the Soviet member of the Council. "Ball," he said, "always sides with the Soviet Union. He is a farmer who speaks his own opinions rather than those of his native Australia or of the British Commonwealth, and his ambition is to occupy elaborate quarters and tower over the Supreme Commander. He complained when GHQ provided him with a twelve-room house, the biggest one he had ever been inside of, and requested GHQ to relax the regulation forbidding foreigners to buy scarce Japanese clothing so that he might acquire striped trousers and a cutaway coat." (Northwestern University professor Kenneth Colgrove, Japanese expert attached to Government Section, interjected that Australia favored a harsher program for Japan than the one General MacArthur was carrying out.) The Chinese member of the council was not spared either; he was lumped with Derevyanko and Ball. "China," said General Whitney, "should follow the advice of Stephen Decatur in all international matters—right or wrong, stand with the United States." One thing was made clear: General Whitney's performance before the Allied Council was dictated by General MacArthur; his sledge hammer tactics had been used advisedly. This whetted our appetite for more insight into the character of this unconventional general.

If Mark Gayn mirrored the views of Japan's Communists and left-wing Socialists towards the occupation and the *New York Times*'s Burton Crane covered the ups and downs of Japan's postwar economy, *Newsweek*'s Compton Pakenham assisted by Harry F. Kern, foreign editor of that magazine, voiced the growing concern of American cold warriors on both sides of the Pacific over the purge of Japanese industrial leaders. *Newsweek* contended that the purge of industrialists exposed Japan to the perils of Soviet Communism; and although, as we have already seen in Chapter 3, Government Section's Charles L. Kades directed the purge program in scrupulous pursuance of Washington's orders and with the full knowledge and approval of Whitney and MacArthur, *Newsweek* nevertheless portrayed Whitney as the villain in that punitive occupation undertaking. According to *Newsweek* for 27 January 1947:

Congress should send a committee to Japan to discover why American capitalist principles are being undermined by American occupation authorities. . . .
The purge originated in the military government branch . . . [which] has long been involved in a four-cornered fight for authority with the G–2 section of Maj. Gen. Charles A. Willoughby, the economic and scientific section of Maj. Gen. William F. Marquat, and the civilian information and education section under Lt. Col. Donald R. Nugent. The relations between these four sections have progressively degenerated as their aims and methods diverged.

Both Willoughby and Marquat are professional soldiers accustomed to operating through channels. . . .

On the other hand, the chief of the military government section, Brig. Gen. Courtney Whitney, went straight to MacArthur with his ideas. Thus . . . a curious feature of the prewar Jap government was revived: The man with direct access to the throne had the best chance of gaining his objectives. Whitney also had the advantage of coming from Manila, a city with which MacArthur has long been associated. There Whitney was a lawyer, a skilled country-courthouse type of orator with the ability to turn dramatics off and on. He is a red-faced man of about 5 feet 6, inclined to be portly and short-tempered. . . .

It is an open question as to the extent to which General MacArthur is aware of the ideological implications of the actions of his military government.

Some four months later *Newsweek* declared: "This purge is deplored in most responsible quarters of the occupation itself. Its motivation and continuance defy analysis." And in June 1947:

One explanation of the purge probably lies in the character of General Whitney. The general is a red-faced, choleric lawyer with an oratorical manner of speaking and a flair for lecturing those who disagree with him. His self-starting temper makes him the terrible-tempered Mr. Bang of Tokyo. Even in his own section of the occupation, Whitney could not be described as a popular figure.

Following nine months more of digging and reflecting, *Newsweek* said of the Government Section chief:

Despite occupation-wide feeling against the actions of the Government Section, other American officials are reluctant to oppose Whitney. A choleric man, he seems to possess the unlimited confidence of General MacArthur. A door is reported to open from Whitney's office on the sixth floor of the Dai Ichi Building directly into the Supreme Commander's set of offices. This unequaled access to the chief and the authority it has given Whitney caused one Tokyo wit to dub him the "poor man's Richelieu."[8]

Newsweek was correct in saying that Whitney was the second most powerful man in Tokyo, that he had ready access to MacArthur, and that he possessed MacArthur's unlimited confidence. But otherwise that weekly newsmagazine's reports on this subject did little more than echo the idle rumor of frustrated middle level officials in other GHQ staff sections who, only partially understanding the mission of the occupation

Emperor Hirohito calls on General MacArthur at the end of the first month of the occupation in 1945. MacArthur regarded the emperor's personal influence as indispensable in effecting Japan's political revolution. *(U.S. Army)*

(1) Alfred C. Oppler, chief of Government Section's Courts and Law Division. His background in German jurisprudence facilitated the democratization of Japan's legal system. (2) Col. H. E. Robison, Government Section executive officer during the first year of the Allied occupation. (3) Guy J. Swope, 1948. The ex-congressman from Pennsylvania was chief of three different Government Section divisions in three years. (4) A 1948 desk portrait of Justin Williams, chief of Parliamentary and Political Division, Government Section, SCAP. *(U.S. Army)*

(1) An informal conference between officials of the Japanese Procurator General's Office and members of SCAP's Government Section, June 1948. *Left to right:* Osborne Hauge, Katsuo Ryozo, Makoto Matsukata, Procurator General Fukui Seita, Frank Rizzo, Charles L. Kades. *(U.S. Army)* (2) A special conference on the Japanese National Personnel Commission, July 1948. Government Section's Civil Service Division Chief Blaine Hoover explains a point to Dr. Asai Kiyoshi, Ueno Yoichi, and Yamashita Okiie, National Personnel commissioners; W. Pierce McCoy, Hoover's assistant, looks on. *(U.S. Army)*

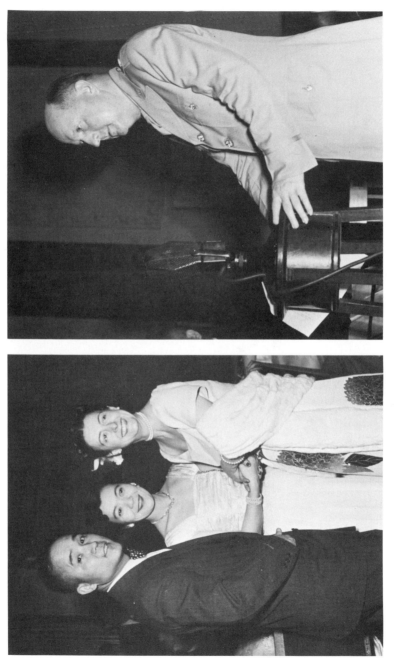

(1) Raymond Aka, Government Section's principal interpreter throughout the occupation, 1949. With him are Mrs. Aka (*center*) and Mrs. Osborne Hauge. (2) Brig. Gen. Courtney Whitney reads General MacArthur's message on the first anniversary of the independence of the Philippines at the Kogyo Club, Tokyo, 4 July 1947. Without Whitney, MacArthur would have been hard put to effect Japan's political revolution. (*U.S. Army*)

and MacArthur's role in achieving it, attributed the reverses of their respective sections to some occult power exercised by Whitney over MacArthur. Actually there was nothing mysterious about Whitney. But for the fact that in his restless middle age he fortuitously found a lofty purpose in life and pursued it relentlessly, he was an ordinary American who, by honesty, industry, and perseverance in the Horatio Alger tradition, pulled himself up by his own bootstraps. He was born in Takoma Park, Maryland, a suburb of Washington, D.C. His father was the first director of the Bureau of Soils of the United States Department of Agriculture. Enlisting in the District of Columbia National Guard in 1917, he subsequently entered the Signal Corps Aviation School and in 1920 was commissioned a lieutenant in the Army Air Corps. While stationed in the nation's capital he earned a law degree by attending Columbia National Law School at night. Following a tour of duty in the Philippines, he resigned his Air Corps commission and moved to Manila to set up a law office. That was in 1927. Nine years later, through the practice of law, prospecting for minerals, speculating in stocks, and making the most of business opportunities, he had become a millionaire. More than a year before Pearl Harbor, sensitive to the danger of war in the Far East, he returned with his family to Washington, D.C.

Entering on active duty in October 1940 as assistant chief of the Legal Division at Army Air Corps headquarters, Lieutenant Colonel Whitney found time to complete the courses of instruction at the Armored Force School and the Command and General Staff School and was on orders in March 1943 to proceed to the Air Corps Intelligence School, preparatory to joining the headquarters staff of the newly activated 14th Air Force under Brig. Gen. Claire Chennault in Kunming, China. Then all of a sudden, the War Department ordered him to report instead to Southwest Pacific Command headquarters in Australia for assignment. It was there, on 24 May 1943, that he had his first contact ever with MacArthur; they were total strangers to each other.[9]

Asked by MacArthur to take the assignment of organizing and directing the Philippine underground movement, an Intelligence operation, Colonel Whitney accepted on the condition that he be permitted to report directly to the Commander-in-Chief. His condition was met. He moved into an office close to MacArthur's Brisbane headquarters and set to work. MacArthur followed the project with keen interest and personally directed or approved every major move that was made. Reports from the radio operators in the Philippines were among the first things he read and evaluated each morning. Five hundred men from Filipino units on the west coast of the United States and in Hawaii were organized into a special battalion in a camp south of Brisbane, where they were put through a rigorous course of training in radio operations and maintenance, intelligence, sabotage, and related subjects. The most difficult task was to find a means of combating the propaganda with which the enemy had saturated the Philippines. Whitney suggested to MacArthur "that various items known to be scarce in the Philippines, such as cigarettes, matches, chewing-gum, candy bars, sewing-kits, and pencils, be sent to the islands by submarine in great quantity for widespread distribution. Each package would bear the crossed American and Philippine flags on one side, and on the other the quotation 'I shall return'—printed over a facsimile of MacArthur's signature. . . . Those three words became the slogan and the watchword of the guerrilla movement." [10] But failing to meet an important deadline, Whitney wrote in a 25 November 1943 memorandum to MacArthur: "On May 29 I said my section would establish direct connection with Manila in six months. I have failed to do so, and deserve whatever punishment you see fit to mete out." Penciled at the bottom of the memorandum were these words: "To Col. Whitney—An excellent job has been done which merits but highest commendation. MacArthur." Before long Whitney had contact with Manila, and his agents there were reporting Japanese military movements, number and tonnage of enemy ships, location of garrison and supply dumps, and even the name of the Japanese marshal (Terauchi Hisaichi) occupying MacArthur's former penthouse suite at the Manila Hotel. [11]

Whether or not a staged affair, as has been alleged, the MacArthur party that waded ashore at Leyte on 20 October 1944 included Whitney. By then, thanks to the success of Whitney's guerrilla movement, there were 134 radio stations and twenty-three weather observatories behind the enemy lines in the Philippines. In addition, there had been sent in hundreds of thousands of arms of all types, great quantities of radio equipment, clothing, food, and medical supplies—all delivered by submarines. Now chief of the USAFE Civil Affairs Section, General Whitney was present on 23 October when MacArthur surprised President Sergio Osmena and his cabinet by restoring to them political control of Leyte, and he was on hand for the progressive restoration of civil power throughout the Philippines during the ensuing campaign of liberation. Whitney sat at MacArthur's side on their historic 30 August 1945 flight to Japan. [12] Whitney wrote the opening speech MacArthur delivered at the 2 September surrender ceremony aboard the U.S.S. *Missouri*. Immediately following that ceremony Whitney returned to Manila to complete for MacArthur the transfer of power from the United States military to the Filipino authorities. That job done, he showed up again in Tokyo in mid-December expecting to become MacArthur's special civil affairs adviser. To his complete surprise, MacArthur made him chief of Government Section, replacing General Crist.

It was then that Government Section sprang to life and began to effect the political transformation ordered by Washington. There followed in rapid succession the twin purge directives of 4 January 1946, a fixed date for a general election, the Government Section debate on the election law and the Supreme Commander's decision to let it stand intact, preparation of a model constitution, revision of laws supplementing the new constitution, reorganization of the executive branch, reconstruction of the court system, elevation of the Diet, and establishment of local autonomy, reforms that had to be made sensibly and expeditiously or not at all.

Contrary to the *Newsweek* opinions previously cited, General Whitney was highly respected and admired by those who got to know him. True, he mingled little with most of his "collaborators," to borrow his expression, probably never learning the names of more than a fourth of us. As between running the shop and concentrating on matters of top priority to MacArthur, he chose the latter, leaving the former to Kades. Even so, he was considerate of everybody in the office, always welcomed a compliment or a complaint, and never barked out orders. Whenever it was brought to his attention that a subordinate was displeased with anything—assignment, pay, location of desk, living quarters—he instructed Kades to take the necessary remedial action. Aware of his concern for their welfare, the staff gave little thought to his aloofness, exulting instead over the fact that he did promptly the things that needed to be done, without red tape but with MacArthur's full approval, and in the manner of a lawyer or businessman rather than an Army general; he was thought to be the type of man that MacArthur as proconsul ought to have around. He got things done, the right things, the way MacArthur wanted them done. He gave standing, prestige, and a sense of usefulness and accomplishment to Government Section. He literally made Government Section MacArthur's strong right arm. He used his assistants to backstop programs of all SCAP sections. It was an ideal if unprecedented setup for him and his staff. In principle, this arrangement seemed to be fraught with danger; in practice, it proved to be just about perfect.

Whitney hoped his staff would share his regard for MacArthur, but he did not demand it. He required only that they give loyal support to the Supreme Commander's policy, that they do nothing to undermine or thwart it. They respected his worshipful attitude toward MacArthur without adopting it, though they greatly admired the Supreme Commander. Except for the Foreword written by Whitney himself, Government Section's *Political Reorientation* showed no special deference to MacArthur; none of the several contributors was under any pressure to praise or even to mention him, and few did.

Whitney was a loner, not the gregarious type like Kades. He was a kind and considerate husband and father. He never found time for golf, tennis, chess, or cards; he was serious-minded, all business. For diversion he smoked Corona cigars, drank Johnny Walker Black Label whisky, collected Oriental art objects, and (before the war) defended, gratuitously, errant American servicemen in Manila police courts. He was as fearless as MacArthur in the face of enemy fire. He was well versed in Anglo-Saxon law, the United States Constitution, and the works of such famous Americans as Hamilton, Adams, Marshall, Webster, and Lincoln. His political philosophy, like MacArthur's, was akin to that of McKinley, Elihu Root, and W. H. Taft. He was a man of integrity, decent, and law-abiding. At age forty-six he welcomed the opportunity of a lifetime to place his talents and know-how at the disposal of MacArthur in the worldwide struggle against totalitarianism. He derived from the association the greatest satisfaction of his life.

Whitney was indomitably faithful to MacArthur and totally under his spell. He had the uncanny ability to correctly read MacArthur's far-ranging mind. He generated viable ideas and developed sound procedures for furthering MacArthur's military and political career. He articulated precisely MacArthur's thoughts on any subject. To him MacArthur was no riddle. With no desire to feather his own nest, he sought only MacArthur's esteem and the privilege of standing in the shadow of his reflected glory; though he was not blind to the fact that the taller MacArthur stood, the larger he would loom in the lengthened shadow. He accompanied MacArthur on his reconnaissance flights over the battle fields during the Korean War, and he was taken by MacArthur to the Wake Island meeting with President Truman in October 1950. History abounds with examples of lesser-known men attaching themselves selflessly and unreservedly to eminent figures. Notable are Damon's attachment to Pythias, Boswell's to Johnson, and Ney's to Napoleon. Like Damon, Whitney would willingly have put up his life as bond for MacArthur's word of honor. Like Marshal Michel Ney, who was shot for renewing his allegiance to Napoleon after Elba, Whitney went into retirement with the dismissed MacArthur. But the Whitney-MacArthur alliance more nearly resembled that between James Boswell and Samuel Johnson. Boswell was thirty-one years younger than Johnson, Whitney seventeen years younger than MacArthur. Both Boswell and Whitney were associated with their respective mentors for exactly twenty-one years. Boswell wrote the definitive biography of the leading literary figure of his age, while Whitney wrote an engrossing, if controversial, partial biography of the most celebrated military figure of the century. Both of the younger men enlarged their faculties through close association with distinguished older men. As Johnson took a liking to Boswell, so did MacArthur to Whitney.

To Whitney every MacArthur whim was a command. Did MacArthur want an early rundown on the daily happenings in the world? Then Whitney regularly obtained and collated the sheaf of overnight radio flashes from the major news services for MacArthur's immediate use upon reaching his office. Did MacArthur want visiting Washington officials, press and radio commentators, noted clergymen, and other dignitaries to receive a sympathetic summary of the administration of the occupation? Then Whitney briefed them in depth. Did MacArthur have in mind a holiday statement to the Japanese people, a letter to the prime minister, an answer to American newspaper or magazine criticism, or a reply to a message from a religious order or a patriotic body? Then Whitney prepared it.

What did Whitney have that MacArthur's other close associates lacked? It was not loyalty alone, for Willoughby, Marquat, Baker, Fellers, Bunker, and others were also passionately loyal. What they lacked was the capacity to fathom the depth and breadth of the old general's mind. They could not grasp the totality of his global outlook, nor his peculiar ties to the American domestic scene, nor the great spiritual forces in which he believed and on which he relied for strength and inspiration. Whitney could. Who else would have accepted the Distinguished Service Star of the Philippines from President Sergio Osmena only on the condition that the record be made to show that "my participation in these operations [of liberation] found both limitation and support not clearly disclosed in your covering citation"? Whitney wanted the record to show that his "participation in those historic operations lay basically in the mechanical implementation of the policies determined upon by General MacArthur to guide these great spiritual forces [underlying the relationship between him and the Filipino people]." [13] Who other than Whitney would have suggested breaking the Japanese constitutional impasse by drafting a democratic model in SCAP, but disclaim credit therefor because "it was MacArthur's responsibility to make the final decision"? The expression "privileged sanctuary," used by MacArthur to describe the interdicted zone in Manchuria during the Korean War, originated with Whitney. He alone, without the concurrence of ESS, wrote MacArthur's thirteen-page reply to *Fortune* magazine's April 1949 article criticizing SCAP's failure to put Japan on the road to economic recovery.[14] He complimented his staff for serving MacArthur well, never for rendering service to him. When I returned at once to Tokyo from Fukuoka on learning of MacArthur's relief by Truman in April 1951, to be of whatever assistance I could to General Whitney, he was deeply touched, but treated my gesture as a mark of respect for MacArthur, not for him. He alone drastically reduced the size of his section in mid-1948 to dramatize MacArthur's desire for more Japanese and less American participation in the administration of that country. Who else on MacArthur's staff could have created the impression, as Whitney did, that his idol was of such stature as to have a "rendezvous with history"? Who else could have correctly diagnosed and successfully magnified MacArthur's own estimate of his power and influence? Who else was so convinced that MacArthur could win the presidential nomination in 1948 and 1952? Thanks to Whitney, MacArthur's vision was a little clearer, his capacity to accomplish results a little enhanced, and his willingness to take calculated risks a little greater. If MacArthur was Whitney's stepping stone to a small place in the sun, Whitney furthered MacArthur's ambition to play a big role on the world stage. MacArthur's gain from their relationship was the invaluable assistance of a versatile civilian, and Whitney's was prestige plus the satisfaction of associating with a great man in a worthy cause.

Whitney made himself indispensable to MacArthur. But for him the political and military purge would have been carried out by G-2, the economic purge by ESS, and the professional purge by CIE, a fragmented purge program that would have been administratively ludicrous. But for him the model constitution would never have been drafted by SCAP. There would have been no Article 9 renouncing Japan's right to maintain military forces. The thirteen-member FEC sitting in Washington would have assumed responsibility for constitutional change; with each of the Big Four nations exercising the veto power, it is doubtful that any substantial revision of Japan's Imperial Constitution would ever have been effected.

Whitney did not share with others the secret of his and MacArthur's affinity for each other. He was fiercely jealous of his unique relationship with the distinguished soldier. Let any other MacArthur lieutenant try to muscle in on his privileged position and his dander was up. In a contest with a rival he asked no quarter and gave none. His main weapon was the lawyer's brief with which he regularly overpowered his soldierly but less erudite rivals in GHQ, notably G-2's Willoughby and ESS's Marquat, both major generals. But if a rival threw at him what he considered a "bean ball," he retaliated with vigor. A case in point was the early 1947 memorandum from Colonel Bunker, MacArthur's aide, advising that all appointments with the Supreme Commander would henceforth be made through the aide's office. Whitney immediately sent the memorandum to MacArthur with the request that he be relieved of his duties in SCAP. MacArthur summoned the offended Whitney and in his presence set fire to the memorandum, simultaneously advising his Government Section chief to come in at will by the side door, bypassing Bunker. When Gen. Matthew Ridgway recommended him for the Medal of Honor for his service to MacArthur as military secretary during the Korean War and the Pentagon offered instead the Legion of Merit, he summarily declined it.[15]

Whitney defended every aspect of MacArthur's administration of the occupation. He would tolerate no hint or expression of doubt on that score. The "old man" could do no wrong. Ordinarily courteous and even tempered, Whitney flew into a passion of rage at the least slight or disparagement of the Supreme Commander. On learning in October 1946 from a junior officer on his staff that a Reuters correspondent (Malcolm Muggeridge) was overheard to say to a visiting State Department official (Warren Hunsberger) during lunch at the Imperial Hotel that MacArthur was egotistical and overrated, he forthwith reported the matter to MacArthur (who promptly ordered both men expelled from Japan).[16] He was less than pleased with me when I told him, in response to his inquiry, that I believed General MacArthur would make no better showing in the Wisconsin primary election of 1948 than either Harold Stassen or Thomas E. Dewey. He never passed up an opportunity to sing MacArthur's praises. Roving correspondents like Stewart Alsop, Doris Fleeson, and Mae Craig characterized his representation of MacArthur as "bilge" and "swill," but others like George Creel and John Gunther were receptive to it. When *Newsweek*'s Harry Kern abruptly rose and departed after listening to a half-hour long Whitney extolment of MacArthur, protesting that he had not come to Whitney's office to be lectured on MacArthur's philosophy, Whitney turned to Kades and Rizzo and said in all seriousness: "Did you ever see such arrogance?"[17]

MacArthur in his way fully reciprocated Whitney's reverence and faithfulness. In his *Reminiscences,* published in 1964, the year he died, MacArthur wrote:

I detailed General Whitney to co-ordinate and direct the entire [Philippine guerrilla movement]. He was ideal for such an assignment. A prominent Manila lawyer, his thirteen years there had made him thoroughly familiar with Philippine conditions and personnel. Rugged and aggressive, fearless and experienced in military affairs, his driving force found full play in charge of a guerrilla army.[18]

Nothing better shows MacArthur's high regard for Whitney than the successive inscriptions on the autographed photographs he gave to his greatest admirer. At five-year intervals commemorating their first meeting on 24 May 1943, MacArthur wrote:

(1948, on photo of MacArthur in uniform)—To Courtney Whitney, with admiration and affectionate regard. Douglas MacArthur.

(1953, on photo of MacArthur addressing Congress in 1951)—After ten years, this day, May 24—with admiration and affection. Douglas MacArthur.

(1958, on photo of MacArthur in uniform)—May 24, 1958, to Courtney Whitney in memory of our fifteen years of devoted comradeship. Douglas MacArthur.

(1963, on photo of MacArthur aboard a destroyer at Inchon, Korea, in 1950)—Twenty years have passed, dear Court, since you joined me, and each has but increased my esteem for your loyal and devoted service. Douglas MacArthur.

On two other photographs, framed and displayed with the above ones in the Whitney home, were these autographed inscriptions:

(1 January 1960, on photo of a painting of MacArthur in his five-star unifrom)—To Courtney Whitney, with admiration and affection. Douglas MacArthur.

(1963, on photo of MacArthur in mufti smoking a pipe and holding a book titled *The Spirit of Old West Point*)—To Courtney Whitney who, as so many times in the past, has been my "right arm" in this venture. Douglas MacArthur.

Though far to the right in American politics, General Whitney had an aversion to Japan's conservative elements, most of whom were identified directly or indirectly with the Liberal party. One reason for this was the strong and persistent opposition of the Liberal party to the major occupation reforms in landholding, labor, education, corporate practices, and both national and local government. Early in the occupation, against the known desires of SCAP, the Liberals exerted themselves to vitiate the provision of the proposed new constitution that transferred the bulk of the Imperial properties to the state. The Imperial Household insisted on expanding the hereditary estates while the Cabinet Legal Bureau advocated restricting them. At the height of this argument, 1 August 1946, a disgusted General Whitney commented heatedly: "Here we have General MacArthur trying to save the emperor institution while Yoshida and his crowd are concerned only with saving the emperor's estates." That night Whitney was to have dinner with Prime Minister Yoshida. I was asked by Mr. Inukai Ken during the afternoon to convey to General Whitney the desire of the prime minister to discuss at the dinner Article 84 of the proposed constitution, which dealt with the property of the Imperial Household. When I reported Inukai's message to Whitney, in the presence of Kades and Robison, the latter remarked wryly to the general: "This will be one dinner you will earn." Whitney then instructed Kades to check Washington's directives to ascertain to what extent the emperor's holdings had to be brought under public control.

Another count General Whitney had against the Liberal party stemmed from the purge. Because the powerful conservative groups in politics and business, hardest hit by the purge, tried with the help of *Newsweek* magazine to discredit Whitney, he used every resource at his command to fight back. He directed his ire at Mr. Yoshida, the personification of the conservative opposition throughout the occupation. Their running feud reflected not only the friction between a staff section of SCAP and the Liberal party but also a clash of personalities between two strong-willed men. Unlike Prime Ministers Katayama and Ashida, who always approached SCAP through Government Section, Prime Minister Yoshida pointedly snubbed Whitney and Kades by making his appointments with General MacArthur through Colonel Bunker, MacArthur's aide, a Whitney rival. This routine somewhat damaged Whitney's image in Japanese circles, hurt his pride even more, and added fuel to his dislike of the Liberal party. The blood between Government Section and the Liberal party became so bad that its leading members in the House of Representatives sought my advice in the spring of 1948 on steps they might take to gain favor with Government Section.[19]

But the conflict had its diverting moments. There was, for example, the time in the fall of 1946 when Mr. Yoshida selected from his night soil-free garden at Oiso two choice melons for General Whitney's table. Three days 'went by and the general asked Cambridge-educated Shirasu Jiro, a top civil servant in the Central Liaison Office, to inform the prime minister that he had "enjoyed the melons to the last bite." The general blushed slightly when Mr. Shirasu, reflecting the Japanese government's intimate knowledge of all that transpired in GHQ circles, said: "That's funny, Sir, the melons are still in your refrigerator." Another time, in mid-December 1948, at the peak of the brouhaha over the budget in which the ruling Liberal party minority in the House of Representatives was pitted against the majority Democratic-Socialist-People's Cooperative coalition—with GHQ's ESS supporting the former and Government Section the latter—Prime Minister Yoshida was embarrassed by a bizarre incident. His Finance Minister, Mr. Izumiyama, only minutes before he was to have been interpellated on the budget at an evening session of the lower house, became dead-drunk in the Diet Building and passed out cold. The next morning, stretched entirely across the top of *Mainichi*'s front page, was a photograph showing the insensate finance minister lying on a couch near the entrance to the House chamber, below which was the caption: "Oh, my aching head." On entering the office that morning, I saw General Whitney seated at his desk with a copy of *Mainichi* on his lap, holding his sides and chuckling over the sorry plight of the man who had been Mr. Yoshida's Finance Minister until a few hours before daybreak.

It is not certain that Mr. Yoshida did not have the last laugh. On 11 April 1951, President Truman removed General MacArthur from his commands, and on 16 April, MacArthur, with Mrs. MacArthur, Whitney, Bunker, and others, departed Japan. "The following day," General Whitney wrote later, "the House of Representatives of the National Diet passed a resolution of tribute and thanks of a nation; it was sponsored by the three major political parties, the leaders of which, with the Prime Minister for the government . . . eloquently extolled MacArthur's inestimable service to the Japanese people." [20] The leaders of the same three major political parties had also agreed to sponsor the following companion resolution of thanks to General Whitney:

Whereas we are deeply impressed by the fact that Major General Courtney Whitney, ex-Chief of Government Section, GHQ, SCAP, has exerted his untiring effort for the cause of the reconstruction of Japan and particularly has given unfailing guidance in elevating the National Diet to the position of the highest organ of state power during his tenure of office of five years and eight months;

Be it therefore, resolved that the House of Representatives hereby express its heartfelt thanks to the general.

The resolution was not adopted. At the Liberal party caucus preceding the plenary session that adopted the resolution for General MacArthur, the prime minister advised that the resolution for General Whitney would be more appropriate at some future session of the House. General Whitney's contribution to Japan, he said, had been so great that it would not do him full justice to pass a resolution today that might appear to be only an annex to the resolution for General MacArthur. The Liberal party caucus accepted the prime minister's suggestion and decided to postpone the Whitney resolution until the next session of the Diet. Because of Mr. Yoshida's continuing opposition, the next session ended without any action being taken on the Whitney resolution, which was never adopted.

Whitney forgave Yoshida for everything in 1964 when the eighty-six-year-old ex-prime minister traveled all the way from Japan to the east coast of the United States to attend General MacArthur's funeral. Whitney was so moved by this gesture that he went to the trouble of preparing a favorable press release for his antagonist of old against the day when the Japanese elder statesman, too, would pass away. [21]

In principle General Whitney held himself aloof from the Japanese. To be sure, like MacArthur, he always welcomed to his office, at their request, such dignitaries as the prime minister, members of the cabinet, justices of the Supreme Court, the attorney general, the Speaker and President of the two Houses of the Diet, and chairmen of Diet committees. But he avoided deliberately and habitually social contacts with the Japanese. One exception that proved the rule was the above-mentioned dinner he had in August 1946 with the prime minister. Another was the dinner he had two months later in the Diet Building as the guest of a four-member subcommittee of the House of Peers Committee on the Constitution. Alarmed over the prospect of a constitutional change in Japan's national polity—for example, the transfer of sovereignty from the emperor to the people—the constitutional scholars of this subcommittee wanted General Whitney to define precisely the rights, if any, of the House of Peers to revise the Bill for the Constitution as already overwhelmingly passed by the House of Representatives. In the face of the Peers's charges that the prime minister's insistence on prompt passage of the measure was the result of SCAP pressure—which might be cited later as justification for revising the charter—Whitney took advantage of the occasion to define General MacArthur's official position on the right of either Diet chamber to exercise its full legislative powers. The Supreme Commander, he said, was actuated by three and only three considerations: faithful execution of his instructions from Washington, evolvement of a truly democratic constitution, and acceptance of it by the "free and untrammeled expression of the will of the Japanese people." Elaborating these principles,

General Whitney pointed out that the Supreme Commander had issued no directive whatever affecting the form, detail or procedure of constitutional revision; that he had left the entire matter to be developed by the Japanese government and people in accordance with democratic processes, while affording to the government, both Cabinet and Diet, counsel and guidance and all other SCAP assistance available. . . . General Whitney . . . pointed out that the . . . Diet is and always has been entirely free to proceed in the exercise of its sole judgment. . . . To evidence the Supreme Commander's complete dissociation from direction of the revision movement, General Whitney advised the Peers that [the Supreme Commander] . . . had most heartily received the report of the final action of the House of Representatives in amending 23 Articles, adding 4 Articles and deleting 1 Article in the course of its action upon the government's draft. . . . In conclusion, General Whitney pointed out that in consequence of the above considerations, the Peers must feel entirely free to accept, to reject, or to modify the constitutional bill before them in the sole exercise of their individual judgments.[22]

In order not to detract in the least from MacArthur's administration of the occupation, General Whitney strictly avoided the news media in Japan. Nevertheless word about him got around. That he was known and respected in Japan was made clear by INS staff correspondent Bob Considine in a *Nippon Times* article (9 January 1951) just three months before MacArthur was relieved. Considine wrote:

> The influential Nippon Times, which seldom goes out of its way to plug Occupation officials, warmly saluted one of these MacArthur aides recently. He is Maj. Gen. Courtney Whitney. . . .
>
> "The Japanese nation sends its congratulations," said the Nippon Times [on the occasion of Whitney's promotion to the rank of major general] "and is grateful for all that General Whitney has done to further Japan's welfare as a stable and progressive democracy. One of the greatest tributes to the success achieved in the democratization of the nation's political setup is the manner in which more and more initiative and controls have been returned to the Japanese Government. The wise counsel and the friendly advice rendered by General Whitney in revitalizing Japan's political life to a point where she may take her place among the free nations of the world are appreciated by a grateful people."

By a curious twist of fate in the first half of 1950, I was able to become better acquainted with Whitney the lawyer and fighter. A delicate situation developed that involved both myself and the general in an extremely personal way. What gave the matter unusual importance was the threat inherent in it to expose to the world the volcanic subsurface tensions produced in some Japanese and American circles by the occupation effort to revolutionize Japanese society. It all started on 12 December 1949, when the Japanese residence occupied jointly by the family of its owner and my family was totally destroyed by fire. For sometime thereafter, in accordance with Japanese custom, gifts were received by my wife and me from scores of Japanese citizens. Exclusive of two packages of Japanese yen, which were returned immediately to the donors, this shower of inexpensive gifts consisted of fruit, flowers, beverages, dolls, pottery figurines, pillows, brocades, kimonos, dishes, lacquerware, glassware, silverware, cloisonné vases, woodcuts, and so forth. Some two and half months later, on 4 March, the Office of the Provost Marshal in a checksheet to the Chief of Staff stated that it had information from a confidential source that Justin Williams of Government Section had allegedly accepted presents of considerable value from individuals in the Japanese government. According to the checksheet, there were persistent rumors in Japanese circles that Williams had accepted from Diet members presents valued at approximately one million yen. The provost marshal requested authorization to investigate the charges. At this point General Whitney took over.

In his own investigation, authorized by the Chief of Staff, General Whitney soon established that the confidential source referred to in the provost marshal's checksheet was ex-Brig. Gen. Frayne Baker, now deputy chief of the Foreign Investment Board, ESS. Forced out as MacArthur's public relations officer in March 1948, he was given a berth by ESS chief, Maj. Gen. William F. Marquat. In December 1948, it will be recalled, he clashed with Blaine Hoover over the pay scale for government employees. To assist General Whitney in his counterattack against Baker, I prepared a sworn statement covering the gifts received, the nonexistence in Japanese circles of the alleged rumors, and Baker's motives for hatching a plot to injure Government Section. In addition, I addressed a letter to General Whitney inviting attention to the complete falsity of all allegations and requesting two things: that action be taken to expunge the allegations from the record, and that I be authorized to file formal charges against Baker for spreading false, malicious, and slanderous rumors against me. General Whitney forwarded my request to the Chief of Staff on 18 April.

The bombshell request threw the Chief of Staff into such a quandary that it took him twenty-four days to act on it. In his 14 May response, without mentioning Baker's name, he found that the motives of the accuser "may reasonably be questioned," and that the charges made "failed to materialize as matters of fact." The provost marshal's request for authorization to investigate the charges was denied on the ground that such an inquiry "would necessarily inevitably result in unfortunate and unwarranted publicity on apparently unfounded insinuations relative to the official relationships existing between officials of General Headquarters . . . and the Japanese Government." My request to file charges against Baker was ignored. To write finis to a disconcerting issue, in other words, to the Government Section chief's persistence, the Chief of Staff instructed Whitney to reprimand me as "admonishment" for knowingly violating SCAP Circular 7 on gift-taking. Typically military, this solution was a smokescreen designed to keep within limits a long-smoldering feud between two MacArthur lieutenants by diverting attention to a third party.

If the Chief of Staff intended to squelch the irrepressible Whitney, he miscalculated. On 1 June, under Whitney's tutelage, I addressed a memorandum to him on my responsibility under SCAP Circular 7 and on criminal charges against Baker. I began by taking exception to an administrative reprimand, "for such action would be based on a presumption of guilt which I deny. Further . . . my very silence would be tantamount to acquiescence in the . . . allegations [made in] . . . the Check Note of 4 March 1950 from the Provost Marshal. . . . Were the reprimand to be administered, it would confirm and perpetuate an unconscionable wrong, for . . . the Chief of Staff's memorandum of 14 May . . . makes no reference whatsoever to the most malicious allegations . . . contained in . . . the Provost Marshal's Check Note."

These damaging allegations, I added, were not based on an anonymous letter as represented but, according to "sworn testimony of the representatives of the Provost Marshal Section . . . on information given to the Provost Marshal by Mr. Frayne Baker . . . who managed, behind the protective designation of 'confidential source' and a secret code number . . . to conceal his role . . . until forced out of cover by your [Whitney's] investigation under the authority of the Chief of Staff. Since Mr. Frayne Baker, when summoned to testify in your investigation, emphatically denied having made these allegations, the record . . . leaves unanswered the question of whether they were fabricated by him or by the Provost Marshal. In either case, my record has not been cleared of these serious accusations." In view of these facts, I continued, it is inconceivable that I should stand convicted by a decision which:

a. Fails to exonerate me of all accusations contained in the Provost Marshal's Check Note. . . .
b. Completely ignores, without so much as mention of the name of the perpetrator, the criminally libelous actions of Mr. Frayne Baker in instigating these charges against me; and
c. Adjudges me guilty of official misconduct based upon an entirely new charge without affording me an opportunity to be heard in my own defense.

I took the position that "not only have I not violated . . . Circular No. 7, but that any other course would have been contrary to the letter and spirit of SCAP Circular No. 23 of 1949 which aims to foster . . . 'the same relationship between the occupation personnel and the indigenous population of Japan as exists between the United States troops and the indigenous population of the United States' and 'to minimize the restrictions on . . . occupation personnel to the maximum possible extent, in order to promote an attitude of friendly interest and guidance toward the Japanese people.'"

Reverting to the heart of the issue, I said: "I cannot believe that the ends of justice would be served by a procedure which adjudges me guilty of actions 'inimical to the objectives of the occupation' without first giving me an opportunity to answer the charge, and which at the same time, by complete silence, implicitly accords to Mr. Frayne Baker continued immunity against the consequences of his criminal actions."

In view of the above considerations, I requested of the chief of Government Section that:

a. I be specifically absolved of the allegations personally made by Mr. Frayne Baker . . . and that the entire Check Note be expunged from the record as having no validity whatsoever;

b. The question of a reprimand be reconsidered, but should that be denied, I be given an opportunity to answer the new charge which has now been introduced of violation of SCAP Circular No. 7 before a competent court or board to permit full consideration of my position upon the evidence of all witnesses having knowledge of the facts; and

c. I be permitted, in the exercise of my right to defend my good name, to file formal charges against Mr. Frayne Baker, who . . . has sought to . . . destroy my professional reputation and official standing.

With this memorandum of 1 June, which he wrote, General Whitney regained the initiative. He put the monkey, so to speak, on the Chief of Staff's back. He could now challenge the Chief of Staff's arbitrary decision to rule out an investigation. He could insist on consideration of the allegations made against me in the provost marshal's 4 March checknote. He could insure a hearing for me before an impartial body qualified to judge whether I had violated Circular 7. And he could make it difficult for the highly placed GHQ friends of Frayne Baker to prevent charges from being filed against him for his malicious and underhanded attack on me. Applicable to the case were pertinent Army regulations and the Army system of justice which the Chief of Staff in Tokyo could not brush aside, and no one knew this better than General Whitney. Wisely, perhaps, General MacArthur, so General Whitney said, never interfered with personnel matters, a custom that would permit the Government Section chief to take my case, if need be, all the way to the Secretary of the Army.

On 25 June 1950, while my 1 June memorandum was still kicking around the Chief of Staff's office, North Korea attacked South Korea, and the case of Williams against Baker and the Chief of Staff dissolved into thin air. I was never administratively reprimanded (punishment meted out for minor traffic violations) by General Whitney, the allegations against me were never expunged from the record, and Baker was never booked for defamation of character. In conversations with General Whitney up to the time he left Japan with General MacArthur in April 1951, and in numerous postoccupation conversations preceding his death in 1969, I never thought to mention the subject, and neither did he. That was the measure of its importance. But the affair provided clearer understanding of why General MacArthur came to regard General Whitney as his "right arm."

6

Origin and Adoption of
Japan's Constitution

Several important aspects of the origin and adoption of the Japanese constitution remain clouded. Still not satisfactorily answered are the following questions: Was it ever the intention of the victorious Allies to let the Japanese people freely choose their own form of government? What was SCAP's position on constitutional revision as of the fifth month of the occupation? Why did he reverse his position? Did he exceed his authority in drawing up a model constitution for presentation to the Japanese cabinet? How was the SCAP draft written? Was it imposed on the Shidehara Cabinet? Were Japanese officials privileged to rewrite any parts of the SCAP model? How did the cabinet justify its sponsorship of an alien political system? What was the attitude of many informed Japanese toward the democratic constition? What were the respective contributions of the Americans and the Japanese to the new basic law? The purpose of this chapter is to clarify these points.

Article 12 of the Potsdam Declaration of 26 July 1945 committed the Allies to withdraw their occupying forces from Japan when a number of objectives had been accomplished, among them establishment "in accordance with the freely expressed will of the Japanese people [of] a peacefully inclined and responsible government." "Responsible government" was the meaningful expression in Article 12, but controversy has centered around the phrase, "in accordance with the freely expressed will of the Japanese people." Interpreting this language literally at the time, Baron Hiranuma Kiichiro, president of the Privy Council and a member of the Supreme Council for the Conduct of the War, saw in it "sinister encouragement to subversive activities calculated to overthrow monarchial government."[1] In later SWNCC directives, the constantly reiterated phrase could have been a reminder to SCAP that he was under orders not to take unilateral action to remove the emperor;[2] or it could have signified the determination of the experts on Japan in the State Department to thwart the design of the China experts, and others, to abolish the throne, regardless of the United States commitment to Japan on that touchy subject. Respect for Japanese feelings was the watchword of the MacArthur administration, but such respect did not derive from the Potsdam Declaration. MacArthur has been roundly criticized for prevailing on the Japanese (i.e., on top government officials) to adopt a form of government that was not in accord with their freely expressed will. Thus, the phrase has been variously construed and exploited. Just what did it mean?

The concept of freely expressed will originated as a psychological warfare strategem to facilitate Japan's surrender. It was inserted in the Potsdam Declaration without enthusiasm and only at the last minute, not to accord the national right of self-determination to Japan but rather, in line with Under Secretary Joseph C. Grew's urging, to smooth the way for Japan's surrender by opening the prospect that the monarchy might be retained. If it had not been for Secretary of War Henry L. Stimson's wholehearted initiative, Mr. Grew wrote, the Potsdam Conference would have ended without any proclamation to Japan being issued at all. But even Mr. Stimson was unable to have included in the proclamation a categorical understanding that unconditional surrender would not mean the elimination of the dynasty if the Japanese people desired its retention. Analysts in the Foreign Morale Division of the Office of War Information thought that the emperor might be turned to good use in breaking the enemy's resistance if Japan's leaders were told that his fate following Allied victory would rest with the Japanese themselves.[3] As Mr. Stimson recalled: "Some maintained that the Emperor must go. . . . Others [Mr. Grew in particular] urged that the war could be ended more cheaply by openly revising the formula of 'unconditional surrender' to assure the Japanese that there was no intention of removing the Emperor if it should be the desire of the Japanese people that he remain as a constitutional monarch."[4] By inserting the freely expressed will phrase in the Potsdam Declaration, Edwin O. Reischauer said succinctly: "We made a bargain . . . American lives for an emasculated monarchy."[5] In its historical context, then, the phrase in question had to do solely with retaining or eliminating the Imperial system, nothing more.

Nevertheless, to repeat, the phrase kept cropping up in Washington directives to SCAP, for no apparent reason other than to prevent SCAP and the China Crowd from doing violence to the Imperial system. The September 1945 Initial Postsurrender Policy directive to SCAP stated that it was "not the responsibility of the occupation forces to impose on Japan any form of government not supported by the freely expressed will of the Japanese people." The fourteen-page State Department paper entitled "Reform of the Japanese Governmental System," which was prepared under the auspices of the State-War-Navy Coordinating Committee and sent to MacArthur on 9 January 1946 as SWNCC 228, employed the freely expressed will phrase no less than five times, but not to ensure that the Japanese could choose their own form of government. Though the paper made it clear that serious consideration should be given to abolishing the throne, it emphasized that the Japanese could keep it if they wanted to.[6] It is to be noted that they could elect to retain the Imperial institution, but not to choose a form of government other than one responsible to the people.

According to SWNCC 228, SCAP should indicate to the Japanese authorities that they were to change the system of government to accomplish seven broad objectives. These objectives were: (1) a government responsible to an electorate based on wide representative suffrage, (2) an executive branch deriving its authority from and being responsible to the electorate or to a fully representative legislative body, (3) a legislative body with full power to reduce, increase, or reject any items in the budget or to suggest new items, (4) no budget to become effective without the express approval of the legislative body, (5) guarantee of fundamental human rights, (6) appreciable increase in local autonomy, and (7) adoption of constitutional amendments or of a constitution to express the free will of the Japanese people. If such radical changes were not freely accepted by the Japanese authorities, SWNCC 228 declared, "the Allies . . . are fully empowered to insist that Japanese basic law be so altered as to provide that in practice the government is responsible to the people." As between this positive demand to establish a responsible government and the contradictory injunction to respect the will of the Japanese people, SCAP was limited to the first alternative. The United States commitment made at Potsdam to let the Japanese people decide the fate of the Emperor institution was not to be confused with the determination of the United States to revolutionize Japan's system of government.

It cannot be overemphasized that SCAP acted on the basis of directives received from Washington. Those directives left no doubt that Japan's political system was to be drastically reformed. SWNCC 228 advised SCAP that the reform program was to be effected in one of three ways. First, the Japanese government should be given an opportunity to initiate and carry out the necessary changes to comply with the Potsdam Declaration. For over three months, with a minimum of occupation interference, the Shidehara Cabinet had been at work on a constitutional revision plan. Second, in the absence of "spontaneous action by the Japanese," SCAP should "indicate" the desired reforms to the Japanese authorities. In October 1945, General MacArthur and Ambassador Atcheson had indicated to Prime Minister Shidehara those governmental reforms deemed necessary by the State Department to achieve a responsible government.

Third, as a last resort, SCAP should issue a directive to the Japanese specifying the reforms to be made. Nothing was said in this connection about the freely expressed will of the Japanese people, nor was SCAP cautioned to refrain from taking action on constitutional revision until he received a directive from the FEC.

SCAP also had advice from the Joint Chiefs of Staff. In SWNCC 228/1, the military offered suggestions on two points, one long-range, the other short-term. The principal short-term military interest was the possibility that implementation of the proposed reforms might foment unrest to such a degree as to require an increase in occupation forces. This served notice on MacArthur that, in effecting the political reforms, he was to avoid violence, civil war, and chaos. The military's long-range concern was that "no nationalistic or military clique or combination should again be able to dominate that country and lead it into a war of aggression."[7] Such explicit language may have influenced MacArthur's thinking on the no-war clause that was inserted in Government Section's model constitution some three weeks after receipt of SWNCC 228/1. The Pentagon expressed no concern over the freely expressed will of the Japanese people. So much for the meaning and employment of that overworked phrase.

As of January 1946, SCAP did not plan on revising the Imperial Constitution. MacArthur believed, as the record shows, that this was a function of the FEC. On 17 January, Government Section officials briefed a visiting delegation of the Far Eastern Advisory Commission (FEAC) on SCAP's political activities. The FEAC, predecessor of the FEC, had been activated in October 1945, without USSR participation, to recommend policies, principles, and standards for the occupation of Japan. Colonel Kades began by reading a prepared statement reflecting SCAP's position. In the presence of General Whitney and nine other Government Section staff members, he told Maj. Gen. Frank R. McCoy, chairman, and six of his FEAC colleagues that so far the Japanese government had not been substantially changed, except for abolition of the military agencies, the Greater East Asia Ministry, and the Board of Information. The Japanese, he said, had made no move to establish a responsible government, had submitted no reform proposals for SCAP's consideration. SCAP's positive actions in the political sphere had been the civil rights directive of 4 October 1945, the purge directives of 4 January 1946, and instructions to the Shidehara Cabinet that led to Diet enactment of the Agricultural Lands Adjustment Law, the Trade Union Law, and the amended Election Law. The amended Election Law lowered the voting age from twenty-five to twenty years, provided for women's suffrage, reduced eligibility of candidacy from thirty to twenty-five years, and changed the election system to allow for a greater degree of proportional representation. These actions, Kades stated, would accomplish politically what had already been achieved militarily. SCAP's policy was to interfere to the minimum extent with the existing Japanese administration, which was expected to change the governmental system through its own administrative reforms. SCAP's objectives at this stage were limited to further demilitarization, encouragement of local responsibility, elimination of feudal and totalitarian practices, and breakup of relations between government and business that continued the Japanese war potential. The forthcoming Diet election, he added, would be a long step toward accomplishing the peacefully inclined and responsible government in Japan contemplated by the Potsdam Declaration. Nothing was said about constitutional revision.

The FEAC members asked a number of questions about financial matters, political parties, the forthcoming election, the Diet, the legal system, and judges and procurators, but their major interest was constitutional reform. "Are you considering amendments to the Constitution?" Senator Thomas Confessor, the Philippines member, asked. "No," replied Kades. "Government Section has understood that that is a long-range problem concerning fundamental changes . . . which is within the province of your Commission." The significant and revealing dialogue thus begun continued as follows:

Q. Senator Confessor: We were given to understand by a headquarters spokesman that your section was studying the Constitution. Is that wrong?

A. Kades: There must have been some misunderstanding. Government Section advises the Supreme Commander on policies pertaining to the internal structure of civil government. . . . It has not considered the Constitution as part of this work. It had been thought that the Constitution was within the terms of reference of your Commission.

Q. Senator Confessor: Isn't it so that the changes being effected in the Japanese way of life by the Supreme Commander will have to be embodied in the Japanese Constitution, thereby requiring the Constitution to be revised?

A. Kades: Whether the written Constitution requires amendment to make the changes permanent is a question I am not prepared to answer since we have not studied the Japanese Constitution from the standpoint of making such revision.

Q. Senator Confessor: Does the present Constitution embody the democratic changes made by the Supreme Commander?

A. Kades: The written Constitution does not embody these changes.

Q. Senator Confessor: I do not understand why constitutional revision is not a part of your work.

A. Kades: Because formal revision . . . would constitute a fundamental change in the Japanese constitutional structure, and as such be within the Commission's jurisdiction.

Q. General McCoy: Is anyone studying the Constitution?

A. Kades: I understand that various groups in Japan are studying the Constitution including citizen groups as well as Japanese governmental committees.

Q. Sir George Sansom [United Kingdom member]: From what you have said about changes taking place in the Japanese government, I gather that the system is not unlike the way we have it in the United Kingdom. Is that right?

A. Kades: It is partly true. Unlike the British system, the Japanese do have a written document. However . . . the day-to-day operations of the government constitute an integral part of the fundamental law.

Q. Senator Confessor: I do not understand how you can amend the Constitution without having a written document.

A. Kades: We do not amend the Constitution as such. However, changes in the governmental structure, reorganization of national and local governmental agencies, the institution of woman's suffrage, the elimination of extra constitutional bodies are, in effect, alterations in the constitutional system of Japan. Directives issued on the basis of recommendations made by Government Section accomplish constitutional development. We are constantly in the process of changing the system of government which, in turn, changes the Constitution in effect, though not in terms.

Q. Francis LaCoste [French member]: I think that the alterations in the Japanese governmental system which are being carried out under the guidance of the headquarters are in fact constitutional changes which should be ultimately incorporated in a revision of the written Constitution. I also think that your methods are entirely consistent with that objective and are satisfactory.

A. Kades: Thank you, sir.

Q. Sir George Sansom: I agree with your distinction. Have you made any formal studies on this?

A. Kades: No, Sir George, we have not.[8]

The foregoing questions and answers should leave no doubt about Government Section's outlook on constitutional reform as of 17 January 1946. There was no thought of amending Japan's constitution. With General Whitney furnishing close liaison between his staff and General MacArthur, Government Section's views were, willy-nilly, those of SCAP. Earlier that month General MacArthur told the FEAC delegation about his previous conferences with top Japanese officials to clarify Allied policy on constitutional reform, "as interpreted in more specific form by the American Government."[9] At MacArthur's final session with the FEAC group on 30 January, he informed them that constitutional reform had been taken out of his hands by the Moscow Agreement of the month before. On 1 February, State Minister Matsumoto Joji delivered to SCAP two papers disclosing the Shidehara Cabinet's ideas on constitutional revision. Two days later, MacArthur instructed Government Section to draw up a model constitution for use by the Japanese. About this MacArthur action the State Department's Professor George H. Blakeslee wrote: "Two days after General MacArthur had stated to the members of the Far Eastern Advisory Commission that he had ceased to take any action in regard to revision . . . he felt forced to take vigorous measures." [10] Dr. Hugh Borton, Blakeslee's assistant, said about Government Section: "[The Commissioners] had been told by General Whitney that the problem of constitutional reform was a matter for the Japanese to consider and that no work was being undertaken by SCAP." [11]

MacArthur's about-face on constitutional revision was triggered by the Shidehara Cabinet's unwillingness to effect substantial changes in the Imperial Constitution. He assumed that the cabinet's revision plan would include, at the very least, the reforms recommended by the State Department to POLAD in October as basic to establishing a responsible government. The list included parliamentary supremacy, an executive branch answerable to the legislature, legislative control of the budget, establishment of fundamental civil rights, elimination of the Privy Council's veto power, and civilian control of the military. [12] Now the cabinet's committee on revision, headed by State Minister Matsumoto, after working for months behind closed doors in strictest secrecy and not once seeking SCAP advice, fell far short of the mark. On 1 February, the day *Mainichi Shimbun* published what was purported to be the Matsumoto committee's draft revision, Dr. Matsumoto submitted to SCAP his "Gist of Revision" and "General Explanation," but not his actual draft revision. [13] Regarding the draft revision, *Nippon Times* for 3 February, reflecting the sharp public reaction to the alleged Matsumoto draft, declared that the cabinet had shown no intention to democratize the constitution. Had the Japanese cabinet defied SCAP? Keeping his cool, General MacArthur advised General Whitney to prepare a detailed answer rejecting the work of the Matsumoto committee. "Further consideration, however, was given to the matter on the 2d and 3d of February by the Supreme Commander and he finally came to the conclusion that the most effective method of instructing the Japanese Government on the nature and application of these principles he considered basic would be to prepare a draft constitution embodying those principles." [14]

Factors other than "Japanese shilly-shallying" prompted MacArthur to reverse his position on constitutional revision. As General Whitney explained: "The first general elections were only two months away, and he was determined that a presentable draft of revisions would be finished so that those elections would also constitute an unofficial plebiscite. If the Japanese continued to hedge and delay as they had for almost four months, the people would have no choice but to vote for or against what was nearly a carbon copy of the old Meiji Constitution." Further to this point, Whitney wrote: "Had MacArthur not moved directly to solve the constitutional problem, Japan would undoubtedly have drifted aimlessly for years under the strictures and limitations of its old constitution, because of the inertia of the Far Eastern Commission sitting under the veto-power threat of the Soviet Union. Thus by timely action this threat was avoided, as was the threat to accomplish by bloodshed what, as MacArthur demonstrated, required only positive leadership to accomplish by peaceful means." [15] General MacArthur said, in retrospect: "It is probably the single most important accomplishment of the occupation. . . . I am certain that it would never have been accomplished had the occupation been dependent on the deliberations of the Far Eastern Commission—with the Soviet power of veto." [16] Thus, MacArthur's sudden decision to revise the Meiji Constitution resulted from Japanese procrastination, the imminent Diet election, and the prospect of filibustering in the FEC. It may have been influenced somewhat by the shock of the FEAC delegation on hearing from Government Section's Colonel Kades that SCAP was not bothering to incorporate occupation reforms in the Japanese constitution. Anyway, just as Foreign Minister Shigemitsu's hurried trip to AFPAC's Yokohama headquarters on 3 September 1945 prevented MacArthur from placing Japan under military government, so did State Minister Matsumoto's feeble constitutional revision plan cause him to have a democratic charter prepared in his own headquarters. It was definitely not a premeditated move.

From SWNCC 228, MacArthur knew precisely what the State Department would propose to the FEC for reforming the Japanese system of government. Now that his hand was forced by the Matsumoto submission, he had to consider whether to proceed at once with constitutional revision on the basis of the existing broad grant of power he had from Washington, or to wait for a directive or directives from the FEC. FEC action might be interminably delayed, and when taken, it might require SCAP to abolish the Emperor system. But did he have the right to pre-empt the FEC at this stage? If he undertook to amend the Meiji Constitution, would he exceed his authority?

Before an impartial tribunal, a good case could be made that MacArthur lacked authority to revise the Imperial Constitution. Under the Moscow Agreement of 27 December 1945, it undeniably became United States policy to have fundamental changes made in Japan's constitutional structure by decision of the FEC. [17] Then, both MacArthur and Whitney informed the FEAC delegation in January that the Moscow Agreement had removed constitutional revision from SCAP's jurisdiction. MacArthur showed that he entertained doubts about the conformity of his contemplated action to United States policy by asking Government Section for an opinion on the matter.

The impartial tribunal mentioned in the preceding paragraph would also have given thoughtful consideration to the case made by Government Section. General Whitney, speaking for himself, Kades, Hussey, and Rowell, all able and experienced lawyers, did not question United States policy on constitutional revision established by the Moscow Agreement. His concern was whether that extension of policy had invalidated other policy positions on the occupation of Japan. After examining the extent of SCAP's power to deal with fundamental changes in the Japanese constitutional structure, he came to this conclusion: "In the absence of any policy decision by the Far Eastern Commission on the subject (which, of course, would be controlling), [SCAP has] the same authority with reference to constitutional reform as [he has] with reference to any other matter of substance in the occupation and control of Japan." Furthermore, "[SCAP's] authority to make policy decisions on constitutional reform continues substantially unimpaired until the Far Eastern Commission promulgates its own policy decisions on this subject." To be sure, "No directive may be issued to [SCAP] by the Joint Chiefs of Staff or any other agency of the United States Government 'dealing with fundamental changes in the Japanese constitutional structure' without 'the attainment of agreement in the Far Eastern Commission.' Neither of the provisions, however, precludes [SCAP] taking action pursuant to existing directives to approve direct constitutional reform." [18]

Professor Blakeslee, in his history of the FEC, supported Whitney's case. He acknowledged that divergent opinions were held by the FEC, SCAP, and the United States government "in regard to the methods appropriate for adopting a new Japanese Constitution," but General MacArthur, he said, "clearly had the authority to lead the Japanese in constitutional reform, subject to any directives which he might receive including . . . decisions of the Far Eastern Commission." SWNCC 228, he wrote, went to MacArthur "for his information and not as a directive," the supposition being that "he would naturally regard the views of the U.S. Government as controlling, especially during the period preceding the formal organization of the Far Eastern Commission." [19]

Whitney's case was not challenged by either the United States government or the FEC. On the contrary, the FEC, including the United States, gave its blessing to MacArthur's revision project by endorsing SWNCC 228 on 2 July and sending it to him as a directive. The FEC also sanctioned the MacArthur no-war clause by not taking exception to its inclusion in the Shidehara Cabinet's constitution revision bill. The several FEC directives on constitutional revision sent to SCAP while the revision bill was under deliberation by Japanese executive and legislative bodies were as scrupulously implemented as they were unwelcome.[20]

SCAP's objectives were decided in Washington, but SCAP's methods for achieving them were devised in Tokyo. It was standing operating procedure in SCAP not to divulge information in advance on planned occupation moves. For instance, SCAP directives on civil rights and the purge were prepared in complete secrecy—"behind closed doors"—and then released to a surprised Japanese government. The same technique was used to set the stage for constitutional revision. Inasmuch as the Matsumoto committee had rejected the democratic reforms recommended earlier by General MacArthur and Ambassador Atcheson, it would have been pointless to instruct the Shidehara Cabinet to try again on the basis of the identical principles contained in SWNCC 228. Yet the rhythm of the occupation had to be maintained. Therefore, it was decided, as General Whitney said, that "the only way to make unmistakably clear to the Matsumoto committee that their recommendations were unacceptably reactionary was to prepare a draft of our own which could be used as the basis for future negotiations."[21]

In embarking on constitutional revision, MacArthur took a calculated risk, for any one of five entities could have scuttled the project. Those entities were the Japanese electorate, the emperor, the Shidehara Cabinet, the United States government, and the FEC. SCAP took for granted that the Japanese voters would give overwhelming approval to the concepts of popular sovereignty, nonbelligerency, and civil liberties by choosing like-minded candidates at the 10 April general election to represent them in the Diet; this was his trump card. He counted heavily on the emperor, too. Had the emperor and the Japanese people not backed him at this critical stage of the occupation, "the results," he said later, "would have been catastrophic."[22] Since he would adhere rigidly to the letter and spirit of SWNCC 228, except for its emphasis on abolishing the throne, he foresaw no serious difficulty with Washington. And if the FEC reacted unfavorably to his move to implement the Potsdam Declaration, he relied on the United States veto to prevent that international agency from causing trouble. The uncertain quantity was the Japanese Cabinet. But that bridge would be crossed when he came to it.

With the decision made, MacArthur gave Whitney full authority to draft a model constitution, with three exceptions. First, the Emperor system would be preserved, but would become subject to the will of the people. Second, the right of belligerency would be renounced, a step proposed to

General MacArthur by Baron Shidehara. Third, all forms of feudalism would be abolished. These provisions were not negotiable; the Government Section staff had to accept them. MacArthur kept control of the operation by keeping in constant touch with Whitney, who in turn kept the situation in hand through his own Steering Committee composed of Kades (chairman), Hussey, and Rowell.[23] It would take a week to do the job.

Government Section undertook to illustrate the principles of democracy by fitting them into the skeletal frame of the Imperial Constitution. To simplify the task, the section's staff were organized into groups based on the chapter headings of that charter. The Legislative group was chaired by Lieutenant Colonel Hays, the Executive group by Dr. Peake, the Civil Rights group by Lieutenant Colonel Roest, the Judiciary group by Lieutenant Colonel Rowell, the Local Government group by Lieutenant Colonel Tilton, the Finance group by Major Rizzo, and the Emperor group by Capt. George A. Nelson. These group leaders and their assistants, using a 1939 volume of the world's principal constitutions (borrowed from Tokyo Imperial University), drew up the provisions for their respective chapters of the democratic model and presented them to the Steering Committee for review and approval. The ground rules laid down by Kades at the start included use of Japanese terminology where feasible, partiality to Japanese institutions and procedures, a unicameral legislature, popular sovereignty, respect for the United Nations Charter, and attentiveness to Washington's guidelines on constitutional revision. Miss Ruth Ellerman, a government analyst, kept notes on the debates, discussions, and decisions, and her eighteen-page "Memorandum for Record," dated 16 December 1947, became the official minutes of the proceedings. The account presented here of Government Section's writing of the model constitution is based largely on that document.

By the second and third days of the operation, the Steering Committee was called on to answer questions raised by various groups. The Legislative group, for example, was not sold on the idea of a unicameral legislature, as had been suggested. After some discussion, the conclusion was reached to propose a unicameral legislature after all. General MacArthur favored it, and Kades thought that the issue might be used as an effective bargaining lever. If we proposed the unicameral legislature, he argued, and the Japanese held out for the bicameral system, we might well yield to strengthen our position on a more important issue. Sentiment favored giving the Diet the right to override decisions of the Supreme Court by a two-thirds vote. Lieutenant Colonel Hays insisted that all Diet deliberations take place in public, with no secret meetings to be held under any circumstances. Returning to the subject of the Diet vis-à-vis Supreme

Court decisions, Hussey made a strong pitch for giving the Supreme Court "absolute power of review," but he was voted down.

Kades expressed fear that in strengthening the legislative and judicial branches too little power would be left to the executive branch. In case the Diet passed a resolution of no confidence, he said, forcing the cabinet to resign, there might be a kind of executive vacuum. Hussey and Peake convinced him, however, that the old cabinet would continue to exercise power during a general election and until the new cabinet took office. To Peake's suggestion that the powers of the executive be specified, Kades objected; he felt that enumerating relatively unimportant powers might require formal amendment of the constitution later to effect procedural changes. Hussey likewise opposed listing the perfunctory duties of the emperor, such as affixing the state seal to documents and opening each Diet session.

Regarding budgetary control, Kades asserted that it would be enough to insert an unequivocal statement in the constitution that no budget could become effective without express approval of the legislative body. Rizzo disagreed, asserting that in the absence of an executive veto there was no way to prevent the legislature from running wild by voting expensive boondoggling and pork-barrel projects. Swope sided with Kades, citing his Puerto Rican experience to the effect that, practically speaking, an executive had the power to refuse to act on legislative appropriations to which he objected. Kades emphasized that the Diet had all powers not explicitly prohibited to it by the constitution.

It was agreed that the means by which the prime minister and the cabinet would be selected should not be specified in the constitution. The majority party or coalition in the Diet would choose the prime minister, and the prime minister would select his cabinet. To Rizzo's concern over defining the power of the Diet, Kades reiterated that all powers not explicitly delegated to the executive and judicial branches resided in the legislature. The supremacy of the legislative body, he said, would become quite clear in Government Section's draft. To Roest's observation that an ideal constitution based on American experience was vastly different from one based on Japanese experience, Kades concurred, but pointed out that "no comparable gap exists between American political ideology and the best or most liberal Japanese constitutional thought."

In the initial discussion of the emperor, the Steering Committee pressed for a strict delimitation of his powers. It decided against a proposed article defining sovereignty, since it was not necessary to amplify the Preamble statement placing sovereignty in the people. Objecting that the term "reign" carried the connotation of "govern" as well, the Steering Committee thought it sufficient for the emperor to be "the symbol of the State and the unity of the people." Negative also was the committee's attitude toward proposals granting initiative power to the emperor, giving him the right to confirm judgments of courts of law, authorizing four Imperial officers, and making it mandatory for the budget to include appropriations for throne expenditures.

The Steering Committee was not pleased with the position taken by Nelson and his assistant, Ens. Richard A. Poole, on amendment procedure. They favored prohibiting all amendments until 1955 and after that requiring a three-fourths majority in the Diet to ratify any amendment. They reasoned that the Japanese people were not ready for a democracy, and that "we are caught in the uncomfortable position of writing a liberal constitution for a people who still think mystically." The Steering Committee countered that no one generation has the right to delimit another generation's freedom to amend its constitution, that a constitution should be not only a fairly permanent document but a flexible one as well, with a simple rather than a complicated amendment procedure. Kades and Rowell differed over whether all international agreements should be submitted to the Diet for ratification. Pointing out that such agreements were all-embracing in their effects on the well-being and lives of the people, Rowell plugged for final Diet control of all treaties. Kades yielded. The Steering Committee was against having the Diet sit as a court of impeachment for hearing charges involving public officials, advising that the use of this procedure be restricted to removal of members of the judiciary. The proposal for an oath clause was withdrawn as having no meaning to a Japanese. A suggested article providing for ratification of the constitution by a two-thirds vote of all Diet members was reworded to read "by a roll-call vote of two-thirds of the members *present*."

Following discussion of "The Supreme Law," Captain Nelson submitted a minority report. He wanted the model constitution to say somewhere that sovereignty rested not only on the will of the people but also on principles of universal morality. "A blunt statement must be made that rectitude as well as physical strength is the source of authority." Kades objected that "the establishment of a kind of universal church has no place in a national constitution. The validity of the constitution stems from the Japanese people and not from any universal morality." Hussey agreed with Nelson. "We have come to recognize," he said, "if rather uneasily, a superior law that governs the people of all nations." Kades was not convinced, but he gave Hussey carte blanche to work out an acceptable statement on universal political morality.

On 7 February, the third day of the undertaking, the Steering Committee met again with groups responsible for the Diet, Finance, the Executive, and the Judiciary. Kades overruled proposals to reduce the present number of seats in the House of Representatives, to define the method and conditions of election for members of the Diet, to require a quorum of a half instead of a third of the membership to transact business in the Diet, and to give the Diet the superfluous privilege of making representations to the cabinet. Kades's proposal to allow more than forty days for a new election after dissolution of the old Diet was rejected by Hussey and Rowell. They also opposed his contention that the Diet should be permitted to make appropriations for any fiscal year in excess of the income provided for that year. The Steering Committee discarded an article providing for a temporary budget in the event the cabinet failed to obtain parliamentary approval for its annual budget. A suggestion to have the prime minister nominated by the emperor was changed to read, "The Emperor appoints as Prime Minister the person designated by the Diet." Kades, Hussey, and Rowell recommended that an article defining the duties of the prime minister be rewritten to emphasize the collective responsibility of the cabinet rather than the executive preeminence of the prime minister. They turned down an article requiring the prime minister and members of his cabinet to subscribe to a pledge on assuming office. Rowell met Kades's contention that the extreme grant of power to the judiciary might lead to a judicial oligarchy by explaining that even a greatly strengthened judiciary would not be able to weaken the prerogatives of the Diet.

On 8 and 9 February, the Civil Rights group gave the Steering Committee a hard time. First, Hussey took issue with a suggested article that reserved unenumerated rights to the people. It was omitted. Then, all three Steering Committee members objected to an article asserting that "no future constitution, law, or ordinance shall limit or cancel the rights guaranteed in this constitution, or subordinate public welfare and democracy to any other consideration." Kades interpreted such language to mean that "amendments to the bill of rights would be invalid and change could come only through revolution." Roest defended the article on the premise that "no future generation should be permitted to abrogate the rights now accepted as inherent in the state of man." Dr. Harry Emerson Wildes backed him by stating that omission of the article "would inevitably open the gates of fascism in Japan." Since no compromise could be reached, it was decided to refer the article to General Whitney for decision. (In the final draft, the article was omitted.) An article giving the people the inalienable right to elect public officials was amended to read: "The people have the right to choose their public officials and to dismiss them." "Freedom of person is the inalienable right of all law-abiding Japanese" was changed to "No person shall be held in enslavement, serfdom, or bondage of any kind." Thrown out was an article forbidding ecclesiastics to participate in any kind of political activity. Slander and libel were disallowed as exceptions to guaranteed freedom of speech. The Steering Committee refused to permit the exercise of freedom of assembly to be hedged by the qualifying phrase, "for peaceful consideration." Kades ruled out the restriction on dismissal of teachers as "procedure impertinent in a constitution and properly belonging in statutory law, if anywhere." Detailed orders for the establishment of social welfare, public health, free education, orderly adoption, and child labor laws were judged to be the proper concern of statutory regulation and not of constitutional law; it was not Government Section's responsibility to set up a complete system of social welfare. The argument of Roest and Wildes that SCAP had a responsibility "to effect a social revolution in Japan and that the most expedient way of doing so is to force through with the constitution a reversal of social patterns" was met by Rowell's comment that "you cannot impose a new mode of social thought on a country by law." No compromise solution being found, General Whitney ruled that the minutia of social legislation be omitted and a general statement substituted providing for social security. Also substantially changed by the Steering Committee and General Whitney were proposals having to do with ownership of land and the general welfare, the right of workers to strike, police supervision of public expression, the right of inheritance, state subsidy of industry, testimony and confession, and the right of counsel to cross-examine witnesses.

In the second meeting of the executive group with the Steering Committee, Lieutenant Esman objected, for one thing, to changes made by that committee in the original draft of the chapter on selecting the prime minister. Because of splinter parties and the improbability of one party gaining a clear majority in the Diet, he argued, the emperor and not the Diet should appoint the prime minister. Kades was not impressed. Any inefficiency and delay involved in Diet selection of the prime minister, he said, was offset by the danger of giving the emperor or his advisers discretionary power. To Esman's second point, that executive power should be explicitly vested in the prime minister and not in the cabinet as a collective body, Hussey, Rowell, and Peake demurred. In Japan, they said, things were done collectively. They won. The model constitution vested executive power in the cabinet.

The paper drawn up by the Local Government group was "discarded as inadequate, and a new one prepared by the Steering Committee." The main objection to the Tilton group's report was that it followed the United States Constitution principle of reserving to local entities those powers not specifically granted to the central government. Japan was, the Steering Committee believed, too small to permit any form of local sovereignty. The revised draft guaranteed a limited local autonomy for metropolitan areas, cities and towns, and other subordinate bodies having taxing power. These local entities were given the right to manage their own affairs within limits defined by the Diet. Provision was made for the election by direct popular vote of local administrative officials and of the members of local and prefectural legislative assemblies, as determined by the Diet. It was assumed that the Diet and the courts would adequately safeguard the principle of local autonomy. Rowell would have given local entities more real power, while Kades would have given them less.

Regarding the Kades-Hussey dispute over sovereignty and political morality, Hussey on 12 February suggested for inclusion in the Preamble these words: "We acknowledge that no people is responsible to itself alone, but that laws of political morality are universal and it is by these laws that we obtain sovereignty." He reasoned that the new United Nations Organization rendered historic notions of Sovereignty "both archaic and foolish," that a basic political morality binding on all nations would be accepted as a self-evident truth within fifty years. Kades clung to the proposition that political morality and sovereignty had nothing to do with each other, that insertion of the Hussey clause would so weaken the draft constitution as to leave it "little more than a gloss of words." He admitted to believing, however, that the clause might very well come to be accepted as a platitude within a hundred years. General Whitney entered the discussion and took Hussey's side of the argument. The slightly modified version of Hussey's draft that he proposed was incorporated in the Preamble of the model constitution.

Before the completed document was mimeographed on 12 February, the articles on Diet control of the income and expenditures of the Imperial Household were tightened. It was explicitly stated that all property held by the Imperial Household and the income from the Imperial estates belonged to the nation, and that all income from the Imperial estates would be paid into the national treasury. Allowances and expenses of the Imperial Household were to be appropriated by the Diet in the annual budget. The stage was now set to take up the model charter with the Shidehara Cabinet.

On 13 February, at the Foreign Minister's official residence, Whitney, Kades, Hussey, and Rowell distributed copies of the model draft to

Foreign Minister Yoshida Shigeru, Dr. Matsumoto, and Mr. Shirasu Jiro, deputy chief of the Central Liaison Office. Whitney explained, as Mr. Yoshida remembered, that the scap draft

> would meet with the approval both of the United States Government and the Far Eastern Commission; that General MacArthur had given much thought to the question of the position of the Emperor, which could best be safeguarded by revising our Constitution along lines laid down in the model version drafted by GHQ; and that if this was not done, GHQ could not answer for whatever might happen to the Emperor. He added that this was not an order, but that GHQ desired most earnestly that the Japanese Government should forward to General MacArthur's headquarters as soon as possible a draft Constitution incorporating the basic principles and form of the GHQ model version.[24]

Taking a quick look at the draft, Mr. Yoshida made note of the provisions pertaining to sovereignty of the people, the emperor as a symbol of the state, and a unicameral legislature. He concluded immediately that the scap draft "was of a revolutionary nature."[25] But he made no mention of Whitney's remark that MacArthur was prepared to lay the issue before the Japanese people if the cabinet failed to approve the revision plan, nor of the fact that Government Section had drawn up a model constitution in secret. According to General Whitney, the effect of the Government Section paper on the Japanese was immediately visible. "Mr. Shirasu straightened up as if he had sat on something. Dr. Matsumoto sucked in his breath. Mr. Yoshida's face was a black cloud."[26] Hussey recorded that the Japanese "appeared visibly surprised and disturbed and said they would have to consider the matter." They received the model charter, he recalled, "with a distinct sense of shock."[27]

But the shock soon wore off. Two days later Mr. Shirasu wrote General Whitney to say that although the scap draft came as a great surprise, Dr. Matsumoto realized that "the object of your draft and his 'revision' is one and the same in spirit. He is as anxious as you are, if not more, . . . that his country should be placed on a constitutional and democratic basis. . . . but . . . there is this great difference in the routes chosen. Your way is . . . straight and direct, [his is] . . . roundabout."[28]

To Japanese conservatives, popular sovereignty was the very antithesis of Japan's centuries-old ethical system of absolute authority and blind obedience. With sovereignty transferred from the emperor, who was at the apex of the political and social hierarchy, to the people, the basic orientation of Japanese society would be thrown into disorder. It would no longer be possible to distinguish between superiors and inferiors and to know where authority lay. The implicit, unquestioning obedience of the masses would not be taken for granted, and the virtually unlimited power

(1) Crowds gather before the Dai Ichi Building waiting for General MacArthur to emerge, 1947. His office was to the right of the second row of windows from the top. (2) Maynard N. Shirven, who succeeded Blaine Hoover as chief of Government Section's Civil Service Division and supervised the writing and passage of Japan's Local Public Service Law. (3) Two major contributors to Japan's democratization, 1948. Baron Shidehara Kijuro *(right)* gave General MacArthur the idea for the no-war clause in Japan's Constitution. Dr. Kanamori Tokujiro rose thirteen hundred times in the Diet to defend the Constitution Revision bill.

(1) Comdr. Alfred R. Hussey, Jr., with two top Japanese Foreign Service officers, *left*, Yamada Hisanari and, *right*, Yokoyama Ichiro, June 1948. Hussey was a key Government Section figure in the drafting of a model democratic constitution for the guidance of the Japanese leaders. *(U.S. Army)* (2) A conference between Government Section's Frank Hays and House of Representatives Speaker Matsuoka Komakichi in March 1948 to discuss black-market activities. *(U.S. Army)*

(1) A conference between Japanese officials and members of SCAP's Government Section to revise Japan's Criminal Code, April 1948. *Seated clockwise:* Judge Mano K., Maruyama D., Prof. Saito K., Prof. Dando S., Baba Y., Hashimoto K., Kiuchi T., Kunimume S., Nogi S., Kawamoto Y., Richard Appleton, Thomas Blakemore, Alfred C. Oppler, Koike X. *Seated far left:* Yjiko D. and Miyashita A. (*U.S. Army*) (2) An informal conference between leaders of the new National Diet and officials of SCAP's Government Section, June 1948. *Left to right:* House of Councillors Secretary General Kobayashi Jiro, House of Representatives Secretary General Oike Makoto, Charles L. Kades, House of Councillors President Matsudaira Tsuneo, House of Representatives Speaker Matsuoka Komakichi, Justin Williams, Frank Rizzo. (*U.S. Army*)

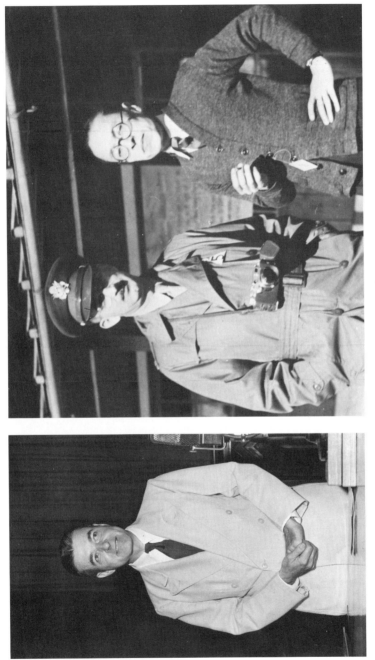

(1) Cecil G. Tilton, chief of the Legal and Government Division, Eighth Army, speaks to the large crowd of allied personnel and Japanese who attended the opening of the three-day conference on the Local Autonomy Law, 1948. The press conference was held at Tokyo University. (*U.S. Army*) (2) Capt. C. F. Guida, member of Government Section's PPD, with Sato Tatsuo, chief of the Cabinet's Legal Bureau (1948). Mr. Sato probably worked more closely with SCAP and Japanese officials on the first draft of the revised constitution than any other Japanese. He later became president of the National Personnel Authority.

of those officials who controlled the emperor would be undermined. The Japanese with whom SCAP dealt in this instance were all veteran bureaucrats, fully conscious of the gulf separating their class from the mere common people. They would defend the emperor's sovereignty to the bitter end, unless the emperor himself commanded them to give ground.

Sentiment in the cabinet was about evenly divided between those who opposed and those who favored SCAP's comprehensive revision plan. Mr. Yoshida spoke for the most conservative members and Prime Minister Shidehara spoke for those who believed that parliamentary democracy could be lived with. Finding SCAP unwilling to yield on any of the democratic principles involved, Messrs. Shidehara and Yoshida, accompanied by Chief Cabinet Secretary Narahashi Wataru, consulted the emperor. This was on 22 February, nine days after the SCAP model had been made available to the top Japanese officials. The emperor resolved the matter by supporting SCAP; whereupon the prime minister instructed Dr. Matsumoto to prepare a Japanese draft based on the SCAP document.[29]

Now the scene shifted to the staff of the Cabinet Legal Bureau. What these officials did between 26 February and 4 March was summarized in 1957 by Sato Tatsuo, deputy chief of that agency. They found the ideas and the expressions in the SCAP draft "thoroughly alien." The provision for renunciation of war "drew special attention." Chapter 3 as a whole, on the rights and duties of the people, was regarded as "something out of the ordinary"; and Article 28—providing that "the ultimate fee to the land and to all natural resources reposes in the State as the collective representative of the people"—was so "out of the ordinary" as to be dubbed "the Red Provision." The chapter on the Judiciary "was considered most extraordinary," particularly the clause permitting the Diet to set aside Supreme Court decisions by a two-thirds majority vote. "No small embarrassment" was the article in the chapter on Finance placing the property and income of the Imperial Household under Diet control.[30]

The Japanese legal experts, according to Mr. Sato, made some changes in the SCAP draft. They undertook to improve the phraseology of Chapter 3 and to add or delete clauses elsewhere thought to be unessential. They deleted the "Red Provision" for nationalizing land and natural resources. They substituted a bicameral for the unicameral legislative system, and authorized the cabinet to legislate by cabinet order in emergency situations when the Diet could not be convoked. The SCAP provisions relating to the Imperial properties were omitted. On 4 March the Japanese draft was submitted to Government Section by Dr. Matsumoto.[31]

Immediate translation of the Japanese submission was begun by Government Section translators, who were assisted by Japanese Foreign

Ministry officials. The work had not progressed far when Dr. Matsumoto and the Government Section lawyers got into a heated debate over the translation of "advice and consent," in referring to the relationship between the cabinet and the emperor, which came out "advice and assistance" in Japanese. It soon became clear that, in addition to the changes mentioned in the preceding paragraph, the Japanese drafters had watered down the rights of the people, empowered a proposed House of Councillors to hobble the House of Representatives, strengthened the cabinet, and authorized the emperor to initiate amendments to the Imperial House Law. The Preamble proclaiming "sovereignty of the people's will" was missing, as was the SCAP provision for terminating the peerage. Freedom of speech, press, and assembly was guaranteed, "to the extent that they do not conflict with the public peace and order." Censorship was not to be maintained, "except as specifically provided by law." People had the right to work, "as provided by law." Workers could organize and bargain collectively, "as provided by law." The SCAP model had been substantially revised.[32]

Working throughout the night and until 4 P.M. the following day, the American and Japanese officials came to an understanding. The Americans approved the Japanese request to delete the "Red Provision" and the provision for Diet review of Supreme Court decisions; they also let stand the provision for a bicameral legislature, on condition that the second chamber would be inferior to the House of Representatives and that its members would be elective. The Japanese negotiators found a satisfactory translation for "advice and consent." Otherwise, except for some language refinements, the conditions of the SCAP model were restored. The next day, 6 March, the cabinet approved the revised draft; an Imperial rescript announcing its adoption was published; and General MacArthur released a statement to the press giving it his unqualified endorsement. Also on that date, Commander Hussey took the precaution to have Chief Cabinet Secretary Narahashi sign thirteen printed copies of the English text of the draft constitution, of which one copy was left with Mr. Narahashi. Made public that evening were a summary in Japanese of the draft constitution and the full text of its English translation.[33]

But the draft constitution was still far from being a finished product. Therefore, at the request of Cabinet Legal Bureau Chief Irie Toshio and Deputy Chief Sato, a number of conferences were held with Government Section officials during the next several weeks to improve it. The nature of these joint meetings was indicated by the questions asked and the answers given. Typical questions raised, in writing, by Messrs. Irie and Sato, with Kades's answers in parentheses, were the following:

Art. 8. (*a*) Does this article apply to gifts by the people to the Emperor? ("Yes").

(*b*) It is interpreted that the article does not apply to gifts to the Emperor as a private individual. ("No").

(*c*) Does "Imperial House" include members of the Imperial Family? ("Yes").

Do the provisions of the article apply to gifts to members of the Imperial Family as private individuals? ("Yes").

(*d*) How about gifts between the Emperor and members of the Imperial Family? ("Yes").

Art. 23. Are not "(Social) Security" and "public health" covered by "social welfare"? When listed side by side with "freedom, justice, and democracy" these two words seem somewhat unbalanced. Would not "social welfare" alone be sufficient here? ("Strike out 'freedom, justice, and democracy' ").

Art. 48. In order to clarify the relation with the next article, would it not be better to revise the present article to read: "An ordinary session of the Diet shall be convened once a year"? ("OK").

Art. 53. Would it not be better to alter the 2nd sentence to read, as in the case of Art. 78, "However, a secret meeting may be held where a majority of two-thirds or more of those members present passes a resolution therefor"? ("Reserved OK").

Art. 84. (*a*) The phrase "the hereditary estates" in the present article is understood to mean the property, personal or real, among the properties of the Emperor to be handed down with the Imperial Throne.

(*b*) If so, can this phrase be interpreted not to include the private property of the Emperor (cars, furniture, scrolls, paintings, villas, etc. for the daily use of the Emperor)? ("Under discussion").

At their next session in Government Section, the Japanese representatives again brought up the question of hereditary estates as covered in Article 84. "At our last conference," they said, "we understood that the word 'estates' should be interpreted to include personal property. In the Japanese text, therefore, we have to use an expression to that effect. However, as it appears the word 'estate' is slightly ambiguous here, we would like to use the word 'property' instead." Kades approved the suggestion.[34]

In the course of these conferences, the Japanese side won an important concession and made an epochal decision. The concession was a new clause providing for the right of the cabinet to convoke the House of Councillors in emergency session when the House of Representatives was in dissolution. The epochal decision was to draw up the draft constitution in spoken Japanese instead of in the traditional literary style of legal language. Thenceforth the spoken language was used for promulgating all laws and ordinances. SCAP had nothing to do with the decision.[35] Thus, by mid-April, the cabinet's constitution revision bill was completed. The problem of the Government Section negotiators was to preserve every democratic principle contained in SWNCC 228, so as to ensure that SCAP would not be reversed by the FEC. The problem of the Japanese officials was to understand the meanings and nuances of some one hundred articles in the draft, to enable them to answer interpellations that would be put in forthcoming sessions of the Privy Council, the House of Representatives, and the House of Peers. Regarding the negotiations with SCAP, Mr. Yoshida had this to say, in retrospect:

> I cannot entirely agree . . . that this post-war Constitution was forced upon us. It is quite true that, at the time of its initial drafting . . . General MacArthur's headquarters did insist, with considerable vigour, on the speedy completion of the task and made certain demands in regard to the contents of the draft. But during our subsequent negotiations with GHQ there was nothing that could properly be termed coercive or overbearing in the attitude of the Occupation authorities towards us. They listened carefully and . . . in many cases accepted our proposals. When it happened that our discussions with them reached a deadlock, they would often adopt the attitude that . . . we might at least give their suggestions a trial and then, if they did not work, we could reconsider the whole question at the proper time and revise the necessary points. And they meant it.[36]

In eleven formal meetings between 22 April and 3 June, the Privy Council thoroughly deliberated the cabinet's bill for revising the Imperial Constitution. In the very first session, State Minister Matsumoto was asked if changes might be made in the cabinet's draft. He replied: "Since the present bill has been announced both in Japanese and English at the same time, it is, I think, politically impossible for the Government to make substantial corrections. The revision right of the Diet is legally recognized, but practically it seems impossible for the Diet to add new provisions, although corrections may be possible with regard to each provision of the bill." Asked whether the cabinet's draft was based on a theory of state sovereignty, popular sovereignty, or Imperial sovereignty, and what was the legal position of the emperor, Prime Minister Shidehara replied that the theory of popular sovereignty proclaimed in the Preamble could not be interpreted to exclude the emperor. The word "people," he said, embraced the emperor, who "was over them as their center." Dr. Matsumoto added that, in a political sense, sovereignty of the people was taken for granted where affairs of state were carried out by the will of the people; but in a legal sense, he said, sovereignty reposed in the state. He interpreted Mr. Shidehara's answer not to mean that the Japanese people included the emperor, but that "the Japanese people unified in one body have the Emperor at the center." Pressed further on this extremely delicate subject, Dr. Matsumoto cut off debate by saying: "Your question gets at the heart of the matter, so I hope you will draw conclusions from the circumstances consequent on our acceptance of the Potsdam Declaration."[37]

Councilor Minobe Tatsukichi, a noted constitutional scholar, pulled no punches in attacking the constitutional revision bill. He declared that Japan's acceptance of the Potsdam Declaration invalidated Article 73 of the Meiji Constitution, under which the current revision was taking place. He ridiculed the cabinet for consulting the Privy Council and the House of Peers on a bill that abolished both bodies. He scoffed at the claim that the proposed constitution represented the freely expressed will of the people, since it was initiated by Imperial command, drafted by the cabinet, and would be promulgated by Imperial sanction when approved by the Diet, "which has the right of revision only within a limited scope." In light of the foregoing, he proposed that the coming Diet concern itself only with establishing sound procedures for revising the existing constitution, and then meet in a subsequent session to carry out the revision. Dr. Matsumoto's rejoinder was that the cabinet could not postpone revision any longer, and even if it did, "we could not but resort to the existing provisions." All members of the Council save Dr. Minobe voted to approve the cabinet revision bill without amendment for submission to the Diet.[38]

Beginning 20 June, the House of Representatives debated the cabinet's bill for two months. As with the Shidehara Cabinet from February to April and the Privy Council from April to June, the discussions in the lower chamber centered largely around the fundamental relationship between the emperor and the people. Next in importance was the no-war clause. Mr. Yoshida, who replaced Baron Shidehara in May as prime minister, and Minister of State Kanamori Tokujiro, who replaced Dr. Matsumoto, bore the brunt of defending the measure in plenary sessions and committee meetings. According to Mr. Yoshida, "despite the fact that the nation was . . . under foreign Occupation, [Japan's foremost authorities in the House] were able to give free expression to their opinion without any restraint whatsoever." SCAP, he said, "maintained in general an attitude of watchful silence throughout the discussions in the Diet, but . . . did intervene once or twice." SCAP intervened to have the Cabinet comply with an FEC directive requiring all ministers of state to be civilians and a majority of cabinet ministers to be Diet members.[39] The FEC also directed that the language of the Preamble be changed to leave no doubt that sovereignty reposed in the people. Though SWNCC 228 did not specify "popular sovereignty," SCAP nevertheless inserted the words in the model constitution; at SCAP's suggestion, before receipt of the FEC directive, the House of Representatives amended the language of the constitution revision bill to clarify this point. Mr. Yoshida repeatedly said in Diet plenary sessions and committee meetings that the substance of the new constitution was required under the terms of surrender, a fact that called for sincere and prudent consideration by Japanese officials and legislators. The House of Representatives approved the cabinet's bill on 24 August by a vote of 421 to 8, after having added two new articles, deleted one, and amended twenty-two.[40] Understandably no consequential contribution to the measure was made on the initiative of the lower house, except to Article 9, as we shall see.

Unlike its warm reception in the House of Representatives, whose members had recently been elected, the revision bill was not enthusiastically received in the House of Peers. Speaking freely for the record, an articulate minority of the members of that body of noblemen and distinguished citizens bitterly attacked the entire revision plan. Dr. Kanamori's reply to them was that "the Meiji Constitution and its lax enforcement caused the downfall of this country. There is no way out . . . except by adopting the democratic system. . . . The Potsdam Declaration provided that the political system of Japan shall be decided by the free will of the people." Mr. Yoshida added: "Although the international situation predominantly overshadowed the drafting of the Constitution, the demands of the people have not been denied."[41] Thus, the inflexible opponent of responsible government in February had become its ardent defender in September. In the process of codifying the new polity of Japan, Mr. Yoshida helped the people shift their allegiance to the new system without losing their national respect and self-esteem.

Mention should be made of an attitude that became more prevalent in informed Japanese circles as facts about the new governmental system sank in. Of course, the tory element remained bitter, but many soberminded Japanese took a more philosophical view of the exotic basic charter, which the people gladly accepted but did not freely choose. Neither had they chosen the German-inspired Meiji Constitution, which resulted in disaster for the nation. For many years preceding the Pacific War, increasing numbers of Japanese admired and copied American ways. Now they were being tendered, gratis, the complete American-British political system in a single package, accompanied by detailed instructions for making it work. With the institution of Emperor partially preserved to give basic orientation to Japanese society, many thoughtful citizens were confident that the new system could be managed so as to minimize its defects and capitalize on its virtues.

It would not be wrong to say that the new governmental system of Japan was established by the United States, with the enthusiastic approval of the elective chamber of the Diet reflecting the feelings of the Japanese electorate. SWNCC 228 supplied the foundation for the basic law, but SCAP added the no-war clause, popular sovereignty per se, the independent judiciary, and abolition of the peerage. But two important provisions of the new constitution were not entirely of United States origin. One of these was the second Diet chamber, the House of Councillors. SWNCC 228 had nothing to offer on this subject. SCAP leaned toward a unicameral legislature. Though not the functional or corporate upper house strongly favored by Japanese conservatives, the elective House of Councillors would not have come into being without the urging of the Japanese side. The other important provision that originated partially with the Japanese was Article 9, the no-war clause. MacArthur decided that Government Section's model constitution would renounce the right of belligerency, but his inspiration for the unusual move can be traced to Baron Shidehara. Professor Theodore McNelly, who thoroughly researched this question, concluded: "Some people believe that Shidehara may have suggested that Japan renounce war as a policy and that it was MacArthur's idea to put the renunciation in the Constitution. In any event, it seems generally agreed that Shidehara and MacArthur did discuss the renunciation of war and that they both held strongly pacifistic views at the time."[42]

As chairman of the House of Representatives Special Committee on the Constitution, Dr. Ashida Hitoshi succeeded in having Article 9 amended to permit Japan to maintain self-defense forces. Article 9 now reads:

Aspiring sincerely to an international peace based on justice and order, the Japanese people, forever, renounce war as a sovereign right of the nation, or the threat or use of force, as a means of settling disputes with other nations.

In order to accomplish the aim of the preceding paragraph, land, sea, and air forces, as well as other war potential, will never be maintained. The right of belligerency of the state will not be recognized.

The Ashida amendments are italicized. In 1951, he declared that his amendments were meant to allow Japan to arm for defense.[43] General MacArthur held that nothing in Article 9 prevented any and all necessary steps for the preservation of the safety of the nation. The article, he said, was aimed solely at foreign aggression.[44]

The Constitution and the
Will of the People

The 1946 Constitution had the approval of the Japanese people as distinguished from the approval given by the Shidehara Cabinet. Some have cited as coercion the method used by SCAP to persuade not the people but the Japanese government to accept the basic principles of the model constitution. Although top Japanese officials were not ordered by SCAP to approve the Western-style charter, they were convinced by occupation authorities that their choice lay between retaining the emperor as a symbol under SCAP's plan and risking having the Imperial system abolished by direction of the FEC. But it was not necessary to put any kind of pressure on the Japanese people.

Following closely the trend of Japanese public opinion, Japan's leaders realized that the salient features of the SCAP draft had the enthusiastic support of their countrymen. They sensed that the masses, consciously or unconsciously, "identified themselves as beneficiaries, rather than victims, of the occupation regime and the new Constitution."[1] They appreciated that both the spirit and the content of the constitution, in spite of their alien origin, met the requirements of a Japanese society involved in a "crisis of redirection and adjustment," that the great majority of the Japanese people "ardently desired to see authoritarianism and militarism extirpated from their society."[2] Some investigators assume that, because of the purge and the chilling effect of the occupation, the Japanese were not free to express their true opinion of the revolutionary political reforms carried out by their government. Others believe that, through the extensive exercise of free speech and freedom of the press, all the essential arguments used by postoccupation advocates of constitutional revision had been raised by the end of 1946.[3] But so far unexplored is the climate of opinion in Japan that emboldened SCAP to effect constitutional reform along lines laid down in Washington. SCAP realized that both Washington and the Japanese people demanded a peacefully inclined and responsible government. Consequently there was no need to order constitutional changes; SCAP was in a position to know that the Japanese people were of a frame of mind to adopt them willingly. The 1946 Constitution has endured because it was popular. The purpose of this chapter is to show that the great majority of the people welcomed it at the time of its adoption and early enforcement.

Constitutional revision was widely discussed during the early months of the occupation. In response to public demand, the cabinet, the newly formed political parties, and many individuals got into the act. One of the individuals, though a resident of Japan for twenty-five years, was not a Japanese national. He was Paul de Gyarmathy, a Kobe businessman of Hungarian extraction (see Chap. 1). Mention was made earlier of his 100-page manuscript, "An Appeal to the Emperor," which was a detailed plan for revising the Imperial Constitution. Although this imaginative and realistic disquisition never received any publicity and reached SCAP too late to influence Government Section's model constitution, it was a faithful representation of the radical governmental changes most Japanese were ready for by the end of the war. It reflected the belief of Gyarmathy and his Japanese business and professional associates that Japan would have to become a genuinely democratic nation, and that the transition would take place "much more easily than generally supposed."[4]

Gyarmathy's project was launched in 1942 when "enforced inactivity" gave him ample time to read and think of "malpractices . . . so deepseated that only a command from the Sovereign could right them." If the 1889 Constitution was a gift from the emperor, he reasoned, then the obvious way to change it was to ask the emperor for another gift. Relying heavily on like-minded Japanese friends and on his extensive personal collection of books and documents, including the texts of thirty-seven Western constitutions, he finished his work before Japan surrendered. "I present it," he wrote, "exactly as it was completed earlier this year . . . before the bombings became too intensive." His collaboration with others was limited, because "prudence and commonsense commanded absolute secrecy, as people got thrown out of third floor windows for lesser crimes than dissecting the function of the Emperor."[5]

Holding with Jefferson, whom he quoted, that "no constitution is good unless it is adapted to a specific people at the particular stage of their mental and moral growth," Gyarmathy, as spokesman for prospective Japanese petitioners, expressed to the emperor their "hopes for an immediate abolition of the present regime, and the appointment of a cabinet which shall possess the confidence of the people, shall bring this hopeless war to an immediate end, and then shall take in hand without delay the timely transformation of the country; a full and definite elaboration of the principles of democracy as regards politics, economics, and justice, in a manner agreeable to the free spirit of the age, and in the general interest of the Nation." [6]

Gyarmathy came close to advocating the democratic principles embodied in SCAP's 1946 model charter. Concerning the form of government, he conceded, as most Japanese would have, that "the supremacy of the Sovereign must forever remain the keystone of the Empire," but inasmuch as "all good and stable governments derive their power from the consent of the governed . . . only the Nation itself through its duly elected representatives assembled in Parliament, shall have the right to advise and to assist the Emperor, and to share his power." This principle, the author pointed out, settled the fate of the Privy Council, Elder Statesmen, Lord Keeper of the Privy Seal, and all other advisory agencies. Executive power would be exercised by a cabinet composed of members of a parliament collectively responsible to parliament. Parliament would have sole power to declare war, conclude peace, ratify treaties, make laws, raise and support armed forces, impose taxes, and appropriate public funds. [7]

Regarding the second chamber of parliament, Gyarmathy's constitution reflected the views of most Japanese savants. Whereas SCAP yielded to Japanese entreaties for a second body, provided its members were chosen democratically and its position made secondary to the House of Representatives, Gyarmathy proposed a Senate of three hundred members, sixty of whom would be appointed by the throne for life. The remainder would be elected for eight-year terms by the following entities:

House of Representatives	60
Senate	60
Prefectures	47
Six free cities	13
Universities	30
Labor	30

Gyarmathy reasoned: "As the lower house is likely to be composed of political mountebanks, let the Senate have some brains." Denied the right to initiate legislation, the Senate would be empowered to veto all measures of the House of Representatives, except the budget. The House of Representatives could override a Senate veto, "though not sooner than six months thereafter." If the Senate vetoed the measure a second time, the House of Representatives would be dissolved. If the newly elected House repassed the same bill and the Senate failed to go along within four weeks, it would, with Imperial assent, become law. [8]

But in other important respects Gyarmathy's reading of the Japanese mood anticipated that of SCAP. He concluded that the people would subscribe to the following recommendations:

1. Women's suffrage—to be realized within ten years.
2. Marriage—to rest on the equality of the rights of both sexes.
3. Civil rights—to be guaranteed. Parliament would make no laws to impede historical research, political studies, academic discussions, and the acquiring of knowledge. The right to assemble would be assured, although restrictions could be placed on meetings held in public places. The right to form associations would be absolute. Religion was a personal affair, not the concern of the state. No person's property could be taken for public use without just compensation. The press would be free. "Every citizen should be conscious of his inherent right to privacy and of his duty not to meddle with another person's."
4. Court system—a Supreme Court to act as guardian of the constitution. It would be the court of last appeal in all civil and criminal cases where the constitutionality of a law was challenged; and it would have power to declare any legislation void if found inconsistent with the provisions of the constitution. The Supreme Court would be composed of a president and twelve justices.
5. Civil service—all government workers would be imbued with the spirit of public servants, employed for the general good.
6. Finance—the power to levy taxes would be vested exclusively in the Parliament, which would delegate part of its power to local governments.
7. Local government—since local institutions constituted the strength of free nations, widest powers would be given to the local authorities. Prefectural governors and the mayors of the six largest cities would be elected by popular and direct suffrage, as would assemblymen and aldermen.
8. Police—in matters pertaining to personnel, training, and discipline, they would be supervised by the minister of Home Affairs; in matters of employment, they would be subordinated to the provincial governments. They could not engage in spying on law-abiding citizens, violate privacy, check free speech, suppress criticism of the government, or interfere with "orderly" public and social amusements. The police would have no power to make bylaws, or to issue ordinances and regulations, except in dire emergencies for a period not to exceed twenty-four hours. The magisterial function would be completely separated from the duties of the police, whose authority would be limited to arresting persons and bringing them before the judge. The use of force would be permitted only to prevent crime, preserve public peace, and bring offenders to justice.

Registration of the movement of the population would be a responsibility of local officials and not of the police.

9. Education—public education would be conducted in accordance with scientifically established principles. Historical instruction would be revised, and the ideas of universal liberty emphasized. Schools should develop personal initiative and self-reliance and teach children to think for themselves.

10. Armed forces—denied a privileged position, they would be controlled by the competent minister. "This control, the Nation hopes, will keep them henceforth forevermore from the possibility of recommencing their old policy which has unloosed the present catastrophe upon Japan." In Gyarmathy's opinion, "once Japan has a truly parliamentary government, all traces of militarism will comparatively quickly disappear."

11. Agriculture—the state would assist tenant farmers in acquiring homesteads on long-term credits, if need be by expropriating, with just compensation, the estates of absentee landowners.

12. Monopoly—the government would not grant monopolies in any industry or trade, except the mails, telephone, telegraph, government railroads, and tobacco.

13. Public welfare—Parliament would enact laws to protect workers, prohibit child labor, and promote public health; and to provide health insurance, maternity care, and old age assistance.

14. Labor—it would be lawful for all employees, urban or rural, excepting only those working for the government, to organize and bargain collectively. The right to strike would be recognized by law.

15. Elections—existing electoral districts, the number of representatives, and the blank ballot would undergo no change.[9]

Had Gyarmathy's home-grown and forward-looking plan been available in late January instead of mid-March 1946, its main effect probably would have been to fortify the strong conviction held in SCAP that the Japanese people were already mentally conditioned for a heavy dose of democracy. Whether it might have influenced the tone or wording of Government Section's model constitution is as problematical as it is immaterial. Its significance stems from its disclosure of the governmental reforms Japan was ready for and might well have brought about if she had been unoccupied and otherwise left entirely to her own devices.

Ironically when Paul de Gyarmathy got his first inkling of the Shidehara Cabinet's draft constitution from *Asahi Shimbun*, he was dumbfounded. "There is plenty of lip-service to democracy in it," he wrote me, "and some play-acting for the benefit of the Americans, but very little hard sense. . . . the whole scheme hardly deserves serious attention." Unaware as yet of SCAP's hand in the matter, he noted that "the Christian Science Monitor has seen through this legal concoction, and called it a booby trap. No constitution is good without some teeth in it, least of all for Japan."[10]

Three days later he wrote me again. "I believe," he said, "the following information is important enough for bringing it to your attention, and through your good offices eventually to the competent section of GHQ." What he had been told the day before in a three-hour interview with the publisher of *Asahi Shimbun*, he continued, "was outright hair-raising." The journalist was convinced that the draft had been written by GHQ, but in Gyarmathy's "honest opinion" it was a fake, and "would not bring this country an inch nearer to democracy." If its sponsors were trying to sell it to the people under the pretext that it came straight from GHQ, he said, then they were just "playing a new variation on the old theme that 'it is the wish of the Emperor' (this time of MacArthur) and thus not subject to discussion." Still insensible to the meaning of the one-two punch delivered by General MacArthur and the emperor in their public statements of 6 March sanctioning the Shidehara Cabinet's draft constitution, Gyarmathy went on: "This is a serious matter, well worth looking into. . . . if this constitution is enacted . . . there will be . . . a major disaster inflicted on the future of Japan. . . . under [it] the policeman in his 'box,' the minister in the Home Department, or Baron Mitsui in his office, would do exactly as they were doing before."[11]

Gyarmathy did not write again. In the end he probably concluded that his revision plan and that prepared by SCAP were much the same, one significant difference between them being that his bore the label, "made in Japan," and SCAP's, "made in U.S.A." Rank-and-file Japanese did not seem then or later to be impressed by this distinction.

Where Gyarmathy in his proposed revision of the Meiji Constitution simply transferred ultimate power to the people's representatives without doing violence to the concept of Imperial sovereignty, SCAP undertook a more complicated fourfold task. At one stroke, SCAP had to overthrow the feudal elite, exalt the masses, preserve the throne, and downgrade the emperor, all without losing the support of the Japanese people or running afoul of the FEC. In the absence of a master plan from Washington for achieving this grand design, it became necessary for SCAP to improvise one on the basis of fortuitous current developments.

The first such development was the highly unfavorable reaction in the United States to Ambassador George Atcheson's October 1945 talks with

Prince Konoye Fumimaro on constitutional revision. Lacking confidence in the chief of his Government Section, MacArthur deferred to his Political Adviser, who had instructions directly from the State Department on the governmental reforms it expected the occupation to carry out.[12] The result was that Far East expert Nathaniel Peffer wrote a letter to the *New York Times* (26 October 1945) blasting the Atcheson-Konoye talks. To allow Prince Konoye to preside at the drafting of Japan's new constitution, he said, was "grotesque," as Konoye stood for everything that had made Japan dangerous to the United States. This was "the worst blunder we have committed." That did it. Unlike Gen. Lucius D. Clay, who shared his authority in Germany with Ambassador Robert Murphy, General MacArthur was the sole administrator in Japan. Consequently he unilaterally disassociated his headquarters from the talks with Konoye and ceased to use the services of the Political Adviser in this sphere. A few months later the Office of the Political Adviser was changed to SCAP's Diplomatic Section and restricted to Japanese external affairs. Thus ended the direct participation of the State Department in the administration of the occupation of Japan, leaving the Supreme Commander entirely free to decide when and how to resolve the issue of constitutional revision under his Washington orders.

(2)   Another propitious development was Emperor Hirohito's renunciation of his divinity. So long as the Shinto doctrine proclaiming him to be a god remained valid, political reforms that might convert Japan to a real constitutional government would be next to impossible to bring about. SCAP's directive of December 1945 abolishing Shinto as a state religion paved the way for Hirohito to issue the historic rescript of 1 January 1946 denying his divinity, declaring false the Shinto doctrine of Japanese racial superiority, and exhorting Japan to "build a new state based on peace and a rational system of government which rules in accordance with public opinion." This rescript took the wind out of the sails of those Japanese diehards in high places who held that, regardless of changes in governmental structure, there could be no question of altering the emperor's status, as his divinity precluded such action.[13] The rescript was an indispensable stepping stone to Emperor Hirohito's decisive support two months later of the SCAP-drafted democratic constitution.

(3)   Constitutional reform was also undoubtedly facilitated by SCAP's civil liberties directives issued during the first two months of the occupation.[14] Lifting of governmental restrictions on open discussion of the emperor, the Imperial institution, and the Japanese government encouraged publication of private Japanese draft constitutions that were vastly more liberal than the one proposed by the Shidehara Cabinet. This presaged the

introduction and widespread discussion of proposals relating to democracy.

(4) Still another timely event was the submission to SCAP in early February 1946 of the Shidehara Cabinet's constitutional revision plan. SCAP's Government Section perceived at once that the cabinet's skill "in fashioning façades involving no structural remodeling was notable." While "all drafts made by political parties and others are demanding the democratization of the Constitution," Commander Hussey wrote, "the Government plan . . . has shown no intention to democratize it. . . . if the Government insists upon the adoption of the Matsumoto draft, public opinion will rise against it." [15] Before receipt of the Matsumoto draft, SCAP had entertained no thought whatever of becoming involved in the process of rewriting the Imperial Constitution. But the work of Dr. Matsumoto and his colleagues was so shockingly short of what the Japanese public was demanding, of what might reasonably have been expected of the Japanese government five months after the occupation began, and of what the fast tempo of the occupation required, that SCAP could not stand idly by. MacArthur had to consider how much more desperate the situation might become if he marked time, perhaps for many months, pending some kind of decision by the still inactivated, eleven-member FEC. After analyzing the situation, he concluded that there was no feasible alternative to tackling the crucial constitutional issue without further delay.

Important as were the foregoing happenings, the sine qua non of constitutional revision was the aroused Japanese public, which clamored for the sweeping liberal and democratic reforms proposed by the newly formed political parties as well as by private groups and organizations. [16] SCAP was caught up in this surge of enthusiasm for radical changes in the political system. The nongovernment draft constitutions were not as thoroughly democratic as the later SCAP model based essentially on SWNCC 228, but they contained the seeds of democratic government nevertheless. Indifferent to local autonomy, women's suffrage, equal rights for women, and guarantees against illegal searches, most of the proposals, like Gyarmathy's, contained provisions for Imperial sovereignty with the prerogatives of the emperor sharply curtailed, a powerful House of Representatives checked by a functional upper chamber, abolition of the Privy Council and the peerage, judicial independence, and guarantees of civil liberties. But these drafts, supplemented by press commentaries, were the best existing yardstick of public opinion.

For SCAP there was no mistaking the attitude of the Japanese people toward political reform during the early months of the occupation. Their ebullient reception of the early occupation directives impressed even the most skeptical and cynical American officials and correspondents in Japan. The prime source of intelligence on the public pulse was the Japanese press, to which SCAP paid the closest attention. Widely utilized by SCAP staff sections to observe and assess the trends of Japanese thought was the invaluable *Press Translations and Summaries*, a stenciled paperback booklet delivered daily (except Sunday) at an early hour. Prepared by G–2's Allied Translator and Interpreter Section (ATIS), which was staffed by around 400 experienced translators, each issue of the publication carried from 100 to 150 items translated from major Tokyo papers, the prefectural press, magazines, and trade, labor, and other special journals. The first section of the booklet contained selected material from that day's Tokyo editions. The other sections consisted of recent articles and editorials from big city and prefectural newspapers and magazines on political, economic, and social subjects. From the scores of newspapers scanned daily and weekly and the approximately 1,500 Japanese language magazines scanned each month, writings of possible interest to the occupation were selected and translated. The Media Analysis Branch of CIE's Analysis and Research Divison used these translations to prepare a daily *Press Analysis* and a periodic *Publications Analysis* on a wide range of topics. One important topic during the first year of the occupation was constitutional revision. Most of what is said in this chapter on the attitude of the Japanese people toward political change is based on the CIE analyses.

Not surprisingly, Japanese thinking on governmental reform became more sharply defined after publication of the cabinet's draft constitution in March 1946 than it had been before. But during the first six months of the occupation, as SCAP's program unfolded step-by-step and the press became less fearful of a return to government thought control, the nature of the political changes demanded by the people came progressively into better focus. In mid-October 1945, CIE press analysts, aware that none of Tokyo's leading newspapers had so far made a serious effort to explain to the people in one syllable words the significance of the MacArthur directives banning restrictions on freedom of thought, noted *Mainichi Shimbun*'s claim that the democratic tendency among the people was very strong. At the same time reference was made to *Yomiuri Hochi*'s observation that the newly formed Socialist party was opposed to revision of the Imperial Constitution solely by officials and scholars handpicked by the government. Not overlooked was that journal's advocacy of democratization of the "fossilized" judiciary along with democratization of the legislative and executive branches. Among other items to which the early

CIE reports drew attention were these: Dr. Minobe Tatsukichi's article in *Mainichi* rationalizing the view of the stubbornly conservative minority that government renovation could be accomplished without changing the Imperial Constitution; a policy statement by the nascent Socialist party that the constitution should be democratized according to the will of the people; *Tokyo Shimbun*'s plaint that the "concrete policy in revising the constitution has not been made clear, however the strengthening of . . . the Diet will naturally be the political trend"; the unanimous opinion of five prominent political figures, reported by *Sangyo Keizai*, that the Imperial Constitution could be revised by other means than "the initiative of the Emperor"; and *Mainichi*'s story on the recently repatriated Communist Oyama Ikuo, Northwestern University staff member during his self-imposed exile, who recommended retaining the emperor but stripped of his power to command the armed forces, giving the Diet the right to conclude treaties, and abolishing the Privy Council and the House of Peers. At the end of October, CIE's newly organized Media Analysis Branch concluded that, although responsible public opinion was not yet sufficiently reflected in the Tokyo columns, all public questions were being discussed more freely.[17]

During the next three months the country's newspapers, in the view of CIE press analysts, became more adept at reporting the public's attitude toward political affairs. For example, editors were thought to be quicker to sense and articulate public dissatisfaction with the government for working in secret on constitutional revision, failing to submit to the Diet a plan to abolish the House of Peers ("a citadel for feudalistic influences, bureaucracy and big capital"), making no democratic moves except when prodded by SCAP, refusing to delimit the sovereignty of the emperor or to tax the imperial properties, clinging rigidly to the fundamental principles of the Imperial Constitution, listening only to reactionaries, ignoring the rapid development of democratic opinion, attempting to "check the development of the democratic revolution by the people," and so on.[18]

It came as no bolt out of the blue, therefore, when the press reacted unfavorably to the Matsumoto committee's ultraconservative constitutional revision plan, which was submitted to SCAP on 1 February 1946. According to CIE press analysts, even the old-line *Jiji Shimpo* found that "this revision does not reflect the opinion of those outside the government." Fukuoka's *Nishi Nippon Shimbun* would have preferred instead a revision based on "the understanding and belief of the people." Tokyo's leftist *Mimpo* characterized the government reactionary plan as the greatest obstacle to democratization and declared that the emperor must remain outside the government.[19] The mounting barrage of criticism directed against the standpat Shidehara government did not appear to be a concerted effort to influence foreign opinion; it had all the earmarks of a normal and natural reaction of most elements of Japanese society to fourteen years of agony under military dominance. In drafting a model constitution for the guidance of the Japanese government, SCAP, thanks to the creditable performance of the Japanese press, was well aware of the nature of the political reforms the Japanese people wanted and were prepared to accept.

As pointed out in the preceding chapter, Government Section officials took precautions to incorporate in the model constitution the democratic principles suggested in SWNCC 228, the State Department paper on governmental reform sent as information to SCAP through the Joint Chiefs of Staff. At the same time they were equally mindful of the customs, feelings, and desires of the Japanese side. Attentiveness to this aspect of the matter was reflected in the official minutes of the section's "constitutional convention," which was held during the week of 4 February 1946. In framing the model constitution, Government Section's lawgivers took account of different shades of Japanese opinion. It will be recalled that they showed a proper regard for the Imperial system, deferred to the desire of Japan's leaders for a bicameral legislature, decided against having Buddhist and Shintoist Japanese officials take a Christian oath to uphold the constitution, allowed the Diet to fix by law the number of members of each House, and respected Japan's election system. That acceptance by the Japanese weighed heavily in Government Section's deliberations on what to include and not include in the democratic model was shown by its rejection of a proposed detailed system of social welfare. Such a system, it was thought, might cause so much resentment that the cabinet would reject the model constitution. Then there was the ruling in favor of collective responsibility of the cabinet to the Diet on the ground that individual responsibility was inconsistent with the Japanese way of doing things. General Whitney objected to the statement in an early version of the Preamble that "by these laws we obtain sovereignty." Put that way, he said, "it takes issue with Japanese beliefs inculcated by two thousand years of training." The wording was changed to read: "obedience to such laws is incumbent upon all peoples who would sustain their sovereignty."[20]

Unfortunately Government Section's concern for Japanese mores did not encompass the wording of the cabinet's draft constitution. This was simply because SCAP meant to preserve at all costs the concessions that had been won from the resourceful and stubborn Japanese negotiators. There was fear of skulduggery in rendering the English of the SCAP draft into legal Japanese. By insisting on a verbatim translation, Government Section knowingly sacrificed conventional and tasteful Japanese to safeguard the principles of popular sovereignty, nonbelligerency, human liberty, and individualism. Even if it be granted that the Japanese government in making a virtually literal translation of the Government Section draft "simply chose the easiest way," as Dr. Takayanagi Kenzo, the eminent authority on British and American constitutional law, claimed years later,[21] the fact is that Japan was encumbered with an inelegantly phrased basic charter. That the 1946 Constitution has survived intact for more than a generation despite this defect attests to the discernment otherwise of its SCAP architects and to the natural aptitude of the Japanese for putting first things first.

Press reaction on 7 March to the cabinet's late afternoon announcement the day before of its draft constitution was "definitely and unanimously favorable." Japanese journals agreed that the most significant sections of the proposed constitution were those dealing with the limitation of the emperor's political authority and with renunciation of war as an instrument of national policy; specifically with democracy and demilitarization, the main points of Washington's occupation policy. *Tokyo Shimbun* (nonpartisan champion of popular causes) expressed satisfaction that the power of government was to be executed by the representatives of the people. *Mainichi Shimbun* (circulation over three million), though not unaware that the proposed revision was "unexpectedly democratic," nevertheless looked on it as "the cornerstone for the reconstruction of the State." *Yomiuri Shimbun* (circulation nearly two million) thought it worthy of note that the present draft was a distinct departure from the draft prepared by Dr. Matsumoto, which was pronounced "unfit for early democratization." *Nippon Keizai* (Japan's *Wall Street Journal*) did not doubt that "a radical revision of the present Constitution was an urgent necessity." *Mimpo* interpreted the move as "pressure from the people" and a bid of the Shidehara government to "ride out the present crisis." *Asahi Shimbun* (largest circulation) saw special significance in the government proposal, "because it has been prepared with the deep understanding of SCAP."[22] No paper viewed the proposal with alarm.

On 8 March, press comment was even more favorable. *Asahi* concluded that the government draft "contains the democratic spirit embraced in the various unofficial drafts so far announced. Moreover, there are some points . . . which even go ahead of those suggested by private circles. . . . the draft has high enough value to warrant discussion and study by the people. . . . the Shidehara Cabinet alone was not capable of drafting it singlehandedly." *Mimpo* thought "it may be well . . . that a progressive draft bill based on the principle of sovereignty in . . . the people has been produced. . . . when compared with this government bill, the reactionary character of the Progressive and Liberal draft proposals becomes obvious." *Nippon Keizai* felt that there should be no objection to it in general even if it was a gift from the Allied powers "as a result of defeat in war." *Tokyo Shimbun* observed sarcastically that the government draft "must be a source of wonder to those who have underrated the ability of the conservative Cabinet to reform the present Constitution. Vesting sovereignty in the people . . . is a marvelous change from the original Matsumoto draft. . . . such a progressive draft would not have been suggested without prodding from SCAP." *Yomiuri* pulled no punches. "The reactionary Matsumoto draft," it said, "has . . . been blown away." CIE's Media Analysis Branch concluded: "The Japanese press unanimously admitted that 'public opinion supports and favors the Government's constitution draft.' Only minor objections were raised and these occasioned no comment."[23]

The Japanese press saw SCAP's hand in the cabinet's draft constitution, and approved. *Yomiuri, Nippon Keizai,* and *Mainichi* reported that Dr. Takano Iwasaburo, an authority on the Meiji Constitution and a strong supporter of the government's action, believed that the "remarkable progressive nature of the new constitution was the product of the Emperor's wish and the Government's close liaison with SCAP." Excepting only the Communist party, the reaction of the major political parties was good. The Progressive party was "favorably impressed. . . . Emperors have never actually held sovereign rights." The Liberal party approved "in principle the draft constitution because it is designed to safeguard the Tenno system. Further, it respects fundamental human rights . . . renounces war as a sovereign right . . . [and is] in complete agreement with the principles [of] . . . the party." The Socialist party felt that the government draft "bears a conspicuous resemblance to the draft revision proposed by this party."[24]

On 9 March, the third day following publication of the government draft, press reaction was again highly favorable. "Along with a growing awareness of the scope of reform," CIE analysts found, "there appeared an increasing realization that the government's draft is of far more progressive character than any proposal made by political parties or other unofficial sources." *Tokyo Shimbun* and *Mainichi* emphasized that the people would now possess the power that formerly belonged to the small group near the throne. *Mimpo* called it "really an epoch-making development in the creation of a democratic Japan." *Shin Yukan* twitted the government. "In giving rights to the people," it said, "the Cabinet is more leftist than the Progressives, Liberals, or Socialists. And by discarding war it is more radical than the Communists." [25]

On the fourth day after the government draft appeared, *Yomiuri* pointed to it as "a measure which will give the people . . . a new psychology and outlook on life." Then there followed, as SCAP's preponderant role in the affair came clearly to light, a period of press bewilderment and disenchantment. Tokyo journals began to print critical articles written by eminent constitutional authorities. *Asahi* objected to a "constitution . . . made by following the advice of America" and declared that "if the people cannot agree with it, we must make another draft." *Jiji Shimpo* was reminded of the guest who, expecting to be served Japanese food, was surprised when foreign dishes were placed before him. That journal feared the consequences of giving the prime minister the powerful functions "controlled by the President of the United States." Like Gyarmathy, an *Asahi* columnist thought the subject should be given much more consideration, "for at present the draft is somewhat ill-fitted, like a borrowed suit of clothes . . . and it cannot serve well the needs of the nation." *Mimpo* printed the following reply of a SCAP spokesman to the many questions raised by metropolitan newspaper reporters: "We are not in a position to offer any explanation . . . for all has been said in the [6 March] statement by General . . . MacArthur. Any further questions will have to be asked of the Japanese government." In Washington, *Asahi* reported, Secretary of State Byrnes declared that "the new draft has been formulated by the Japanese Government itself, according to its own rights, and it was not planned by the will of the Allied powers." One can easily imagine the embarrassment to the Shidehara government and the disillusionment of the Japanese people if SCAP and the State Department had publicly accepted credit for framing the draft constitution. Even so, *Mainichi* urged the exercise of special care "so that the problem of this constitution will not be used as a means of keeping the Shidehara Cabinet in power." In a front page article the highly respected *Jiji Shimpo* sounded a note of caution by pointing out that "the most serious question of the revised constitution is the Tenno system." The Soviet Union, Australia, New Zealand, and the Philippines, it said, "are likely to insist upon [its] abolition." [26] Viewed in this light, what really offended the press was not the substance of the government draft but its unfamiliar terminology.

Taking its cue from other Japanese journals, the English language *Nippon Times* put the government draft in proper focus. Owned by the Japanese government, published for the benefit of the English-speaking community in Japan, and edited by an American-educated Japanese political scientist, that newspaper, professing to know the Japanese mind, undertook, unofficially, to reflect the views of the Japanese government, SCAP, and the Japanese people. On 2 March, four days before the government draft was released to the press, *Nippon Times* declared: "It is absolutely essential that Japanese society be made completely peaceful and nonmilitaristic." A week later, *Nippon Times* (9 March 1946) supported the government draft in these words:

This document is indeed a "new and enlightened constitution" the like of which the world has heretofore never seen.
The feature which makes [it] outstanding is the provision by which Japan renounces war. . . .
Less revolutionary . . . but revolutionary enough from the standpoint of Japan's historical background are the provisions unequivocably vesting sovereignty in the people. . . . this arrangement . . . is eminently wise, for there is no question that the overwhelming majority of the Japanese people of today desire and need the Imperial Throne. . . . the two factors have . . . been reconciled in a statesman-like manner to assure both the democratic powers of the people and the stability of the state. . . .
Revolutionary for Japan are the provisions guaranteeing . . . the fundamental human rights. . . . These will constitute a veritable Magna Charta for the common man in Japan. . . .
So responsive is the constitution "to the most advanced concept of human relations" . . . that there can be no objections of any substantial character from any source. . . . the nonofficial efforts at drawing up alternative drafts have been rendered superfluous.

Another week went by and *Nippon Times* began to have second thoughts about the matter. Paradoxical as it may seem at first glance, it said in a 16 March editorial:

the true aims of the draft constitution may well be better advanced by a healthy and vigorous questioning . . . than by a too docile and unanimous approval. . . . The Japanese people were already predisposed toward welcoming a constitution of this sort. . . . The approval of the new constitution is therefore spontaneous and sincere. But there is danger that this approval may be too uncritical and therefore too superficial. . . . a thing which is too glibly accepted may at some future time be too easily abandoned. . . . also . . . reactionaries opposed to the aims of the constitution may be able at some future time to capitalize on the pretext that it was imposed by an arbitrary authority. . . . The people should therefore suggest changes in phraseology which, while retaining the essential significance of the original, will make the meaning more comprehensible and seem more intimately familiar to the Japanese mind than the unaccustomed phraseology of the present draft.

Like other journals, *Nippon Times* (21 March) quickly became reconciled to the popularity of the government's draft constitution despite its "irrelevancies of phraseology," "wordiness and redundancy," "didactic

passages," and "conspicuous consciousness of the late war and its consequences." On 2 April it concluded: "There can be no question that the
majority of the people . . . heartily welcome the advent of democracy. In
fact, so unconditional is the popular sentiment in favor of democracy that
this very enthusiasm gives rise to doubts as to whether the people really
understand what it is they are now so glibly favoring." *Jiji Shimpo* echoed
Nippon Times's qualms with these comments: "This is not a Japanese
constitution. . . . its expression, rather than its idea, is utterly lacking in
Japanese characteristics. . . . only a constitution written by and understood by the Japanese will be recognized and protected." In a later issue,
the same paper became more specific in its criticism, objecting to the
"verbosity of the text," insisting that contradictory expressions, needless
reiteration, and meaningless words be struck out, and questioning
whether the Preamble was "suitable to be attached to the constitution of
an independent country." [27] Significantly press discussion was concerned
with technicalities rather than general principles.

The determinants of the kind of constitution Japan would have were the
United States government, SCAP, the FEC. the Japanese government, and
the Japanese people. As the principal source of occupation policy, the
United States government naturally backed SCAP's administration of the
occupation. SCAP had to be heedful of Joint Chiefs of Staff directives, FEC
policy decisions, the intentions of the Japanese government, and the
attitude of the Japanese people. FEC policy decisions could be made only
with United States support and concurrence. The Japanese government
was at the mercy of SCAP, the FEC, the emperor, and the Japanese public.
Though their country was under foreign occupation, the Japanese people
were beholden neither to SCAP, nor to the FEC, nor to the Japanese
government; they were free to express themselves on the kind of constitution they wanted. Had they been opposed to parliamentary democracy,
SCAP would not have drawn up a model constitution. If it had not been for
the enthusiastic backing of the Japanese people, the SCAP constitution
would not have survived the FEC's effort to discredit it. To the Japanese
people belongs credit for forcing the major Japanese political parties to
support the government's draft constitution bill in the Diet.

The striking thing about the Diet debates on the constitution bill during
the long, hot summer of 1946 was not their effect on the contents of that
measure, which was negligible, but rather their confirmation of the irre-
sistible demand by the general public for a democratic and pacifistic basic
charter. As the debates progressed from one chapter of the draft to
another, opinion favorable to its adoption became more pronounced. This

trend can be clearly detected in the press coverage of the deliberations. It was first seen in the reaction to a statement made by Prime Minister Yoshida following formation of his first cabinet in late May 1946, when he served notice that with the new constitution his government would lay the foundation for democracy, "taking into consideration the general world trends and paying due regard to the general will of the people" (*Nippon Times*, 23 May). *Nippon Times* for 25 June rapped his knuckles for thus trying to ward off opposition to the bill. "The Diet must . . . rephrase and even . . . change drastically the proposed draft," it said, "whenever it seems advisable. There should be no predisposition to accept the draft constitution as it is simply because it has been presented with the endorsement of the highest authorities." And again two days later (27 June): "It is unfortunate indeed to create the impression, however unintentionally, that these terms [of the Potsdam Declaration] are being accepted reluctantly under pressure and that they are embodied exclusively in the proposed draft constitution which consequently must be adopted without question. . . . the terms of the Potsdam Declaration . . . are actually being accepted with joy and enthusiasm by the vast majority of the Japanese people."

Disinclined at first to comment on the sovereignty question, which was discussed at great length in the Diet, leading journals soon began to express their views quite freely on this and other sensitive issues. In the opinion of *Dai Ichi Shimbun*, "We give too much trouble to the Emperor; we do not want to give any more responsibility to him." *Tokyo Shimbun* derided the House of Peers for trying to salvage some authority for the emperor. Under the new constitution, it said, the emperor's political responsibility would be greatly reduced "and there will be no more danger of his being used as a puppet." The same paper thought it rather humorous that titles of nobility were protected while the army and navy had been abolished, the zaibatsu dissolved, and "the nation itself is undergoing a tremendous change." Although the SCAP model and the cabinet's revision bill permitted all present members of the peerage to retain their titles as long as they lived, *Mainichi* noted that "all parties had agreed unanimously to abolish the system immediately." *Mainichi* was also pleased to note that all political parties in the House of Representatives had reached agreement on Article 84, which stipulated that the properties of the Imperial family would revert to the state. The influential *Nippon Keizai* expressed astonishment at the Liberal party view, "which advocates extension of the rights of the Emperor." Doubting that the Yoshida Cabinet had a passion for its own constitution revision bill, that paper viewed democratization as "what we, the people, should accomplish, regardless of the Potsdam Declaration." *Mimpo* pointed out that the old system, under which the Tenno exercised substantial political power, was not derived from the will of the people. Just after the final vote of 421 to 8 on the revision bill was taken in the House of Representatives, a *Jiji Shimpo* reporter became conscious of "a tense feeling such as never had been known before." [28]

Nippon Times, delivered free of charge to SCAP officials, was not averse to offering gratuitous advice on constitutional matters to SCAP as well as to the Yoshida government. It was not by chance, therefore, that on the day set for convocation of the Ninetieth Diet that the journal featured the FEC's three-point basic policy on constitutional revision calling for adequate discussion, legal continuity, and public support. The third point was considered most important, according to the International News Service dispatch from Washington quoted in Tokyo, because of "criticism that the proposed constitution borrowed too much from foreign political ideas and broke too far from Japanese ideas." Dr. Kazuo Kawai, the brilliant editor of *Nippon Times*, had no way of knowing that the FEC had raised objections only to those proposed reforms in the draft constitution that had not been specifically recommended in SWNCC 228: removal of the emperor from political power, renunciation of war, and provision of "safeguards to the individual which are new to Japan" (*Nippon Times*, 16 May 1946). It can only be concluded from this that the faraway FEC had difficulty in understanding that all three points were included in SCAP's model constitution simply because the Japanese people wanted them.

As of 16 July, *Nippon Times* was no longer worried about the points raised by the FEC. From his soundings of Japanese opinion, Dr. Kawai had come to believe that the situation was completely under control. "The Diet's handling of the problem of . . . revision," he wrote, "seems to have settled down at last to a sensible and practical basis. . . . sounder heads seem to have taken over the proceedings. . . . the new Constitution . . . is eminently sound in its essential characteristics. . . . certain passages . . . might be re-phrased. . . . [However] the major parties, for the most part, unerringly found these points." And when finally the draft constitution bill was passed, *Nippon Times* (10 October 1946) said: "There can be no question that its adoption represents the fervent desire of the great majority of the Japanese people. . . . It provides for the peaceful policy which is the heartfelt longing of the people. . . . its flaws are of no significance."

Some of the popular enthusiasm for the new constitution ultimately rubbed off on the sponsoring Yoshida government, if we can accept the verdict of *Nippon Times*. After it was promulgated on 3 November 1946, the government issued a comprehensive statement pointing out how strictly its policies conformed to the spirit of the new charter. "By identifying itself with the new Constitution which is decidedly democratic in character," the newspaper (6 November 1946) said: "The Yoshida Cabinet apparently hopes to convince its critics that there can be no question of its own democratic character. . . . The Government's intention of educating the people widely concerning the . . . new Constitution, of reforming and extending the school system, of liberalizing the administrative system, of expanding local self-government, of rehabilitating the national economy, and of stabilizing labor relations and safeguarding social security can meet with nothing but the hearty approval of everyone. . . . there is every reason to believe that the Yoshida Cabinet is utterly sincere in its desire to pursue progressive, democratic policies."

Thirty-five-year-old Teramitsu Tadashi was an able and personable member of the House of Peers secretariat. Why he quit his position when the House of Peers was superseded by the House of Councillors, he kept to himself. Twenty-eight years after the effective date of the new Constitution, Mr. Teramitsu, a Tokyo lawyer and a teacher of constitutional law at Asia University, was asked for his candid opinion of the Constitution of Japan and its chance of survival. He welcomed the opportunity to do so. Article 1 should be amended, he said, to make the emperor "head" instead of "symbol of the State." Furthermore, Article 9, which renounces war, and Articles 31–40, which embrace the humanistic precepts and procedures of Anglo-American criminal law, should be abolished. Finally, the Preamble should be rewritten in "genuine Japanese." But he despaired of ever seeing these changes come about. In the course of nearly thirty years, he said, the "American Constitution of Japan" had become "fixed" in the minds of the people. As for present-day Japanese law students, he said further, their attitude was not formed by the traumatic events of 1946, but rather by what the history books have to say. It was his belief that the conservative Liberal-Democratic party had lost public support and that the opposition parties, lacking a feeling of nationalism and patriotism, were foolish and misguided. He thought highly of the Takayanagi Commission's 1958–1965 study of the constitution and the reports it published on the subject in 1961 and subsequently. He did not expect the constitution to be amended before 1985 or 1990. It would be amended ultimately, he predicted, either by a triumphant Japanese Communist party (notwithstanding its long record of defending the present constitution), or, at a time of emergency, by an aroused public moved by loyalty and devotion to country.[29]

The substance of Teramitsu's point of view was fully articulated by experts on constitutional law in the course of the 1946 Diet debates on the draft constitution bill. The Japanese press duly reported but did not editorially support the arguments of the traditionalists, except in the matter of syntax. On the contrary, Japanese journals consistently upheld the three points made in a 1947 article in *Daigaku Shimbun* by Dr. Nambara Shigeru, president of Tokyo Imperial University, (1) that the new constitution was "Japan's declaration to the world abandoning war and proclaiming our ideal of a peaceful country," (2) that it shifted political power from "a small number of leaders . . . into the hands of . . . the people at large," and (3) that, comparatively, it was "markedly thorough in establishing the basic human rights of the people as eternal and not to be violated." [30]

The situation in Japan when the enforcement of the new constitution began in 1947 resembled in some important particulars what existed in the United States when Andrew Jackson became president in 1829. If Jackson's election signaled the shift in the balance of power from the original thirteen states east of the Appalachians to the newer states to the west, Japan's democratic charter marked the undoing of the powerful minority that had ruled since the Meiji Restoration and the rise of the masses from the rank of *shimmin* (subjects) to the rank of *jimmin* (the people). Even though the general public had little understanding of the democratic way of life, it sensed this shift of power with gusto. Popular sovereignty was widely hailed in articles and editorials. The most characteristic feature of the new constitution, wrote Dr. Tsuneto Kyo, president of Osaka Commercial College, in *Jiron,* "is the sovereignty-in-the-people principle . . . [a] fundamental reform . . . carried out by the freely-expressed will of the people. . . . Although it cannot be said that the national thought has changed thoroughly . . . it is obvious that [it] has begun to change." The transfer of sovereign power to the people, Dr. Minobe acknowledged in a *Sozo* article, constituted a change in the national structure. And because the reduction in the power of the emperor was not required by the Potsdam Declaration, he added, the change was effected by the Japanese themselves. Dr. Royama Masamichi, in an *Asahi Hyoron* article, observed that "the new Constitution has placed the bureaucratic system under the control of the political parties through the Diet"—a significant step toward popular rule. [31]

Appraising the constitution on its first anniversary, 3 May 1948, magazine writers changed their emphasis from specific provisions to basic principles. Much democratic progress had been made, they conceded. An *Oriental Economist* staff writer thought that "results of the 'democratic revolution' during the year . . . cannot be overestimated." [32] To *Nippon Keizai* it was "the one thing Japan can be proud (to show) the world." "Without doubt," in the opinion of *Asahi*, "[its] historical significance is its renunciation of war." *Jiji Shimpo* considered it "too early" to discuss the appropriateness of revision, as suggested by the FEC. [33]

By the second anniversary of the constitution, the Japanese people were becoming attached to it, so much so that the FEC decided not to issue a directive to have it revised. The Yoshida Cabinet and the Diet also announced that they had no intention to revise it. "The new Constitution was . . . a subject of heated discussion immediately before and after its promulgation," *Yomiuri* recalled, "but after its enforcement, debates switched to its interpretation and practical application, and the general criticisms have been softened." According to Tokyo *Nichinichi Shimbun*, Representative Higai Senzo, speaking for a number of thoughtful people, remarked: "Even if some points may not fit at the present time, the Constitution will be assimilated . . . with the passing of years, and there is no need at the present time to get perturbed over these points of incompleteness." In the opinion of Diet Library director Kanamori Tokujiro, the former state minister who rose 1,300 times to defend the government's draft constitution in the Diet, the same journal reported, "nothing is more strange than to think first about changing the Constitution and then looking for points that can be changed." *Asahi Shimbun*, reminding its readers that the feudalistic way of thinking "is still deeply rooted in the minds of citizens throughout the country . . . [and] that there still remain vestiges of a desire to revive the fascistic system," urged the people to make "even greater efforts . . . to develop democracy . . . at an accelerated pace." *Jiji Shimpo* took a more philosophical stance. "The Japanese people," it said, "have not yet come to a satisfactory understanding of democracy. . . . However, it is unfair to demand that the people achieve an ideological metamorphosis in only two years. There is no precedent for such a thing in the world's history. . . . the Japanese people today are enthusiastically making steady strides toward the democratization of the nation." *Nippon Keizai* advised against tampering with different clauses of the constitution while disregarding its fundamental spirit. "There is no room for revision with respect to democracy and pacifism," it declared. This comment by a university lecturer, published in *Tokyo Shimbun*, probably expressed the opinion of most Japanese: "A law would lose dignity if it were such as to require constant revisions; how much more would be the loss to . . . the basic law of a nation. Though it may contain shortcomings, a Constitution should be given a flexible interpretation and its revision avoided." [34] If the press was a reliable reflector of public opinion, the democratic constitution was slowly but surely becoming a structural part of Japanese society. The people's estimation of it appeared to be increasing in proportion as their understanding of it deepened.

SCAP's Role in Restructuring the Diet

SCAP's earliest actions relative to the Imperial Diet are described in Chapter 2. Those actions included a request to the Japanese government for continuing information on legislation, preparation of a manual on Diet rules and procedures, development of a plan for maintaining close surveillance over the Diet, formulation of a limited program of parliamentary improvement, initiation of a series of written reports on Diet activities, and negotiation of a pay increase for Diet members. Other than the last mentioned move, no Diet organizational and operational reforms were effected during the first year of the occupation; but by the end of June 1946 the lower house Speaker had been persuaded to appoint a select committee to investigate the fitness of that body to function under the new constitution. Soon after that step was taken, Comdr. Guy Swope, my immediate supervisor, departed for the United States, leaving me to carry on as chief of the Legislative Branch. On 1 August 1946, I was officially assigned the four-fold task of improving the election system, keeping SCAP abreast of goings-on in the Diet, expediting the passage of SCAP-sponsored legislation, and reforming the Diet's organization and procedures. This chapter deals with parliamentary reform.

Immediately apparent were two major obstacles to Diet reform, one in the Diet itself and the other in Government Section. The leaders of the House of Representatives, with ingrained dedication to the traditions and aspirations of the fifty-six-year-old Imperial Diet, were not favorably disposed to parliamentary innovation, and, save Lieutenant Esman and myself, no Government Section official was giving thought to the Diet as the highest organ of state power under a revised constitution based on popular sovereignty. Nowhere in SCAP, it should be noted, was there so much as a scrap of paper from Washington on how the Diet should be structured. With Esman soon to quit the section, I was left to carry on alone. I believed that the Swope-Esman Diet reform program as approved by Kades and Whitney was on the right track but was inadequate. I was therefore obliged to draw up a more comprehensive plan and then sell it to my superiors. Only then would I be in a position to sit down with the veteran politicians of the House of Representatives.

In their May 1946 memorandum, "Reform of Diet Structure and Procedures," Swope and Esman maintained that SCAP "should not endeavor to create a model legislature," that the Diet's organization and procedures "should be left to develop under native auspices resulting from experience gained in meeting the daily problems of legislation." From SCAP's standpoint it would be sufficient, they thought, for ex-congressman Swope to "contribute his knowledge and experience in legislation as an adviser on legislative procedure."

Dependence on entreaties and demands by SCAP individuals to effect the required changes in Japan's political system was, in my view, not enough. Equally if not more important than personal suasion was an all-embracing and practical set of specifications that Japan's politicians could take or leave. Just as Government Section spelled out in a model constitution the basic principles of popular sovereignty, nonbelligerency, human liberty, and division of powers between the different branches of government, so should it, I believed, sharply delineate a suitable organizational and procedural framework for the new National Diet. With this in mind, I prepared and submitted to Kades on 3 September a twenty-five-page draft memorandum on the subject. Of the fifteen innovations proposed, including five previously recommended by Swope and Esman, Kades approved all but one; he objected to my suggestion that Diet members should make public the amount and source of their income.

With Kades's overall approval of my draft memorandum, "Major Handicaps of the Diet under the New Constitution," I took one final precaution, before resubmitting it, to ensure its soundness. I had it appraised by a prewar acquaintance, University of Minnesota Professor Harold S. Quigley, recognized authority on Japanese government and politics who, at that time, was a temporary employee of General Willoughby's G–2 Section. Though rankled because Government Section had not sought his advice in drafting the model constitution, he was glad to review my memorandum—*in camera,* of course. He thought some of my statements were a bit strong, but found my overall case to his liking. His more trenchant comments will be given below.

The problem, as I stated it in the 10 September 1946 memorandum, consisted of four handicaps of the Diet, as follows:

First, it possesses neither the dignity nor the prestige essential to a national legislature. Second, it lacks the machinery required to direct the affairs of a modern state. Third, its increased grant of power under the revised Constitution is in danger of being curtailed by supplementary laws. Finally, present political leaders neither desire nor intend to give the Diet ascendancy over the feudalistic bureaucracy which dominates the national government.

The first point was pretty self-evident. To support it I stated some widely accepted facts: the Diet had never been a national legislature in the Western sense, it had never been the center of political gravity, it had never reflected the national will, it had never made nor supervised the execution of national policy; that back of it were no lofty traditions, no noteworthy performances, few great names. It was esteemed, if at all, only as an impotent debating society. So far during the occupation it had made no effort whatever to increase its power or prestige, even though, under the democratic constitution about to be adopted, it would assume policymaking and supervisory powers traditionally exercised by such bodies and offices as the Imperial Conference, Elder Statesmen, Senior Statesmen, military boards, Lord Keeper of the Privy Seal, Minister of the Imperial Household, and Privy Council.

To support the second point about the paucity of legislative machinery, I compared the skimpy facilities of the Diet with the sophisticated apparatus of the United States Congress under the recently enacted Legislative Reorganization Act. My purpose was not to suggest that Japan should copy the American model in preference to Continental systems or an indigenous system, but rather to emphasize the weak points of the Diet as a national legislative body. If Congress had to modernize its machinery and procedures to avoide an imminent breakdown of the legislative branch, how much more imperative was it for the Diet to undergo extensive restructuring!

To substantiate my third point, I cited the fifteen or more laws to supplement the constitution, including the all-important Diet Law, then under revision by the executive branch. Mention of Diet Law revision by the government was a reminder of the manner in which the Meiji oligarchs had rendered the Imperial Diet ineffective. The framers of the Imperial Constitution wrote the Diet Law in 1890 as an additional safeguard against the nascent legislature. Under that law neither House could freely pick its own chairman, select its own chief secretary and sergeant-at-arms, issue notifications to the people, summon witnesses, correspond except through a state minister with any government office or local assembly, or receive petitions for amending the constitution. The Diet Law fixed the pay of members, permitted the government to prorogue either House for fifteen days, and allowed the respective Budget Committees only twenty days to examine the annual budget. Three times in the 1930s the House of Representatives passed a bill to liberalize the Diet Law, but each time the House of Peers rejected it. I indicated that the first tentative draft of the revised Diet Law drawn up in mid-August 1946 by the government's Special Provisional Legislative Investigation Committee was consistent with the original law; framed by the Cabinet Legal Bureau, it was still an instrument for restraining the people's representatives, not one for serving the needs of a national legislature.

Regarding the fourth handicap, the negative attitude of top legislators, many experienced politicians of postwar Japan, including some of those who had supported the reform efforts of the House of Representatives during the previous decade, incredible as it seemed, were now reluctant to back moves intended to enhance the power and prestige of the Diet. For example, the able and respected Ashida Hitoshi told me in all seriousness that it would be unwise to increase the pay and raise the prestige of Diet members, because "capable officials would leave the Government and become members of the Diet." Resisting Swope's recommendation that he appoint a committee to revise and liberalize lower house rules and procedures, Speaker Higai pleaded that the House was too busy with legislative matters, that funds to finance such a project were unobtainable, that custom required the government to draft laws and rules for House approval, and that any revision committee of House members, following party lines, would end up in deadlock. Not until informed of SCAP's concern over his persistent obstinacy did Mr. Higai agree to appoint a Diet Law study committee. Thanks in particular to the Social Democrats and members of other minor parties, this committee—the Diet Law Inquiry Committee, as it was called—though empowered only to make a study, soon began, on its own initiative, to rewrite the Diet Law, notwithstanding the considerable progress along this line already made by the Provisional Legislative Investigation Committee.

On the basis of the foregoing analysis, my memorandum concluded that unless positive steps were taken to strengthen the Diet, the bureaucracy would retain control of the machinery of government and occupation reforms would more easily be nullified in the future. To increase the dignity and prestige of the Diet and to provide it with necessary legislative machinery, I requested SCAP authorization to take up with Japanese political leaders the fitness of the following proposals for inclusion in the revised Diet Law:

1. Appropriate pay scale for members.
2. Secretarial assistance for each member.
3. Office for each member.
4. Franking privilege for members.
5. Independent contingent fund for each House.
6. Diet library.
7. Legislative bureau and reference service.
8. Legislative council of the Houses.

9. A standing committee for each ministry.
10. Qualified experts for each standing committee.
11. Public hearings by committees.
12. Provision for free discussion by members.
13. Limitation of interpellation time.
14. Elimination of practices degrading to members.

Professor Quigley's criticism of the memorandum was to the point. On my characterization of the Imperial Diet as an impotent debating club, he commented: "In general true but might well be qualified; the Diet could embarrass the oligarchs and sometimes did." To my assertion that policymaking was a cabinet not a Diet function, he countered: "Not entirely." If the House of Representatives was powerless, as I implied, he wondered how its members managed to repay their benefactors. "Pretty strong" was his reaction to my assertion that the function of the Diet Budget Committees was to rubber-stamp the government's budget. He doubted (mistakenly) my claim that the Diet Budget Committees were denied access to Board of Audit reports. To my contention that powerful politicians were bent on keeping the Diet weak and ineffectual, he mentioned only Mr. Inukai Ken as an exception. After my correct statement that the yearly stipend of a Diet member was, until recently, ¥3,000, he placed a question mark. For my declaration that the House of Peers "effectively protected" the feudal system, he suggested "helped to protect." My warning that unless SCAP lent support to a positive program for shoring up the Diet the bureaucrats would retain control of the government drew from him an approving "Amen!" Regarding revision of laws supplementing the new constitution, he asked: "Why cannot SCAP insist upon dealing only with Diet committees in the matter of drafting the Law of the Diet?" About the memorandum, he wrote: "Your recommendations appeal to me as wholly desirable with the exceptions noted." His endorsement was heartening.

Kades bucked the memorandum to Rod Hussey with this comment: "Executive Branch of Government affected materially; also question of time and legal aspects involved. In cooperation with Col. Hays, please go over recommendations and then with Mr. Williams, we will have a conference." Hussey and Hays concurred in the entire list of recommendations. With Government Section's go-ahead signal, I turned my attention to the Diet.

At the Diet Building just after the 3 November promulgation of the revised constitution, I discussed Diet reform with Speaker Yamazaki Takeshi,

Mr. Higai's successor, Vice-Speaker Kimura Kozaemon, and Chief Secretary Oike Makoto. Unlike the House leaders a few months before, these leaders were, thanks to the character and background of Yamazaki and to a better understanding generally of SCAP's program for Japan's political reorientation, genuinely friendly and cooperative. They asked numerous incisive questions about the Western parliamentary practices and facilities that I presented for their consideration and approval or disapproval. Their reaction was highly favorable, and Mr. Yamazaki vouched personally for acceptance of the entire package by the Diet Law Inquiry Committee. A draft of the new Diet Law, they assured me, would be ready by the middle of the month. In my reports on these talks to Colonel Kades, I stated that Speaker Yamazaki was "particularly encouraged . . . by the knowledge that Government Section approved Diet Law revision by the Diet itself, rather than by the Government," and that, concerned about "the low popular esteem of the Diet," he was committed to improving its status.

On the first day of December, I submitted to General Whitney a five-page memorandum on the progress of Diet Law revision. Covered first was the work of the House Diet Law Inquiry Committee since its establishment on 4 July, including its unexpected and unprecedented assumption of responsibility for writing the law, its translation into Japanese of the United States Legislative Reorganization Act of 1946, and its submission to Government Section on 29 November of the fifth and final draft of its proposed Diet Law bill. Then I indicated the extent to which the draft bill differed from the 1890 Diet Law. "While 69 of the 99 articles in the 1890 Law are retained," I said, " . . . they are concerned primarily with such routine matters as discipline, police, resignations and retirement, relations between the Houses, petitions, and election of officers. In the revised draft, 54 of the 123 articles are either radical modifications of corresponding articles in the old law or else are entirely original." Continuing in this vein, I wrote: "The 24 articles of the old law retained and fundamentally modified . . . are designed to remove the shackles imposed on the Diet by the Meiji Constitution and the laws supplementing it, to increase the dignity and prestige of both Houses, and to establish the supremacy of the House of Representatives over the House of Councillors." Further, "The 30 new articles . . . are designed . . . to equip the Diet with essential aids, devices, and facilities required by it to direct the affairs of a modern state. . . . While far from perfect," I concluded, "the proposed Diet Law is a vast improvement over the Meiji Law, retaining many of the usages of the past and incorporating a number of the soundest practices of Western democracies."

In recapitulating the story of the Diet Law, a Government Section "Diet Report" of 17 December said:

The fifth and final bill supplementing the Constitution and scheduled for enactment into law during the 91st Extraordinary Diet Session, the bill for the Diet Law will be introduced tomorrow afternoon in the H.R.

[The measure was drafted] by an unofficial committee . . . representing . . . the 7 parties and groups in the lower chamber and carefully refined by the legal specialists of the Cabinet Bureau of Legislation. . . .

The main features incorporated in the 133 articles of the revised draft, entirely lacking in the 99 articles of the Meiji Diet Law, are the following:

1. *Adequate machinery for directing the affairs of the nation:* (a) a system of 21 standing committees; (b) joint hearings by parallel standing committees of both Houses; (c) open hearings . . . required on budget and all revenue measures; (d) each House elects its own officials; (e) contingent fund for each House; (f) a 150-day session; (g) joint-legislative committee; (h) power to subpoena witnesses and to conduct investigations; and (i) establishment of a Diet library and legislative reference service.

2. *Increased dignity of Diet members:* (a) salary not less in amount than that for highest career officials; (b) retirement allowance; (c) franking privilege; (d) office space and clerical assistance.

3. *Safeguarding minority rights:* (a) free and open discussion . . . every two weeks during a Diet session; (b) minority reports . . . to be printed in the Record of Proceedings; (c) any member can introduce bills; (d) at the request of 20 members, a bill . . . must be placed on the agenda of the House; (e) any member's proposed interpellation . . . must be entered in the Record of Proceedings.

The revised Diet Law . . . removes . . . degrading practices . . . such . . . as court rank for members of the Secretariat, appointment of House officials by the Emperor, prorogation of either House by the Emperor, time limit on budget deliberations . . . addresses to the Throne and representations to the Government, petitions in the form of a prayer, prohibition of Diet correspondence with Government offices, and remarks by Diet members implying disrespect for the Imperial House. The word "Emperor" is omitted . . . and the expressions "Imperial Rescript" and "Throne" are used only in connection with Diet convocation and promulgation of laws.

Because of the support of all factions, the bill for the Diet Law will be passed by the H.R. in record time.

The leaders of the House of Representatives seemed to take enormous pride in their handiwork. In introducing the Diet Law bill on 18 December, Mr. Tanaka Manitsu of the Progressive party said, according to the "Diet Report" for 20 December: "Since under the revised Constitution the Diet will be the supreme organ of state power, a new Diet Law, written by the Diet itself, is necessary. . . . It is epoch-making that this most important bill was framed by members of the House, a fact which will have a profound effect on the future of constitutional government. . . . Revolutionary ideas are introduced by provisions for a system of powerful standing committees and for public hearings on important measures. . . .

The sole purpose of the revised law is to strengthen the Diet." Before the thirty-six-member special committee of the House to which the bill was referred, Chief Secretary Oike said on 19 December regarding its genesis:

The first meeting of the House group was held on 6 July 1946. Throughout the remainder of the harried Diet session, the members carried on vigorous debates and drafted a Diet Law bill consisting of 19 chapters. On the basis of this draft, codification of the bill was taken up in earnest following the close of the Diet session on 12 October. Each member freely expressed his opinions and deliberated on all articles with great seriousness. At ten or more of these meetings, to which numerous government experts were invited, discussions were carried on in a spirit of harmony, with the result that this final draft received the approval of all twenty members of the House committee. Government Section of GHQ rendered every assistance throughout the period . . . encouraging the committee to frame a genuinely democratic Diet Law, and offering suggestions on numerous occasions for increasing the authority of the National Diet, for which the entire membership of the committee is most grateful.[1]

The House of Representatives passed the bill on 21 December without a dissenting vote and immediately sent it to the House of Peers, where it ran into unexpected trouble. This was one day after the two top officials of each House had lunched with the emperor for the first time in Japanese history.

If the House of Representatives, anticipating the exercise of its incredibly enhanced power, was in an expansive mood during the Ninetieth and Ninety-first sessions of the Imperial Diet extending from June through December 1946, the moribund House of Peers was downcast and prone to be picayunish. In their examination of the draft constitution bill and the host of laws supplementing it, the learned gentlemen of the upper chamber came closest to losing their cool in the course of their deliberations on the Diet Law bill. Because of the light it throws on the attitude of the most conservative circles toward the political revolution then taking place, their manner of treating this particular bill was an important event in the occupation drama.

Most members of the House of Peers, if outwardly philosophical about the imminent demise of that body, were deeply resentful of the exalted position soon to be attained by the House of Representatives, which they despised. They winced at the various provisions of the democratic constitution that subordinated the House of Councillors, successor to the House of Peers, to the House of Representatives. Among these were Article 59, which stipulated that the House of Representatives may either override a negative decision by the other House on a law bill or call for a conference of both Houses; Articles 60, 61, and 67, respectively, which gave the House of Representatives final word on the budget, treaties, and designating the prime minister; and Article 69 under which only the House of Representatives could pass a nonconfidence resolution in the cabinet. Article 101, a supplementary provision of the constitution, authorized the House of Representatives to function as the Diet "until such time as the House of Councillors shall be constituted," that is, until the House of Representatives saw fit to approve legislation to activate the House of Councillors. It was in connection with Articles 59 and 101 of the constitution that the House of Peers, while considering the Diet Law bill, threw the legislative process into commotion.

Not a few Peers surmised that the Diet Law bill, drafted and passed by the House of Representatives contrary to provisions of the Imperial Constitution and the Imperial Diet Law, was utilized by senior politicians of the lower house to square some old accounts between the Houses. That the bill contained provisions for impressing on proponents of a second chamber the inferior position of the House of Councillors in the new National Diet did not escape them. They could not help but note that the Opening Ceremony of the Diet, traditionally presided over by the President of the House of Peers, would henceforth be chaired by the Speaker of the House of Representatives; that in case of disagreement between the two Houses over the term of a session, the decision of the House of Representatives would prevail; that Diet-enacted measures requiring promulgation would be tendered to the throne through the cabinet by the Speaker of the House of Representatives; and that designation of the prime minister would be communicated to the throne by the Speaker of the House of Representatives through the cabinet. It was, however, the Diet Law bill provision permitting the House of Representatives alone to request, under certain conditions, a meeting of the constitutionally pre-scribed joint committee of the Houses that the Peers elected to challenge.

The Imperial Constitution made no mention of a joint committee of the Houses. The Imperial Diet Law provided that either House in case of disagreement could demand a conference, and "the other House cannot refuse it." But not so under the new democratic dispensation. Article 59 of the constitution gave the House of Representatives the right to override by a two-thirds majority a negative decision on an ordinary piece of legislation by the House of Councillors; but the same article, in a para-graph inserted at the behest of the House of Peers, "does not preclude the House of Representatives from calling for the meeting of a joint committee of both Houses, provided by law." No such right was reserved to the House of Councillors. Consequently, the House of Representatives in drafting the Diet Law bill assumed that the House of Councillors was denied the right to demand a joint committee. The House of Peers took the opposite view, holding that it was the intent of the framers of Article 59 of the constitution to respect the traditional right of either House to demand a joint committee. Neither side would yield, and the Diet Law bill was put aside by the House of Peers on the final day of the Ninety-first Diet, creating an awkward state of affairs.

Tokyo newspapers traced the shelving of the bill by the House of Peers to four causes. First, that body was resentful of the three-day time limit placed on its deliberation of such an important measure. Second, State Minister Uehara Etsujiro insulted the dignity of the upper chamber by threatening to stymie the House of Councillors Election Law bill in the House of Representatives unless the House of Peers passed the Diet Law bill. Third, during the preceding Diet session, State Minister Kanamori Tokujiro had taken an equivocal stand on the right of the House of Councillors to demand a joint committee. Before the House of Peers Subcommittee for the Draft Constitution he had said on 2 October when asked why Article 59 should not be amended to make a joint committee compulsory in case of disagreement between the Houses: "The House of Representatives had nothing like it in mind when it passed the draft constitution bill. To insert such a provision would do violence to the fundamental spirit of the new Constitution. Besides, Article 59 is concerned only with bills initiated by the House of Representatives; it says nothing about bills initiated by the House of Councillors. Provision for the latter can be made in the Diet Law without violating the Constitution, and the Government intends to do just that." [2] Fourth, the House of Representatives which drafted and passed the Diet Law bill rejected a House of Peers proposal to amend Article 84, claiming that a change could not be made at that stage without loss of face. Regarding the impasse, *Yomiuri Shimbun* charged in a 26 December editorial that the failure of the House of Peers to pass the bill was shortsighted. Thwarting passage of "the most important bill" of the Ninety-first Diet session, it said, was motivated largely by wounded vanity resulting from Uehara's "slip-of-the-tongue and from the small amount of time allowed the upper house to deliberate the bill." The same day *Jiji Shimpo* reported that the House of Peers "took a firm stand [in October] in deliberating Article 59 of the Constitution and finally succeeded in winning a commitment from the government to assure the House of Councillors the right to call a conference. The government's failure to honor the commitment, as State Ministers Shidehara and Kanamori explained to the House of Peers Diet Law Bill Committee, could not be helped, because the House of Representatives had drafted the bill in such a way as to deny that authority to the House of Councillors.

The government offered a compromise plan calling for passage of the bill on 25 December in its present form with the understanding that it would be amended to suit the Peers at the next session. The House of Peers, however, rejected the compromise plan." *Tokyo Shimbun's* slant on the confused situation could have given comfort only to the House of Representatives. It said in its 27 December issue that:

the point at issue resolves into the essential question of whether or not the absence of the right of the House of Councillors to call a meeting of a joint committee really acts as an impediment to the fulfillment of the duties of the House of Councillors. . . . even though the House of Councillors may make amendments to bills passed by the House of Representatives, if the latter again passes such bills in their original shape and form by a two-thirds majority vote, the House of Councillors would have to accept them. If the House of Councillors wishes to come to a compromise on a certain bill, it would present a motion to that effect at a meeting of the joint committee. If the House of Representatives sees no possibility of the bill being passed by a two-thirds majority vote, it will naturally respond to such a proposal for compromise. . . .

If the House of Representatives is confident of repassing the bill and has no intention of coming to terms with the House of Councillors on the disputed bill, it will surely reject the convocation of the joint committee. In these circumstances, as a practical problem it would be quite in order for the House of Peers to accept the mooted stipulation in its present form.

Unlike the press, the political parties made no pretense of being objective and charitable toward the action of the House of Peers on the Diet Law bill. Spokesmen for the Liberal and Progressive parties thought it regrettable that the Peers ignored the unanimous opinion of the House of Representatives, which acted in behalf of all the people. The late submission of the bill to them was no justification for their conduct. They were swayed by emotions. The same bill would be submitted again at the beginning of the next session, and they could deliberate it to their heart's content. As the Social Democratics saw it, the upper house was displeased that the lower house was the first to discuss the House of Councillors Election Law bill. For the same reason, it was annoyed that the lower house took up the Diet Law bill first. Thus, in shelving the bill the upper house was swayed by sentiment.

Government Section's "Diet Report" for December 26 described the uproar over the stalled Diet Law bill in a single paragraph, as follows:

Refusal of the H.P. special committee to approve the Diet Law bill on the last day of the session (25 December) resulted in the failure of that measure to be enacted into law. The proposed modification by the Peers of Article 84, which permits the H.R. to request a joint committee meeting in case the Houses disagree on legislation, was to accord the same right to the House of Councillors; but the H.R. would not agree to this change, preferring instead to carry the fight over to the next session. The real objection of the Peers to the bill was that they had had no part in drafting it.

The day after this report was distributed within GHQ, Speaker Yamazaki, together with Vice-Speaker Kimura and Chief Secretary Oike, called on General MacArthur to present a lower house resolution of thanks for recently American-financed deliveries of vehicles, salt, coal, and petroleum to Japan. I represented Government Section at the meeting. After listening attentively to extended observations and pronouncements on Japan's labor troubles made by the general, and then reading the resolution of thanks, the Speaker brought up the subject of the checkmated Diet Law bill. He said:

Under study by members of every political party since last July, the measure was unanimously passed by the House of Representatives. We received invaluable assistance from Government Section officials, who gave most generously of their time and knowledge. On a number of occasions they remained at the Diet until late at night, showing a keen understanding of the Japanese legislative system and explaining to us additional aids and facilities required by the Diet to exercise its powers under the new Constitution. The Diet Law bill was approved by all 466 Representatives, and it is regrettable that the Peers failed to pass it.

To the general's inquiry as to why the Peers balked, the Speaker said that there must have been a hidden reason, because the cabinet offered to extend the session for their convenience. Obviously well-informed about the bill in question and its treatment in both Houses of the Diet, General MacArthur asked whether it would be reintroduced during the next Diet session. "Yes indeed," replied the Speaker, "on the first day, so that the Peers may have all the time they wish to discuss it." "Will the lower house pass it?" the general wanted to know, and the Speaker assured him it would. Then, with his head slightly tilted to produce a quizzical effect, the Supreme Commander asked: "Will the House of Representatives pass it exactly as it is now?" And the Speaker said: "We will not change a word." Pleased with the answer, the general turned to a subject dear to his heart, the women Diet members.

The reader may be interested to know how the aggressive House of Representatives and the dispirited House of Peers unscrambled the mess over the Diet Law bill. SCAP made no move to resolve the issue, for no important democratic principle was involved. But the outcome may have been influenced indirectly by SCAP. To get at the bottom of the dispute, I conferred at length on 13 January 1947, during the Diet recess, with the chief secretaries of the two Houses, Oike and Kobayashi Jiro, in the former's office. Long-time Diet officials, natives of Nagano prefecture, and warm personal friends who freely discussed official problems between themselves, they talked without restraint to me. According to Mr. Kobayashi, the House of Peers, "without intrigue or hidden motives of any kind," failed to approve the bill on 25 December for three reasons: insufficient time, dissatisfaction over Article 84, and awareness of the forthcoming annual Diet session which would precede the effective date of the new constitution, 3 May. He dismissed State Minister Uehara's "veiled threat" to delay passage of the House of Councillors Election Law bill as having no impact whatever. I accepted his invitation to attend a meeting the following day of a small group of Peers selected to examine all aspects of the controversy, and assured him, in response to his inquiry, that General Whitney would gladly consult with them at their convenience.

What I desired to learn from Oike and Kobayashi was why it would not be in order for members of the two Houses to meet informally before the Diet reconvened and iron out what appeared to be relatively minor differences between them. Since the Diet Law bill gave the House of Councillors the right to demand a conference in connection with the budget, treaties, and selection of a prime minister, I said, what objection could there be to extending that right to cases involving ordinary legislation? The power of the House of Representatives would not be affected one whit, I went on, while opportunities for the second chamber to offer constructive suggestions would be increased. Mr. Kobayashi was certain that the Peers would welcome an informal meeting on the matter, but Mr. Oike pointed out that Representatives could not engage in such talks without implying "surrender" on certain questions, that is, without losing face. To my suggestion that he himself might appear with me before the small group of Peers the following day, he demurred, saying that Speaker Yamazaki, then ill at his home in Ibaraki prefecture, had instructed him to make no commitments and to attend no meetings of the kind suggested. Even were the Speaker here, Mr. Oike added, he would not commit the House of Representatives to any agreement with the Peers, because "the Diet Law bill is now controlled by the seven political parties and groups of the lower house and not by the Speaker." According to Mr. Oike, Speaker Yamazaki took the position that the political parties "would not support him should he arrange a compromise with the House of Peers, and if for any reason the lower house was urged to yield, the high morale of its members would be broken." Furthermore, Mr. Oike said, "the Supreme Commander favors the bill as it was passed by the House of Representatives . . . and has the Speaker's promise to pass the identical draft in the regular session." Both Oike and Kobayashi agreed that the Diet Law bill would most likely be passed again by the House of Representatives, without change, early in the regular Diet session, be amended by the House of Peers to permit the House of Councillors under Article 84 to demand a joint committee, and then be referred to a joint committee of the Houses, where a compromise solution would be found.

At the Diet Building the following day I sat down with four Peers, as scheduled. The discussion was to have been recorded, but I objected and the two shorthand secretaries left the room. These distinguished men— Professors Takagi Yasaka and Takayanagi Kenzo and Messrs. Ohki Misao and Shimojo Yasumaro—were, I thought, more than a bit cynical. To my question, "How many present members of the House of Peers might in the future stand for elective Diet seats?" they shouted in unison, "None!" They sneered at the provision in the Diet Law bill to increase the allowances and perquisites of Diet members, saying it was ignoble for legislators "to stoop to paying themselves as much as government officials received." As for informal negotiations with members of the other chamber, they echoed the message Mr. Kobayashi had brought back from the meeting with Oike and me the day before, that such talks were taboo for fear of shattering the solidarity of the political groups in the House of Representatives and inviting news media charges of "a deal." It was not until they alluded to the Diet Law bill as the only major legislation to originate in the House of Representatives that I sensed what was probably the true purpose of the meeting. I concluded that they hoped SCAP pressure would force "those people" in the other House to yield on the joint conference issue. They did not seem to appreciate that such a move would have been contrary to SCAP's rule of deferring to Japanese conventions to the greatest possible extent. When it became clear that I would not undertake to do their bidding, they pinned their hopes on General Whitney, with whom I agreed to arrange a conference for them.

On 17 January, General Whitney received in his Dai Ichi Building office the four Peers with whom I had conversed three days before. He listened patiently to their interpretation of Article 59 of the constitution and their version of Article 84 of the Diet Law bill, and then gave them the same advice he had given another delegation of Peers three months before regarding their right to amend the draft constitution bill: that SCAP had not dictated the contents of the Diet Law bill nor suggested that any particular Japanese agency draft it; that he had left the matter to be developed by the Japanese side in accordance with democratic processes while affording to the cabinet and Diet counsel and guidance and all other SCAP assistance available; that the Diet was entirely at liberty to proceed as it saw fit; and that, accordingly, the Peers should not hesitate to accept, reject, or modify the Diet Law bill before them in the sole exercise of their individual judgments.

Thenceforth the Diet Law bill was handled in a strictly Japanese way. Following an extended recess, the Ninety-second Diet reopened on 14 February and, at the conclusion of interpellations on the prime minister's policy speech, the House of Representatives unanimously repassed the original Diet Law bill and sent it to the House of Peers. This was 21 February. By the end of the month the House of Peers Special Committee on the Diet Law Bill had completed its study of the measure and was prepared to do business with the House of Representatives. According to Government Section's "Diet Report" of 5 March,

Eight members of the H.R. Diet Law Committee—Ashida (L), Yoshida (P), Nakamura (SD), Uda (DC), Suzuki (People's), Hososeko (Indep.), Shiga (Comm.), Ito (Japan Farmer's)—met informally yesterday with the H.P. Diet Law Committee for the sole purpose of obtaining an exact copy of the 20 or more amendments proposed by the Peers. . . . There was no discussion of any kind, only a formal informality by which the Houses do business. The H.R. Committee will now study the specific amendments and recommend to the lower house the attitude that should be taken toward them. The H.P. will be notified "informally" later of the results. Should the H.R. take a determined stand against amending the bill, the H.P. will have the choice of yielding, continuing formal negotiations, or passing its version of the bill and requesting a joint conference. Because of "face," the Houses do not resort to a joint conference unless an agreement has been reached beforehand, a practice which, in effect, obviates the necessity for a joint conference. In this particular dispute, the H.R., having framed and passed this measure unanimously on two occasions, holds the whip-hand.

On 18 March, Count Hashimoto Saneaya, chairman of the House of Peers Committee on the Diet Law Bill, told its members: "Even though a committee meeting . . . has not been held for some time, during this period various studies have continued where many political problems have been taken into consideration. Therefore we are able once again today to hold a special committee meeting. If there are any other questions concerning this entire Diet Law bill, we would like to hear them. . . . Since there are no other questions, I would like to close this inquiry if there are no objections." There were no objections. Then Mr. Ohki explained the amendments as informally agreed upon by the negotiators for the two Houses. His explanation, which became a part of the history of the legislation, included the understanding that when a legislative bill initiated by the House of Councillors should be amended by the House of Representatives, the House of Councillors, if it disagreed with the amendment, could request a joint conference.[3]

For interested GHQ officials, Government Section's "Diet Report" for

18 March 1947 described the finale of the controversy in these words: "The Diet Law bill, with 10 articles amended, was passed unanimously by the H.P. today and will be returned to the H.R. for repassage tomorrow." Regarding Article 84, the most contentious item, the report said: "The following paragraph will be added: 'In spite of the preceding paragraphs, the H.C. may, with its notification of disagreement, request a meeting of the Joint Committee of both Houses, only when the H.C. has not agreed to a legislative bill referred thereto by the H.R. However, on this occasion, the H.R. may refuse the request for a meeting of a Joint Committee of both Houses.'" This was face-saving language for both sides without changing anything of substance. The primacy of the House of Representatives was maintained, and the right of the House of Councillors to demand a conference was recognized. On 28 April the Diet Law, countersigned by all members of the cabinet and approved by the Privy Council, was promulgated in accordance with Articles 6, 55, and 56 of the Imperial Constitution. How close this typically Japanese settlement of a ticklish problem came to being muddled by the Far Eastern Commission sitting in Washington was never disclosed to the Japanese side.

Though both SCAP and the FEC were pledged to implement the United States basic directive of 3 November 1945, they had deviant approaches to Japan's democratization. This was because SCAP dealt with the real Japan and the FEC with an imaginary Japan. Long after SCAP became immersed in constructing the democratic Japan of the future, the FEC was still preoccupied with teaching a lesson to the Imperial Japan of old. Nothing better reveals the immense difference between the way the occupation was actually run and the way outside Allied officials felt it should have been run than the tiff between SCAP and the FEC over a couple of purely technical items in the Diet Law bill.

During January 1947, while the Ninety-second Diet was still in recess and the House of Peers Diet Law Special Committee was conducting informal negotiations with the Diet Law Inquiry Committee of the House of Representatives, members of the FEC had the bill under study. At an FEC committee meeting on 20 January, Major J. Plimsoll, the Australian member, took exception to the rendition of the Japanese into English. He thought that an "emergency" session of the House of Councillors would more correctly be translated "urgent" session, that the title "Speaker" should read "President," that "one-fourth or more" was preferable to "more than one-fourth," and so on. But the Commission as a whole was more concerned with three provisions that linked the pay of Diet members to that of top government officials, permitted an official of the government other than a minister of state to speak at Diet plenary sessions and committee meetings, and gave more emphasis to "interpellations" than to "free discussion." Regarding the third point, the Commission believed it "essential to the parliamentary system . . . that there be a 'question time' during each day's business in which members . . . can ask questions of ministers and receive answers. . . . Matters of policy and opinion should also be discussed by Diet members at some point in the day's business. The Commission doubts that an 'interpellation,' in Japanese parliamentary practice, meets the above requirement." But it was in connection with the other two points that the Commission wanted SCAP to have the Japanese make changes.[4]

Article 69 of the Diet Law bill, first of the two provisions about which the commission complained to SCAP, read: "The Cabinet may, with the approval of the Presidents of the Houses, appoint representatives of the Government to assist Ministers of State in the Diet." After lecturing SCAP on the desirability of strengthening the legislature, the Commission advised: "It would seem to be undesirable for a representative of the Government other than a Minister of State or a member of the Diet to have the right to speak before the Diet. . . . it is essential that ministers themselves, or Diet members appointed as their parliamentary deputies, should be present in the House to explain and defend the actions of their Departments and the legislation they are sponsoring, and that they themselves should participate in the Diet debates. If persons other than members of the Diet were allowed to attend and speak in the place of ministers, it would be contrary to the principle of Cabinet responsibility to the Diet." To this SCAP replied:

The provision contained in Article 69 of the Diet Law is in accord with long established custom and practice in Japanese legislative history. It is a provision which was inserted on the sole initiative of the House of Representatives and unanimously approved by that chamber—a legislative body which has shown the most zealous desire to secure and preserve in the fullest detail its power in government accorded by the new constitution. The provision is merely one within the body of rules established by the Diet to govern its own procedures, and is susceptible to amendment should experience deem amendment necessary. As it is not violative of any democratic principle and cannot possibly compromise the principle of cabinet responsibility to the Diet, I consider it a most dangerous departure from established occupational policy to force a change upon the Diet in such detail.

SCAP went on to say:

The interpretation given by the Far Eastern Commission is not in accord with past Japanese practice nor with the intent of the article, namely, that the cabinet members would delegate their representative authority to the Diet. On the contrary, it is intended to permit them to bolster themselves by the technical aid of civil service subordinates of the respective ministries in presenting in complete detail factual matters which might be demanded by the Diet. While it differs somewhat from the British parliamentary procedure, it can hardly be said that it is less democratic or less efficient. I do not believe, under the circumstances, that it would be possible to persuade a voluntary modification.[5]

The second FEC complaint to SCAP had to do with Article 35 of the Diet Law bill. This article provided that "members shall receive an annual allowance not less in amount than the highest pay for government officials in general." (The formula had been approved the previous July by Speaker Higai and Minister of Finance Ishibashi Tanzan at the urging of Milton Esman and myself.) The commission was "uncertain as to the effect of the provision linking the allowance of Diet members to the salaries of government officials, as 'kanri' may be interpreted to include all appointed officials of the Government, even those of the highest rank such as the Chief Justice. Would this provision be likely to prevent adequate remuneration being offered to those holding the most senior and important government posts?" SCAP replied:

With respect to the allowances for Diet members prescribed under Article 35 of the Diet Law, our interpretation here and the interpretation and intent of the Diet itself is that the provision questioned is not that "a government official's allowance shall be limited to that of a Diet member," but that "a Diet member's allowance shall equal that of a common or ordinary national government official's highest allowance"—in other words, that pertaining to the highest official under the civil service, viz., Vice Minister. Thus, there is no limitation placed upon the remuneration of any government official; the article only provides a minimum basis for the remuneration of Diet members. This too is a provision merely concerned with internal administration without involving any democratic principle and in which interference by the Allied Powers would be most difficult of justification.[6]

This exchange brought out above all the place of Japanese usage in the judgment of SCAP and the FEC. SCAP made respect for Japanese ways a matter of utmost importance, the determinant of whether occupation political reforms would last. Mr. F. C. Everson, the United Kingdom member of the Commission, dismissed regard for "past Japanese practice" as a valid argument. The Australian member objected to SCAP's use of past Japanese practice as a means of throwing the burden of proof that a procedure was undemocratic on the Commission; he also questioned the Supreme Commander's statement that it would not be possible to bring about a voluntary modification of Article 69. The Australian and Soviet members stated that they were prepared to support a motion for a policy decision requiring that all who have the right to speak before the Diet be cabinet ministers or Diet members. Though Mr. G. G. Dolbin, the Soviet member, favored calling on scap to act immediately, the Chinese, French, Indian, and United States members supported the United Kingdom member's proposal to leave the matter for further consideration, "particularly at the time the Commission formally reviews the Japanese Constitution." Not again was the subject brought to scap's attention. As for Article 35 relative to the pay of Diet members, the fec Constitutional and Legal Reform Committee agreed to recommend that no further action be taken at that time, thus laying the issue to rest.[7] Four days later, the House of Representatives, unaware of this peripheral ferment, repassed the Diet Law bill.

In restructuring the Imperial Diet as in revising the Imperial Constitution, scap had limited objectives. The constitution was revised not to give Japan the British parliamentary form of government or the American system of checks and balances, but rather to effect the reforms recommended by the United States government in swncc 228. Had scap been directed to revise the Meiji Constitution without benefit of Washington guidelines, then scap would have asked the Department of the Army to dispatch to Japan a group of constitutional authorities to perform the task, as he did in the case of Japan's education, library, and civil service systems. Similarly the Imperial Diet was not made over in the image of the British Parliament or the American Congress. It was restructured with no other thought than to strengthen it vis-à-vis the Japanese bureaucracy for the more responsible role it was to play under the democratic constitution. Both the new constitution and the National Diet Law contain features borrowed from the British and American systems of government. To those Japanese leaders who were dubious about mixing parliamentary and presidential democracy, scap's advice to them was always the same: try the new system, keep what is good, discard what is unworkable.

Most of the exotic provisions contained in the National Diet Law were easily absorbed by the Japanese legislature. Of course, the benefits to individual members—higher pay, office space, secretarial assistance, franking privilege, dignity of position—were taken in stride. Acceptable were such innovations as public attendance at plenary sessions and committee meetings, the contingent fund for each House, and the National Diet Library. The Diet adopted the old and successful American practice of open hearings, which permits popular participation in the lawmaking process. The most discussed subject during the House of Representatives examination of the Diet Law bill, the idea of having scholars and other expert witnesses testify in open Diet committees, was at first repugnant to a stubborn minority. Three important innovations were scrapped in due time. These were the Legislative Council, used by a limited number of American state governments to facilitate cooperation between their legislative chambers, the system of free discussion (open debate), designed to encourage rank-and-file members to speak their mind for the record, and the right of a single member to introduce a bill. In 1955, both Houses concluded that "these systems are not compatible with the parliamentary system of our government."[8] *— effectively shuts up the minority parties*

Special mention should be made of two particularly important innovations that were successfully assimilated by the National Diet. These are the system of standing committees and the legislative reference service of the National Diet Library. Without them the legislative branch would have had little chance of holding its own against the executive branch. Assisted by the Research and Legislative Reference Department of the National Diet Library, the sixteen standing committees of each House, institutionally adapted to the Japanese scene, perform precisely the task SCAP had in mind for them, that of checking the arbitrariness of the powerful bureaucracy. By thoroughly scrutinizing cabinet-drafted legislative bills, by interpellating government officials, by filibustering, by appealing to the public through the mass media, and by sometimes influencing minority factions of the ruling government party, the opposition parties in the standing committees keep pressure on the cabinet to compromise. In any event, by having the last word on every piece of legislation, the Diet, thanks to the standing committees, lives up to its billing as the sole lawmaking organ of the state. With the source of its strength in the standing committees, the Diet has made the position of the bureaucracy an uneasy one; it accounts for the admittedly great improvement that has taken place between the government and the people. For those who feel that the British system of generalized committees should replace the National Diet's standing committees, Yale's Professor Warren M. Tsuneishi has this to say: "The argument is theoretically sound, but in the upside-down world of practical everyday politics in Japan, the adoption of the British committee system could very well be disastrous to parliamentary government. Such a change would increase the influence of an already too powerful executive by permitting even stricter control of pending legislation than is the case today."[9] In short, there would be greater danger of Japan's present "one-and-one-half-party system" becoming a one-party system.

9

The New Face of Japanese Politics

In the opinion of Woodrow Wilson, "to know anything about government, you must see it alive."[1] For more than six years I was privileged to see alive and at close range the Japanese political system in all its ramifications—cabinet, bureaucracy, legislature, political parties, electorate, electioneering, voting. With free and easy access to cabinet ministers and other high government officials, the Speaker of the House of Representatives and the President of the House of Councillors, Diet members and the staffs of the Diet secretariats, politicians of every political party, newspapermen and college professors, and a representative cross section of ordinary people, I was afforded an opportunity few foreigners have ever had to study firsthand the labyrinth of Japanese politics. These personal sources were supplemented by available literature on the subject and particularly by the G–2 Allied Translator and Interpreter Section's massive translations of leading Japanese newspapers and magazines, a veritable goldmine of information on Japanese politics during the occupation.[2] If the 1889 Constitution was, as Prince Ito Hirobumi said, concerned with the "preeminent importance . . . of safeguarding the sacred and traditional rights of the Sovereign,"[3] the 1946 Constitution assigned, by contrast, preeminent importance to the sovereignty of the people. My quest was for evidence of the extent to which the people understood and appreciated the shift of emphasis from the old to the new basic charter and valued the unprecedented powers, rights, and responsibilities to which they had fallen heir.

Equal importance was not attached to each of the main components of the reformed political system. The traditionally strong bureaucracy, for example, was not, in my estimation, the decisive factor. In a contest for power the dominant political party, exercising the people's sovereignty in the House of Representatives, would inevitably have the last word with government officials, who had been downgraded from masters to servants of the people. Nor did the cabinet appear to be the key to the situation, because the prime minister owed his position to the majority party in the lower house and retained his office at the pleasure of that party. Though backed by laborers, tradesmen, and intellectuals, the new left-wing political parties—Socialist and Communist—could not be regarded as the wave of the future, for most Japanese were unsympathetic to radicalism, revolution, and ideological mass movements. But these parties could make a significant contribution by capitalizing on the constitutionally guaranteed rights of freedom of speech, freedom of press, and freedom of assembly to gain support for their "struggle" against the "tyranny" of the conservative majority. Not crucial one way or the other to the democratic experiment was the election system, the efficacy of which had been demonstrated in the general elections of 1946 and 1947 and would be further demonstrated in subsequent occupation-monitored general elections. That leaves the electorate. Were the "untutored masses" still so politically immature, still so subservient to Shinto-Confucian-Buddhist-feudal ideals of paternalism, loyalty, place, communal sanctions, supra-partisanship, and the like that they would not entrust the making of domestic and foreign policy to professional politicians in an elected assembly? Recalling the antagonism of the political parties in the 1890s "to the fundamental national policy decided upon by His Imperial Majesty at the time of the glorious Revolution," Prince Ito observed: "A sound electoral body is essential to a sound chamber of deputies." [4] His observation was axiomatic; and the electorate's postwar soundness or unsoundness would be reflected, I thought, in the parliamentary body of its choosing.

It is difficult to imagine a better preparation for understanding the initiation of democratic rule in Japan than an on-the-spot study of the National Diet from May 1947, when the new constitution was launched, to April 1952, when the occupation ended, a period of almost exactly five years. The National Diet was central to the process. Its 716 members (466 Representatives, 250 Councillors) had direct contact with the people through elections, with the cabinet and with their respective political parties through participation in drafting party policy. The National Diet could not establish democracy; that condition of society could only be the product of evolutionary growth. But it afforded the best means for making a critical judgment of Japan's democratic potential.

Before the advent of democratic government the Diet Building in the heart of Tokyo was not a center of attraction for Japanese sightseers. It symbolized little to the people, and no unauthorized person could enter its portals without a special permit. But within two years of the enforcement of the new constitution the situation was reversed. The building was open to the public, and people from all parts of Japan were flocking to it. According to a 26 March 1949 *Seiji Shimbun* article, a steady stream of sightseeing buses discharged daily in the plaza facing the visitors' lounge an average of 1,600 citizens, who were as interested in seeing the assembly hall of the House of Representatives as that of the House of Councillors, where the Imperial Throne is located. The convocation of the Fifth National Diet, it said, attracted 1,800 persons, the largest crowd on record for a plenary session.

By the winter of 1951–1952 the imposing edifice had become a mecca for peripatetic Japanese. *Pacific Stars and Stripes* (1 November 1951) referred to it as "the center of Japan to the country at large—even more so than the Dai Ichi Building in the days of General MacArthur." Kyodo News Agency (2 January 1952) had an explanation for the phenomenon of the building's popularity. "In the ruin, the despair and the flux of postwar Japan," it said, "the white, majestic Diet Building has come to be the number one scenic attraction in the capital of a renascent nation. It has replaced the Meiji Shrine, the Yasukuni Shrine, and the *Sengakuji*, most revered spots in prewar Tokyo to out-of-towners and Tokyoites alike. The first is one of the most important religious places in Japan; the second . . . is likened to the national final resting places of the war dead in other countries; and the last is where the souls of the 47 ronins are perpetuated." (The forty-seven *ronin* were a band of masterless samurai who, early in the eighteenth century, committed mass hara-kiri after having avenged their deceased lord, all in keeping with the feudal code.) "At the height of the sightseeing season," it went on, "over 20,000 persons visit the Diet daily. Last year . . . 560,000 persons visited the upper house and 470,000 the lower house. These figures do not count the number (estimated quite large) who passed through the building by the introduction of the legislators themselves."

The Kyodo article also pointed out that the stately Diet Building was completed in 1936 at a cost of ¥26,500,000, "a stupendous figure then." (On hearing this figure from the guide, an ex-Japanese naval officer remarked: "Hmph! Just enough to build one ten-thousand-ton cruiser.") Furthermore, the building's monthly power consumption was equal to that of a city of eighty thousand inhabitants, its telephone facilities matched those of a city of forty thousand, five miles of carpeting covered its hallways, and sixty million pages of printed matter were run off the Diet presses the past year. The writer concluded: "With full independence gained for Japan, the Diet will take on added importance. Parallel with this, more and more people are expected to rivet their eyes on the Diet, with the result that there will be a lot more visitors to the already popular Diet Building." Those visitors with an inquisitive turn of mind would naturally become curious about what went on inside the building.

What went on inside the building would tell whether Japan had generated enough individualism to give parliamentary democracy a better than even chance to succeed. There were, to be sure, manifold difficulties, the greatest single one being the people's confrontation with a political order that exceeded their experience and strained their imagination. They would need to become conscious of their sovereignty, to appreciate why "objective" government officials had one function and politically minded Dietmen another, and why the former should be selected by competitive examinations and the latter by popular vote. They were dubious about the bureaucracy ever taking directions from the Diet or the Diet from them. Even many educated persons, including university professors of political science, were baffled by the new political setup.

Illustrative of the confusion was a Japanese newspaperman's feature story in 1951 on Diet recesses. Though presumably an authority on Diet procedures, he was at a loss to know why a legislative session of 150 days was authorized for the Diet when by his reckoning all Diet business could easily be accomplished in seventy-five days or less. After convening the previous 10 December, he wrote, the Diet took a year-end recess that lasted until 25 January. Then, in late March, after passing the annual budget and 153 legislative bills, the Diet recessed again until 7 May, when it was to reconvene and extend the session for two weeks to accommodate the cabinet, which by that time would have additional bills ready for submission to it. Why give Diet members a daily hotel allowance of ¥1,000, or approximately three dollars, and spend large sums for Diet operations, he asked, "when half the session is withered away in play?" Moreover, he felt it was "the acme of stupidity to want to prolong the session after holding a lengthy recess." His final complaint was about the manner in which the Diet handled legislation. "A few days before recessing," he said, "both Houses rushed through dozens of measures. . . . a budget of ¥100,000,000 . . . was presented on the last day before the present recess and went through both Houses on the same day. At such speed, a session would need to be only 30 days." Quick passage of the budget, he found, resulted from an informal discussion on 31 March between members of the Liberal, Democratic, and Social Democratic parties. "Discussion is another name for blackmarket transactions," he concluded. "Everything is decided in about an hour by a group of 10 or so men. Can such maneuvering be called democratic?" Four full years after the democratic constitution became operative, not a little of the press comment was still on the level of this 6 April 1951 Kyodo article.

On 31 August 1947, after the First National Diet had been in session for three months, I undertook to put its performance in some kind of perspective for interested GHQ officials. So far, I wrote in a "Diet Report" of that date, the Diet had not become the highest organ of state power; it had failed thus far to originate either an important piece of legislation or bring about an administrative reform of any consequence. Most of its members appeared to be adrift, taking guidance as usual from the government. Admittedly the presence of the occupation forces was a psychological deterrent to Diet initiative, but less so than the heavy hand of the past. The tradition of playing second fiddle to the bureaucratic-military-big business oligarchy was still strong.

But it would be incorrect to assume that the Diet had only marked time, I said, for that body had been methodically grooming itself for a more active role. Most of the standing committees had already selected qualified specialists to assist with research. Progress had been made in setting up the bill-drafting and reference service, and most members had been assigned a clerical assistant. The annual postage allowance for each member had been quadrupled, the secretariat staffs of the House of Representatives and the House of Councillors expanded from 371 to 597 and 160 to 420, respectively, and a request made to SCAP for American experts to assist in planning and setting up the National Diet Library. Construction would soon start on office buildings for Diet members.

Already, I continued, the Diet had done some serious testing of the new power structure. It had, for instance, successfully challenged the cabinet on both procedural and substantive matters. After having bested the cabinet in a dispute over the source of authority to extend legislative sessions, the Diet—more precisely the House of Councillors—had taken exception to the conventional government practice of legislating by cabinet order. In the bill establishing the Labor Ministry, which the House of Representatives had passed unanimously, the House of Councillors substituted Diet approval for cabinet order as the requirement for increasing the number of bureaus in the new ministry. Spurred by the Social Democrats, the House of Representatives sought, unsuccessfully, to muster the necessary two-thirds vote to reject the amendment, not on the merits of the case but because the "upstart" House of Councillors had dared to contest the dominant House of Representatives. Privately most members of the lower house favored the House of Councillors amendment, which had the effect of alerting all standing committees of both chambers to clauses in government bills perpetuating the unrestricted power of the bureaucracy to legislate by cabinet order. At the very least, the amended Labor Ministry Law disproved the contention of those political experts who viewed the elective House of Councillors as nothing more than a second House of Representatives, unable to correct hasty decisions made by the lower house. Time would tell, I said, whether the

House of Councillors would be more, or less, conservative than the House of Representatives, but that it would not be a puppet body had been clearly indicated.

Even as the press harped on Diet inactivity and the public contemplated the uncustomary good conduct of Diet members, the forty-two standing committees of the two Houses went methodically about the business of making a going concern of the legislative branch.

These miniature legislatures, the work-shops of the Diet, [I wrote] . . . are as new to Japan as the concept of popular sovereignty. . . . they are investigating everything inside and outside the Diet. They are subpoenaing witnesses. . . . They are talking back to bureaucrats. . . . Early in August, on the demand of the Diet, each ministry released an automobile to . . . a Diet standing committee chairman. In the same manner standing committees obtained military vehicles which had been purchased by the Transportation Ministry from the U.S. Eighth Army. . . . in Japan . . . motor transportation for Diet committees symbolizes the rise of the Diet to a position of power. . . . More important, of course, are the investigations being carried on by the committees. . . . This month, for the first time, sub-committees made on-the-spot studies of national conditions; they inspected coal mines, rehabilitation centers [for repatriated soldiers], flood-damaged areas, child welfare institutions, recreational facilities, hydroelectric power sites, hoarded commodities, perishable foods, and the police system, and on their return made full reports to their committees in the presence of the state ministers concerned, suggesting actions to be taken by the government and proposing remedial legislation. The state ministers and their underlings now attended committee meetings when summoned. The time may not be far distant when standing committees, as expert on public problems in their respective spheres as government officials, will be the instruments for making parliamentary government a reality in Japan.

The two public hearings conducted in August by Diet standing committees, Japan's first ever, were as professional as their prototypes in the United States Congress, the only other parliamentary body in the world that invited the people thus to particpate in the legislative process. To testify on the adultery clause of the Criminal Code bill, the House of Councillors Judicial Committee had invited ten nationally known jurists and social workers together with twenty of the 133 persons who had responded to newspaper notices and radio announcements of the hearing. The biggest committee room in the Diet Building was too small to accommodate the crowds that gathered to hear what their fellow countrymen had to say on the subject. A short time later the House of Representatives Judicial Committee conducted an equally professional and successful hearing on various aspects of the Civil Code bill. Public hearings were also held by the Budget Committees of both Houses, meeting jointly on a ¥70 million supplementary budget.

Less successful than the work of the standing committees was the novel system of free debate inaugurated by both chambers in July. Since then, Diet members had assembled to discuss the housing problem, control of foodstuffs, sale of nonquota rice, local autonomy, and other questions of vital concern to the Japanese people. Though no less alien to Japanese legislators than public hearings, I said in the "Diet Report," the open debates held thus far had not been promising. In past years stalwarts of the respective political parties, making effective use of interpellations—questions and critical remarks carefully prepared by party policy councils to embarrass the government in power—had never cultivated the dying art of debate by which members of the British Parliament and the American Congress once sought to convert political foes and influence public opinion. Interestingly enough rank and file Diet members were eager to "debate," but on mounting the rostrum they invariably delivered previously prepared speeches which had no relation to what had been said in the preceding set speeches of their opponents. To encourage give-and-take discussion the Management Committees of the two Houses changed the procedure for each biweekly session, but to no avail. *Asahi Shimbun* for 8 July 1947 said of the first free discussion held in the House of Representatives: "The sweltering galleries were filled to capacity. . . . every political party seemed to have picked its most spirited speakers. . . . Contrary to expectations, the . . . discussion lacked vigor." *Jimmin* (8 August) commented: "Members have wasted these ten days by holding free discussions and meetings." I did not imply in my report that successful parliamentary government hinged on the use of any particular form of elocution for airing policy differences between opposing political parties. It soon became obvious that the system of interpellation, which was wholly compatible with Japan's political experience, was to the Diet what Question Time was to the House of Commons and committee interrogation was to Congress. On the first anniversary of the new constitution the subject of free discussion was publicly ventilated by Matsuoka Komakichi, Speaker of the House of Representatives, and Abe Shinnosuke, a critic. Mr. Abe declared that questions involving party principles were too delicate for uncontrolled public talkfests in the Diet. Mr. Matsuoka concurred, adding that free discussion could be carried on only in areas "not decided by the party council." Should members in the course of their remarks contravene party policy, he said, they would be charged with showing "contempt for political principle." Therefore, he concluded, "free discussion cannot become lively; the old custom of settling everything by party council cannot be revised overnight"

(*Mainichi Sunday Magazine*, 2 May 1948). Open debate simply was not the Diet's cup of tea. But rowdyism was something else.

Violence is almost unheard of in the British House of Commons. Strongly committed to constitutionalism and naturally inclined to liberty, members of the majority party simply do not goad the minority to the point of rebellion. Nor is violence associated with lawmaking in the United States Congress. The work of that body is conducted with decorum, even when in the upper chamber, the Senate, the minority party employs obstructive parliamentary tactics (the filibuster) to have its will prevail over the majority. Other safeguards against a potentially despotic majority in Congress are the presidential veto and the Supreme Court's power to declare acts of Congress unconstitutional. But public assemblies in all English-speaking and most Western European countries, with or without such safeguards, operate on the principle of majority rule.

Though committed to parliamentarianism and majority rule, the Japanese Diet during the occupation was not in all respects a model of propriety and good taste to a Western observer. A scattering of its members, especially in the lower house, had a reputation of being raucous and coarse. Their behavior was fairly represented by Mr. Uyena Yoichi, a qualified specialist employed by the Diet, in the following letter he wrote to Blaine Hoover, chief of Government Section's Civil Service Divison:

In the knowledge that the 5th Diet will be sitting soon, may I take the liberty to state some of the impressions I received from the 3rd and 4th Diets?

Boisterous is the word to describe the Diet, abuse and outcry being its chief characteristics. Whenever a member begins to speak, the opposition heckles him with all sorts of hooting accompanied by tumultous noise made by banging their desks with their name plates so as to drown out the voice of the orator. They do not seem to have a particle of interest in what is being said. At a Waseda-Keio baseball match, however clamorous the rooting may be, one side allows the other to play the game. Could not the Diet maintain the same level of dignity?

During the sittings of various Diet committees the attitude of members toward government officials is something like that of a prosecutor toward an accused. The lamentable lack of decency in their bearing is often bitterly felt. . . . Their ungentlemanly attitude so vexed one qualified specialist as to cause him to resign his post.

On one occasion during the 4th Diet I had to remain all night with my committee. Such sessions often invite too much drinking. I believe no sitting should extend beyond 10:00 P.M.

It would be very much appreciated if Dr. Williams would take appropriate steps to correct these evils. I rely on your discretion whether or not to forward this letter to him.

Hoover forwarded the letter to me by a crisp memorandum which said, facetiously: "I am surprised!"

Bad manners were one thing, while the use of physical force in lawmaking was another. As Japan, like Germany, well knew, dictatorship could result from violence inside and outside of legislative halls. Actually the Diet was the scene of relatively little rough-and-tumble during the occupation. Of more than fifteen hundred laws enacted in the years 1947–1952, all except a negligible percentage were passed in accordance with prescribed rules of procedure, without rowdyism or fisticuffs. This meant that a near enough consensus was reached through negotiation and compromise on most measures to preclude minority charges of majority tyranny. The minority was seldom outraged to the point of revolting against majority rule, or, stated differently and probably more accurately, only infrequently did the majority provoke the minority to employ strong-arm methods. But sometimes individuals and groups in the Diet carried violence so far as to raise doubts in the minds of some whether the Japanese were capable of governing themselves, and to evoke the specter of postoccupation reversion to authoritarianism under the leadership of depurged ultranationalists. Credence was lent to this feeling of uneasiness by three concrete examples of brawling in the House of Representatives. One of these grew out of intense left-wing opposition to the Yoshida government's March 1947 bill to amend the election law. Another resulted from strong right-wing opposition to the Katayama government's September 1947 bill for temporary state control of coal mines. The third was an unpremeditated act committed on impulse by a couple of aggrieved members.

Taking the last case first, the aggrieved individuals were forty-seven-year-old Democratic Liberal Konishi Toramatsu, a third-term member from Osaka, and forty-one-year-old Communist Tachibana Toshio, a first-term member from Hyogo. Konishi, a higher elementary school graduate, was a building construction boss, and Tachibana, a Tokyo University graduate, was chairman of the Communist party branch in Kobe. Approaching its close was the long Fifth Diet, in which many unpopular bills required to carry out the belt-tightening nine-point economic stabilization program dictated by the United States government were under deliberation. At the plenary session of the House of Representatives on 19 May 1949, Social Democrat Asanuma Inejiro denounced the Yoshida government for having inserted in the National Tax Board bill the phrase, "at the request of the Allied Powers." It was cowardly and irresponsible, he said, to pass the buck to GHQ in this manner. A government delegate's answer that the offensive phrase was inserted by mistake and would be deleted so offended the opposition parties that it touched off a fifteen-minute brouhaha between the Communists and the Democratic Liberals, which was described by some newspapers as the most spectacular battle in Diet history. In the course of the disturbance a side argument arose between Kamiyama Shigeo, Communist, and Sasaki Hideyo, Democratic Liberal. To silence other Democratic Liberals who were heckling him, Kamiyama faced them and shouted "fools," whereupon Konishi, in the excitement of the moment, attacked Kamiyama and began to strangle him by tightening his necktie. Springing to the defense of Kamiyama, Tachibana threw a hard right to the head of Konishi. Unable to restore order, Speaker Shidehara adjourned the session and immediately called a meeting of the House Steering Committee. The Democratic Liberal party blamed the Communists for the trouble and demanded that Tachibana be referred to the House Disciplinary Committee, while the Communist party blamed the Democratic Liberals and insisted that Konishi be referred to that committee. The Social Democratic party traced the outbreak to the government's "unscrupulous" attempt to shift to GHQ the onus for an unpopular bill, and the anticoalition Democrats criticized both the Right and the Left "for beclouding the future of parliamentary government" (*Jiji Shimpo*, 20 May 1949). This was only the start of the affair.

Showing up at the Democratic Liberal party meeting held immediately after the brawl ended, Shiga Yoshio, one of the Communist "Big Three," forced Tachibana not only to apologize profusely to Konishi but to invite from him a retaliatory blow on the head. "In his fury Konishi landed two blows on Tachibana's head" (*Asahi Shimbun*, 23 May 1949). Appearing later before the Steering Committee Tachibana apologized for his conduct, while Konishi only boasted of the restraint he had exercised. "Inasmuch as my opponent was a Communist—not a Socialist or People's Cooperative—he would have lost his life," he said, "if the incident had taken place outside the Diet." That evening Konishi summoned from Osaka twenty of his *kobun* (henchmen). At noon two days later in the Diet dining room, Shiga and Tachibana, fearing a vendetta by Konishi, again apologized unstintingly to him in the presence of Hirokawa Kozen, chief secretary of the Democratic Liberal party, and the Konishi gang from Osaka. The act was described as "a ceremony of amicable settlement of the dispute in a manner practiced by gangsters" (*Jiji Shimpo*, 22 May 1949). On the recommendation of the Steering Committee the House voted thirty days' suspension for Tachibana and seven for Konishi

(*Mainichi Shimbun*, 25 May 1949). Because of the unfavorable press reaction, the Democratic Liberals considered expelling Konishi from the party.

Japanese newspapers were all but unanimous in condemning the Tachibana-Konishi fight, and they judged the method of settlement to be as ignominious as the tumult itself. *Jiji Shimpo* (22 May) complained that the Communists had bowed down before Konishi in complete disregard of the prestige and authority of the Diet. Other papers interpreted adjudication of the ruckus under the code of chivalry as a reflection of the nation's true character. Kaneko Yobun, a member of the House of Councillors, traced the violence in the Diet to Japan's low cultural standard, "the traditional, feudalistic, and fascistic character" of the Democratic Liberal party, and the "utterly despotic character" of the Communist party. "The fact that a compromise was quickly sought and an honest and righteous attempt to face the issue squarely was avoided resulted in the disgraceful feudalistic agreement," he concluded. One paper saw behind the threatening language used by Konishi "the terrorism and militarism that prevailed throughout Japan not so long ago." Another viewed the spectacle of Konishi's henchmen openly conspiring in the Diet as "more a disgrace to that body than the fact that some Diet members exchanged blows at the plenary session." *Yomiuri Shimbun* (25 May) bemoaned the fact that "scandalous events" such as the Konishi affair, occurring so often, appear to shock the nation "only slightly." If passage of bills must be accompanied by "fist fights or strangling," *Shin Yukan* (25 May) commented in a jocular vein, "we would rather vote for judo champions and boxers."

The underlying cause of the Tachibana-Konishi fight, as with other battle royals in the Diet, was, according to Japanese critics, reliance of the government party on numerical superiority to enact legislation. An editorialist of at least one highly respectable journal took issue with the "majority tyranny" argument of the opposition parties, citing it as an admission that they would accomplish their purpose by fair means or foul. But most commentators found a close relationship between majority arbitrariness and violence. The strategy of the government parties to pass bills by force of numbers, said *Sekai Keizai Shimbun* (25 May), turned the Fifth Diet into "an arena of filibustering and free-for-alls rather than a place to carry out sincere deliberations." *Asahi Shimbun* (25 May) was more blunt. "If the majority, whether right or wrong, runs riot in disregard of minority views," it asserted, "it must be remembered that acts of violence will be incited."

Despite what the Japanese press said over and over, the significance of the Tachibana-Konishi encounter seemed to lie elsewhere than in the alleged predilection of the majority in the Diet for oppressing the minority. That isolated action was prompted by excited individuals, not by the machination of any party. As a bit of melodrama intended—by Konishi, at least—to rekindle in the public mind the spirit of loyalty and revenge immortalized in heroic tales of the past, it was taken as an insult to the intelligence of the people. Scathingly rebuked from the rostrum of the House of Representatives by spokesmen for the opposition parties and repudiated by his Democratic Liberal colleagues, Konishi became a pitiable object of shame, totally out of step with the times. The treatment accorded him and Tachibana by the House demonstrated rather conclusively that the Japanese people were far more sophisticated than Lafcadio Hearn had found them to be at the turn of the century. This was a hopeful sign.

Entirely different from the Tachibana-Konishi outbreak was the violence associated with the Yoshida Cabinet's March 1947 project to amend the election law. Although SCAP was not disinterested, a hands-off position was maintained in regard to this controversial issue. The account here is confined to the conflict in Japanese circles. To the 2 May 1947 "Diet Report" reviewing the work of the Ninety-second Diet, prepared by the staff of the Legislative Divison, I contributed an analysis of the "Filibuster on the Election Law Amendment." On March 23, I wrote, four days before the session was to have closed, several measures, including the election law amendment bill, were scheduled for passage in the lower house. Making only routine technical adjustments in election procedure, the election law bill had the support of all political parties; prior agreement on its terms had been reached through informal discussion and compromise, the Japanese way. Nevertheless the Social Democrats, People's Cooperatives, Communists, and Independent Club members, in the knowledge that the conservative majority was playing a foxy game, blocked the bill's emergence from committee. It was the plan of the Liberal-Progressive coalition to win committee approval of the uncontested technical changes and then, immediately following the committee chairman's report in plenary session, introduce and pass an additional amendment substituting the single ballot and medium-size electoral district for the existing limited piural ballot and large constituency, the system under which so many newcomers to the Diet, including thirty-nine women, had been elected in 1946. The nongovernment parties objected strenuously to this strategem, condemning above all else the complete lack of sincerity shown by the majority. When this question was raised earlier in the session, the government parties had pledged not to propose important changes in the election law without first consulting all other parties. This explained why the minority parties had bottled-up the election law bill in committee, and why for several days running the House Steering Committee, whose decisions required unanimity, was unable to alter the agenda to permit consideration of other and more pressing legislation.

Actually the Social Democrats did not, as some believed, strongly object to the projected Liberal-Progressive amendment, which merely restored the prewar election system, the only system on which the political parties could agree after the adoption of universal manhood suffrage in 1925. Under the limited plural ballot and large constituency plan accenting proportional representation, which was adopted in December 1945 at the urging of SCAP's POLAD, the Social Democrats won ninety-three seats in the April 1946 election, whereas, under the single ballot and medium-size electoral district system they won 143 seats in the election of 1947. When they came to power three months later in coalition with the Democrats and People's Democrats, they made no move to restore the 1945 election system. Of far greater moment from the standpoint of parliamentary government was the bitter brawling accompanying the election law change. If it was scandalous and shocking, as the press charged, it was also instructive. With the strong backing of Prime Minister Yoshida, Home Minister Uehara, State Minister Shidehara, and the party bosses, the Liberal and Progressive parties made no secret of their fixed purpose to reestablish the pre-1945 voting system. Accepting the challenge, the nongovernment parties vowed to employ every conceivable parliamentary tactic to resist the "trickery and underhandedness" of the majority. Their aim was to block passage of the election law bill until 27 March, when the session was scheduled to end.

In the eighteen-member Election Law Committee the minority members proved to be skilled parliamentarians as well as accomplished rough-and-tumble artists. To delay action on the bill, they consumed two days debating a motion to enlarge the committee membership. Then they introduced and debated for hours a motion of nonconfidence in the committee chairman for having cut short an interpellation by a Social Democrat. They consumed still more precious time discussing motions to hold committee hearings in a larger room and to recess for meals and party conferences. They served notice that they would introduce in plenary session a dreaded resolution of nonconfidence in the Speaker, which took precedence over other business, unless the government parties divulged the details of their still undisclosed amendment. They warned, moreover, that lengthy interpellations would be made on all bills placed on the agenda of the House and also that amendments without end would be offered and debated. Predictably fists soon began to fly, and then pandemonium broke loose. The chairman suffered contusions on the face and head, stenographers' tables were overturned, inkwells hurled, and visitors incited to enter the fray. So tense did the situation become by 26 March that it was rumored the government might ask the Supreme Commander for armed forces to prevent further disorder.

On 27 March the six-day deadlock ended as suddenly as it had begun. The cabinet extended the Diet session four days, and the government parties acceded to the face-saving demand of the Social Democratic party to deliberate in committee, in accordance with long-established parliamentary practice, all intended amendments to the election law, including the one for medium-size districts and the single ballot. This permitted the several parties to introduce their respective amendments at the House plenary session and then discuss them in an enlarged committee of thirty members. By a sixteen to fourteen vote in each instance the minority parties' amendments were defeated and those of the government parties approved. The bill as amended was unanimously passed by the House on 30 March, consigning to history another rhubarb in the Diet.

Where a Westerner eyed this brawling as a rather unsavory parliamentary spectacle, the Japanese viewed it as a technique of parliamentary government. Supposedly they abhored violence, but actually they did not; they accepted it as an integral and necessary part of Japanese-style parliamentary proceedings. They cheered the left-wing parties for demonstrating with vigor that the ruling conservative elite's steamroller was stoppable. The willful and deceitful ploy of the majority to gain an advantage in an election that was only a month away, they sensed, was a harbinger of similar moves to scuttle civil liberties, end collective bargaining, revive militarism, subvert the school system, reimpose thought control, and so forth. As von Clausewitz regarded war as continuation of diplomacy by other means, the Japanese recognized violence as continuation of a filibuster by other means. Only by the filibuster could the people be made the court of last resort—at the next election—for judging a struggle in the Diet. Animated proceedings, it should be noted, did not prevent the Diet from performing its proper legislative functions; the unwritten law that the legislative show must go on was dutifully obeyed. Had the donnybrook precipitated by the election law issue wrecked or seriously impaired the government's overall legislative program, the people would not have dismissed it as just another tiff between the majority party and the opposition; they would have questioned the soundness of the parliamentary system.

The rowdyism attending Diet deliberations on the bill for state control of coal mines was generated by the opposition Liberal party to checkmate the majority coalition of Social Democrats, Democrats, and People's Cooperatives. Having committed itself before the April 1947 general election to establish government control of the country's coal mines, the Social Democratic party was able to get the backing of its coalition partners only for an extremely weak coal control bill. Still, the measure was regarded as a test case for the gradual socialization of a major industry. A number of coal mine operators organized a nationwide opposition movement to prevent submission of the bill to the Diet. The Liberal party spearheaded the drive to defeat the proposal in the Diet, and counted on defection to its side of many Democrats. That more coal was urgently needed no one denied. General MacArthur examined the cabinet's mine control bill and authorized its "presentation to the Diet . . . without prejudice of any kind from this headquarters." [5] The bill was submitted to the Diet on 25 September 1947. A hard fight was forecast.

On 22 November, I wrote a "Diet Report" on the subject under the title, "Coal Bill First Acid Test of Representative Government Under the New Constitution." The Liberals, I said, relying on the parliamentary skills of veteran politicians like Ono Bamboku, Hoshijima Niro, Uehara Etsujiro, and Yamazaki Takeshi, set out to wage a successful delaying action until 9 December, beyond which date the session could not be extended under any circumstances. The battle was joined on 20 November when the government parties decided that the time had come to wrest the bill from the deadlocked Mining and Industry Committee, which Liberals and dissident Democrats then controlled by a seventeen-thirteen majority, and bring it to the floor of the House for a decision. This required a House resolution requesting an interim report on the committee's deliberations by the chairman. After wrangling all day, the Steering Committee reached an agreement at 7:00 P.M. on three items for the agenda, the third of which was the resolution on the interim report. Soon after the opening of the evening session, the Speaker had a Liberal party member evicted from the chamber for attacking a Social Democrat. This caused most of the Liberals to walk out, but they returned when the Speaker announced the presence of a quorum. The mood of the House was described as "ugly." The first order of business was a report on the Employment Security bill, a measure in which SCAP was interested. Refusing to approve this item by the usual voice vote, the Liberals called for an "open vote" (roll call followed by individual balloting). Ordinarily a half hour exercise, the open vote on this occasion—because of time consumed by Liberal members plodding down the aisle, stopping to chat with old cronies, and bending to

General MacArthur leaves his headquarters at the Dai Ichi Building, Tokyo, in March 1948. On his left is General Whitney, his closest associate and adviser. Behind him is Col. L. E. Bunker, his aide. *(U.S. Army)*

(1) National election for members of the House of Representatives, April 1947. Socialist Nishio Suehiro campaigned and won in Osaka. (2) Sakurauchi Tatsuro, chairman of the House of Councillors Budget Committee, hosts a dinner party for members of Government Section's PPD (1948). *Clockwise from left:* Mr. Sakurauchi, Justin Williams, Mrs. Justin Williams, Inagawa Jiro, Capt. C. F. Guida, Helen Loeb, Teramitsu Tadashi, Carlos Marcum, Mildred Fisher, Mrs. Sakurauchi.

A view of the Diet Building from the Imperial Palace grounds.

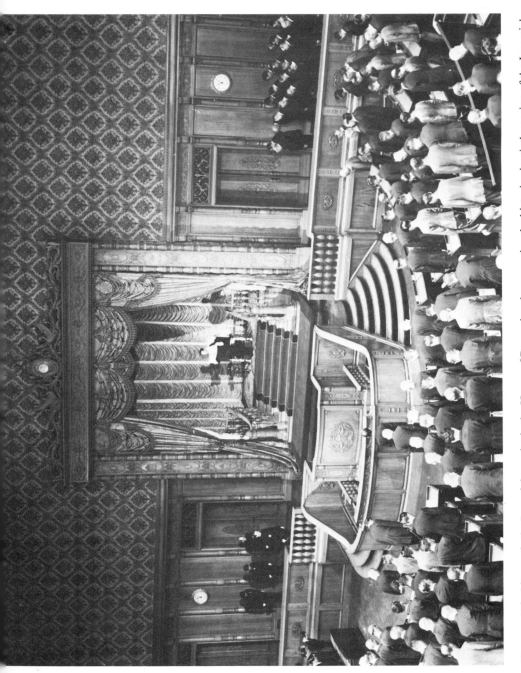

Emperor Hirohito reads the Imperial rescript in the House of Peers chamber, opening the historic ninetieth session of the Imperial Diet in June 1946. This was the Diet that adopted the democratic Constitution. (*U.S. Army*)

tie their shoe laces—took an hour and a half. Before the vote could be tabulated a Liberal challenged its validity on the ground that the member evicted two hours before had cast a ballot in violation of House rules and demanded that another open vote be taken. The Speaker acceded to the demand. By the time the second vote had been tabulated, it was too close to midnight, the end of the calendar day, to proceed with the second item on the agenda. The Liberal strategy of placing an important piece of legislation first on the agenda and so manipulating it to delay action on other items had worked.

On 21 November the Liberals again held the initiative. While Speaker Matsuoka was closeted with the secretaries general of the four major parties arguing the legality of the proposed committee interim report on the mine control bill and discussing compromise suggestions—all to no avail—a rump meeting of the seventeen opposition members of the Mining and Industry Committee was held and a motion of nonconfidence in the committee chairman approved, the logic being that a deposed chairman could not make an interim report even if the House adopted a resolution requesting it. News of this "coup" brought quickly to the committee room husky Social Democrat Asanuma who, despite a vow to avoid rowdyism, took a healthy swing at a Liberal member. When the plenary session finally opened at 9:40 P.M., an alert Liberal moved to adjourn, and only then did the napping Social Democratic floor manager move to place the interim report on the next day's agenda. Voting first on the motion to adjourn, by open ballot, the House was again subjected to the slow-motion routine of the night before, and reached the end of the business day without acting on the second motion. The conduct of the Liberals and several Democrats on this occasion was nothing less than scandalous. They were guilty of hooliganism, drunkenness, and disobedience of the Speaker's orders. One member committed a nuisance in the chamber. The disorder was described by the 25 November *Chubu Nihon Shimbun* (Nagoya) as "nothing more than a squabble between the government party and the opposition." The wily Liberal minority appeared to be outsmarting the clumsy coalition majority.

For 22 November the House Steering Committee succeeded in scheduling five twenty-minute speeches on the motion to request the interim report from the Mining and Industry Committee. When Kanda Hiroshi, speaking for the Liberal party, asked for an additional five minutes, obtained it, and then demanded still more time, his request was refused and he was ousted by the guards after a half-hour struggle. No sooner were the scheduled speeches finished than the Speaker shocked the Liberals by announcing a thirty-minute limit for taking an open vote on the motion. The motion was carried, the interim report was made, and the Mining and Industry Committee was instructed to conclude its deliberations on the coal mine control bill within two days. The presiding officer's firmness marked the turning point in the struggle.

In a Steering Committee meeting at noon on 25 November, Chairman Asanuma urged all parties to outlaw fighting and carry on in a gentlemanly manner. By now resigned to the bill's passage, the Liberals decided to end their filibuster. Accordingly all confidence and nonconfidence resolutions were withdrawn, the Mining and Industry Committee concluded its deliberations, and at 9:30 P.M. the House passed the bill by the lopsided vote of 233 to 155—thus climaxing, as the 25 November 1947 issue of *Nippon Times* said, "two weeks of interparty and intraparty wrangles [ending] in savage parliamentary fist fights."

Under the caption, "Diet or Zoo," the same *Nippon Times* editorial, expressing the reaction of the Japanese press to the tumult accompanying House passage of the coal mine control bill, continued:

Nothing quite like this recent manifestation of rowdyism has ever been seen before in the history of the nation's legislature. . . . the systematic blocking of business through organized rough-house tactics, the slugging of the chief sergeant-at-arms by a Diet member, the near grappling of the secretaries general of two major parties, and the unseemly conduct of some of the Diet members who were obviously under the influence of liquor constitute a new high—or low—in shocking legislative manners. . . . If the Japanese legislators should persist . . . it would cast serious doubt on the competence of the Japanese nation to operate successfully a democratic type of government.

Japan's competence to operate a democratic type government was, of course, the sixty-four-dollar question, the gamble the United States government took when it directed the Supreme Commander to democratize the country. But before addressing this point, a concluding comment on Diet brawling is in order. For one thing, Ubakata Daikichi, the Democratic party member who committed the nuisance in the House chamber at the height of the filibuster, was forced to resign his Diet seat. His act was considered criminal, not "moral." His own political party disowned him, and the press felt free to print his name, showing that some forms of filibustering were repugnant. In the second place, the Liberal minority resorted to violence not because the party's welfare was at stake, not because of majority tyranny or deceit, not to win concessions or to save face, but to comply with demands made by the coal mine owners, an important segment of the conservative establishment. To demonstrate to the mine owners the genuineness of its effort to defeat the measure, the Liberal party was obliged to employ standard filibustering tactics, including violence. But in going all-out against the bill the party conspicuously did not throw all caution to the wind. It was not by happenstance that its filibuster fell palpably short of unduly antagonizing the voting public, of wrecking the government's legislative program, or of jeopardizing the parliamentary system. The Liberal party never lost sight of its ulterior purpose, which was to win the next election and regain control of the government.

The cases of brawling examined here, and numerous others, showed that violence in the Diet was not an aberration but rather a Japanese parliamentary innovation, a distinctive contribution to the science of government. Without it, representative government in Japan would not be truly Japanese, and probably would not work. With it, parliamentarianism was as permanent a fixture of Japanese culture as journalism, capitalism, and other Western adaptations. The violent aspects of the filibuster simply reflected party loyalty, the intoxication of battle, and racial volatility; the rigid Japanese code of personal behavior did not hold good in extrinsic settings like public conveyances, sports arenas, and legislative halls. Far from being a threat to parliamentary government, violence could very well prove to be its salvation. Violence in the Diet could hardly lead to dictatorship, for one-man rule is totally alien to the still viable Japanese family-group-nation concept. The main threat to parliamentary government was dictatorship of a conservative majority in the House of Representatives, which the minority parties realized they could not prevent except by recourse to violence. How much violence? Enough to give the majority a deserved rebuke plus something to think about.

On 15 December 1951, shortly before Japan regained her independence, I addressed the political science faculty of Waseda University on Japan's parliamentary system. My remarks revolved about two key questions: Would it last? Would it work?

Some authorities, I said, answered the first question in the negative, holding out little hope for the survival of responsible representative government. In the opinion of Sir George Sansom, the Japanese, being an Asiatic race, lacked the genius for self-rule. Throughout Asia, peasant masses were governed by a small class of warriors, priests, or officials. Their form of government might be monarchial or aristocratic, feudal or bureaucratic, even republican, but in essence it was always despotic.[6] Much the same melancholy thesis, with a shift of emphasis, was advanced in the early part of the century by present Representative Uehara Etsujiro, who declared in his doctoral dissertation: "In the government of Japan bureaucracy is, indeed, the most salient feature. The body of civil officials exercises an almost unlimited power. . . . they do not serve the people, but rule them. . . . political pessimists . . . prophesy failure for constitutional government in Japan." [7] I also cited a recent newspaper editorial to the effect that current lawmaking was a farce in which the political parties bowed as always to the bureaucrats. My listeners were thoroughly familiar with the following stereotyped sentiments frequently expressed by commentators and critics:

1. "If there is an M.P. who cannot get financially fat, he must be an idiot."

2. "There is no M.P. who thinks and feels things from the viewpoint of national interest."

3. "Party and personal interests are matters of their first and foremost consideration. They want titles and degrees to show that they are somebody and they love to blow and brag."

4. "Post-war M.P.s are all tasteless, thoughtless, and imprudent."

5. "Key positions in the Liberal Party are held by bureaucrats who should have remained as public servants."

6. "All Japanese political parties have flashy signboards but the articles they sell are not trustworthy."

7. "Women Diet members? Simply hopeless."

8. "Diet members waste much time keeping in touch with their constituents, and they always treat visitors from home with decency, even to the point of shopping for them at Mitsukoshi's Department Store."

Obviously, I concluded, these cynics took a dim view of the people's representatives, if not of parliamentary government. They seemed to forget that Japan's parliamentary system was the fruition of an indigenous democratic movement, which had been accelerated by the occupation. Apparently the recent shift in the locus of power had not impressed them.

With power now reposed in the National Diet by virtue of popular sovereignty, a constitutional amendment would be required to change it. In the foreseeable future it would be extremely difficult to muster a two-thirds vote of the full membership of each House for any amendment proposal to alter the present form of government. Start worrying about the lastingness of the parliamentary system, I counseled, when the Diet and the people seriously consider any proposal that would nullify the civil rights provisions, extinguish the House of Councillors, create a defense ministry, subordinate the Supreme Court to a newly constituted ministry of justice, deprive women of the ballot, and restore sovereignty to the emperor.

Much could be said against the quality of Diet members, I acknowledged, but I questioned whether their endowments would materially affect the permanence of the parliamentary system. Able members would, of course, have to be recruited to fill party, cabinet, and Diet positions. The postwar scramble of top bureaucrats for Diet seats pointed to one means of supplying the talent required for successful party government. But would not that bring back authoritarianism under a different name? The answer was that once an ex-government official emerged from the rigors of an election campaign, his vaunted arrogance and arbitrariness would be somewhat tempered; and when he undertook to perform his Diet or cabinet duties, his outlook would no longer be that of a vice-minister or a bureau chief. If he had difficulty getting used to respecting public opinion and rubbing elbows with professional politicians, his new environment—the party caucus, for example—would have a sobering effect. He would soon become a party man and yield to party discipline. Concerning Diet membership in general, one body of 716 would at a given time act and react in much the same manner as another similar body, for the simple reason that the internal and external conditions with which any government had to wrestle were what they were.

Bureaucrats, I said, were the target for many a caustic and irresponsible utterance. Everybody seemed to regard them as the enemy of parliamentary government. But were they? In the past, they ruled rather than served the people. Now the order of rank was reversed, the people having become sovereign with officials occupying the position of public servants. Policymaking was now a party responsibility. The party leadership in the cabinet was answerable to the Diet and the people, not to the bureaucracy. After every clash between the bureaucracy and the government party, the bureaucracy would be weaker and the party stronger. Take the current issue of personnel reduction, I said. The prime minister and his cabinet, themselves nearly all ex-bureaucrats, claimed that unwarranted bureaucratic influence brought to bear on members of the House of Councillors had resulted in emasculation of the government's personnel bill. Would the cabinet yield to the alleged superior power of the bureaucracy? Apparently not. The prime minister had ordered an investigation to establish whether public servants lobbied against the government's legislative program in violation of the National Public Service Law. Little by little the bureaucracy would surely become reconciled to parliamentary government.

The keystone in the arch of parliamentary government was the electorate. Japan's original parliamentary system, which remained very much alive under extremely adverse conditions for fifty years and then survived World War II, represented at the very least a people who have the necessary unity, temperament, and character to govern themselves. Although in the 1946 and 1947 elections for members of the House of Representatives the voters were not fully aware of the meaning of the ballot, having cast it so often in a vacuum, they revealed a surprising degree of political awareness in the general elections of 1949 and 1950 for Representatives and Councillors, respectively. Granted that many electors were ignorant and confused, they knew enough to follow the advice of well-informed leaders in farm and fishing associations, labor unions, business circles, and the like. Such leaders constituted the small but dynamic and influential political community in all countries where responsible government existed. The essential point was that the Japanese had a demonstrated capability for self-rule.

In answering the second question, whether parliamentary government would work, attention was directed to the National Diet, which held the key to the success or failure of the experiment. An examination of the twelve Diet sessions under the new constitution showed a remarkable degree of progress in the development of this representative institution. The National Diet was equipped with a variety of internal administrative and technical services, staff facilities, and physical arrangements that were lacking in the Imperial Diet: a legislative reference and bill-drafting service, expert committee consultants, National Diet Library, offices, clerical staff, franking privilege, retirement allowances, dormitories, reception halls, contingent fund. Its standing committees made on-the-spot investigations, conducted public hearings, summoned witnesses and took testimony under oath, obtained documents from any government agency, and demanded the presence of government officials. With powers and prerogatives equal in all respects to those of the most advanced Western assemblies, it should be judged by whether it fulfilled the three basic functions of making the laws, supervising their administration, and representing the people.

Since May 1947 the National Diet had enacted 1,344 laws, passed many resolutions, adopted the various budgets submitted to it, and approved several treaties, including the Peace Treaty and the Security Treaty signed at San Francisco. That a considerable portion of this program was occupation-sponsored or -inspired is of less consequence than the fact that the Diet gained experience with every facet of the lawmaking process. There was much fumbling in 1947 and 1948, but after that the standing committees of each House, with the expert assistance of their own qualified consultants and of the Diet Legal Bureaus, became quite proficient in detecting and correcting flaws in government-drafted bills. There had not been and probably would not be much legislation sponsored by Diet members. Actually little or no legislation of any consequence was written by members of the United States Congress or the British Parliament. Most legislation to implement the policies of the party in power, whether in the United States, the United Kingdom, or Japan, would of necessity be prepared by the heads of state, their cabinets, and expert staffs. But that fact did not detract from the importance of the legislature. Middleton Beaman, father of the congressional bill-drafting service in the United States, wrote: "What is to be desired is that when the legislation is enacted it express accurately, down to the last word and comma in it, the intention of Congress in passing it. . . . If it meets that test 100 percent, it makes no difference where it comes from, if it comes from heaven, from an executive department, or is written in our office or some other place." [8] Robert Heller, another United States authority on the legislative process, said that "Congress should not be criticized as a 'rubber stamp' if it approves most legislation sponsored by the executive branch, so long as Congress has participated in the formulation of that legislation." [9] Even under occupation conditions the Diet had amply demonstrated that it participated in the formulation of legislation, that the enactment of laws was a function it controlled (or would soon control) exclusively, and that it contributed to the lawmaking process the popular will and its own knowledge and judgment.

John Stuart Mill said that the primary function of a representative assembly was to watch and control the government. [10] Obviously the Diet was making substantial progress in this direction through the conduct of investigations by its standing and special committees. The Education Minister's recent "moral code" project was dropped after experts testifying before the House of Councillors Education Committee exposed it to full public view. The case of the Ginza bathhouse, the construction of which violated building codes and materials control regulations, was exposed by a House of Councillors standing committee. Another committee of the upper house "persuaded" the Welfare Minister to abandon his announced plan to discontinue the government's program of BCG antituberculosis innoculations. A House of Representatives Special Administrative Inspection Committee opened hearings on a suspected misappropriation of ¥15 billion by the Salt Monopoly Corporation, and the same committee reportedly uncovered a ¥100 million misappropriation by the Japan Monopoly Corporation. Investigations were being made by Diet committees entirely on their own initiative. This was something new. The famous "Hoarded Goods" investigations by a Diet committee in 1947–1948, which among other things caused the downfall of the Ashida government, were for the most part the result of SCAP prodding. Thereafter the committee lapsed into inactivity, but within the past year had been revived without a prod from any outside source. The record of Diet watchfulness so far was encouraging.

There were unmistakable signs that the National Diet was increasingly deferential to the people. Under the old dispensation successful candidates for Diet seats disregarded their constituents after one election until the eve of another when they would show their concern by making a generous donation to the primary school and the local temple. Now Representatives and Councillors, despite the important duties they had to perform, took time to go shopping in Tokyo with visiting constituents. But it was such things as Diet galleries daily filled to overflowing, public attendance at committee hearings, alignment of labor unions and agricultural societies with political parties, increasing adjustment of political party platforms to public opinion, prominence given Diet activities in the press, widespread sampling of the people's views on current topics by newspaper polls, occasional "fireside chats" by the prime minister, and the heavy turnover in Diet membership at each election that reflected the sovereignty of the people, the potency of the ballot, and the new sense of responsibility acquired by Diet members.

Would parliamentary government work? The widespread public interest in and support of the National Diet in the exercise of its legislative functions offered the best possible answer to the question. In the final analysis, of course, successful parliamentary government rested on the political morality of public officials and the political maturity of the electorate. The voters had consistently confounded the higher critics by exhibiting a rare degree of political horse sense, a quality that would influence the political morality of elective and appointive officials in the years ahead.

During the question and answer period following my address, I sensed that the members of Waseda's political science faculty—because of the low status of political science under the Meiji Constitution—were poorly prepared to accept my thesis that popular sovereignty and parliamentary rule were the wave of the future in Japan. But they were not dogmatists; they demonstrated a willingness to think about what they had heard.

10

Parliamentary and Political Division

While officials of SCAP and the Japanese government addressed themselves to the realities of the situation in postwar Japan, United States and FEC officials in Washington were preoccupied with the Imperial Japan that had attacked Pearl Harbor and overrun Southeast Asia. Outsiders had little notion of how the occupation was conducted. And only slightly more knowledgeable of what the occupation was all about were the more than two thousand civilian employees of SCAP. They were for the most part compartmentalized technicians, mindful only of the areas of their specialization. One of the few exceptions to this generalization was a small group of officials in Government Section, the Parliamentary and Political Division (PPD). Unlike most SCAP subdivisions, PPD was brought into close contact with Japanese politicians of all parties, Japanese officeholders at all levels, and a cross section of officials in the general and special staff sections of MacArthur's headquarters. PPD was a kind of ringside seat from which middling officials observed the occupation's routine, noted its foibles and banalities, and contemplated its human side. Mostly unrecorded, these down-to-earth aspects of Japan's political revolution must soon fade into oblivion. With the thought of preserving some of the atmosphere and flavor of the occupation, this chapter on PPD's functions, personnel, and range of activities is written.

Government Section's defunct Political Affairs Division was merged with the Legislative Division in February 1948 to form PPD. PPD's main responsibility was to carry out SCAP policy in all matters pertaining to the establishment of parliamentary government. But this carried with it such corollary functions as coordinating relations between agencies of the Allied powers and the Diet, securing SCAP clearance of legislative bills for introduction in the Diet, and ensuring passage of legislation in the form desired by SCAP. Of nearly seven hundred bills cleared by SCAP during the twenty-one-month period following convocation of the Ninetieth Diet in June 1946, four hundred were enacted into law. Since the effective date of the constitution in May 1947, over three hundred cabinet orders were cleared. Occupation objectives could be attained through the "Potsdam Ordinance," under which the cabinet acted without regard to Diet legislation, or through laws enacted by the Diet. Employment of the latter method, which the Supreme Commander preferred, was facilitated by PPD's understanding of occupation objectives, the organization and operation of GHQ, Diet procedures, Japanese political parties, and Japanese officialdom.

PPD performed numerous other functions. In addition to evaluating the leaders, platforms, and practices of political parties, it encouraged Diet leaders to draft legislation for reducing political corruption and promoting cleaner elections. PPD consulted with the chairmen of the forty-two standing committees in the Diet, made continuing analyses of the national political situation for the Supreme Commander and the chief of Government Section, and supplied a spokesman for Government Section on current political trends and developments. The division assisted the Diet in obtaining SCAP approval for funds to start construction of the National Diet Library, which would ultimately cost over ¥3 billion and employ a staff of more than one thousand, and of ten new Diet office buildings costing ¥400 million. PPD supported the Illegal Property Transactions Special Committee of the House of Representatives in its effort to track down the post-war disposition of public supplies and materials valued at an estimated ¥100 billion. Just before he left Japan with General MacArthur in April 1951, General Whitney commended PPD for contributing to the success of parliamentary government in Japan, helping to gain the support of Japanese political circles for the aims of the United Nations in the Korean War, and planning and conducting the Diet Leaders Mission to the United States in 1950.

During the final year of the occupation under General Matthew B. Ridgway, the duties of PPD were little different from those of Government Section itself. Frank Rizzo, General Whitney's successor, listed as the main duties of the section the clearance of legislative measures for submission to the Diet, review of cabinet orders implementing SCAP directives and Diet-enacted laws, cooperation with political parties to facilitate accomplishment of occupation objectives, supervision of the conduct of general elections, and analysis of election results. He advised General Ridgway that continuation of the functions performed by PPD would be required until the close of the occupation.

The personnel strength of PPD never varied from four professionals and two secretaries. Between 1946 and 1952 only ten individuals, five in each category, saw extended duty with the division. The secretaries were Misses Margaret Haverty, Mildred Fisher, Virginia Sheriden, Ruth Grahamslaw, and Virginia Sutherland. Besides myself, the professionals were Miss Helen Loeb and Capts. R. G. Brown, Crescendo F. Guida, and

Charles Norris. Each of them understood occupation policy, SCAP's relations with the Japanese government, and the importance of getting along with Japanese officials and politicians.

The members of the PPD staff were assigned specific tasks. As chief of the Diet Operations and Analysis Branch, Miss Loeb advised Diet leaders on SCAP legislative requirements, resolved differences over legislation between Diet committees and their SCAP counterparts, supervised the work of the Japanese liaison staff in each House covering Diet activities for Government Section, and prepared reports on legislation and politics for GHQ dissemination. Until he left Japan in December 1948, Brown, assisted by Guida, headed the Legislative Liaison Branch. On succeeding Brown, Guida was joined by Norris. The branch kept the Diet informed of SCAP-cleared bills and amendments, advised the Attorney General's Office on the issuance of cabinet orders, compiled a cross-reference index of laws passed during the occupation, maintained a biographical roster of sitting Diet members, arranged conferences between visiting Allied dignitaries and Japanese political leaders, and forwarded copies of Diet-enacted laws to the Department of the Army. Actually there was no sharp division of duties in PPD; except for preparing Diet reports, each member of the staff performed any of the above-mentioned functions, and many more.

Parliamentary and Political Division relied heavily on the assistance of the two Japanese liaison groups located in the Diet Building, one for each House. The thirty or so diplomats, translators, and typists in each group, answerable to the presiding officers of the respective Houses, were to all intents and purposes members of PPD. Their offices were connected to ours by direct telephone. The chiefs of the two groups, in addition to making arrangements for monitoring Diet plenary sessions and committee meetings, kept in touch with Diet and political party leaders, served as interpreters at meetings between Diet members and SCAP officials, delivered daily resumes of Diet committee meetings to Government Section, and performed a multitude of chores for PPD and the Diet. Their task was not an easy one. Not until Messrs. Shima Seiichi and Inagawa Jiro, both in their thirties, became heads of the lower and upper house groups, respectively, in 1947, were the positions filled by Japanese officials endowed with just the right blend of temperament, resilience, and patience to meet the heavy demands placed on them. Enjoying the complete confidence of successive lower house Speakers Yamazaki, Matsuoka, Shidehara, and Hayashi Joji and upper house Presidents Matsudaira Tsuneo and Sato Naotake, and of all Government Section officials, they did their work exceedingly well. By including them in the Diet Observer Group attending the San Francisco Peace Conference in 1951 the Yoshida government recognized their valuable contribution to the smooth working relationship that existed between Japanese and American officials during a major portion of the occupation. Not surprisingly, some years after Japan had regained her independence, both were named to ambassadorial posts.

Neither in the mountains of manuals and regulations of the United States Army and Navy nor in the millions of documents published by other United States government agencies was there a particle of advice on how to deal with the complex of affairs engendered by the Allied military occupation working through the Japanese government. Consequently SCAP officials and their Japanese counterparts had to improvise ways to cope with situations of every kind that arose and demanded attention. Steps taken by PPD to meet some of these situations will interest readers who care to know more about how the occupation railroad was run.

Curiously there were a couple of brushes between Diet members and American GIs. In July 1946 three enlisted men commandeered Japanese government auto no. 1125, which was assigned to State Minister Shidehara. Shortly after the distinguished statesman had entered the Marunouchi office of the Mitsubishi Bank, the soldiers, "one showing a revolver," forced the waiting chauffeur to drive them about Tokyo for an hour or so. In the meantime the overdue state minister made his way on foot to the Diet Building. As soon as the chauffeur showed up and explained what had happened, Mr. Shima telephoned Government Section. Since the chauffeur was unable to identify any of his sightseeing passengers, nothing could be done about this regrettable incident. Of a different sort was the other event in which House of Representatives Budget Committee chairman Kambayashiyama Eikichi, following a December 1948 conference in the Meiji Building with members of A. C. Oppler's Legal Divison, was taken into custody by the Air Force guards. Although he remonstrated that his presence in the Diet was required to expedite passage of a multibillion-yen supplementary budget, he was detained for having in his possession nine American-made cigarettes, in violation of military regulations. To make matters worse, he was forced to disclose that the cigarettes were a gift from Representative Kaji Ryosaku, parliamentary vice-minister for the Attorney General's Office. No sooner did Mr. Kambayashiyama, on orders from the guards, telephone Mr. Kaji in the Diet that he was to report next day to a certain Air Force captain in the Meiji Building than Mr. Shima notified Government Section of the bizarre occurrence. I immediately telephoned Col. Alva Carpenter, chief of Legal Section, who had Kambayashiyama released and the summons to Kaji cancelled. Then I wrote a memorandum to General Whitney stating that until Air Force Headquarters guards were properly indoctrinated, meetings between Legal Division lawyers and Japanese officials would be scheduled in the Dai Ichi Building instead of the Meiji Building. General Whitney brought the matter to the attention of GHQ's Chief of Staff. There were no more incidents of this kind.

As the international cold war progressively heated up in the late forties, PPD was repeatedly called on to defend the Diet against officials of GHQ's general staff sections in their frenzied pursuit of Japanese Communists. First, in July 1948 G–2's Civil Intelligence Section (CIS) ordered the Diet to submit its publications for censorship. Colonel Kades approved the recommendation of PPD to have the Diet disregard the order. A month later CIS began needling Government Section to halt Communist campaigns to overthrow Japanese prefectural governors. Typical was its report on the campaign against the governor of Shimane prefecture. Activities to date, it said, had been confined to public speech meetings and open forums, newspaper advertising, and distribution of handbills, inspired for the most part, it was surmised, by three Communists on the staff of the *Shimane Shimbun*. Inasmuch as this and other current recall campaigns were perfectly legal under the SCAP-approved and Diet-enacted Local Autonomy Law of 1947, General Whitney agreed that the issue raised was inane and should be ignored.

In 1949, G–3 requested that Government Section have Councillor Hosokawa Karoku, a Communist, arrested and tried in a United States military court under SCAPIN 16 of September 1945 for making malicious and derogatory remarks about the United States Army's repatriation of Japanese prisoners from Russia. General Whitney's reply to G–3 (9 April 1949) said:

1. Investigation by this section reveals that statements made by Hosokawa . . . in the House of Councillors on 17 November 1948 concerning the condition of Japanese repatriates arriving at Maizuru . . . do not constitute "false or destructive criticism of the Allied Powers" under paragraph 3 of SCAPIN 16. . . . Hosokawa's remarks . . . fall more appropriately under paragraph 2 of SCAPIN 16, in which the Supreme Commander decrees "an absolute minimum of restrictions upon freedom of speech . . . unless such discussion is harmful to the efforts of Japan to emerge from defeat as a new nation entitled to a place among the peace-loving nations of the world."

2. Speaking in support of a Resolution for Acceleration of Repatriation, Hosokawa said, according to the official Proceedings of the House of Councillors, "We have received information that among those repatriates who arrived at Maizuru . . . between the 1st and 4th of November there took place serious violence. . . . What have the Allied Powers' authorities done about this?" It did not occur to Matsudaira Tsuneo, President of the House of Councillors . . . that

there was anything malicious or derogatory in his comments. The ensuing investigation conducted by the . . . Repatriation Special Committee . . . showed that 25 persons from the Eihiko-Maru, 52 from the Keizan-Maru, and 365 from the Takasaga-Maru were hospitalized at Maizuru upon debarkation, some requiring treatment for injuries sustained from violence aboard ship. . . . Reports growing out of such conditions are ample justification for a member of the national legislature to . . . demand an investigation.

    3. There is no basis for action in this case.

That ended the matter.

What might have happened to parliamentary government had Japan's democratization program been carried out by the general staff sections was shown again in May 1949 when the House of Representatives Repatriation Committee requested, through Government Section, SCAP authorization to present a petition on repatriation to the Soviet Mission and the Allied Council. Diplomatic Section's Cabot Coville advised that the committee should make its own arrangement to call on the Soviet Mission, and that the Diplomatic Section would receive the petition on behalf of the chairman of the Allied Council. But within minutes after PPD asked G–2's Foreign Liaison Branch to notify the Soviet Mission of the Repatriation Committee's request, G–3's Repatriation Branch informed Government Section that, under revised SCAPIN 927/17, dated 9 March 1949, G–3 objected to the proposed visit of the Diet committee to the Soviet Mission. However, an exception might be made in this instance if Government Section would write G–3 a check note explaining the circumstances. General Whitney approved PPD's suggestion to handle the matter informally as proposed by Mr. Coville.

Defending National Diet librarian Kanamori Tokujiro against CIS charges of authorizing publication of a Communist-inspired document was one of several such tasks that fell to the lot of PPD. The document, translated and mimeographed by the Diet Library in July 1949, was a record of events in China from August 1945 to March 1949, taken from the Hong Kong Communist newspaper *Wen Hui Pao*. Many issues of the paper contained lies, distortions, and misrepresentations intended to poison the minds of Chinese readers against the United States. In consequence of complaints registered by conservative Diet members, Kanamori was investigated by Speaker Shidehara and President Matsudaira and found innocent of any wrong doing. Having got wind of the rift in Japanese circles, CIS requested Mr. Shirasu Jiro, an assistant to Prime Minister Yoshida, to supply information about "a certain document" published by the National Diet Library. Shortly thereafter, that agency laid the matter on Government Section's doorstep, implying that the document was part of a Communist plot to discredit the United States in the eyes of the Japanese at a later date. At issue from the standpoint of GHQ was whether the Diet Library had violated an early occupation directive forbidding Japanese criticism of Allied nations and their nationals.

To get at the bottom of the charges PPD obtained Dr. Kanamori's side of the story. The document was published with his approval, he said, solely for future use by the Diet Standing Committees for Foreign Relations. The leak of the highly classified paper to CIS he traced to two disgruntled ex-officials of the Diet Library, who had been fired as mischief-makers and conspirators. Since the institution employed no Communists, he was convinced that the commotion in Japanese circles was brought about by reactionary elements opposed to a free and independent library. In defense of Kanamori, a PPD memorandum of 22 November 1949 pointed out that, though not a librarian by profession, he had grown in stature since assuming his present position in the spring of 1948. A close friend and associate of Japan's leading bureaucrats and jurists and formerly chief of the Cabinet Legal Bureau (not to mention the fact that as a state minister he had spoken around thirteen hundred times in defense of the new constitution during Diet debates thereon), "he has absorbed . . . some of the spirit of the postwar system of government established here. . . . he has been influenced by his association with leading American scholars, and is beginning to be recognized as a pillar of strength by those Japanese elements susceptible to enlightenment. If a man of this character, conservative but intelligently liberal, cannot be . . . supported, at least by occupation officials, it must be admitted that those minimum fundamental changes envisaged . . . as requisite to establishing popular government were merely pipe dreams." PPD recommended that Government Section inform CIS that no action would be taken against Diet Library officials and that Dr. Kanamori would be advised to discharge forthwith any remaining officials on his staff guilty of conspiring to destroy the usefulness of the Diet Library as a great public institution. No further inquiries were received from CIS about the questionable Diet Library document.

Throughout the year 1951, particularly after the departure from Japan of General MacArthur and General Whitney, G-2 kept steady pressure on Government Section to stop Communist Diet members from holding meetings in Diet office buildings. Though fully aware of these activities, Government Section had to respect the attitude of Diet leaders toward the problem. As PPD informed Frank Rizzo in April 1951 regarding G-2's complaint that Communist meetings in Diet office buildings "may be inimical to the occupation and to the Japanese government," these and other left-wing gatherings in different Diet buildings had long since been brought to the attention of the presiding officers of the two Houses and through them to their respective Steering Committees. Both committees concluded that, while Communist and other left-wing members abused the privilege of using the buildings for meetings with their constituents, it would be impossible to suppress them without contravening the rights of all other members. The logical step, they believed, would be to ban the Communist party either by Diet law or SCAP directive; but such action, they confessed, would not prevent Communist sympathizers from meeting in Diet office buildings under the auspices of left wing members. Diet officials were thankful that Communist groups now held their meetings in the newly constructed "Members Halls" rather than in the corridors of the Diet Building itself where until recently they had roamed at will. So long as Communist party members were enabled to reach an audience of eighty million Japanese from the rostrum of each House, conservative members refused to get worked up over small Communist gatherings in the Diet auditoriums. Nor were they of a mind to stir up a hot controversy involving the constitutional Bill of Rights by proscribing such meetings. It seemed obvious that Government Section should think twice before creating a far greater problem than the existing one by undertaking to prevent left-wing meetings on Diet premises. Rizzo assured G–2 that Government Section would continue to watch the situation carefully.

Three months later the Tokyo Metropolitan Police Bureau protested to Diet leaders that Communist-sponsored meetings in Diet office buildings circumvented Tokyo ordinances relative to public assemblies. This was an ominous maneuver by G–2. The presiding officers of the two Houses, Liberal party officials Hoshijima Niro, Masuda Kaneshichi, and Yoshitake Eichi, Chief Cabinet Secretary Okazaki Katsuo, and State Ministers Sato Eisaku and Nemoto Ryutaro were all in agreement on the following points, which PPD passed to Government Section chief Rizzo in a 13 July 1951 memorandum:

a. The Metropolitan police must not intrude on Diet premises lest the function of representative government be weakened and the way cleared for return of the Peace Preservation Law, Thought Police, the Imperial Rule Assistance Association, and all other trappings of the former Police State by means of which the totalitarian elements destroyed the prewar Imperial Diet.

b. Discriminatory regulations designed to restrict the use of Diet Members Halls by Communist members would not effect the desired purpose inasmuch as Communists and fellow travelers could still meet under the auspices of other Diet members.

c. The respective Steering Committees, which reflect the relative numerical strength of all political parties, will not adopt more stringent regulations than existing ones. Should the presiding officer of either House take any action without prior approval of his Steering Committee, he would be subjected to a resolution of nonconfidence.

The only way to stop the Communist-sponsored meetings on Diet property, the PPD memorandum said, was by SCAP order. But such an order "would be difficult to justify in view of the Supreme Commander's desire to encourage the fullest development of responsible representative government through constitutional processes even while Japan is under the occupation." PPD recommended that GHQ take no action that would impair the authority of the Diet. Again the wishes of the Diet were respected.

A few days later lower house Secretary General Oike was visited in his Diet Building office by a Mr. Momii of the Counter Intelligence Corps. Momii requested that he be supplied regularly with information on Communist-sponsored meetings in Diet buildings. A stop was put to this nonsense by reminding G–2 that Momii's action violated Staff Memorandum No. 29 of March 1947 charging Government Section with staff responsibility for all matters relating to the Diet.

To strengthen Government Section's position against G–2's unremitting campaign to have Communist meetings in Diet halls banned, PPD asked Secretaries General Oike and Kondo Hideaki to lend a helping hand, first, by having a secretariat official attend and accurately report the proceedings of each such meeting, and second, by forwarding to Government Section a summary of each report. They were glad to cooperate. From the day G–2 began receiving copies of these reports through Government Section, its harassment of the Diet ceased.

Setting up and attending meetings between visiting Allied dignitaries and top Japanese officials was, in contrast to protecting the Diet against G–2's annoying tactics, an uncomplicated and pleasing function performed by PPD. It devolved on PPD to accommodate several delegations of United States Senators and Representatives, the United States Vice-President, two presidential aspirants, a party of Australian parliamentarians, and others. Typical was the August 1946 visit to the Diet by six members of the House Military Affairs Committee, headed by Representative R.L.F. Sikes of Florida. They spent forty-five minutes in the Speaker's salon of the lower house conferring with twenty-one Japanese Representatives, thirty minutes with Prime Minister Yoshida and State Minister Shidehara, and ten minutes in the House of Peers gallery looking down at the throne. A year or so later Congressman Francis E. Walter, a conservative Democrat from Pennsylvania, arrived just in time to be invited to Prime Minister Katayama Tetsu's luncheon honoring Diplomatic Section chief William J. Sebald, chairman of the Allied Council. (Among the guests were Foreign Minister Ashida, Economic Stabilization Board director Wada Hiro, Chief Cabinet Secretary Nishio Suehiro, Maj. Gen. Edward N. Almond, Chief of Staff, and Government Section's Kades and Williams.)

In 1951 Speaker Hayashi and President Sato gave a reception in the House of Councillors for Vice-President Alben W. Barkley. The standard arrangement was made for former Minnesota Governor Harold E. Stassen in December 1950 and New York Governor Thomas E. Dewey in July 1951. When an agent of the Japan Broadcasting Company abruptly slipped a microphone into the hands of Governor Dewey at the conclusion of the session in the Speaker's salon, that two-time Republican nominee for the presidency spoke extemporaneously for five or six minutes, informing his nationwide Japanese audience of the "interesting and valuable discussion" he had just finished with their distinguished Representatives and Councillors and of his joy and satisfaction over meeting again the fourteen members of the Diet Delegation whose acquaintance he had made the year before in Albany. Entering the Army sedan waiting for him in front of the Diet Building, he raised a questioning eyebrow at the "VIP" (very important person) sign displayed on the windshield. Then he shook hands with the GI driver, a Texan, and told him that Mrs. Dewey was from Sherman, Texas. He asked me to identify the Japanese Diet member at the conference who "kept asking such sharp questions." He meant Nozaka Sanzo, the brilliant Moscow-trained Communist who was noted for having successfully brainwashed Japanese prisoners of war at Yenan, China, toward the close of the Pacific War. "Today," the Governor confided, "I received far more enlightenment from the Japanese politicians than I did yesterday from a delegation of bankers and businessmen headed by the governor of the Bank of Japan."

What transpired at a conference in the House of Representatives with a Soviet trade mission was routinely reported to PPD. A Communist party circular announcing the meeting said that during the past five years of the occupation Japanese-Soviet trade had amounted to $24 million, with Japan exporting to Russia wooden ships, locomotives, freight cars, repair parts for ships, and ice producing machines and importing from Russia coal, fertilizer, paper, pipe, and metals. The Japanese M.P.s present were under the impression that the Soviet trade expert would offer his views on trade. But that official, accompanied by a political adviser, was under the impression that he had been invited to hear the views of Diet members. According to Secretary General Oike's report, Representatives Uehara and Kawasaki Hidejo left the conference in disgust. It was revealed that Russia could not supply Japan with desperately needed raw cotton, salt, iron ore, and light metals, and the Soviet trade official was unable to state that his country would export petroleum to Japan.

Mention should be made of meetings between the emperor and "visiting firemen" (foreign dignitaries). The Supreme Commander controlled all intercourse between outsiders and the emperor, and only G–2 could authorize a GHQ official to enter the palace grounds. To accommodate General MacArthur, General Whitney drafted me three times during the occupation to go along with foreigners for audiences with Emperor Hirohito in the administration building of the Imperial Household Ministry. On one occasion I accompanied Mr. John Hausserman, an elderly mining entrepreneur from the Philippines who was a personal friend of both General MacArthur and General Whitney. On another occasion it was a United States congressional delegation led by Representative W. Sterling Cole, New York Republican. The third such audience was for five parliamentarians from Australia. At each of the affairs the proper amenities were observed. Tea was served. Nothing was discussed. The obviously bored Tenno, like his guests, had no regrets when the brief and perfunctory proceedings were finished. The thing about these meetings that clung to my memory was the fact that three of the Australian parliamentarians were unseated at the next election, presumably for having called on the Emperor of Japan.

The Diet looked to Government Section for protection against arbitrary and capricious acts of Japanese and GHQ bureaucrats. How the Diet and the PPD teamed up without guile or craft to stymie such incongruous proposals as a political parties law and an American-style election law is explained in the next chapter. One case will suffice here to show the Diet's ability to exercise its constitutional power even under conditions of military occupation. Three months before the effective date of the new constitution, lower house Speaker Yamazaki came to PPD with a request to see the Supreme Commander on a matter of "extreme urgency." The previous year, he said, the Japanese government inaugurated a five-year program for recovery of silkworm production and promised farmers ¥252 per *kan* (about eight pounds) of cocoons. When last year's crop was in, however, the government paid the farmers only ¥98 per *kan*. Now, Mr. Yamazaki went on, over strong protests by the silk culture associations, the Ministry of Agriculture and Forestry was on the verge of arbitrarily fixing the price for the 1947 crop at ¥154 per *kan*. Responding to the demands of the silk farmers, the House set up a special committee to

intrude, for the second time during the occupation, on ground traditionally
reserved to the government. (The only other such intrusion was attempted, successfully, by the House of Representatives Diet Law Committee.) Mr. Yamazaki had in mind persuading General MacArthur, with
whom he had already established a friendly relationship, to prevent the
government from announcing the price until the special House committee
could complete its study of the problem. His message was conveyed to
General Whitney on a Friday.

The following Monday General Whitney, Maj. Gen. William F. Marquat, chief of ESS, and a PPD staff member met with Mr. Yamazaki, six
members of the special committee, and two experts on cocoons. General
Whitney explained that General MacArthur was always available to
Japanese parliamentarians, but because of the technical nature of the
subject at hand, it was thought advisable for Government Section and ESS
to represent him at this stage. Mr. Yamazaki pointed out that since
sericulture directly engaged a million families and silk reeling ten million
more, and since the government and the producers differed widely over a
fair price for cocoons, the question had become political. To circumvent
the customary government highhandedness, he said in conclusion, the
Diet had come to GHQ for "helpful hints." Next, Representative Ishiguro
Takeshige, former vice-minister of Agriculture and Forestry, ably explained the fascinating economics of silk production and sale. General
Marquat complimented Ishiguro for his erudite presentation, but noted
the absence of officials from the Price Control Board and Economic
Stabilization Board. He stressed that the silk problem was part of the
overall economic situation. But it was General Whitney's assurance to
Yamazaki that the Supreme Commander was less interested in setting an
immediate price for cocoons than in having the issue settled democratically that signalled victory for the astute Speaker. Continuing the discussion in the following weeks with officials of ESS and the Japanese Price
Control Board, he and his Diet associates won some important concessions.[1] The Diet, thanks to the good offices of Government Section, had
successfully challenged the all but invincible ESS-backed Japanese Finance Ministry and its affiliated agencies.

PPD carried out a miscellany of dissimilar assignments. These included
such things as preparing letters of sympathy for General Whitney's signature when distinguished Diet members died, and representing SCAP at the
funerals of House of Councillors President Matsudaira Tsuneo (1949) and
House of Representatives Speaker Shidehara Kijuro (1951). When SCAP
ordered the establishment of a 75,000-man National Police Reserve in

1950, it devolved on PPD to obtain the sympathetic understanding of the opposition parties in the Diet for the project, for which appropriated funds were disbursed by the cabinet under provisions of the SCAP order. PPD drafted a set of remarks for General Ridgway's use in greeting the fifteen-member Diet Observer Group on its return from the San Francisco Peace Conference in 1951.

On a different level were the special papers prepared by PPD on a variety of subjects. One of these was a reply to the British Mission's claim that two 1947 Japanese laws (No. 53 for disposing of religious properties by the state and No. 125 denying to aliens the benefits of Article 17 of the constitution) were unconstitutional. In this instance GHQ refused to substitute its own judgment for that of the Japanese government, which held that the laws in question were constitutional. Another paper was a statement of Government Section's position on the 1949 proposal of the FEC's Australian member to have inserted in the Japanese constitution a new article forbidding a Diet member to introduce a financial bill without cabinet authorization. On SCAP's recommendation, the Australian proposal was tabled by the FEC. Still another paper defended General MacArthur against attacks in 1949 for telling the Allied Catholic Women's Club of Tokyo that he had had no part in Japan's birth control legislation of 1948 and 1949. The paper quoted him as saying that population control was not prescribed by Allied policy or considered any part of his executive responsibility or authority.

PPD prepared an analysis of the House of Representatives election in January 1949, when the Communist party increased its Diet seats from four to thirty-five. In the analysis it was pointed out that the two conservative parties had registered a gain of seventy-four seats. The gains of both the Communists and the conservatives were made almost entirely at the expense of the Social Democratic party, which lost ninety-four seats. Significantly the Social Democrats and the Communists combined polled 63,508 fewer votes in 1949 than in 1947. There was less voter confusion in 1949 than in the previous two postwar elections for the lower house, proof being that for the first time during the occupation a single party—the Democratic Liberal—won a clear majority of the 466 seats. No longer could anyone doubt that Japan was overwhelmingly conservative.

Shortly before the occupation ended PPD did a special paper for General Ridgway on Japan's unhappy experience with extraterritoriality before 1900. The story of the people's resentment against the special treaties exempting foreign residents from the jurisdiction of Japanese law courts went far to explain the country's unyielding opposition to granting discriminatory rights to American military forces committed to her protection after the restoration of independence. It was important for the commander of our soldiers, sailors, and airmen in the Far East to understand why the United States had no choice but to conclude with Japan "an agreement on criminal jurisdiction similar to the corresponding provisions of [the 1951 NATO] Agreement." [2]

PPD fueled Government Section's relentless and partially successful campaign to minimize GHQ interference with the Japanese legislative process. The main offender was the oversized and unmanageable ESS. By withholding clearance of legislative bills for reasons other than noncompliance with occupation objectives, ESS—and occasionally other staff sections—preempted the National Diet's role under the new constitution. *Tokyo News* had this in mind when it said on 8 May 1952, ten days after the occupation ended: "All decisions of the government and all measures to be submitted to the Diet were subject to GHQ approval. . . . even the size of the signboard of a local government agency had to be determined by occupation authorities." No sooner was the First National Diet convened in 1947 than Chief Cabinet Secretary Nishio, referring to excessive control by GHQ of the legislative process, told PPD that the main difficulties facing the Katayama Cabinet were the following: the Diet's impatience with the cabinet for late submission of legislation; slowness of SCAP sections in clearing ministerial bills for final cabinet decision; and the cabinet's lack of freedom under the new constitution, particularly in the matter of legislative details such as language refinement.

General Whitney and Frank Rizzo made some headway in rectifying this situation between 1947 and 1952, but they had an uphill struggle all the way. SCAP staff sections, including Government Section itself until most of its divisions were liquidated or transferred elsewhere in mid-1948, intransigently rejected the proposition that the Diet should have first preference in eliminating the imperfections, including unconstitutional provisions, from Japanese legislative proposals. Consequently SCAP sections not only precensored legislation but delayed for weeks and even months clearance of bills, any one of which a competent SCAP official could have examined for deviations from occupation policy in an hour or less. How much worse the situation might have been had Government Section not kept steady pressure on the Chief of Staff for corrective action is left to the judgment of the reader.

The Chief of Staff, typically, sought a compromise solution. He favored precensoring economic and fiscal measures by GHQ and simultaneously having the Japanese government operate under the democratic procedures prescribed in the new constitution. The initial test case was the

Bicycle Race bill of 1948, to which ESS objected on such grounds as possible monopolistic practices and poor draftsmanship. The question was whether or not bicycling was a purely Japanese affair. General Whitney referred the matter to the Chief of Staff for decision, taking the position that ESS rejection of a bill sponsored by fifty-eight members of the House of Representatives was a wholly arbitrary suppression of the legislative initiative. Let it be introduced, he said, and deliberated by the appropriate committees of the two Houses. The very corrections that ESS proposed to make in the bill could better be left to the action of the Diet itself with any SCAP assistance it might require. The Chief of Staff ruled that the Bicycle Race bill should be left to the discretion of the Diet, and Government Section cleared it. Thus, a precedent was established. But since this was only a stopgap solution of the problem, Government Section kept goading the Chief of Staff to approve a positive and realistic procedure for handling legislation. The section's position was that all bills, whether originating with the cabinet or a member of the Diet, should be permitted to be introduced without precensorship by GHQ. Whitney reasoned as follows (3 September 1948 check note):

It has for some time been the established policy of the Supreme Commander [he told the Chief of Staff], and indeed that of the United States, to shift to the Japanese themselves responsibility for solution of their own domestic problems and to intervene therein only to insure against any violence to basic Allied objectives. . . . Existing practice tends to perpetuate a situation found at the start of the occupation wherein the Diet was confined to little more than a puppet role. . . . During this advanced phase of the occupation, such improvements as staff sections may deem advisable in legislative bills, where there exists no direct involvement of basic policy, should be "sold" to the responsible legislative committee . . . through consultation and advice, rather than through the more rigid procedure of formal SCAP action. No possible disadvantage could result from thus freeing the legislative process. Before any bill becomes law, it must run the gamut of open hearings in a standing committee of each House, where it is examined clause by clause, with the advice and assistance of a Diet Legal Bureau and of special committee consultants, after which it is brought up in plenary session in both chambers for final debate and action by the entire membership. If a government bill, it must, even before its introduction in the Diet, be drafted by the legal experts in the appropriate ministry (who invariably coordinate with the SCAP section concerned), then be discussed and approved by the whole Cabinet, and finally be examined by the Attorney General's Office to determine that it does not traverse any directive of the Supreme Commander, conforms to the provisions of the Constitution, and is technically sound from the standpoint of legislative draftsmanship. In the course of the legislative process, there is ample time and opportunity for this headquarters to advise with the responsible ministry or Diet committees as to any proposed legislation. Should such safeguard by any chance fail to prevent an enactment which . . . conflicts with basic occupation policy, a formal directive setting the law or any provision thereof aside would be adequate.

Maj. Gen. Alonzo P. Fox, deputy chief of staff, was favorably disposed to most of Whitney's thesis. He was particularly impressed by the point that introduction of over a hundred bills, "few of which by any stretch of the imagination were related to occupation objectives." was delayed until the last ten days of the most recent Diet session, because staff sections and even divisions within sections could not agree among themselves. He concluded that GHQ could dispense with precensoring member bills, but not cabinet bills. The flaw in this arrangement, Whitney pointed out, was that if individual legislators were accorded the full right to introduce bills without prior SCAP approval, while denying the cabinet the identical right, the cabinet might very well hit on the idea of circumventing prior SCAP approval by having all legislation introduced by members of government parties. Accordingly he recommended that the policy statement proposed by General Fox be changed to read:

After Japanese government-sponsored legislation, which has received Cabinet approval, or legislation sponsored by a member or members of the National Diet is introduced in the Diet, copies submitted to this headquarters . . . will be distributed by Government Section to the interested staff sections. Comment by the interested sections will be submitted to Government Section promptly, and will be concerned with principles, not details of draftsmanship. . . . the comments will specify the particulars, and Government Section will refer them to the proper Japanese government ministry and to the Diet committees concerned for consideration. Unless a proposed bill manifestly contravenes SCAP policy, there should be no objection to its enactment by the Diet. If it is considered that the legislation, if enacted, would contravene SCAP policy or be detrimental to the accomplishment of occupation objectives, the comments and recommendations will be submitted through Government Section to the Chief of Staff for consideration. If deemed necessary or appropriate, a formal directive to the Japanese government in draft form will be attached. Such draft directive will specify the occupation objective or directive of the Supreme Commander contravened in the proposed legislation.

But for United States Interim Directive No. 96 of December 1948, known as the economic stabilization directive, Whitney's plan for handling legislation would in all probability have been approved by the Chief of Staff. Pending the Chief of Staff's decision, which was not handed down until the spring of 1951, Whitney unilaterally cleared eighty-one bills, a third of the total introduced in the Fifth National Diet, over objections interposed by one or more staff sections. Interestingly enough, not a single request was made to the Chief of Staff to invalidate any of the bills thus cleared and subsequently enacted into law. Amendments were handled in much the same way. Except in the field of public finance they were also unilaterally cleared, after which SCAP officials' findings were channeled through the Legal Bureau of each House to the various Diet committees.

(Dr. Sherwood Fine, ESS special assistant, regarded a Diet-proposed amendment to the cabinet-approved 1948–1949 budget as nothing more than a diabolical plot of the opposition political parties to "mess up what had been a perfectly sound budget when handed to the Diet." That the Diet might rework the figures within the framework of a balanced budget did not appeal to him.) Reflecting Washington's belated decision to relax occupation controls generally, the Chief of Staff in a July 1949 policy statement lent moral support to Whitney's actions by forbidding "interference with the Japanese Government in the performance of its functions" and "authorizing only that surveillance . . . necessary . . . [to ensure] attainment of occupation objectives."

The procedure for clearing legislation under the March 1947 staff memorandum proved to be flexible enough during five National Diet sessions in 1949 and 1950 to safeguard fundamental occupation policies without giving rise to loud cries by the Japanese of excessive control. But the one previously mentioned difficulty, that of precise and detailed directon by GHQ in the single area of public finance, would be the main cause of trouble in the future. PPD warned General Whitney, specifically in connection with the general budget for 1951–1952. No sooner was that budget presented to the Diet than ESS served notice that amendments thereto and legislative measures requiring funds not clearly earmarked for the purpose would be disallowed. Only in this way, ESS insisted, could Washington's stabilization directive be effectively carried out.

To this General Whitney emphatically demurred. Without questioning the United States stabilization policy, he protested to the Chief of Staff in a 10 February 1951 memorandum that the ESS procedure was "unduly rigid, out of step with the present stage and trend of the occupation, and destructive of other fundamental objectives." Since, he said further, "this difference of opinion involves the whole delicate mechanism of occupation control over Japanese governmental processes and the manner of its settlement entails immediate political consequences of grave import not only to the Japanese but to the authority and prestige of the Supreme Commander, the need for a command decision is urgent." The 1951–1952 budget draft then before the Diet, he contended, was not the only possible combination that would satisfy the requirements of the economic stabilization directive. Variations could be devised within the framework of that directive and within the meaning of the Chief of Staff's check sheet of 24 April 1950, enunciating the new United States policy of relaxed control. "It has been the consistent policy of the Supreme Commander as communicated to the undersigned," he said as a clincher, "that he would not concern himself with the minutia of government appropriations so long as provision was simultaneously made for adequate revenue to maintain a true budgetary balance." Not only was relaxation of occupation controls in order after more than five years of occupation, he went on, but a fundamental occupation objective, that of strengthening democratic tendencies, was at stake. The ESS procedure, he said, restricted the Diet to "enacting the budget exactly as presented by the Cabinet or precipitating a political crisis by rejecting it." The corrosive effect of such an ineffectual role

inevitably robs the legislative branch of all integrity and reduces it to the very status of a "talk club" which it occupied under the Meiji Constitution and the Tojo regime. Specifically in point is the [SWNCC 228] policy instruction transmitted to the Supreme Commander by the United States Government as early as 7 January 1946 which included among the objectives to be accomplished in the reform of the Japanese governmental system "a legislative body, fully representative of the electorate, with full power to reduce, increase or reject any items in the budget or to suggest new items."

On the basis of the foregoing, Whitney recommended that Diet budgetary amendments and other legislative proposals be reviewed and cleared by GHQ if they did not violate SCAP's budgetary policy.

In a three-point policy statement, the most comprehensive ever made on this subject, the Chief of Staff, employing much of Whitney's language verbatim, directed in a 30 March 1951 check sheet

a. That all amendments to the Government's budget, proposed by any member of the Diet . . . be reviewed by the Economic and Scientific Section under the same general standards as governed the review of the Government's budget draft and that they be cleared . . . if they do not violate the SCAP's budgetary policy.

b. That other legislative proposals . . . which contain budgetary implications be cleared provided that appropriate budgetary measures . . . have been assured.

c. That legislative proposals having budgetary implications made after a national budget has been passed be cleared provided the funds are legally included . . . in the existing budget. Should no funds be available consideration of the bill should be withheld until the next supplementary or regular budget preparation period.

Prompted by the favorable climate thus created, Government Section moved decisively during the Tenth Diet session to release major legislative bills from the grip of SCAP sections. Representative of the actions taken was clearance of the Hokkaido Port Construction Bill, which Civil Transportation Section (CTS) had held up for more than six months. The measure had the support of all political parties, the Hokkaido Development Agency, the cabinet, the Ministry of Transportation, and the House of Representatives Committee for Transportation. Appropriations for its implementation had already been made. CTS did not contend that its passage would contravene any occupation policy or directive. Violent repercussions in Japanese circles were a distinct possibility in the event GHQ disapproved it. According to a 31 March 1951 Rizzo memorandum:

On 19 February 1951 . . . Mr. Osmand of CTS . . . was informed that GS . . . felt compelled to clear the bill . . . and would proceed to do so unless specifically instructed to the contrary by the Supreme Commander or the Chief of Staff. In view of the strong opposition to this bill consistently expressed by CTS, however, GS would hold up its action for 24 or 48 hours if the Chief, CTS desired to request that special instructions be issued. . . . Mr. Osmond . . . stated that Colonel Miller appreciated the opportunity to appeal the proposed clearance but had decided not to do so. Accordingly, the bill was cleared the same day.

The Mutual Loans and Savings Bank bill was likewise cleared over ESS objections. So also was the Vocational Educational bill, but only after PPD obtained from the chairman of the House of Representatives Education Committee a statement, witnessed by Finance Minister Ikeda and certified by the Budget Bureau chief, that "expenditures . . . shall be defrayed within the limit of already appropriated budget of the Ministry of Education" (Williams memorandum, 31 March 1951).

Climaxing the protracted tug-of-war between Government Section and ESS over draft legislation was the case of the Trust Fund Bureau Fund bill, prepared by the Finance Ministry to implement a recommendation made by Mr. Joseph Dodge, special consultant on economic stabilization, and cleared by SCAP on 1 March. Three weeks later the fireworks started when the Finance Committee of the House of Representatives offered an amendment to the bill which ESS disapproved on the ground that it was in violation of a Dodge recommendation. Government Section referred the matter to the Chief of Staff, emphasizing that SCAP's refusal to clear the amendment might bring about an embarrassing situation not unlike that of 1950 when the Diet, much to the Supreme Commander's chagrin, killed the Local Tax bill following GHQ's flat rejection of certain amendments. "At the very next Diet session," Whitney said, "when GHQ permitted certain amendments to be introduced, the bill was readily enacted with large majorities in both Houses." It was his opinion that the principle involved in the current Dodge recommendation would best be implemented by adopting "a reasonable attitude" toward the Diet's right of legislative deliberation (Whitney check sheet, 29 March 1951).

In a five-page 31 March check note to the Chief of Staff ESS hit back, concentrating on what it called the "inaccuracies and false concepts" contained in Government Section's papers on the subject. Instead of addressing himself to the question in dispute, the right of the Diet to deliberate, General Marquat, ESS chief, offered such non sequiturs as these:

No nation will impose austerity upon itself especially if the United States can be forced to meet all costs of its aspired luxury standards. . . . The thought that according license to the Diet members to attack Occupation policy will prevent shifting of responsibility by the Japanese to the headquarters would appear to be the height of naivete. . . . I do not recognize the authority of the Government Section to act upon the decisions of ess within its operational area as inherent in the exercise of the perfunctory function of transmitting bills to the legislature. This is an assumption by Government Section of a top position in the chain of command transcending that of the Chief of Staff. The Government Section is not qualified to analyze economic matters . . . ; its surveillance responsibilities should be confined to a check on form and legislative policy only. . . . It is manifest that the series of allegations being advanced by Government Section is a harassing campaign designed to crack existing economic policy. . . . The concept that the Supreme Commander will permit the reversal of the economic stabilization accomplished in Japan through the investment of approximately $2 billion of U.S. funds in acceptance of the academic premise of liberalizing freedoms which up till now have been in no way unduly restrictive or penalizing would appear to be most tenuous.

On the day he received the above check note, the Chief of Staff notified ess and Government Section that his policy statement of 30 March applied to the Trust Fund Bureau Fund bill. Accordingly General Whitney forthwith cleared the proposed amendments, and the Diet immediately enacted the amended bill into law.

Thus, as of April 1951 (the month MacArthur and Whitney departed Japan), scap had at last a firm policy on legislation. Under it ess was responsible for interpreting and implementing United States economic directives. ess gave orders to the Japanese government, which carried them out either by Potsdam Ordinance, the occupation-approved device for bypassing the Diet, or by Diet-enacted legislation. Under the new democratic dispensation the Japanese government, unless ordered to the contrary by scap, had no choice but to implement ghq instructions by the legislative route. And here Government Section's jurisdiction over legislation came into play. It unilaterally cleared all legislative proposals that, in its judgment, violated no United States or scap directives, subject to review by the Chief of Staff on appeal from a staff section. In January 1952, Government Section obtained the Chief of Staff's approval, over ess protest, to clear any legislation to which objections had not been registered within forty-eight hours of its receipt by interested staff sections. Shortly thereafter the Chief of Staff approved another Government Section recommendation to restore full legislative freedom to the Japanese cabinet and Diet, "reserving only the scap's right to interpose formal objection within a 24-hour period to any proposed legislative measure which would clearly violate a policy directive of continuing applicability."

Of 1,637 bills processed in the three-year period 1948–1951, Government Section cleared 179 over objections raised by different staff sections. In no instance did a staff section appeal a Government Section clearance action to the Chief of Staff.

Of its manifold responsibilities, PPD gave high priority to that of preparing daily reports on Diet activities for the Supreme Commander and other interested GHQ officials. Unlike the ATIS translations and news analyses and similar endeavors by CIE and Government Section's Public Affairs Divison, all of which contained an abundance of valuable information on the doings of the Diet, PPD reported on the basis of firsthand and unimpeachable sources precisely what was transpiring in the Diet and what lay immediately ahead. Through these reports the Supreme Commander and others followed the hearings on the draft constitution, the Diet Law bill, land reform and labor legislation, Yamazaki's bid for the post of prime minister, defeat of the Local Tax bill, political crises, and debates on the San Francisco Peace Treaty. Many of the 722 Diet reports made by PPD during the occupation were devoted to the status and progress of legislation, but many more dealt with political personalities and current political developments. To forestall charges or insinuations of his having tampered with the reports for an ulterior purpose, General Whitney required prompt delivery of the original of each to General MacArthur over the name of the individual in PPD who prepared it. General Ridgway received the reports over the name of the Government Section chief. As instigator of the reports, General Whitney thought they made a valuable contribution by supplying the Supreme Commander with pertinent information on Japanese political trends basic to important high-level decisions.

Continuity of United States Policy

To some observers in Tokyo, United States occupation policy toward Japan underwent so drastic a change in 1948 as to take on the character of a "reverse course." Miriam Farley, a SCAP labor specialist, had the impression that the occupation's original aim of democratic reform gave way to the urgent need to place Japan's economy on a self-supporting basis.[1] To Mei Ju-ao, China's member on the International Military Tribunal, 1948 represented a transitional period in American policy vis-à-vis Japan. Democratization of the country was no longer of concern to the United States. The economic deconcentration program had been abandoned altogether, and the zaibatsu were regaining their prewar prestige and power. The purge program had degenerated. Japan was drifting toward fascism.[2] W. Macmahon Ball of Australia, the Commonwealth member of the Allied Council, wrote in early 1948 that American policy now aimed at establishing Japan as the workshop of East Asia, so as to make her self-supporting and not a permanent burden on the American taxpayer.[3] On the basis of these and other contemporary expressions of opinion, Professor Theodore McNelly wrote this terse synopsis: "The image of the Occupation suffered from the so-called reverse course, when American policy shifted from the democratization of Japan to the rebuilding of the country in order to contain communism."[4] In whose estimation the image of the occupation suffered and in what way policy shifted from democratization, he does not say.

The reverse course concept—the idée fixe of sympathizers with radical socialism in Japan, the "emancipation movement" in China, and the Labor governments of Australia and Britain—does not stand up under close scrutiny. Its exponents wrongly suppose that the inevitable evolution and timely adjustment of United States policy was a reversal of policy. The purpose of this chapter is to show that, far from being reversed, the policy of democratization continued without interruption to the final day of the occupation.

On 9 October 1948, President Truman approved a set of National Security Council decisions known as NSC 13/2, the most important United States policy statement respecting Japan since 1945. NSC 13/2 reflected the determination of the government to proceed full steam ahead toward fulfillment of America's basic aims in Japan. Those aims, as President Roosevelt clearly defined them in his famous October 1937 quarantine speech at Chicago were to curb the "fascist disturbers of mankind" and to bring about the "removal of barriers against trade." [5] With the completion of the demilitarization and democratization programs in Japan by 1948, ensuring against the future rise there of totalitarian disturbers, one stage in United States relations with that country ended and another began. The time had arrived, regardless of the cold war, to consider implementing Article 11 of the Potsdam Declaration, which promised "eventual Japanese participation in world trade relations," and Article 12, which placed the Allies under obligation to withdraw the occupation forces once the country had met the conditions imposed on it. The result was NSC 13/2, which reaffirmed and updated but did not reverse American policy; its aim was to ready the new democratic Japan for entry into the free world community of nations as a self-supporting trading partner. [6]

The avowed purpose of NSC 13/2 was to "concentrate our attention on the preparation of the Japanese for the eventual removal of the regime of control," that is, removal of SCAP, the FEC, and the Allied Council of Japan. It contained twenty recommendations for achieving this goal. Six of the recommendations having to do with the terms and timing of a peace treaty, post-treaty defense of Japan, fortification of the Ryukyu Islands, leasing of Japanese naval bases, and the International Military Tribunal—all beyond SCAP's authority—were not concerned with the occupation policy of demilitarizing and democratizing the country. Strictly administrative in character were nine other recommendations bearing on the occupation: disposition of United States tactical forces in Japan, relaxing SCAP controls and reducing SCAP personnel, limiting the scope of the FEC's authority, continuing the Allied Council without changing its functions, SCAP's relations with the Japanese government, assimilating past occupation reforms, lessening occupation costs, and establishing programs for interchange of persons and propaganda broadcasts to Japan. Regarding the recommendation for assimilating occupation reforms, SCAP was advised to intervene "only if the Japanese authorities revoke or compromise the fundamentals of the reforms." This phrase left no doubt that the policy of democratization was not to be relaxed or reversed. Still another recommendation had to do with control of Japan's war potential; far from reversing the policy of demilitarization, NSC 13/2 declared that Japan would be forbidden to manufacture weapons of war and civil aircraft. The remaining four recommendations pertaining to the police establishment, the purge, economic recovery, and reparations were the only ones with occupation policy implications. The question, then, is whether or not United States policy relative to these four areas was shifted or reversed.

NSC 13/2 suggested that SCAP strengthen the Japanese police establishment by reinforcing and reequipping the present forces and expanding the national police organization. When the original draft of the NSC paper was submitted to him in June 1948 for his views, SCAP commented that any further expansion of the police could be expected to have very explosive international reactions; also that expansion clearly beyond actual police necessity would be most difficult to defend without FEC clearance. Replying to a December 1948 Department of the Army request for a report on his implementation of specific NSC determinations, SCAP said that the police establishment was at full legal strength, engaged in intensive training, and making progressive improvement. Six months later, addressing himself to the Department of the Army's inquiry concerning police equipment, training, strength, effectiveness, and financing, SCAP noted that the potential effectiveness of the force had been increased by the acquisition of 125,000 United States revolvers, necessary ammunition and spare parts, and approximately 150 motor vehicles from Japanese industry. Furthermore, he said, 82,000 men had received in-service training at local, prefectural, and national training schools in 1948, with 75,000 others scheduled to receive like training in 1949. All policemen had already received formation and riot control training. With SCAP's moral support, he said, the Japanese police were capable of handling any anticipated internal disturbance without intervention of occupation forces. He did not foresee any pay reduction for police personnel.[7] The foregoing is sufficient to show that U.S. policy regarding Japan's police establishment underwent no fundamental change prior to the outbreak of the Korean War in June 1950.

Maintaining that the purpose of the purge had been "largely accomplished," an early draft of NSC 13/2 advised not only that the program be extended no further but that purged individuals who had held relatively harmless positions should be made eligible for governmental, business, and public media positions. In addition, the cases of certain individuals purged by category should be reviewed, and screening for public office of persons below a certain age should be dispensed with. To this proposal SCAP took strong exception. "The administration of the purge program has now been completed," he said, "except insofar as concerns the screening of future applicants for public office." Moreover, he reminded Washington, the purge policy had been drawn from the Potsdam Declaration, the 1945 United States directive to SCAP, and the 1947 FEC basic

Diet delegation arrives in Honolulu to begin United States mission, January 1950. *Top row, left to right:* Shima Seiichi, Hatano Kanae, Takada Hiroshi, Onogi Hidejiro, Kanamori Tokujiro, Asanuma Inejiro, Oike Makoto, Makoto Matsukata. *Bottom row, left to right:* Matsumoto Takizo, Yamazaki Takeshi, Sakurauchi Tatsuro, Iwamoto Nobuyuki, Imamura Chusuke, Kondo Hideaki, Shiikuma Saburo, Justin Williams. (*Honolulu Advertiser*)

Secretary of State Dean Acheson chats amicably with members of the Diet delegation in February 1950. Second from left is Yamazaki Takeshi, who as Speaker of the lower house pressed for adoption of the democratic Constitution and the Diet Law. Shaking hands with Mr. Acheson is Matsumoto Takizo, English-speaking ambassador of goodwill who had the confidence of all Japanese political factions and all sections of GHQ. The other Japanese are *(left to right)* Sakurauchi Tatsuro, Asanuma Inejiro, Shima Seiichi, and Shiikuma Saburo. In 1945 Mr. Acheson vowed that Japanese society would be radically changed. *(U.S. Army)*

(1) At the Imperial Preserve, 1950. *Left to right:* Maj. C. F. Guida; Capt. Charles Norris, PPD; and Capt. William Curtis, who became the fourth and last executive officer of Government Section. (2) An outing at the Imperial Preserve, 1950. Justin Williams *(left)* with Maj. Jack Napier, Government Section executive officer, 1948–51.

(1) General MacArthur shakes hands with Japanese notables at Tokyo's Haneda Airport just before his departure for the United States on 16 April 1951. Justin Williams, SCAP official, assists the general by identifying each Japanese leader for him. Behind Williams are Arthur, the general's son, and Maj. Anthony Storey, his pilot. *(Asahi Shimbun)* (2) Japanese notables see General MacArthur off at Haneda Airport, 16 April 1951. Among them were Prime Minister Yoshida Shigeru *(with hat raised)* and House of Councillors President Sato Naotake *(with hand raised)*. Between them is House of Representatives Speaker Hayashi Joji. *(Asahi Shimbun)*

post-surrender directive. "The directive of the Far Eastern Commission is explicit in this matter," he concluded, "and I question the authenticity of SCAP action in positive derogation thereof until the Commission has altered its directive accordingly." [8]

After NSC 13/2 was approved, there followed an exchange of radio messages in which the Department of the Army pressed for some attenuation of the purge program and SCAP clung tenaciously to the purge policy it had evolved. Requested by the Army—in a message addressed to CINCFE (Commander-in-Chief, Far East)—to inform the Japanese government that no further extension of the purge was contemplated, and to modify the purge along lines laid down in NSC 13/2, MacArthur replied with a discourse on existing Allied policy. As CINCFE, he said, he lacked authority to implement the nonmilitary features of NSC 13/2, which were under SCAP's jurisdiction. He expressed sympathy for the apparent United States aim of restoring unilateral control over Japan, which the Secretary of State had surrendered at Moscow in December 1945; but he was aware of no single expedient by which this could be done. But if the United States breached the Moscow Agreement by unilaterally rescinding Allied policy, he warned, such action would establish a legal and moral basis for the USSR to extend its own unilateral influence over Japan—and "it is doubtful that we could successfully resist any thrust it might decide on against Hokkaido." As for reversing the purge policy, he went on, it must be done formally and openly, for the Japanese could not act in that area without another SCAP directive, a move in which the Allied Council and the FEC would have a consultative and reviewing interest. [9]

In an 18 December 1948 radiogram, MacArthur again reminded the Army that NSC 13/2 had not been sent to him in the manner prescribed by the Moscow Agreement. He also pointed out that every member of the FEC was on the alert for any misstep that might leave him vulnerable to impeachment for improper stewardship of his international responsibility. The United States should firmly insist on the right to shape policy, he said in a 26 December follow-up message, but repeated the importance of doing so openly and within channels, as in the case of the 11 December economic stabilization directive. [10]

Army Under Secretary William H. Draper agreed with MacArthur that the desired purge modifications could not be accomplished by informal action. But he emphasized that relief should be obtained in those cases where specific FEC policy would not be contravened. He felt that it would be permissible within FEC directives to follow the universally accepted American concept of justice, which held that a person was innocent until proved guilty. This was a reference to the SCAP criterion of purge by category, under which certain individuals were guilty until proved innocent. To resolve the conflict between NSC 13/2 and the 3 November 1945 basic directive, the United States government in January 1949 rescinded paragraphs 5b, 23, and 40 of the latter. These provisions required SCAP to assume that, in the absence of satisfactory evidence, all persons who had held key positions in government and industry since 1937 were active exponents of militant nationalism and aggression. Army Secretary Kenneth Royall informed MacArthur that appropriate purge cases could now be reviewed on the basis of harmless positions held or the youth of the individuals concerned. In July 1949 the Army queried SCAP on the number of cases reviewed and the actions taken since 1 December 1948.[11]

In his answer, SCAP acknowledged that the conflict between the United States basic directive and NSC 13/2 had been removed, but not the conflict between NSC 13/2 and the pertinent controlling policy decisions of the FEC. (It was FEC policy to exclude from public office and from any other position of substantial private responsibility persons who had been active exponents of militarism and militant nationalism.) Within the policy limitations, there had been a constant review by the Japanese government of purge action previously taken, with a resultant reinstatement of eligibility to hold public office of approximately one thousand persons since 1 December 1948. Cabinet order number 39 of 8 February 1949 established a public office qualifications board to hear appeals based on errors or injustices. As of July 1949, this board had before it 31,190 appeals for review.[12]

Tipped off by the grapevine that the purge policy was about to be radically altered, Prime Minister Yoshida disclosed in a press interview (*Mainichi Shimbun*, 11 January 1949), while the election campaign for members of the House of Representatives was in progress, that his government was contemplating a large-scale clearance of purgees in political, financial, and local government circles. A sort of general amnesty was expected, he said. Less than a week after his Democratic-Liberal party won that election by a landslide, he asked General MacArthur to approve the appointment of two purgees to cabinet posts, expressing the belief that "it would not prove too embarrassing to you if they are now exempted from the application of the Purge Directive." General MacArthur replied: "It would not be within the proper scope of my authority to sanction purgees for Cabinet posts without concurrence of the Far Eastern Commission which it would be quite impossible to secure." A few weeks later General Whitney told members of the newly formed Public Office Qualifications Appeal Board that in spite of rumors and counterrumors there was no alteration of purge policy by the FEC either at hand or contemplated. Over a year later—on 4 June 1950—General MacArthur informed a conference of his section chiefs that there would be no relaxation of the purge, that the January 1946 purge directive (SCAPIN 550) would be strictly enforced, and that all actions of the Japanese government on purge matters would continue to be reviewed by Government Section. When Fujinuma Shohei, a purgee, bypassed the Japanese government and SCAP and appealed directly to Washington in 1949, the Department of the Army sent him this reply: "Through the proper agency of General Headquarters you were determined to have been an active exponent of militant nationalism and . . . were barred from public service. Such action is final and conclusive and is not subject to review by . . . the Japanese government . . . since the power and authority of the Supreme Commander over the government and the people of Japan is plenary." Of the 31,190 appeals reported by SCAP in his 28 July 1949 message to the Army, the review board had recommended by October 1950 that 10,090 of the applicants be reinstated. By the end of the year, 15,010 of a total of 207,740 purged individuals had become eligible to hold public office. It was not until 3 May 1951, soon after General MacArthur had been succeeded by General Ridgway and when John Foster Dulles was making good progress in working out the terms of a Japanese peace treaty, that the Japanese government was authorized by SCAP to "review existing ordinances issued in implementation of [purge] directives." [13] In June of that year a government council began reviewing the cases of the remaining purgees. Thus, while clear cases of injustice were redressed, the original purge policy was adhered to by SCAP and the Japanese government until the end of the occupation was in sight. There was no reverse course in this sector.

NSC 13/2 made economic recovery, second only to United States security interests, the primary objective of United States policy in Japan. Massive American financial aid would be provided and the United States government agencies concerned would cooperate to eliminate obstacles to the revival of Japanese foreign trade. To be successful the program would require increased Japanese production, a high export level, a minimum of work stoppages, internal austerity, and a balanced budget. Army Under Secretary Draper spearheaded a drive in the final months of 1948 to win approval of official Washington for the stabilization plan. Large-scale United States funding would be ineffective, he was told by officials of the Departments of Commerce and Treasury and the Federal Reserve Board, unless actually accompanied by a stringent and realistic program to combat and reverse the present inflationary trend. The result was United

States Interim Directive No. 96 of 11 December 1948, which required SCAP to impose on the Japanese the rigorous stabilization program suggested in NSC 13/2. The directive was prepared by the Department of the Army in accordance with Section III–3 of the Terms of Reference of the Far Eastern Commission (The United States "may issue interim directives . . . whenever urgent matters arise not covered by policies already formulated by the Commission"), concurred in by the National Security Council, and duly transmitted to SCAP by the Joint Chiefs of Staff. Subsequently rescinded was the provision in the 1945 basic directive that reads: "You will not assume any responsibility for the economic rehabilitation of Japan or the strengthening of the Japanese economy." [14] Did these actions constitute a shift from democratization to containment of communism?

The case of the Japanese Marxian socialists for the reverse course concept is valid in this instance only if their major premise, that United States policy originally aimed at establishing a socialist state, is accepted. There is no denying that a sprinkling of populist, New Deal, and radical ideas—for example, trust-busting, collective bargaining, violent overthrow of government—found their way into the United States basic directive. But it is little less than grotesque to imagine the world's leading "bourgeois capitalist democracy," represented in Japan by an archconservative Supreme Commander, rejecting the time honored principles of private property and rugged individualism and undertaking to rebuild Japan as a socialist showplace. The revision of the National Public Service Law in 1948 to deprive public employees of the right to strike, frequently cited as a major policy change by the United States, represented at most a difference in outlook between Government Section's internationally known civil service expert, Blaine Hoover, who subscribed to the 1935 Wagner Act's exemption of public employees from the right to strike, and ESS's American Federation of Labor agent, Jim Killen, who opposed that provision of the Wagner Act. In deciding for Hoover, whose original National Public Service bill of 1947 had been emasculated during his absence from Japan, General MacArthur merely endorsed a principle underlying the most progressive labor legislation in United States history. In this connection it should be pointed out that SCAP's prevention of the Communist-planned general strike set for 1 February 1947 represented no change of policy, despite the legitimate inference by Japanese leftists that the 1945 United States basic directive permitted and favored the use of force by the people to overthrow a feudalistic and authoritarian government. SCAP was on firm ground in assuming that United States policy never aimed at establishing by force in Japan the people's republic demanded by the Moscow-controlled Japanese Communist party. From first to last American policy was to establish not a dictatorship of the proletariat but a parliamentary form of government which would represent the electorate, including the nation's workforce.

A case can also be made for the reverse course viewpoint if we accept the hypothesis that the occupation was to last indefinitely. But such an assumption cannot be made. Paragraph 3c of the 1945 United States policy document advised SCAP that surveys dealing with the economic, industrial, financial, social, and political conditions would be constantly made for effecting modifications of policies to promote the ultimate objectives of the Allied powers. One ultimate objective of the FEC was to permit Japan "to purchase from foreign countries raw materials and other goods . . . [and] to export goods to pay for approved imports." [15] Thus sooner or later economic rehabilitation would become absolutely indispensable to restoring Japan's independence. Was not the economic stabilization directive of 1948 a tacit admission that the totally demilitarized and substantially democratized former enemy had fulfilled the requirements laid down in the Potsdam Declaration for ending the occupation? Did not Japan's evolution, as planned, necessitate adjusting not reversing United States policy to make her self-supporting? This required heavier infusions of United States funds. As one of several conditions for appropriating these funds, Congress insisted that all available Japanese resources, including properties heretofore earmarked for reparations but necessary to Japanese recovery, be made available to the Japanese economy. The arguments for stopping Japanese reparations removals were, as Army Assistant Secretary Tracy Voorhees radioed SCAP, the likelihood that the occupation would be protracted, the changed international situation, particularly in the Far East, and the necessity of relieving the burden on the American taxpayer for occupation costs.[16] Despite the 1945 United States admonotion to SCAP to assume no responsibility for rehabilitating the economy of the country, General MacArthur at the outset of the occupation directed his staff to work out necessary plans to "make Japan self-sufficient as soon as . . . humanly possible." [17] NSC 13/2, then, did not establish the policy of rehabilitating Japan's economy, but gave higher priority to a policy that had actually been in effect from the beginning, an action that neither reversed nor downgraded the primary policy of democratization.

Fifteen years after the occupation ended, George F. Kennan, chief architect of the 1948 NSC policy decisions, wrote: "How, at what stages, and in what degree these decisions finally found realization in the actions and practices of SCAP, I cannot tell." [18] As a matter of fact the Washington decisions, including the one on economic recovery, made no major impact on the occupation because, as SCAP informed the Department of the Army, "The United States policy position enunciated in NSC 13/2 for the most part parallels policy long guiding the occupation." [19] That the NSC decisions regarding the police establishment, the purge, and the economy brought about no basic policy changes is pointed out above. In other areas SCAP took certain administrative actions ostensibly in response to Washington's bidding, but none that might not well have been taken without outside prodding. Little more than window dressing was the 16 July 1949 GHQ staff memorandum notifying all civil and military units that, inasmuch as the character of the occupation "had gradually changed from the stern rigidity of a military occupation to the friendly guidance of a protective force," the occupation forces would henceforth "continue to advance the transition as rapidly as the Japanese government is able to assume the attending autonomous responsibility." Six months earlier SCAP had told Washington that the NSC decision to place "a steadily increasing degree [of responsibility] in the hands of the Japanese government" had been progressively in force throughout the occupation until receipt of the interim directive on economic stabilization, "which has for the time at least . . . placed the Japanese government under rigid occupation control in all matters affecting the Japanese economy." [20] Occupation administration, then, not occupation policy, was affected by the economic recovery program.

SCAP reported to Washington a number of actions taken to show compliance with NSC 13/2 decisions. Among these were the following: reduction of GHQ and Eighth Army United States civilian employees in 1949 from 3,660 to 1,950; discontinuance of the prefectural Civil Affairs teams in 1949 and reduction of Civil Affairs personnel from 2,758 (2,179 military, 579 Department of the Army civilians [DACs]) to 526 (111 military, 415 DACs); relinquishment or scale-down of SCAP control of the Japanese export and import trade, foreign exchange funds, foreign businesses, the communications equipment industry, the International Postal Service, customs and immigration responsibilities, the Japanese National Railways, mined stocks of precious metals, and so forth; the requirement that occupation personnel be charged for such fringe benefits as Japanese servants and bus transportation. These and other moves were already in the works and would have been made in due course without the NSC decisions. SCAP's evaluation of the exercise was given in this April 1949 reply to a Department of the Army request for a report on his implementation of NSC 13/2: "Insofar as possible all provisions have been accomplished or are being practiced as current routine performance." [21]

Nor did the NSC decisions have any noticeable effect on the prosecution of occupation reform programs. Despite the fact that NSC 13/2 advised SCAP not to press on the Japanese Government any further reform legislation, and notwithstanding SCAP's assurance to Washington that no additional reforms were contemplated (save reformation of the tax structure), SCAP staff sections, though checked somewhat by the balanced budget requirement, continued as usual to foster policies for the evolution of defeated Japan into a demilitarized, democratic, friendly, ultimately self-supporting nation. Nothing better illustrates this than SCAP's late 1948 involvement in the project to revise the National Public Service Law (NPSL).

The NPSL revision controvery started with SCAP's 22 July 1948 letter to Prime Minister Yoshida (written by Blaine Hoover, chief of Government Section's Civil Service Division) advising that strikes and collective bargaining by public servants be disallowed. [22] The Japanese government reacted by issuing at once a Potsdam Ordinance, which was to remain in effect until superseded by formal Diet legislation. By the time the necessary draft legislation had been readied for submission to the Diet the scandal-ridden Ashida government fell, bequeathing the issue to the new Yoshida government. Designated Prime Minister on 14 October, Mr. Yoshida planned to amend the NPSL, dissolve the House of Representatives, and call for an election. The three opposition parties, commanding a majority vote in the House, countered by demanding a substantial wage increase for government employees as the price for passing the NPSL no-strike revision bill, and challenged the right of the prime minister to dissolve the House until the adoption of a nonconfidence resolution in the cabinet. In consequence of these differences the Diet required seven weeks to approve the no-strike ban and three weeks more to pass the related wage bill, a ten-week period that coincided with Washington's finalization of the NSC decisions to prevent SCAP sponsorship of further reform legislation, reduce GHQ operations as rapidly as possible, and place responsibility for administering the occupation to a steadily increasing degree in the hands of the Japanese government. Ironically it was at this very time that GHQ intervention in Japanese affairs reached unprecedented heights, characterized by SCAP seeming to run afoul of Washington's instructions, the minority party government doing battle with the majority opposition parties, the Temporary National Personnel Commission assuming powers traditionally reserved to the Budget Bureau, Government Section clashing with ESS, and General Whitney tilting with

Prime Minister Yoshida. These mix-ups are examined here in some detail to show that there were no signs whatever of changes in United States policy or occupation routine.

NSC 13/2 did not take note of SCAP's project for prohibiting strikes and collective bargaining by government employees. It was not until late October that United States interest in the subject surfaced. According to an Associated Press dispatch reported in the 27 October 1948 issue of *Nippon Times,*

> The United States may act soon to head off a right to strike, no collective bargaining labor law for Government workers in Japan.
> Officials here said yesterday three American Government departments—State, Army and Labor—are giving urgent study to ways of getting the U.S. off the spot that has been getting hotter for the past three months. . . .
> General MacArthur has been backed up publicly on his original stand by Army Secretary Kenneth Royall and by the American spokesman on the Far Eastern Commission, Major General Frank McCoy. There has been no hint of any order reversing General MacArthur.

Yoshida said that he had repeatedly consulted GHQ on the NPSL bill and was assured that the United States government fully supported General MacArthur's stand on the measure. Washington, then, gave higher priority to the principles of the Wagner Labor Relations Act of 1935, which denied public employees the right to strike and bargain collectively, than to the recent NSC dictum that SCAP stop sponsoring reform legislation.

When it became clear that the United States government would not oppose SCAP on the labor question, Prime Minister Yoshida threw additional light on his government's attitude toward the three critical issues of NPSL revision, higher wages for public servants, and Diet dissolution. Positive that revision of the NPSL was fundamental to Japan's welfare, he was vague about a supplementary budget to cover wage increases. Diet dissolution, in his opinion, should be based on the constitution, but he declined to amplify that point. Sharply divided on the dissolution question, the government and opposition parties campaigned energetically for SCAP support of their respective positions. While former Prime Minister Katayama was closeted with General MacArthur and Attorney General Ueda Shunkichi with Legal Section chief Alva C. Carpenter discussing the right of the cabinet to dissolve the Diet under Article 7 of the constitution, Government Section was known to be in sympathy with the stand taken by the famed parliamentarian, Ozaki Yukio. Mr. Ozaki had said publicly that if the prime minister elected by the Diet dissolved it, disregarding the Diet which represents the will of the people, it would be like a servant dismissing his master.

By this time the situation had become tense, the lines hardened. Leaders of the opposition parties doubted that Mr. Yoshida respected Article 69 of the constitution, which, they asserted, "authorizes dissolution only in case the House votes nonconfidence in the government or refuses a vote of confidence." Word was around that Irie Toshio, chief of the Legal Bureau of the House of Representatives, and Kanamori Tokujiro, who had steered the constitution through the Diet, had both advised Mr. Yoshida that, like the British prime minister, he could unilaterally dissolve the lower house. In a 19 November memorandum, I informed General Whitney that two enterprising Japanese newspaper reporters had overheard the prime minister say to a Democratic-Liberal party conference: "My 15 November speech . . . in which I said that this session was called solely to consider the NPSL and related measures and that on their passage the House would be dissolved, had been approved beforehand by the Supreme Commander. . . . My policy on dissolution following enactment of the NPSL and companion laws still holds. . . . Don't be misled by General Whitney . . . and foreign news agencies. Have confidence in me and General MacArthur."

What brought the controversy to a climax was my 26 November memorandum to General Whitney on a two-hour discussion I had had that day with Tokyo University president Nambara Shigeru. The distinguished educator wished to speak frankly and in the utmost confidence, since he had spent several hours the day before with Mr. Katayama. The essence of what he said was this: SCAP should settle this question by imposing the correct interpretation of the constitution on the cabinet and the political parties, as SCAP did earlier in the occupation by cracking down on the government right and left. The press was solidly back of Mr. Yoshida solely because he had successfully defied General Whitney. Yoshida had the opposition parties backed into the corner because he had made them believe that General MacArthur was on his side of this dispute. It was Mr. Yoshida's plan to have the NPSL bill passed and then to dissolve the House, denying the opposition parties a chance to act on the supplementary budget for wages. Mr. Katayama saw no way out of the tangle except for the House to defy the cabinet by refusing to be dissolved, even if Mr. Yoshida attempted to dissolve it under Article 7, a move that would place Japan in a state of revolution. And that was precisely what could be expected unless SCAP clarified its position on the relation of the wage issue to the other six bills. Dr. Nambara did not believe the Social Democrats could be persuaded to separate the supplementary budget question from the requirements for legislation imposed by the 22 July letter. He asserted that the real issue was representative government against one dangerous, arrogant, old-time bureaucrat. Dissolution in the near future, he said, was necessary, but as an issue it was secondary in importance. The opposition parties were at a disadvantage because of the SCAP requirement that six bills be enacted into law by next Tuesday; SCAP silence on the seventh measure, the wage bill, deprived the opposition parties of the one weapon with which they could defend themselves. If SCAP insisted on passage of the six bills by 30 November, then SCAP should prevent arbitrary dissolution of the House until the supplementary budget could be deliberated.

At 9:30 the next morning General Whitney, accompanied by Colonel Kades, went to the prime minister's official residence to—using Dr. Nambara's expression—crack down on Mr. Yoshida. General Whitney expressed to Prime Minister Yoshida the Supreme Commander's fear that an attempt to dissolve the Diet without alleviating the salary conditions of the government employees would create an explosive political situation; further, that for the cabinet to utilize the emperor as the device for effectuating the dissolution would raise the grave question among the Allied powers as to whether or not an attempt was being made to restore governmental power to the emperor. Therefore, it was felt that the prime minister should work out a compromise with the opposition parties, using for that purpose the good offices of the Supreme Commander and the chief of Government Section. According to Colonel Kades's 27 November 1948 memorandum on the conference,

> The Prime Minister responded that he did not understand the point about the Emperor because the Constitution provided that, with the advice and consent of the Cabinet, the Emperor could dissolve the Diet. General Whitney replied that this, of course, was a ministerial function to be performed after the constitutional basis was laid by the House of Representatives through either the passage of a vote of nonconfidence or the failure to pass a vote of confidence. . . .
>
> The Prime Minister then said to General Whitney, "What do you suggest as the way to dissolve the House of Representatives?" General Whitney replied, "Mr. Prime Minister, the question is not what I suggest. I am not here as the chief of Government Section; I am here as a messenger for General MacArthur."

General Whitney suggested as a compromise that once the present program plus the pay bill was enacted into law, the opposition parties would raise no further barrier to the dissolution of the Diet by passing a resolution of nonconfidence under Article 69 of the constitution. General Whitney had to repeat the suggestion several times before Mr. Yoshida understood it. Then, Kades reported,

> As soon as he did understand it, Mr. Yoshida said that the reason there was a delay in the pay bill was that the Economic and Scientific Section had informed the Finance Minister that the government should not approve the recommendation of the National Public Service Authority [for a monthly wage base of ¥6,307], but

urged a substantially lower increase in government workers' salaries, and that until this issue was resolved no "money bill" could be presented. . . . General Whitney said that he was not speaking of the seventh bill as a complete supplementary budget but only that portion relating to the increase in government workers' pay and the sources of revenue to meet that single item. . . . Mr. Yoshida stated that if this is what SCAP desires, he would obey.

Two days later Speaker Matsuoka announced that an agreement had been reached between the government and opposition parties concerning the NPSL bill and related measures. The agreement called for passage of the NPSL package, completion of deliberations on a new wage scale budget, and adoption of a resolution of nonconfidence in the government. On 30 November the NPSL legislation was enacted into law.

That left the wage bill and the motion of nonconfidence in the government. Regarding the pay standard, the government proposed a ¥5,300 level while the opposition parties adopted the ¥6,307 base recommended by the National Personnel Authority. The spread between the two figures represented the intensity of the conflict between Government Section's Civil Service Division and ESS's Public Finance Division, which culminated in a bizarre attempt by two GHQ factions to order the Diet around just two months after Washington had formally decided that SCAP should not press on the Japanese Government any further reform legislation.

The government and opposition parties were pledged to pass the wage bill and the nonconfidence resolution on 13 December. That evening, at a dinner party for members of the lower house Finance Committee, Finance Minister Izumiyama Sanroku, the host, became intoxicated, flirted with two female Diet members, collapsed on a sofa, and failed to make a scheduled appearance before the Budget Committee. Thrown into a state of excitement and indignation which lasted until dawn of the next day, by which time Prime Minister Yoshida had accepted Mr. Izumiyama's resignation from the cabinet, the House never got around to deliberating the two measures. But the disconcerting Izumiyama affair was only one episode of "that night to remember." Another was the unpublicized interference of rival SCAP factions with the normal processes of the Japanese government.

Throughout the night the lower house Steering Committee was harassed by conflicting "orders" given by Blaine Hoover, Civil Service Division chief, and Frayne Baker, a special assistant to General Marquat. Claiming to speak for SCAP, Hoover encouraged leaders of the opposition parties to hold out for the ¥6,307 wage level, while Baker, also in the name of SCAP, demanded that they support the ¥5,330 government wage offering. Just after midnight, the chairman of the Budget Committee burst into the office of Speaker Matsuoka to say that Mr. Frayne Baker had requested the presence at his residence of Prime Minister Yoshida and the leaders of the opposition parties to be given ESS's final stand on the wage standard issue by General Marquat. At about 1:00 A.M., Chief Cabinet Secretary Sato Eisaku and Transportation Minister Ozawa Saeki made the same request to members of the Budget Committee, warning that failure of the opposition leaders to appear at Baker's home would be interpreted to mean that they favored the government wage bill. Diet officials declined to go, saying that their contacts with GHQ were limited to those arranged through Government Section. The confusion resulting from the alternating hourly demands of Hoover and Baker could have been avoided if GHQ had provided them with a definitive statement on the wage issue.

General MacArthur could no longer stand aloof from the struggle. Later that morning, on the basis of a decision made by him, I informed Speaker Matsuoka that the Diet had full freedom to adopt whichever wage plan it desired. *Mainichi Shimbun* for 16 December reported: "The government decided yesterday to revise the new wage bill, setting the basic wage for government employees at ¥6,307 within the limit of the ¥26.5 billion wage budget. The decision came following Prime Minister Yoshida's call on General MacArthur. . . . Government Section Chief Whitney and Economic and Scientific Section Chief Marquat participated in the conversation." The Diet passed the new wage bill on 21 December, the supplementary budget on 22 December, and the nonconfidence resolution on 23 December, after which the House of Representatives was immediately dissolved in accordance with Articles 69 and 7 of the constitution, paving the way for a national election to fill all seats in the lower house.

It would not have been feasible in the situation described above for SCAP to follow the hands-off policy prescribed in NSC 13/2. Such were the mode and momentum of the SCAP regime at the end of three years that any perceptible change in occupation administration could have thrown into a dangerous state of confusion the highly disciplined but nervous Japanese population and seriously jeopardized the democratic gains of 1945–1948. This would have been no less true had MacArthur been chief of the State Department Policy Planning Staff and had George F. Kennan held the post of Supreme Commander for the Allied Powers. Hence a massive shift in United States policy or a fall-out in the revolutionary content of SCAP's activities was simply out of the question.

SCAP used two approaches to occupation reforms, which were not affected by NSC 13/2. If the reform was Washington-directed, like economic stabilization, SCAP instructed the Japanese government to enforce it. But if the reform was hatched up in GHQ, the Japanese government was at liberty to accept or reject it. Belonging to the first category was the local tax bill of 1950 and to the second category the 1947 political parties bill and 1949–1950 proposals to revise Japan's election law. A brief discussion of these three reform projects will suffice to show that SCAP's administration underwent no important change midway in the occupation.

Next to the NPSL wrangle, the local tax bill of 1950 caused SCAP more anguish than any other occupation reform, not excluding the making of the democratic constitution. Out of deference to Washington's opposition to further reform, SCAP informed the Department of the Army in July 1949 that, with the exception of the reformation of the local tax structure, no additional reform measures were contemplated. In September SCAP instructed Prime Minister Yoshida to draw up legislation incorporating the recommendations of the Shoup Mission to place local government finances on a firm footing.[23] Within six months the terms of the local tax bill had been hammered out between the Finance Ministry and ESS. But there was a caveat. The prime minister wrote SCAP that, with the inflexible rates proposed and the "June election for the House of Councillors looming," the local tax bill would have "hard going." Accordingly Mr. Yoshida suggested a more flexible rate which was, he said, "as economically sound as it is politically efficacious."[24] What he meant was that certain rates could be made flexible without loss of revenue. On hotels, for example, regardless of the rate, the hotel owner paid a lump sum fixed by the tax assessor. Nevertheless SCAP's reply to the prime minister's suggestion, dictated by ESS and concurred in by General Whitney, directed that the legislation be enacted "without modification."[25]

In more than one PPD "Diet Report" General MacArthur and General Whitney were flagged that the local tax bill was in trouble. By 1 May, one day before the Diet was to adjourn, it became clear that the House of Councillors would defeat the measure and that the Liberal party majority in the House of Representatives lacked the necessary two-thirds majority to override the upper house decision. Immediately after the Councillors voted down the bill by 102 to 73, the House of Representatives requested a joint committee of the Houses to try to save it. No progress was made. Forty minutes before midnight on 2 May the House of Councillors telephoned to Government Section an entirely new substitute proposal approved by all factions, with the explanation that there was still time for the joint committee to act thereon if quick clearance could be obtained. The proposal was immediately referred to General Whitney who found it unacceptable as violating the budgetary requirements imposed by the

Economic Stabilization Program. A few minutes later the seventh session of the National Diet was brought to a close.

At 9:00 the next evening Marquat, Whitney, Rizzo, and myself appeared before a wrathful Supreme Commander to explain what went wrong. After hearing first Marquat and then Whitney make the excuse that many Councillors anticipating the June election feared their constituents more than a united ESS and Government Section, he asked for my version of what went wrong. Instead of telling him the unvarnished truth of which he was already aware, that the uncompromising inflexibility of two of his staff sections was the root of the trouble, I told him that sooner or later his enlightened policy of encouraging the national assembly to become in fact as well as in theory the highest organ of state power made inevitable a negative vote in the Diet. With that the discussion ended. Now fully composed, General MacArthur turned to General Whitney and said: "Court, get out a press statement for the morning papers. Say that the House of Councillors was entirely within its right to reject the local tax bill, that in a democracy it sometimes takes a little longer to conduct the nation's business."

The next evening I escorted to General MacArthur's office two of Japan's most eminent elder statesmen, Shidehara Kijuro, Speaker of the House of Representatives, and Sato Naotake, President of the House of Councillors, both proficient in English. An hour later, going down in the elevator with them, I asked casually, to break the silence, "How was it?" assuming that the three dignitaries had had a serious but friendly discussion. In a grave and trembling voice Mr. Sato replied: "Dr. Williams, it was just awful." Unless one or both of the Japanese statesmen left a record of what transpired at that closed meeting, it will never be known what General MacArthur said to them.

A day or two went by and General Whitney asked me to assume responsibility for ensuring passage of the local tax bill at the next Diet session in July. In order to comply, I told him, I would need some bargaining leverage together with an ESS assistant qualified to deal with tax matters. As to bargaining power, he said that General MacArthur was willing to sacrifice an unlimited amount of revenue—¥10 billion, ¥20 billion, ¥30 billion—so long as the principle of sound local financing was established. "Of course," he added with a smile, "some revenue should be collected." Harold Moss, an ESS official on leave from the Internal Revenue Service, was named by General Marquat to work with me, and equally felicitous was Mr. Yoshida's selection of Sato Eisaku to complete the team. We worked together in perfect harmony. By large majorities both Houses of the Diet passed the amended bill and, according to Moss, without sacrificing any revenue. The authors of NSC 13/2 who advised SCAP to relax pressure steadily but unobtrusively on the Japanese government in connection with reforms could not have had a very clear notion of how things were done in occupied Japan.

Government Section's political parties bill and the Yoshida government's election law amendment bill, both of which originated in the winter of 1946–1947, were good examples of what SCAP meant when, concerning an early version of NSC 13/2, the Department of the Army was told that the general concept of leaving to the Japanese people a maximum of freedom in the administration of the internal affairs of their government had long guided the occupation. Sponsored by Pieter Roest, who in the eventful January 1946 debate with Milo Rowell had argued against "democratizing" Japan's election law by GHQ fiat, the political parties bill aimed at checking the "inordinate multiplication" of political parties and introducing an American-type printed ballot. The purpose of the Yoshida government's election law revision scheme was to replace the large-size constituency and plural ballot system, which had been adopted by the Diet in December 1945 on instructions from the Office of the Political Adviser, with the more practical prewar medium-size constituency and single ballot system. Consistent with its rule in such matters SCAP refused either to sponsor Roest's project, which the Japanese found unpalatable, or to kill the Japanese government's, which Roest and several other Government Section officials opposed.

The Government Section debate on the election law, it will be recalled, led to SCAP's fundamental decision not to demand correction of the minor imperfections of that statute, which SCAP deemed basically sound and democratic, because it reflected Japanese thought and would withstand nationalistic pressures that might later be placed on it. In March 1947 the Diet amended the law, which T. A. Bisson construed as SCAP intervention directly on behalf of the old parties by granting Yoshida permission to make the change.[26] If on the advice of Government Section officials GHQ had refused to clear the election law amendment proposal of the Yoshida government, would Bisson by the same logic have referred to direct SCAP intervention on behalf of the left-wing parties to thwart the will of the Diet majority? SCAP neither championed the cause of the Japanese conservatives nor sought to place the Japanese liberals at a disadvantage. SCAP merely undertook to ensure GHQ neutrality, as we shall see.

The Yoshida government informed Government Section in November 1946 of its intention to change the election law. In December Speaker Yamazaki explained to General MacArthur that the modified proportional representation system forced on the Japanese government a year earlier had been tried in Japan many years before and found wanting, that the medium-size constituency and single ballot system had best served the nation's electoral needs in the past. In January 1947 a group of top Government Section officials carefully examined the Home Ministry's draft bill for amending the election law, and recommended retention of the existing scheme of restricted plural voting and the large-size election district. Instead of following this suggestion of Roest, Bisson, Hussey, Wildes, and others, General Whitney informed Prime Minister Yoshida that the proposed election law amendment was a matter concerning which SCAP felt the National Diet should have sole discretion as it involved but a selection between two democratic alternatives. This was his way of counterbalancing the efforts of his subordinates to throw the weight of SCAP on the side of the opposition parties. After a violent struggle in the Diet the conservative parties reestablished the medium-size constituency and single vote system. When Katayama became prime minister three months later his Social Democratic party made no move to restore the large-size constituency and plural vote system.

Although General MacArthur refused to give his blessing to the political parties bill, he took no exception to Roest's recommendation that the Japanese government be encouraged to prepare the draft of a political parties law for submission to the Diet. The four major parties in the lower house took over from the Home Ministry the burden of drafting the necessary legislation. Whereas all occupation "must" legislation was drawn up by the government and submitted to the Diet bearing a GHQ imprint, bills originating in the Diet carried no GHQ label; they could be freely criticized by the Japanese.

Japanese opinion was distinctly unfavorable to limiting the number of political parties by law and to adopting the untried printed ballot. The leader of the minuscule Farmers party declared that the measure would wreck his party. Some politicians objected to the stipulation that a newly formed party could not be placed on the printed ballot until it had obtained the signatures of two percent (i. e., 800,000) of the 40 million votes cast in the last election. Their objection was not so much the enormity of the task as people going around asking for signatures, thus giving prospective opponents an opportunity to make publicity about themselves prior to the opening of the campaign. The most caustic criticism of the bill came from the venerated Saito Takao, who told a Democratic party caucus in September 1947 that since a political party, an association of kindred spirits, was guaranteed under the constitution, it was absolutely impossible to prohibit it by law. No country, he said, had ever enacted a political party law. Following this blast, the political parties ceased considering the measure.

If SCAP in this instance had not taken a neutral stance, Japan might have been saddled, at least for the duration of the occupation, with a printed ballot. One can imagine some of the problems that might have arisen with such an alien voting instrument. On the blank ballot, the voter enters the name of a single candidate, using for the purpose Japanese, Chinese, or Korean characters, Japanese phonetic symbols (*kana*), *romaji* (Roman letters), or braille. Would a printed ballot have carried the names of all candidates in these familiar language forms, or would *romaji* alone have been required? What about the positioning of parties and candidates on a printed ballot? Would the complications of a printed ballot have kept many voters from the polls? If the printed ballot were suited to Japanese use, it would have been tried sometime in the past. More congenial to the nature and outlook of the Japanese is the blank piece of paper on which, at the polls, they have only to write the name of the candidate to whom in one way or another they have become committed and can turn for favors. Had the printed ballot been adopted under occupation pressure it would probably have been the first democratic reform to go down the drain after the peace treaty became effective.

SCAP's 1946 decision to maintain intact Japan's home-grown election system came under severe attack in later years. During the national election campaign of January 1949, and again during Diet deliberations on the Public Office Election bill a year later, Japanese newspaper editors, encouraged by occupation officials, so bitterly assailed restrictive provisions of the election law as infringing constitutional rights that SCAP could not remain on the sidelines. General Whitney temporarily stilled the complaints by advising representatives of Japan's Election Commission (established in December 1947), the Attorney General's Office, and National Rural Police Headquarters at a meeting with CIE and Government Section officials to "construe all laws which you are called on to administer in the light of constitutional mandates . . . to insure preservation of individual liberties guaranteed by the Constitution." Following the meeting the Election Commission issued this ambiguous statement: "The Constitution guarantees the press freedom to express opinion [which] . . . imposes . . . the obligation to perform its functions as a responsible medium of public information . . . giving paramount importance to the promotion of the interests of the people." [27] In their effort to have the restrictive provisions set aside by a Potsdam Ordinance, thus avoiding the legislative route, Japanese newspapers charged that the election campaign was exceedingly dull and that the vote would be the lightest ever. Following a field trip with the chairman of the Election Commission, I informed General Whitney that voter interest appeared to be high and that the turnout on election day would be as great as usual. (Actually the turnout exceeded that of April 1947.) By chance, at the very time that Dan Imboden, CIE press officer, was quoting Voltaire and Jefferson on freedom of the press, the Japanese government had to suppress the distribution by *Akahata,* the Communist newspaper, of 100,000 sheets carrying the pictures of 117 Communist candidates in clear violation of regulations restricting posters. Had SCAP forgiven this violation as "freedom of the press," all Japanese and most American newspapermen would have attributed the large Communist party gains at the polls to GHQ interference with age-old election customs.

Responsible Japanese, including the big daily editors, believed in a degree of press regulation at election time. Retired Tokyo University professor Royama Masamichi advocated an election press code to prevent newspapers from going "wild." Democratic party leader Kosaka Zentaro observed that certain newspapers of doubtful character tinged with yellow journalism, affiliated with one particular party or faction, and opposed to democracy should be strictly supervised. Veteran Democrat Chiba Saburo favored freedom of the press but felt that there were many instances where some newspaper published slanderous reports of a vicious nature about individuals with a view to ruining their election chances. Restrict newspaper comment on individuals but permit criticism of political parties and platforms, he said. Socialist Suzuki Mosaburo and People's Democrat Ide Ichitaro were agreed that inasmuch as many small newspapers sprang up on the eve of an election campaign solely for election purposes, some delicate questions arose regarding unconditional freedom of the press. In the belief of the nine-member Election Commission, complete freedom in printing and distributing campaign literature would bring about utter chaos. *Akahata,* ignoring custom and common decency, would publish large extra daily and weekly editions in support of Communist candidates knowing that *Yomiuri, Asahi, Mainichi,* and scores of prefectural dailies would observe certain ethical standards required of genuine newspapers. Communism versus freedom of the press in a country where the people lack powers of discrimination was the dilemma yet to be resolved. Though a strong advocate of freedom of the press, *Yomiuri Shimbun* (31 March 1949) conceded that, since free electioneering could be carried to an extreme, it was necessary to have "some degree of restriction."

In April 1949 the cabinet approved and referred to Government Section for GHQ clearance the National Election Administration Commission

Establishment bill which had been drawn up by the Election Commission. Immediately the House of Representatives, which had not been consulted by the ex-Home Ministry election commissioners, unanimously adopted a resolution to set up a special committee to revise and consolidate all election laws. It being my responsibility to recommend approval or disapproval of the government bill, I advised General Whitney to clear it so as to force the lawmakers to make a choice.

Several days later, in response to a request of the House of Representatives Election Committee for my views on election restrictions, I offered the following suggestions:

1. Complete freedom of speech and press.
2. Complete freedom of voters to participate.
3. Unrestricted freedom of candidates to make house-to-house visits, distribute name cards, use megaphone squads, substitute speakers, telephones, loudspeakers, autos, boats, personal letters, handbills, and poster boards.
4. Limited but realistic restrictions on total individual campaign expenses, individual and party newspaper advertisements, and posters.
5. Absolute prohibition with severe penalties for vote buying, distributing gifts, serving food and alcoholic beverages, distributing false, libelous, and obscene literature and drawings, and employing minors for electioneering.
6. State support for posters and postcards, election bulletins, newspaper advertisements, radio appearances, transportation, competitive speech meetings, and get-out-the-vote publicity.

Having shelved the government bill, the House in December 1949 referred to Government Section for clearance the Public Office Election bill, an omnibus measure drafted by Diet members and concurred in by every political party and faction. On the basis of views expressed during the past eight months by university presidents, college professors, newspaper publishers, political commentators, election administration officials, politicians, and the general public (through a *Mainichi* poll), the Special Committee produced a comprehensive bill which, though not exactly democratic by American standards, was the most liberal election code in Japanese history and one that could be understood and supported by all classes of Japanese society. It aimed at eliminating wasteful duplication of effort, encouraging greater voter participation, and affording would-be candidates of limited means an opportunity to stand for election. The Japanese Press Association took exception to Article 148, which fell short of granting full editorial freedom to newspapers. Under pressure from the newspaper publishers, the House Committee changed the text to allow "unrestricted comment and criticism by legitimate news publications." This kind of pressure was preferable to GHQ fiat. As I told General Whitney in a 6 December 1949 memorandum:

GHQ interference with this strictly Diet-drafted measure might easily produce diametrically opposite results from those desired. . . . enforced changes would unquestionably destroy the complete agreement now existing between political parties. . . . . the original plan of the National Election Commission . . . to draft and introduce an omnibus election bill as a Cabinet-sponsored measure dissolved in the face of the Diet members' opposition to such unwarranted interference with the legislative branch. GHQ efforts to rewrite the Committee draft could have the effect of discrediting the bill's sponsors.

Though placed, as in January 1946 and again in January 1949, in the position of defending election regulations that limited criticism by the press and restricted candidates' use of such things as autos, posters, and newspaper advertising, General Whitney clung to the MacArthur principle of leaving to the Japanese a maximum of freedom in their internal affairs. The people themselves, not GHQ, he told members of the lower house Election Committee, "should correct any imperfections after the example of the Japanese Press Association which by vigorously attacking the proposed Article 148 of the bill . . . [had] forced the Committee to rewrite it." [28] It was in this manner that the Public Office Election bill, without any GHQ-directed refinements, became law in April 1950, at last ending attempts by GHQ officials to Americanize Japan's election system.

Such was the way SCAP carried on both before and after Washington decided that responsibility should be placed to a steadily increasing degree in the hands of the Japanese government.

12

The Diet Mission to the United States

Among the October 1948 recommendations of the National Security
Council to prepare Japan for eventual independence was one for a cultural
exchange program under which approved national leaders could study
and observe American techniques and the ways of American democracy.
Soon SCAP began processing Japanese participants under this program.
Organized into groups of five or less, fifty-five national leaders in education, health, agriculture, recreation, transportation, communications,
labor, diplomacy, commerce, justice, and public safety were ready by
mid-1949 to begin study tours of the United States, and during the remainder of the occupation hundreds of other Japanese men and women leaders
were thus exposed to the American scene.

Unique among the many planned undertakings comprising the exchange of persons program for Japan was Project No. 33: Diet Delegation.
This was a group of fourteen Diet members and Diet officials selected to
study and observe for fifty days in early 1950 the United States Congress
and the operation of its committee system, the organization and operation
of state legislatures, and the operation and functioning of political parties
for comparative study in connection with the development of Japan's
parliamentary system. From the standpoint of cost, publicity, high-level
interest, and amenities the Diet delegation surpassed every other Japanese reorientation project.

Such a study mission was first proposed in the summer of 1948 by the Diet
Committees for House Management. On 10 August, Speaker Matsuoka
and President Matsudaira addressed a joint letter to General Whitney
appealing for favorable consideration to dispatching a small group of Diet
members to the United States, and perhaps to Great Britain and France, in
order to obtain firsthand information on various parliamentary problems,
management of proceedings, and the spirit by which the lawmakers were
guided. According to *Yomiuri Shimbun* (29 June 1949), the letter reflected
the concern of many Diet members over

various difficulties in Diet management that previous Diets had not known. . . .
The Diet under the Meiji Constitution was called the "approving Diet" because its
only power was to approve bills presented by the government, but since the
sovereign power now resides with the people the Diet should control the govern-

ment by laws made by the Diet itself. From the 1st to the 5th session, however, this ideal was achieved only to the extent that the Diet decided pros and cons with respect to the bills presented usually by the government. . . . How is the Congress managed in the United States where the people have true sovereignty?

General Whitney was favorably disposed toward the request but thought it advisable to withhold his approval until United States funding became available and the Diet gained more experience under the new constitution.

The timely issuance of NSC 13/2 together with successful completion of five National Diet sessions improved the prospect of sending a Diet delegation to the United States. So much so that in the spring of 1949 Parliamentary and Political Division recommended to General Whitney that SCAP endorsement be given to the project as a means of promoting one of the major objectives of the occupation.

As the second year under the new Constitution draws to a close [the 20 April memorandum said] the National Diet is strongly desirous of sending . . . a delegation of 15 Representatives and Councillors, together with 6 officials of the Diet secretariat, to study the operation of the United States Congress and the Canadian Parliament and to investigate methods and management of political parties in both countries. . . . On returning home the delegates could do incalculable good by radio addresses, newspaper articles, press conferences, and lectures . . . contributing thereby to the political education of Japan and to better international understanding. . . . United States policy . . . permits Japanese to go abroad for . . . purposes that are "recognized as democratic and . . . will contribute towards the process of reorientation." . . . members would not engage in political or commercial activities. . . . eligibility will be restricted to committee chairmen and committee directors.

Concurring in the recommendation, General Whitney radioed the Department of the Army (DA) for its approval and asked that accommodations for the delegation be arranged and appointments scheduled on the basis of a study program to be furnished by SCAP. SCAP proposed that emphasis be placed on everyday, down-to-earth practices and procedures of Congress and its components. Textbook information and learned discourses were less important than opportunities to observe closely congressional machinery in operation together with willingness of congressmen and clerical staff to answer patiently specific questions that would be asked by Diet members. Questions could be expected about fixing the daily agenda, allocating speaking time, composing differences between parties, respecting minority rights, drafting and introducing bills, selecting committee members and chairmen, deciding length of session, filibustering, recruiting staff assistants, interrogating cabinet members and other government officials, enhancing the prestige of congressmen, fixing congressional pay and allowances, using library reference and research materials, keeping stenographic records, operating political party headquarters. Only by actually observing the Dietmen in action after their arrival in the United States were officials able to understand that the visitors from Japan would accomplish most in free, informal question and answer discussion with practicing legislators and practical politicians.

DA approved the proposal in principle, but questioned the psychological effect on the United States public and Congress of a large Japanese delegation. It was suggested that separate groups of approximately five Dietmen would not arouse questions concerning expense. SCAP replied that in the interest of economy and to keep the size of the escort to a minimum, it was impractical to send groups of five. Therefore he proposed sending one group of fourteen with two DA civilians. DA not only agreed but suggested a "long" newsreel to cover the Dietmen's visit as well as a chartered plane for travel in the United States. To ensure cooperation by United States authorities, DA advised that a personal message from General MacArthur to various officials who were to receive the members of the Diet (Majority Leader of the Senate, Speaker of the House, state governors, presiding officers of state legislatures to be visited, mayor of New York City, and the United Nations secretary general) would be of great value. SCAP's compliance with the request set the stage for the delegation to study firsthand the United States Congress, the Canadian Parliament, and the legislatures of South Carolina, Massachusetts, and New York.

In December 1949, GHQ issued orders for two Government Section officials, myself and Makoto Matsukata, and the following fourteen Japanese nationals: Representatives Yamazaki Takeshi, Iwamoto Nobuyuki, Asanuma Inejiro, Imamura Chusuke, Shiikuma Saburo, and Matsumoto Takizo; Councillors Sakurauchi Tatsuro, Onogi Hidejiro, Hatano Kanae, and Takada Hiroshi; Oike Makoto and Kondo Hideaki, secretaries general, respectively, of the lower and upper house; Kanamori Tokujiro, director of the National Diet Library; and Shima Seiichi, chief of the House of Representatives Liaison Section. The delegation left for the United States in mid-January 1950.

The Japanese themselves picked the fourteen members of the delegation within the framework of GHQ's guidelines. When *Akahata,* the Communist party organ, objected that it was improper to exclude members of a specific political party, key political leaders were informed of Washington's dictum that foreign nationals whose friendship and regard were questionable should not be permitted to visit the United States, at its expense, in any guise. In line with a suggestion made by Senator

H. Alexander Smith on the occasion of his visit to Japan in October 1949, an informal invitation was extended to Speaker Shidehara and President Matsudaira—and, on the sudden death of the latter, to his successor, Sato Naotake—to head the mission, but they declined for reasons of age, health, and the pressures of office. Thus, while no single member of the Diet delegation as finally constituted was selected on the recommendation of GHQ, GHQ made the political parties responsible for designating only individuals qualified to represent the new Japan.

The ten Diet members in the group—six Representatives and four Councillors—were top drawer among the 716 members of the two Houses. Two were in their early sixties (Yamazaki and Sakurauchi), seven were between fifty and fifty-four, and one was forty-eight (Matsumoto). The group included four Democratic-Liberals (Yamazaki, Iwamoto, Imamura, Onogi), two Democrats (Shiikuma and Sakurauchi), two Socialists (Asanuma and Hatano), one People's Democrat (Matsumoto), and one Green Breeze Society member (Takada). Only three had been prewar members of the House of Representatives, but they carried no taint of militant nationalism or aggression. All were college graduates. Two had been postwar cabinet ministers (Iwamoto and Hatano). Four were or had been Diet committee chairmen or directors (Asanuma, Imamura, Sakurauchi, Takada), three parliamentary vice-ministers (Yamazaki, Shiikuma, Matsumoto), three college professors (Imamura, Matsumoto, Hatano), and five central committee members of their respective political parties (Yamazaki, Imamura, Asanuma, Sakurauchi, Iwamoto). Yamazaki was Speaker of the lower house when the new constitution was adopted, and Iwamoto was Vice-Speaker. Onogi was the only millionaire and Matsumoto the only one who spoke English.

The success of the mission would be due in no small measure to the individual contributions of Yamazaki and Matsumoto. A thoroughly seasoned politician from Ibaragi prefecture, the white-thatched Yamazaki, an early MacArthur favorite, would charm his American audiences by telling them what they wanted most to hear. Interpreting for Yamazaki, the affable Matsumoto, longtime prewar resident of Fresno, California, graduate of the Harvard School of Business, and master of the American idiom, would put the best possible construction on Yamazaki's statements, and on those of his other colleagues, omitting or rephrasing what he considered inappropriate.

Uninstructed by SCAP as to what they should say or do in the United States, the group prepared the following statement for their guidance abroad:

Our object is to inspect and study Congress and the political parties in order to contribute to the future development of the Japanese Diet. . . . there is nothing whatever of a political character to our visit. We come not as politicians but as a study group.

Certain difficult problems have arisen in the Diet under the new Constitution that were unknown under the old system. Although we have been favored with the helpful advice of SCAP officials, we deem it essential that Diet members themselves study the fundamental features of the Congressional system.

The function of the three members of the Diet secretariat—Oike, Kondo, and Shima—was to further the aims of the mission during its travels in the United States and on its return to Japan. The fourth non-Diet member, Dr. Kanamori, director of the recently established National Diet Library, was, like Yamazaki, a figure of national repute. A former chief of the Cabinet Legal Bureau and the state minister who guided through the Imperial Diet in 1946 the bill for revising the constitution, his task was to gather information and ideas from directors of relevant public and private libraries in the United States.

The Japanese public was put on notice that the Diet delegation was an out-of-the-ordinary project. Shortly before the party left Japan the Armed Forces Radio Station in Tokyo twice broadcast the recording of a fifteen-minute interview on SCAP's reasons for sending a group of Japanese politicians to the United States. Of the many cultural exchange projects set up by SCAP, only the members of this one were given a personal send-off by General MacArthur. On this occasion, Democrat Shiikuma thrust an autograph book before Japan's proconsul and commanded him to "sign, sign," an order with which the surprised Supreme Commander complied—with a grin. "You will see both good and bad in the United States," General MacArthur told them, "but I can assure you that you will be well received."

Owing to pressure generated by a very enterprising local chamber of commerce, the first stop of the delegation was at Honolulu. During their thirty-hour stay there the members showed up at a chamber of commerce luncheon, called on the mayor and the acting governor, visited the 442nd Battalion Memorial Hall and the Punchbowl Cemetery, and attended a cocktail party at the Pearl Harbor residence of Admiral Arthur Radford, Pacific Fleet Commander. The enthusiastic welcome given them in Hawaii indicated that the new democratic Japan was not held responsible for the consequences of the surprise attack on Pearl Harbor eight years before.

At San Francisco the show got on the road. There a DA contingent composed of Col. George P. Lynch, officer in charge, Lt. Col. Robert V. Shinn, publicity director, Capt. C. B. Baker, fiscal agent, and Frank Vail, newsreel cameraman, joined the mission, and Maj. Gen. Carter B. Magruder, deputy to Army Assistant Secretary Tracy S. Voorhees, was on hand to deal with any unforeseen occurrence. Three hours after arriving the Dietmen assembled at the St. Francis Hotel for their first press conference. Their answers to pointed questions on such subjects as the menace of the Japanese Communists, Red China's threat to Formosa, early withdrawal of the occupation forces, balancing Japan's budget, and writing a peace treaty were satisfactory. It was noteworthy that, whereas the National Security Council feared a possible Communist takeover in Japan, Mr. Yamazaki told the San Francisco newsmen that as yet communism offered no threat to his country. General Magruder, who had worried lest the new breed of Japanese politicians might be unequal to the merciless interrogation by cynical American reporters, radioed General Whitney to put his mind at rest regarding the ability of the Dietmen to handle themselves under crossfire of questions from an unfamiliar press; at San Franciso, he said, they gave an impressive performance that reflected great credit on the occupation. The next day a lively discussion on local government was held in the office of San Francisco's mayor, after which a scholarly but dry lecture on federal and state government relations was delivered by a Stanford University professor.

At Sacramento the sympathetic and warmhearted Governor Earl Warren made a hit with the group. Patiently answering one question after another about legislative processes, budgets, taxes, and other subjects asked by the Japanese lawmakers through Representative Matsumoto, he turned aside their apologies for taking so much of his valuable time, assuring them that they could question him as long as they wanted. He confessed to enjoying the occasion and thanked the group for coming to his state. The war was over, he said, and Americans wanted to be at peace.

After three strenuous days in San Francisco and Sacramento the visitors relaxed for three days, mingling briefly with a few nondescript movie colony people in Beverly Hills and then spending a leisurely weekend in New Orleans before landing at Columbia, South Carolina, on their seventh day in the United States.

For the next five days in Columbia, local and state government officials, state senators and assemblymen, university leaders, and private citizens extended themselves to oblige the grateful and hardworking Japanese. Only one favor was refused them. When Kyoto silk tycoon Onogi expressed a desire to inspect a local textile plant, former Secretary of State James F. Byrnes, who had driven down from Spartanburg to greet the visitors, amiably demurred, citing a prewar rejection by Japanese textile manufacturers of a similar request made by him on a visit to Japan. Roaring with laughter, Mr. Onogi conceded that a textile expert, by simply walking through a mill, could easily detect and make mental note of the slightest improvement in conventional production techniques. Of course, to the battery of Pentagon and local reporters and cameramen trailing the delegation, every gathering, engagement, interview, tea, luncheon, and banquet was grist for the news media in a few South Carolina cities and in every city of Japan. I wrote Frank Rizzo on 23 January:

> We are ten days out but it seems like two or three, so fast and furiously are we being put through the paces. . . .
>
> Yesterday I got your message requesting me to radio daily reports. So far I have filed two reports. . . . When the press representative from DA's New York Field Office objected to my sending radiograms per your instructions, I asked Colonel Lynch if I should obey SCAP or would he assume responsibility for countermanding SCAP's request to me. He advised me to obey SCAP's order. . . .
>
> So far there has been no serious mishap. Most members, confused by the menu, ordered every item on it for breakfast the first morning at the St. Francis Hotel. Several of them found St. Francis Hotel keys in their pockets when we reached Los Angeles. At the hotel in New Orleans Mr. Sakurauchi fell asleep in the *benjo* (toilet), causing a forty-five minute holdup of the boat ride on the Mississippi. But the members are all doing remarkably well.

At the end of the first day in Columbia I dispatched the first of many radio messages to General Whitney on the doings of the delegation. In addition to describing the warm reception they received in South Carolina, I mentioned Matsumoto's assertion to 175 Columbia Rotarians that Japan's political reformation was on the order of Magna Carta, the French Revolution, and American Independence, and Yamazaki's observation before 150 Civitans that the Diet operated on the same principles as the United States Congress and that General MacArthur "excels in statesmanship, kindness, and understanding." Where Lieutenant Colonel Shinn in his messages to GHQ's Public Information Office focused on South Carolina dignitaries and South Carolina institutions, I tried to emphasize the activities and reactions of the Japanese. Regarding South Carolina hospitality, I cited the free cinema tickets furnished the members, their invitation to a square dance, their fascination with parking meters, and their continued bafflement by restaurant menus.[1]

My second message from Columbia noted the visiting Councillors being introduced from the rostrum of the Senate chamber standing beneath a life-sized painting of John C. Calhoun, and Representative Yamazaki throughout a two-hour session of the Assembly sitting on the rostrum beside the Speaker. I pointed out that the Dietmen were impressed by the

South Carolina legislators' unrestricted and spontaneous debate, decorum, respectful attention, avoidance of catcalls and violence, and membership in the single Democratic party. Then I made reference to the three-column photo of the Japanese on the front page of the Greenville, South Carolina, *News,* along with a feature article on, among other things, Yamazaki's statement that Communism was making "no great progress in Japan," and Matsumoto's prediction that "within five years Japan will be a democratic nation to marvel at."

By the time I had made my fifth report to General Whitney, the Diet delegation's thoughts were turning to Boston, the next stop.

A single minor incident at Boston saved the mission from being little more than a grand tour, ballyhooed all over Japan but scarcely noticed in the United States outside the few cities visited. Thanks to the backfiring of a cheap publicity stunt concocted by demagogic members of the Boston City Council, an aroused American public, by rushing to the defense of the embarrassed and discomfited Japanese, convinced a dubious White House and Congress that, to quote from an editorial appearing in the *San Francisco Chronicle* less than two weeks before (18 January), "we mean to engage in no adventurous folly that would permit Japan to be taken over into the Moscow camp," that "our present job in Japan . . . [is] to develop the great middle lying between the extremes of Communism . . . and reaction," and that "both self-interest and mutual interest must be taken into account by the United States as it approaches the question of writing a Japanese peace treaty." In short, let the United States enter into a partnership with the new Japan as symbolized by the dignified and unpretentious Diet delegation.

The facts in the case, as one newspaper said, were almost too silly to be believed. A group of ten members of the Diet and four of its secretariat were in Boston on a guided tour authorized by Congress and based, as the escort stated, on Gen. Douglas MacArthur's desire that the legislators should have a chance to see at first hand the inside workings of the democratic process. But a member of Boston's City Council had the happy inspiration that the Japanese were probably here taking pictures of fortresses and trying to learn all they could about the A-bomb. His motion to bar them from the Council room carried eleven to eight.

The Associated Press account of the incident was carried in lengthy stories in the American press. A great New York daily quipped that Massachusetts State officials welcomed the Japanese with open arms and allowed them to take pictures of the Sacred Cod, Paul Revere's Horse,

and other "secret installations." GHQ's press release in Japan noted that
while Boston's newspapers devoted headlines and space to the action,
they also devoted big headlines and far more space to the criticism of the
Council's action, the subsequent honors accorded the visitors by the
governor and the state legislature, and other activities engaged in by the
Dietmen.

My 31 January message on the subject to General Whitney contained
these observations:

Most cordial meeting with Mayor Hynes, City Hall, at two P.M. Replying to
mayor's question, "How do you like General MacArthur?" Sakurauchi said,
"Hundreds of children in neighborhood of Embassy bow to the general several
times each day, and the general always bows back."

First unfortunate incident occurred 3:30 P.M. at City Hall when delegation went
upstairs per arrangement made with Council president two weeks ago to attend
session of City Council. Since one councilman caused fifteen-minute embarrassing
delay objecting to Japanese attendance, DA request was cancelled and delegation
left City Hall after receiving profuse apologies from Mayor Hynes. Many photog-
raphers and reporters surrounded Dietmen on way out. Accompanying PIO immediately released the following statement: "The Department of the Army wishes
to emphasize that the present mission . . . is based on General MacArthur's desire
that these legislators . . . see at firsthand the inside workings of democratic
processes. The establishment of the new Japan with a government modeled to a
large extent on our own is . . . insurance for a lasting peace in that part of the world
which is so . . . important to our country." Dietmen unperturbed by incident
saying this apparently falls under heading of the bad side of United States which
General MacArthur instructed them to study.

My 1 February message contained these items:

Every edition of Boston papers yesterday gave top front page headlines to action
of Boston City Council on January 30. . . . Council . . . taking severe drub-
bing. . . . Christian Science Monitor article says: "The reception on Beacon Hill
took on international significance in the light of the snub." Governor Dever
reception of delegation . . . went out over nationwide radio hookup. . . . In
replying Yamazaki . . . avoided mention of Council's rudeness . . . said for first
time on tour that Japan has become a democratic nation . . . that delegation
members represent new Japanese democracy. . . .statement made deep impression on big crowd in Governor's office. . . . Dietmen . . . cheered by visitors all
walks of life coming to Bellevue Hotel to apologize for Council's action.

And the next day I radioed:

Ordinary front page headlines this date as follows: "Incident Makes City Laughing
Stock" . . . "Abashed Boston Warmer Host." . . . *Herald* editorial says: "Boston
might ask General MacArthur for permission to send eleven of its Councilmen for
indoctrination in Japan." . . . Yamazaki and SCAP representative honored by
sitting on rostrum beside Senate president throughout session. Delegation oc-

cupied distinguished visitors gallery underneath oil painting of Calvin Coolidge and immediately above Captain Parker's musket which fired shot heard round the world. . . .numerous invitations [including one from Mrs. Theodore Roosevelt, Jr.] to private dinners.

Other highlights of the Boston visit included a meeting with Harvard President Conant, a chamber of commerce luncheon at which Red Sox stars Cronin, Dowd, Pesky, and McDermott autographed baseballs for the entire delegation, and a belated newspaper headline, "Jap Communists Hail Hub Council," based on a Tokyo UP quotation from *Akahata*. Needless to say, Paul Revere's ride and Bunker Hill came to life. One paper commented that the Dietmen found themselves lifted from the obscurity of a routine Cook's Tour to that of full-blown national celebrities.

While New York state and local officials at Albany, not unmindful of the recent Boston City Council gaffe, went all out to be neighborly and kind to the visitors from Japan, the Dietmen themselves continued their relentless study of the techniques and spirit of American democracy. They displayed a keen interest in local affairs and asked searching questions. Like the legislators of South Carolina and Massachusetts, New York's senators and assemblymen warmly welcomed the Japanese and gave them special floor privileges. One high court official remarked that they possessed a degree of skill in cross-examining that would have been exemplary anywhere. A common question asked by friendly New Yorkers was: "When will SCAP permit the Diet to start functioning?" At the chamber of commerce luncheon Dietman Asanuma, a Socialist, citing the American penchant for using superlatives, claimed for Japan the best constitution in the world. Representative Matsumoto on the same occasion noted that Americans failed to realize the vast social transformation Japan had undergone under General MacArthur. The Dietmen were at a loss to explain why they were getting better press coverage in the United States than in Japan. Though DA's information officer and photographer were supplying four thousand words of copy and numerous pictures to GHQ each day, Albany papers were more generous with their space than were Tokyo's *Asahi*, *Mainichi*, and *Yomiuri*, copies of which were mailed to the Dietmen by SCAP's Government Section.

In New York City the situation was different. To be sure, the Japanese participated in the usual things—a press interview, discussions with New York's mayor and the United Nations secretary general, a visit to the Statue of Liberty, an evening in the Oyster Bay home of Mrs. Theodore Roosevelt, Jr., a stop at the *Reader's Digest* plant at Pleasantville, a

Bankers Club luncheon, sukiyaki dinners at Miyako's, the view from the top of the Empire State Building, church invitations from Francis Cardinal Spellman and John Foster Dulles—but they were confronted for the first time on the tour with American business tycoons. Former Florida governor David Sholtz hosted a party for them in his Savoy Plaza apartment. Among those present were, in addition to the acting mayor and a federal judge, Vice-President A. E. Schumacker of Chase National Bank, President George Hall of Union Carbide, and Vice-President Frank Goedeke, Jr., of International Steamship Lines. Autographed photos of General MacArthur and Prime Minister Yoshida were prominently displayed on the mantle.

To climax their tour the delegation spent a busy two-week round of activities in Washington, D.C., which was interrupted to permit an overnight trip to Ottawa, Canada. They were officially received by Secretary of Defense Louis Johnson, Army Secretary Gordon Gray, Army Assistant Secretary Tracy S. Voorhees, Secretary of Agriculture Charles F. Brannan, and Secretary of State Dean Acheson. Vice-President Alben Barkley invited them to the Senate floor as senators stood and applauded. Majority Leader Scott Lucas's address of welcome was seconded by nine other senators. Senate Secretary Leslie Biffle's luncheon for the party was sponsored by the Senate Foreign Relations Committee. At a round table conference lasting all afternoon, ten senators patiently answered their pointed questions on the upper chamber's modus operandi. House Speaker Sam Rayburn received them as friends not enemy nationals, and the House membership gave them a standing ovation. The Diet delegation witnessed the House in session, attended hearings of the Ways and Means and Armed Services Committees, and took part in a three-hour conference with eight members who gave detailed answers to questions on procedures and practices. Mr. Voorhees radioed SCAP that the visit was proving most successful.

The delegation spent the better part of two days in the Library of Congress discussing with officials there the composition and operation of Congress, how a bill became a law, and the research services furnished to congressmen. Dr. Kanamori, director of the National Diet Library, devoted most of his Washington stay to studying the makeup and functions of the Library of Congress.

Being particularly interested in United States political parties, the Japanese made special visits to the national headquarters of the two major parties. The principal subjects discussed were permanent party organization, functions, membership, fund raising, limitations on campaign expenditures, and the role of women. They offered no resistance to suggestions that they pose for pictures with likenesses of the Democratic donkey and the Republican elephant.[2]

On 23 February the delegation, minus the DA contingent, broke away for a two-day study of the Canadian parliamentary system. Ottawa hospitality matched that of Washington. A luncheon was given by Secretary of State for External Affairs Lester B. Pearson, a dinner by Minister of Fisheries R. W. Mayhew, a reception by Speaker of the House Ross MacDonald, and both Houses of Parliament extended a cordial welcome. In each instance expressions of goodwill were exchanged, with Yamazaki speaking tactfully, as usual, and Matsumoto interpreting at his diplomatic best. At the interview by top reporters of the Canadian press the Japanese legislators, no longer frightened by the conference method of discussion, were in a happy and confident mood. For example, to a question as to whether General MacArthur had instructed them, "as he is said to have done," to exercise care in what they said and did, Matsumoto replied with some heat that General MacArthur had told them to look for both the good and the bad in the United States and Canada and to feel entirely free to speak to any and everyone, ask whatever questions they desired, and draw their own conclusions about everything.

In his final report to the Under Secretary of the Army on the visit of the Diet delegation, Colonel Lynch said that the project undoubtedly did much to awaken the American people to their responsibilities in Japan and to develop a friendlier and more cooperative feeling toward her people. He said further that the future activities of individual members of the delegation and their ability to guide the Japanese people toward a stable democracy would measure the extent to which the mission of the project was successfully accomplished.[3] The effect the participants had on the Japanese public was impossible to measure, just as it was impossible to ascertain what effect the tour had on the participants. The pro-capitalist majority of the delegation were no doubt duly impressed and favorably influenced by the open and sincere welcome they received; but who was to say whether or not the two Socialist members might have had their suspicions confirmed, that the American system was the very antithesis of their notion of the ideal society?

Concerning the reaction of the Japanese to the widespread publicity about the tour of their countrymen, the skeptical ones may very well have looked on the official receptions in the state capitals and Washington as stage-managed affairs without real significance. But the most cynical must have been moved by the spontaneous response of the American people to what happened in Boston. *Nippon Times* for 28 February 1950 credited the American treatment of the Dietmen with "giving the Japanese people a spiritual boost . . . toward completing their national reconstruction. . . . the picture of the militaristic Japanese of former days will contrast sharply with the Japanese as they are now with their new vigor and new resolve to win a place among the friendly and democratic nations of the world."

Whatever the effect of the publicity, the returning Dietmen were treated as conquering heroes entitled to be paraded up and down the main streets of their country's cities and towns. General MacArthur told them that the opportunity their trip afforded the American people to assess Japan's new leadership had provided immeasurable encouragement to the many who saw in new Japan a potential bastion of liberty and peace for the free world. In a lower key, *Nippon Times,* after complimenting the members for accomplishing their mission in a thoroughly creditable manner reminded them that they faced an equally important task to relay faithfully to the Japanese people the valuable lessons they had learned during their tour.

This task the Dietmen willingly undertook with relish and gusto. They enjoyed showing off their knowledge of the American method of serving a meal. Their conduct was as exemplary in every way as it had been during the American tour. Each member received hundreds of invitations throughout Japan to address farm and labor unions, chambers of commerce, civic clubs, and groups of prefectural officials; some delivered as many as seven speeches a day. Eight newsreels covering the trip ran for weeks in two thousand Japanese theaters. Thus, what began as a technical study of American legislative practices ended as an exercise in democracy and international goodwill.

But an effort, however ineffective and little noticed, was made to apply a number of American legislative practices to the operation of the National Diet. The delegation formally recommended to House of Representatives Speaker Shidehara that these four reforms be realized at once:

1. Initiation of all legislation by Diet members through their respective political parties, except bills based on the constitution or other laws. (This practice proved to be unsuccessful, and was soon dropped.)

2. Consolidation and replenishment of the National Diet Library and the Legislative Research and Reference Bureau.

3. Alteration of the Diet chambers to reflect the sovereignty of the people.

4. Classification of the Diet secretariats under the special civil service, "as heretofore."

Other recommended reforms were:

1. Punctuality in attending committee meetings and plenary sessions.

2. Better utilization of public hearings "for determining the people's will."

3. Restriction of urgent interpellations at plenary sessions to "pertinent questions."

4. Authorization for committee qualified specialists to ask appropriate questions on matters under deliberation.

5. Provision for a democratic seating arrangement in committee meetings to eliminate any impression that members were placed in an inferior position vis-á-vis government delegates.

6. Approval only of petitions recognized as being in harmony with national policy.

7. Prevention of inspections by members outside the Diet during a session except in extraordinary cases.

8. Use of the gavel by the Speaker and committee chairmen to restore order.

9. Maintenance at all times of a clean chamber, "inside and outside."

10. More attention to amenities in the Diet dining room.

Clearly the foregoing recommendations were limited to technical and procedural matters. The Dietmen were unable to agree on such basic reforms as outlawing violence, relaxing party discipline, and encouraging free debate, Western usages that could not be easily—or, for that matter necessarily beneficially—transplanted to the Orient. In any event, the United States government got a good return on the $37,000 that DA originally earmarked for this project.

13

Japanese Politics and Politicians

On the occasion of his becoming Speaker of the House of Representatives, six years after the occupation ended, long-time politician Hoshijima Niro wrote me the glad tidings. Received in audience by Emperor Hirohito, he was asked whether it was advisable for the government party to monopolize the key parliamentary posts of Speaker, Vice-Speaker, and committee chairmen. Mr. Hoshijima laid blame for the practice at my feet. The chief of SCAP's Parliamentary and Political Division advised, he told His Majesty, that all these positions should be held by members of the majority party.[1] That the emperor regarded the division of Diet posts as an ethical matter revealed that representative government in Japan functioned in a totally different atmosphere from that of the United Kingdom and the United States. Equally instructive was the excuse used by Mr. Hoshijima to avoid having to justify majority rule under Japan's moral code.

Actually, the leadership of the dominant Liberal Democratic party did not need a suggestion from an outsider as an alibi for controlling all key positions in the legislature; Japan's seasoned politicians know the meaning of power. I mention the Hoshijima letter to indicate my friendly relationship with the Japanese political community. That relationship gave me a rare opportunity to explore an area that Japanese scholars shun like the plague. In exploring the area, I stumbled on some aspects of Japanese politics that have not found their way into print, aspects with certain implications for the functioning and success of parliamentary government. It is to a few of these sidelights that this chapter is addressed.

Of the six presiding officers of the Diet with whom I had extensive official contacts—House of Representatives Speakers Yamazaki, Matsuoka, Shidehara, and Hayashi Joji and House of Councillors Presidents Matsudaira and Sato—Matsudaira was the most intriguing. A relic of the feudal past, he was very much a part of the living present. Born in 1877, he had the bearing of a great daimyo or a shogun. His father, Matsudaira Katamori, was the last Lord of Aizu. The brother of a count and a viscount and married to a daughter of the last feudal lord of the Saga Clan, Matsudaira Tsuneo elected to be a commoner. But his daughter Setsuko married Prince Chichibu, the emperor's oldest brother, and a son married into the family of Prince Tokugawa, last President of the House of Peers. Entering the foreign service in 1902 after graduating from Tokyo Imperial University, he became in 1924 Ambassador to the United States and in 1929 Ambassador to Great Britain, where he served concurrently as delegate to the London Naval Conference, the Geneva Disarmament Conference, and the London Monetary and Economic Conference. He held the post of Imperial Household Minister from 1936 to 1945, resigning to accept responsibility for destruction by American bombs of part of the Imperial palace. According to a 1945 War Department Intelligence document, this distinguished Japanese statesman was considered to be "very sane, wise, experienced, and absolutely opposed to militarists . . . possessed of fine character . . . friendly attitude toward United States."[2]

No one could conduct official business with Mr. Matsudaira without being greatly impressed. Eminently fair, but firm, and unaffectedly cordial, he understood what the occupation was all about and never hesitated to use the authority of his office to further its aims. Political factions in the House of Councillors were loath to challenge his decisions. He never felt the need to call on General MacArthur to demonstrate his importance or to enhance his prestige. But when General MacArthur sought a Japanese political figure to represent him at a 1949 conference in Geneva, he decided on President Matsudaira, who was noticeably moved by the gesture, but had to decline the invitation for reasons of health. For the same reason he declined SCAP's invitation to him to head the Diet mission to the United States.

It struck me as being strange that of all the top Japanese officials, politicians, and scholars who had been jailed, expelled from the Diet, dismissed from university positions, or otherwise persecuted for opposing the government's policy of militant aggression in years gone by that Mr. Matsudaira alone should have gone scot-free. Why was that? I asked Inagawa Jiro, who headed the Diet Liaison Section in the House of Councillors. The explanation, he said, lay in the fact that Matsudaira's father, the Lord of Aizu, had held out against the abolition of the shogunate in 1868 until his forces were routed by those of the emperor. The result was that Lord Matsudaira, in yielding to the superior strength of the new Choshu-Satsuma dispensation, had established a precedent for opposing the Imperial order, which he and his descendents had since been free to follow. Consequently Matsudaira Tsuneo, while opposing the policy of the military aggressors, was able to retain the post of Imperial Household Minister. There will be no more like him.

No Japanese do I remember with greater affection or hold in higher esteem than Yamazaki Takeshi, the veteran politician from Ibaragi prefecture. His name appears more frequently in these pages than that of any other of his countrymen. From the summer of 1946 to the spring of 1947, when he was Speaker of the House of Representatives, he gave me the full benefit of his long parliamentary experience, sound judgment, and perfect understanding of the postwar international situation. At a dinner party during that period he made me the present of an artistic, signed specimen of his calligraphic skill, which translates, truthfully: "I am not inferior to anyone in the matter of sincerity." In the fall of 1948, I consulted closely with him on what came to be known as the "Yamazaki Affair," an unsuccessful maneuver by Government Section to have him succeed Ashida Hitoshi as prime minister. He teamed with Matsumoto Takizo to make an outstanding success of the Diet mission to the United States in 1950. While I cannot cite any particularly good turns I did for him, I am vividly aware of a most important favor he did for me. It was to affix his seal to an unofficial list of Diet reforms I submitted to him in November 1946 and thus assume personal responsibility for having them incorporated in the Diet Law bill, which a special committee of the lower house was drafting.

Regarding Diet reform, I had taken the unconventional position in Government Section that the House of Representatives instead of the cabinet should draft and sponsor the new Diet Law bill. This would be the best possible evidence, I argued, of that body's genuine desire to strengthen itself. But was the lower house eager to assume that responsibility? Suppose Speaker Yamazaki had balked at signing my paper. Only a few months before, Yamazaki's predecessor, Speaker Higai, had adamantly opposed taking steps suggested by Government Section's Guy Swope to invigorate the legislature; and shortly thereafter Ashida Hitoshi, an influential member, had told me that a strong Diet would attract high government officials to it and thus weaken the executive branch. These former government officials preferred a Diet Law bill drafted by the Cabinet Legal Bureau. I was, therefore, more than a little relieved when Speaker Yamazaki made no production whatever of putting his seal on my paper, which listed eleven new provisions for inclusion in the projected Diet Law; in fact, he seemed to welcome the opportunity. (The provisions are listed elsewhere in this book.) Yamazaki's action left no doubt that the professional politicians were now in the saddle and welcomed my paper as the GHQ greenlight they had been hoping for. Henceforth, the influence of the bureaucratic elements in the House diminished. I was able to assure General Whitney and Colonel Kades that the leading politicians would take the necessary steps to make the Diet the "highest organ of state power."

In July 1951, the PPD staff wrote a brief message to President Sato of the House of Councillors to congratulate him and his companions on their escape from serious injury in the fall of their auto over a fifty-foot cliff in Nagano prefecture. He appreciated the gesture.

Slender and frail, Sato Naotake, a graduate of the Tokyo Higher Commercial School, entered the Foreign Service in 1905. Fluent in English and French, he served between 1921 and 1945 as Counselor of Embassy in France, Minister to Poland, Ambassador to Belgium, Ambassador to France, Japanese Foreign Minister, and Ambassador to the USSR. In 1947, he was elected to the House of Councillors from Aomori prefecture, and in 1949, on the death of Mr. Matsudaira, he was unanimously elected President of that chamber. His prewar American diplomatic acquaintances rated him as extremely intelligent, liberal, and courageous enough to express opinions that he knew to be unpopular. Hugh Wilson, American Minister to Switzerland, said of him in 1937: "He is one of those rare Japanese able to animate Westerners with a feeling of affectionate confidence. He has the most intimate conviction of the necessity for harmonious cooperation between Japan and other nations." Sato was known to regard Japan's attack on Pearl Harbor as a "regrettable mistake," which would "end disastrously for Japan." [3] My association with him, beginning in 1947, bore out these prewar estimates of his character and outlook. Our friendship became more than casual as a result of the Hagiwara incident in October 1947.

Hagiwara Toru, director of the Foreign Office Treaty Bureau, was dismissed by the Katayama government for having allegedly told Sato's House of Councillors Foreign Affairs Committee that Japan had not been conquered. According to Associated Press Bureau chief Russell Brines's account of the firing in *Pacific Stars and Stripes* for 27 October, the dismissal "followed a request by SCAP headquarters for an explanation of [his] remarks but without headquarters pressure for his removal, informants [Whitney and Kades] said. . . . Informants expressed the belief that the government was making Hagiwara the 'scapegoat' for an adverse international reaction to his remarks." Government Section leaders based their request for an explanation of Hagiwara's remarks on an article that appeared in *Stars and Stripes* on 23 October, under the following headline: "JAPAN UNBEATEN, DESERVES TREATY ROLE," DIET TOLD: FOREIGN OFFICE OFFICIAL URGES USE OF DIPLOMACY IN GAINING PEACE AIMS. The purport of the article was, first, that the Japanese did not admit that they had surrendered unconditionally, second, that the Japanese were trying to maintain the fiction that they had never been defeated, and third, that the Japanese intended to play the Allies against each other in order to get the best possible terms at the peace table.

Hagiwara's dismissal by the Japanese government to placate GHQ and the Allied world was none of my business, but the nature of his testimony in the Diet was. Certain in my own mind that the chairman of the House of Councillors Foreign Affairs Committee would not permit a government official to make remarks likely to hurt Japan at a future peace conference, I immediately got in touch with Mr. Sato. Being, of course, already familiar with the *Stars and Stripes* story, he said: "Why, Hagiwara's testimony was nothing like that." I concluded from this that the career of the forty-one-year-old official was being destroyed by a sensational and erroneous AP report carried by the only American newspaper published in Japan. Since it was normal procedure to furnish written reports to the Supreme Commander on Diet committee hearings, I invited the universally respected chairman of the upper house committee in question to fill me in on what Hagiwara had said, and he gladly accepted.

Through most of the night of 23–24 October, at my residence in Shibuyaku, Mr. Sato, assisted by Matsumoto Takizo, related the facts in the Hagiwara case, and I took notes. Matsumoto translated the 21 October articles in *Mainichi, Nihon Keizai,* and *Yomiuri,* from which the *Stars and Stripes* article was taken, while Sato gave me the background of the incident. Some seven weeks before, according to his account, he, Shidehara, Yoshida, and Matsudaira had met at the official residence of the President of the House of Councillors to discuss the treaty question, with Hagiwara attending as a treaty expert. The views expressed by Hagiwara on that occasion, taken from a standard work on international law published in 1920, were essentially the same as those he expressed to the House of Councillors committee. If Hagiwara had made an inappropriate remark before the committee, Sato told me, he, as chairman, would have been the first to object. While stenographic reports of informal committee meetings were not kept in either House, Sato went on, he had requested a clerk to take notes of the proceedings in question. He was certain that those notes would support his contention that no questionable, embarrassing, injudicious, or offensive remarks—from the standpoint of any nation—were uttered by Hagiwara or any member of the committee.

Following an American breakfast prepared by my wife, Mr. Sato went his way and I went to my office, as usual, in the Dai Ichi Building. By noon, on the basis of the Japanese newspaper articles and Mr. Sato's explanation, I had completed for limited distribution—to General MacArthur, General Whitney, and Colonel Kades—a special five-page paper, titled: "DELICATE INTERNATIONAL SITUATION" UNDULY DISTURBED BY INFLAMMATORY ARTICLE IN "STARS AND STRIPES." Both Whitney and Kades, convinced by my report, they told me, that Hagiwara had been unjustly railroaded, said that they would recommend his reinstatement as soon as the international excitement had died down. General Whitney informed the Yoshida government early in 1951 that there would be no adverse international reaction if Hagiwara were appointed to an important government post.

I never met Mr. Hagiwara, nor did I ever receive word from him that he was aware of the quiet attempt made by Sato, Matsumoto, and me to save him from a rank injustice.

If Showa Denko was not Japan's greatest scandal of all time, as some believed, it was her greatest scandal during the occupation. It had its origin in the Japanese government's 1946 decision to more than double the production of fertilizer. Central to the success of the project was Showa Denko, the giant electrical-chemical company, and the Reconstruction Finance Bank (RFB), the main source of public credit for such ventures. With loans totaling ¥2,358,000,000 ($6,550,000) from the RFB, Showa Denko achieved the goal set for the output of fertilizer by the summer of 1948.

Just weeks before that time, the charge was made that Showa Denko had obtained the loans illegally. In April 1948, at a secret session of the House of Representatives Illegal Property Transactions Committee, a member of the opposition Democratic Liberal party asserted that Prime Minister Ashida and Economic Stabilization Board director Kurusu Takeo had pocketed millions for facilitating RFB loans to Showa Denko. Getting into the act shortly thereafter, the Tokyo Procurators' Office ultimately indicted for bribery, fraud, and perjury thirty-eight persons, including, among others, Democrats Ashida and Kurusu, Democratic Liberals Ono Bamboku and Matsuoka Matsuhei, Socialist Nishio Suehiro, Showa Denko president Hinohara Setsuzo and several of his underlings, Industrial Bank vice-president Ninomiya Motoshigo, former Agriculture-Forestry vice-minister Shigemasa Masayuku, and numerous bank clerks and middle level government employees. Although the press speculated that Showa Denko had expended at least ten percent of its huge loan for bribes, gratuities, and hush money, the Tokyo procurators, after questioning two thousand suspects and taking forty thousand pages of testimony, arrived at the figure of ¥76,628,817 ($212,858), or three and a quarter percent of the loan principal.

Of the political bigwigs in the case, Ono and Matsuoka convinced the court that they had accepted ¥200,000 and ¥100,000, respectively, not as bribes, but as "a gift between friends" and "a mere loan." Still pending when the occupation ended were suits against Ashida for accepting ¥2,000,000 ($5,556), Kurusu for accepting ¥3,750,000 ($10,417), and Nishio for accepting ¥1,000,000 ($2,778). Each rested his case on the standard and previously successful defense used in political scandals, that the money was presented as political party donations and not as bribes to influence government officials or to hush up rumors of corruption in political circles. Total payments to them, it should be observed, amounted to slightly less than ten percent of the total illegal expenditure that Showa Denko was charged with making. It was the remaining ninety percent, or roughly ¥70,000,000 ($194,444), that interested me. I wanted to know whether this outlay for commissions, or whatever, was legal and proper in the context of Japanese custom, and whether, had politicians not been involved, the basis existed for a great scandal. For answers to these questions, I turned to Shima Seiichi and Inagawa Jiro, the brilliant young Foreign Office officials who headed the Liaison Sections of the House of Representatives and the House of Councillors.

Recently, I explained to them, Gen. Albert C. Wedemeyer, returning home from China, stopped briefly in South Korea and Japan. Asked in Tokyo about the average rake-off by Chinese and South Korean officials on American military and civilian aid, he said that it ran to at least ninety percent in China and around forty percent in South Korea. Japanese officials were, by comparison, quite honest, Wedemeyer was told, for they took ten percent or less. Was this story applicable to the Showa Denko Affair?

Shima and Inagawa said no. Although the Oriental practice of cumshaw, or squeeze, was, they assured me, common enough in Japan, it did not explain the principle underlying the great majority of payments made by Showa Denko for entertainment, gifts, and special allowances. Those payments were, they said, ostensibly for liquidating Showa Denko obligations, that is, for reciprocating, in keeping with an ancient and unique Japanese tradition, favors received by Showa Denko. They meant the tradition, as Basil Hall Chamberlain described it, of giving *les petits cadeaux qui entretiennent l'amitié* (little presents that sustain affection), and as Ruth Benedict explained it, of meeting obligations to preserve one's reputation, honor, and peace of mind.[4] Note, they said, that

¥15,600,000 ($43,333), or twenty-two percent, went for gifts and enter-tainment of government officials and "guests" (for example, GHQ functionaries). Regarding the large sums allegedly paid to Industrial Bank vice-president Ninomiya, Shima and Inagawa pointed to Showa Denko president Hinohara's explanation, that apart from intimate friendship, he wished to thank him for the efforts he made in accommodating the com-pany with loans. In December 1947, he gave him ¥200,000 ($556) as an expression of gratitude for his good offices. In similar fashion, in De-cember 1947 and January 1948, Hinohara gave Maruyama Jiro, managing director of the Yasuda Bank, four kakemono (hanging scrolls) and a total of ¥100,000 ($277), remembering that, when the electric power supply in the Fukushima prefecture plant was on the verge of suspension, they were able to tide over the difficulty because of Maruyama's help. By the same line of reasoning, they continued, Fujii Takashi, chief of Showa Denko's General Affairs Section, gave to each of five loan officers of the Sanwa and Yasuda Banks—"for their favorable consideration in granting loans"—an average of ¥27,000 ($75).

But in its application to the Showa Denko case, Shima and Inagawa agreed, the foregoing argument had two defects. First, it was not in order to reward government officials for approving loans of public funds. Sec-ond, in any event, the recompense was excessive. As every Japanese knew, an obligation was to be met with the mathematical equivalent of the favor extended. But Showa Denko had repaid everyday favors with unheard of commissions. The gratuities were far out of proportion to the favors rendered. Lacking sophistication, the Showa Denko people were less concerned with meeting their obligations than with paying bribes for loans obtained.

Would any Showa Denko gratuities at all have been legal and appropri-ate? Shima and Inagawa thought that "reasonable" payments would have been acceptable. What was reasonable? That depended on the loan aggre-gate, they said. The larger the amount, the lower the percentage for obligations incurred. Japanese understood the fine distinction between meeting an obligation and giving a bribe. Aside from the political contribu-tions, had Showa Denko shown better taste and judgment in being thoughtful of those who had been deferentially helpful, the percentage of the total loan devoted to gratuities would have been closer to a half percent, or ¥11,790,000 ($32,750), than to three percent, or ¥70,740,000 ($196,500)—and no scandal would have resulted.

Fukushima Shintaro, a top Foreign Office official who became Deputy Cabinet Secretary in the Ashida government, was under considerable pressure from Democratic party leaders in the late summer of 1948 to stand for a seat in the House of Representatives at the next general election, which appeared imminent. Offered a "safe" constituency in a Tokyo election district, he was sorely tempted to toss his hat into the ring; but he resisted the temptation, then and later.

At a social gathering one evening, I took the liberty to ask him if he would tell me precisely how he would conduct his campaign in the event he decided to run. A professional politician would have been reluctant to answer this question, but Fukushima, being more outgoing and less reserved than most Japanese, was glad to oblige. As I took hurried notes, he listed the following requirements, which were familiar to every politician:

1. Select an experienced campaign manager.

2. Accumulate ¥2,000,000 ($5,556) for the short campaign period only.

3. Recruit thirty intelligent, enthusiastic, and reliable young men to run the office, contact key people, make speeches, arrange speaking engagements for the candidate, play host to visiting electors, etc.

4. Enlist the support of two influential local politicians in each subdivision of the district.

5. Make the acquaintance of a few leaders in each neighborhood and through them obtain the support of local factory owners, businessmen, and others.

6. Select an able speech writer to draft appropriate addresses for radio and competitive meetings, and to instruct the candidate and his assistants.

7. Obtain one big truck and three Datsuns.

8. Procure a powerful loudspeaker for each vehicle for announcing speech meetings and for informing electors, "inside their homes," of the candidate's qualifications.

9. Cultivate local newspaper reporters, who make their influence felt through their articles and pictures.

10. Bring in a cabinet minister, a famous politician, or a top government official to stump the district.

Tucked away in a 16 September 1971 *Asahi Shimbun* article on SCAP and the Katayama government was mention of a parliamentary stratagem I had recommended to Diet leaders in 1947 to facilitate passage of the Economic Deconcentration bill. With the opposition Liberal party skillfully filibustering to prevent passage of the bill before midnight, when the session ended, I hinted to Mr. Nishio that he might stop the clock to allow more time for the legislation to be enacted. He took the hint. According to the article, the Liberal Democratic party has employed the clock-stopping tactic ever since.

Nishio Suehiro, Chief Cabinet Secretary at the time, for years to come identified me with the above incident, which the Liberal party then denounced as being immoral. But it was another experience in connection with the same bill that has kept Mr. Nishio fresh in my memory.

With Washington breathing down his neck, General MacArthur was especially concerned over the bill in question. Consequently, I made one of my rare visits to the Diet Building to consult the affable Mr. Nishio about the prospects of the bill's passage. "Have no fear," he said, "I will see that it passes." When I asked if he would set a dependable deadline for its passage, he replied without hesitation, "Two weeks from today." I reported to SCAP that the deadline would be met.

It was not met, and I made another trip to the Diet Building to ask Mr. Nishio for an explanation. "There's nothing to worry about," he said, "the bill is going to pass." "How could I be sure," I asked, "since he had fallen down on his solemn promise to have it enacted a day or so before?" At that, he leaned back in his swivel chair, raised both arms high into the air, then slapped his knees, and roared with laughter. "Oh," he explained, "there is a misunderstanding over the word sincerity, or *makoto*, which does not mean exactly the same thing in English and Japanese." Then, he went on to say that he did not mean that the bill would actually be passed by a certain calendar day, but that it would be passed absolutely at that Diet session. "It is my commitment that counts," he said, "not a particular day of the month. I gave you my word, in all sincerity, that the bill would pass, and it will. Whether today or tomorrow is of no consequence."

On 6 August 1945, the first atomic bomb was dropped on Hiroshima, causing about 130,000 casualties and devastating 90 percent of the city. Almost exactly a year later, through the headquarters of the British Commonwealth Forces, the mayor and council of Hiroshima City asked GHQ to make available two American experts on town planning to redesign the city. Because the precedent would lead to many requests from other communities, which could not be granted, General MacArthur, on the advice of Government Section, Diplomatic Section, and Eighth Army, turned down the petition.

But Hiroshima's Mayor Hamai Shinzo, himself a victim of the bombing, was a man with a bulldog tenacity. Following the general election of January 1949 for members of the House of Representatives, he found that sentiment in the Diet was now favorable to his plan for reconstructing

Hiroshima as an international peace city. But there was still the GHQ bottleneck. To get a sounding from that quarter, Mayor Hamai, Council President Nitoguri Tsukasa, and Representative Matsumoto Takizo from Hiroshima, called at my Shibuyaku residence one evening in March 1949. After hearing their case in great detail, I encouraged them by saying that I personally favored their proposal and would see that General MacArthur would be sounded out for his reaction. The next day I explained the situation to General Whitney, who forthwith discussed it with General MacArthur and obtained the go-ahead signal. The three Hiroshima leaders were highly pleased when I told them a few days later in my Dai Ichi Building office of General MacArthur's approval of their project. At that point, they said there still remained the important matter of transferring title to some ten acres of land, valued at ¥10 million, from the national government to the city. GHQ's Natural Resources Section had jurisdiction over the land, they said, because much of it was devoted to rice cultivation. Whereupon, in their presence, I telephoned Mark Williamson, an old friend from military government days, to set up an appointment for them, and told him that General MacArthur had already given his blessing to the peace city project. With Williamson's prompt assurance to them that Natural Resources Section would interpose no objection to transferring the land to Hiroshima City, the Diet was free to proceed at will.

At the beginning of May 1949, the House of Councillors submitted to Government Section for clearance a bill for Construction of Hiroshima as the Eternal Peace Commemorating City, sponsored by Socialist Yamada Setsuo (later to become mayor of Hiroshima) and sixty-five other Councillors. Actually all parties and factions in both Houses were in favor of the measure, I informed General Whitney in a 3 May 1949 memorandum. Public-spirited citizens, local officials, and Diet members of Hiroshima prefecture had been working on the project for over a year. To prevent the draft bill from getting bogged down in GHQ red tape, I added that it called for no appropriations or the allocation of any construction materials. "It does stipulate . . . that the government may transfer public property— meaning the land used as a national arsenal—to Hiroshima City and Hiroshima-ken, which . . . shall bear the expenses necessary for execution of the construction enterprise. There is nothing in the bill that would require examination and coordination by GHQ staff sections. . . . A high level policy decision would seem to be all that is needed." Immediately cleared by SCAP, the bill was passed by the House of Representatives on 10 May and by the House of Councillors on 11 May.

That the foregoing account of how Hiroshima achieved the legal status of an international peace city lacks dramatic content is explained by the fact that, from my standpoint, there was nothing dramatic about it. But from the standpoint of the Hiroshima parties concerned, the story was different; they were as excited as participants usually are after a hard-earned victory. Or so it would seem, if we are willing to accept a version of my role in the affair first published in German, then in French, and here a translation from the French:

The elections of January 1949 having resulted in a sharp swing to the left, the moderate government party, somewhat shaken by the shift, realized that it would have to pay more attention to its popularity. Thereupon, when he returned to Tokyo in February, [Mayor] Hamai met with a reception of unexpected civility on the part of the deputies of the conservative and government party. . . .

The mayor undertook personally to obtain the necessary concurrence of the occupation authorities. Together with Deputy Takizo Matsumoto, who had spent many years in the USA, and Nitoguri, president of the municipal council of Hiroshima, he went to see Mr. Williams, representative of MacArthur vis-à-vis the Japanese Parliament. After Matsumoto had painted a brief picture of the situation for the benefit of the American, the latter was shown a copy of the Hiroshima Peace Memorial City Construction Act, and he began to examine it with as much scruple as circumspection.

Time seemed to have stopped while Mr. Williams "attentively and without batting an eye" studied the document. He kept a complete silence and there was not the slightest indication what his decision would be. The persistent efforts of the Allied censorship to efface the memory of Hiroshima from the public conscience made a positive decision most improbable. However, the words pronounced by MacArthur at the time of the Peace Celebration of August 6, 1947, and the echo of these words throughout the world left the door still open for hope.

Hamai evokes in these words the nearly intolerable minutes of the waiting: "I was on tenterhooks. I watched the slightest movements of his face in order to try to guess his reactions. Let him say *No* and the whole plan for Diet legislation would be killed. But when he took his eyes from the paper, he exclaimed: "This is wonderful. It will be a capital political event, on the international as well as the domestic level. You must do everything possible immediately to get your project debated and adopted. As soon as the Diet has approved it, I will submit the text of the law to General MacArthur for his signature."

The three Japanese, overflowing with joy, exchanged vigorous handshakes. "It's in the bag," repeated Nitoguri while leaving GHQ. "Now the law will go through. There is no longer doubt about it." [5]

If, in retrospect, Hamai and Nitoguri romanticized my part in their parleying with GHQ to win approval of the peace city project, I remembered the exercise for its having set in motion a series of steps by which some insight was gained into the way money was passed from a grateful constituent to an accommodating Diet member in satisfaction of an obligation. Just as I automatically directed the Hamai party to Natural Resources Section's Mark Williamson for resolution of the land transfer matter, so Representative Matsumoto had automatically brought his

Hiroshima clients to me for advice on obtaining GHQ approval of their plan. No other Japanese could match Matsumoto's knowledge of the complex interrelationship between the Japanese government and GHQ. That was the source of his great influence in both Japanese and American circles.

Japanese politicians were reluctant to discuss their political financing, and Matsumoto was no exception. Like his close friend, Fukushima Shintaro, he talked freely about how to organize and conduct a successful election campaign, sidestepping only questions about campaign costs and how he met them. Nor did he care to discuss how a Diet member, any Diet member, shouldered the heavy financial burden of his office.

One day in a friendly meeting with Matsumoto, our conversation drifted from parliamentary politics to Mayor Hamai. For no particular reason, I casually asked him if Mr. Hamai had appropriately discharged the heavy obligation to him for lobbying the peace city bill through SCAP. And without hesitation, he explained exactly how the obligation had been met. The subject was understandably personal and confidential, but he did not ask me not to repeat what he said. I feel that, if he were still living, he would grant me permission to recall our conversation of some thirty years ago. On a day when Mr. Matsumoto was tied up at the Diet Building, Mayor Hamai called at the Matsumoto residence in Tokyo. After a brief chat over tea with Mrs. Matsumoto, he left. Some hours later Mrs. Matsumoto discovered behind a *shoji* (sliding door) a sizeable envelope containing about ¥500,000 in currency. It was the amount Matsumoto had expected, even though there had been no agreement or understanding of any kind. It represented around five percent of the value of the national land transferred to Hiroshima City. In no sense was the cash a bribe or a payoff. The whole thing was routine, the way things are done in Japan. It was a concrete example of how a Dietman's clients, big and little, public and private, take care of obligations for favors rendered. After all, elections are costly, and Diet members cannot serve their constituents on their legislative salaries. The equivalent of $1,389 left at the Matsumoto residence was an expression of Hiroshima City's appreciation for valuable services rendered to it; the recipient was not left with a feeling of guilt.

Nozaka Sanzo, the one-man Communist braintrust, was by any standard a most remarkable Japanese. As I point out elsewhere, his 1944 five-page paper titled "The Program of the Japanese Community Party," made available to American Foreign Service officials in Yenan, China, was to a surprisingly large extent incorporated in the 1945 United States Initial Post-Surrender Policy for Japan. At a July 1951 roundtable of Diet members in the Speaker's salon, he captivated visiting Governor Thomas E. Dewey with his penetrating questions and pertinent comments on the international situation. By meticulous reporting to Government Section on repeated violations of civil rights by the American military and the excessively harsh treatment G–2 agents and military government personnel meted out to numerous Communist activists, he mitigated the situation somewhat. Our Intelligence community never obtained evidence to refute Nozaka's contention that the Japanese Communist party was completely free of Moscow. Though SCAP felt compelled in 1946 and again in 1947 to prevent left-wing elements from overthrowing the conservative Japanese government, high SCAP officials not only had considerable admiration for the leadership and organizing skill of Nozaka, but an off-the-record conviction that his followers would fight hardest and most effectively to sustain the new democratic system. Just how prophetic a 1947 Nozaka statement to a Government Section official on protecting democracy would prove to be could not be fully appreciated at the time it was made. But neither could it be ignored. He said, according to a 10 March 1947 Roest memorandum to Whitney:

While . . . in the past there was no chance to carry out a socialist program through parliamentary means, there *is* now. Hence the Communists now favor the parliamentary method of bringing about political, social and economic change, and in this respect can join the Socialists. But there is one fundamental difference: the Socialists do not recognize the use of mass action outside the Diet as a proper instrument, while the Communists do. They use extra-parliamentary mass pressure . . . as a necessary auxiliary weapon.

A new dimension of Japan's postoccupation political process, mass demonstrations have been used effectively to defeat a number of legislative proposals for reviving prewar authoritarian practices and institutions.

In the period before the Korean War, Nozaka's strong support of most occupation reforms, combined with his apparent independence of Moscow, gave Government Section leaders food for thought. Why not strike a blow for democracy in Japan and simultaneously score a victory for the free world against international communism, they speculated, by having the Japanese Communist party publicly declare its freedom from Russia and its allegiance to Japan? Where the State Department's George F. Kennan conceived "demilitarization and collection of reparations" to be the major objectives of the occupation, SCAP had engineered Japan's political reorientation from the beginning of the occupation on the assumption that democratization was a main objective. And where Kennan, at the time of his conferences with MacArthur in the late spring of 1948, held that SCAP had rendered Japanese society "vulnerable to Communist Party pressures," paving the way for "a Communist takeover," the SCAP people knew better.[6] Anyway, it was in this atmosphere that I drew the assignment in March 1948 to sound out Nozaka, with whom I had been on good terms ever since he arrived from China in 1946, on his outlook and freedom of action. Our recorded discussion of 18 March 1948 in the Diet Building was as follows:

Williams: Is the Japanese Communist Party connected with the Comintern?
Nozaka: No.
Williams: Does the Party take orders from Russia?
Nozaka: No.
Williams: If there should be a war between Japan and Russia, which side would your Party take?
Nozaka: That is an impossible question. The Constitution outlaws war.
Williams: Then suppose the U.S. and Russia were at war, with Japan a U.S. ally, what would be the attitude of your Party?
Nozaka: Japan should side with neither country; Japan must remain neutral. The Japanese people do not wish to be involved in any war. If all other Japanese political parties favored joining the U.S. against Russia, my Party would still oppose going to war on either side.
Williams: Does your Party stand in the same relationship to Russia as that of Czechoslavakia?
Nozaka: No. Unlike Czechoslavakia, Japan must not be dominated by any country.
Williams: Your Party suffers because its name connotes subservience to Russia, which you deny. Then, would you clarify your position by changing the name of the Party?
Nozaka: I admit that the name may give the wrong impression. In East Germany, Poland, and Roumania, the Communists adopted the name Labor Party. Such a name might be contemplated for Japan in the future. But not now, for that would give our workers the wrong impression.
Williams: What is your feeling about GHQ's attitude toward your Party?
Nozaka: Frankly, it's not good. Since the spring of 1946, it has become worse.
Williams: Do you think that changing its name might help dispel GHQ's dislike of your Party?
Nozaka: I don't think it would help, but we will consider it.
Williams: If the Yoshida conservative people came to power, would they revive the old repressive measures?
Nozaka: No. Labor is too strong, and there is no support for fascism today. Communist leaders would not be jailed, for nothing would be gained by it; we now have thousands of capable leaders.
Williams: If your Party came to power, would you suppress the Liberal Party?
Nozaka: No. We are a people's party, but others would remain free to organize opposition parties.
Williams: Would you be interested in continuing this discussion with Colonel Kades, maybe General Whitney, and others on what your Party stands for?
Nozaka: Gladly.

In his questioning of Nozaka, Kades got no further than I did. If the Communist leader was too cagey to antagonize GHQ further by flatly refusing to demonstrate by positive action his party's independence of the Soviet Union, he was also too shrewd to take a step that would permanently alienate world communism. But Government Section's efforts to capitalize on what appeared to be Nozaka's independent status may not have been altogether naive; for while the astute Japanese Communist leader had to bow finally to Cominform pressure in January 1950, he was able in subsequent years, by stressing nationalistic sentiments, to persuade the party "to think in terms of Japanese needs rather than foreign Communist demands."[7]

Hasegawa Koichi, professor of political science at Waseda University, was a gifted and durable friend. With a diploma from the High School of Commerce in San Franciso, a Bachelor's degree from Miami University (Ohio), and a Master's degree from Columbia University, he was strongly oriented to the United States. My wife and I helped him, and he helped us. He was our authority on things Japanese—history, art, pottery, *No* and *Kabuki* theater, education, merchandise. He translated papers of mine into Japanese and Japanese articles of interest to me into English. He was instrumental in having Waseda invite me to make two campus addresses, one to the student body, the other to the political science faculty. He assisted me in making contacts with the Japanese intellectual community, and I reciprocated by helping him make contacts with American and Japanese officials. We never gave each other a gift of any kind.

Instead of supplementing his inadequate university pay by writing for magazines, as a number of professors did, he turned his knowledge of the English language and American customs to good account. One evening he telephoned me at home to ask if it would be in order for me to make an appointment for him and his client to see a certain United States Army colonel from Okinawa, who was registered at the Imperial Hotel. The colonel, whose mission in Tokyo was to buy composition shingles for military warehouses on Okinawa, was, of course, delighted to have my telephone call introducing a prospective bidder. Months later, I asked Mr. Hasegawa if he had an understanding with this particular client regarding suitable compensation for his services. Yes, he said. He received a flat ¥3,000 ($8.33) for the introduction, with a promise of ten percent of the first million of sales and two percent of the gross in excess of that figure. I did not ask if his client got a contract for shingles, and he did not volunteer to tell me.

Two months before the end of the occupation, I invited four Japanese intellectuals to dinner. They were Baba Tsunego, publisher of *Yomiuri Shimbun,* Yamaura Kanichi, columnist for *Tokyo Shimbun,* Yabe Teiji, retired Tokyo University political scientist, and, of course, Mr. Hasegawa, who had informed the others in advance of what the gathering was for.

The day following the dinner, Mr. Yamaura devoted his entire column (*Tokyo Shimbun,* 1 March 1952) to that event. At one point in his commentary he said:

I have had no social intercourse with any American nationals residing in Japan. I have entertained no desire to be on visiting terms with any of those occupation authorities. I still recall how the swash buckling Japanese once showed off clumsily their superiority in the Japan-occupied areas. . . . My language difficulty is . . . secondary.

Thus I became for the first time Mr. Williams's guest. Having come to know Mr. Williams, who is unassuming in manner, I am prone to reflect if my mind has been a bit too warped in this regard.

Obviously not a sycophant, but a writer with an open mind, Mr. Yamaura said of the purpose of the get-to-gether:

Two political scientists and two political commentators were invited to dinner at the Williams residence the other day. Lively talks ensued for over four and a half hours. It was his intention to draw out comments mainly from his guests. I found that the questions put to his guests were pertinent and poignant, hitting the mark.

Regarding the questions discussed, he wrote:

Once independence is restored to Japan, the ponderous weight of GHQ will naturally be removed. . . . [Williams] is anxious to know what element in the Japanese social strata will eventually fill this power vacuum.

This is a very difficult question to answer. . . . It is unbelievable . . . that the Japanese Emperor will have this supreme political power restored to him. . . . This view was aired by one of those present at the party. Another predicts that this new leadership will be taken over by newly created zaibatsu. . . . politics requires money. There are no longer the Mitsuis and the Mitsubishis. . . . The new rich will step into their shoes. This is quite a realistic interpretation. . . .

Mr. Williams . . . raised a question as to whether Japan and the United States would be capable of working together . . . sincerely and honestly in the future. He claims . . . the Diet stenographic records of the interpellations on the Administrative Agreement under the U.S.-Japan Security Treaty . . . gave him the impression that anti-American feeling would be latent in the minds of the Japanese. Let me explain about the matter. . . . We like to reprimand the government for its culpable negligence in accepting the Administrative Agreement which bears the character of extraterritoriality. We are leveling criticism against the Japanese government, but not against American friendship.

In an earlier chapter I discuss the scholarly paper I presented to the Waseda political science faculty in December 1951 on the prospects of representative government in Japan. Translated into Japanese and distributed by Mr. Hasegawa, the paper was liberally documented, drawing from studies on the subject by British, American, and Japanese authorities and from my knowledge of the National Diet under the democratic constitution. Though I was generously complimented by the members of the largest and ablest political science group in Japan for my familiarity with the Japanese political scene, their questions and comments made it perfectly clear that the Western concept of popular sovereignty and democratic rule was beyond their range of comprehension. They obviously stood aloof from Japanese politics and politicians. They demonstrated what Professor Maruyama Masao had written about their discipline in 1947, that

> Japanese political science . . . never had the corrective experience of shaping and being shaped by political realities. . . .
> The sterility of Japanese political science is . . . essentially an outcome of the political structure established after the Meiji Restoration. . . . Any inquiry into the ultimate source of political power became taboo.
> . . . important national decisions were made outside the Diet . . . [where] nothing was to be seen but personal brawling.
> . . . the political scientist who . . . turned to a problem of everyday politics . . . was about on the same level as the political reporter . . . virtually confined to expressing platitudes.
> . . . [Though] the task of political science is to grasp "the currents and trends in the life of the state" . . . there has been little, if any, progress in regard to communication between political scientists and practical politicians.[8]

Most Japanese political scientists, though strong supporters of the democratic constitution, have difficulty in adjusting to the thought of popularly elected representatives shaping the country's internal and external policies.

14

MacArthur: Statesman

Normally United States foreign affairs are conducted by the State Department. For the political reorientation of Japan, however, this practice was not followed. The Department of the Army was the focal point of United States policy in Washington, and a professional soldier was given the post of civil administrator in Japan. By reason of this exceptional arrangement, the unique talents of Gen. Douglas MacArthur as a civil leader were brought into play. For five years and seven months under United States policy directives, he was engaged in changing Japan from a semifeudal to a democratic society, or, as *Time* magazine (9 May 1949) put it, in "fostering a social revolution far bolder than anything colonial powers of the past have attempted in Asia." During the latter part of his administration, he experienced considerable difficulty in dissuading Washington policymakers from materially altering the character of the democratic structure he had methodically erected. In this chapter, an effort is made to portray MacArthur as he appeared to Americans associated with his venture in Japan, and to evaluate his contribution to that country's political reorientation.

Unquestionably a complex individual, MacArthur was also a paradox. Besides being a brilliant military leader, for instance, he could also very well be remembered as an illustrious statesman. No American soldier had ever been so roundly denounced and passionately defended by his contemporaries. In Japan he was liberal in his political views, yet he was the darling of know-nothing elements in the United States. His substantial personal power was better appreciated by the leftists, who feared him, than by the rightists, who mistakenly took him for granted. Autocratic in some respects, he was a staunch advocate of representative government. As Supreme Commander for the Allied Powers, he won the plaudits of the peoples of the world, yet was relieved of his post by an American President whose popularity was at a record low.

There were those around MacArthur in Japan who had not forgotten him as a highly decorated American officer in World War I, as a member of the military court that sacked General Billy Mitchell, an early exponent of the airplane, as the Army Chief of Staff during the Hoover administration who suppressed the bonus marchers with great swiftness, and as a bosom friend of isolationist newspaper publishers William Randolph Hearst and Robert R. McCormick. But that picture gradually faded away as MacArthur the proconsul skillfully and patiently coaxed Japan into the twentieth century and placed her under the protection of the United States, accomplishments chalked up while Secretary of State James F. Byrnes, Gen. Lucius D. Clay, and Gen. George C. Marshall, respectively, fared badly negotiating over Eastern Europe, administering the American Zone of Germany, and mediating China's civil war. Except in Japan, there appeared to be utter confusion everywhere in the conduct of our postwar foreign affairs.

MacArthur projects two images, one malign and one godlike. He is loathed by his detractors and revered by his admirers. Mark Gayn as well as anyone represents the detractors and Courtney Whitney the admirers. Reviewing Whitney's book about MacArthur for a liberal, intellectual weekly publication, Gayn described it as "petulant and bellicose pamphleteering," which "served MacArthur ill . . . served history worse." [1] He wrote for those liberals who hailed the hatchet job, *The General and the President,* done by Richard H. Rovere and Arthur M. Schlesinger, Jr., in 1951. [2]

But Whitney's book was practically unanimously acclaimed, except by the left wing, which reacted predictably. It was the only book in publishing history to be reviewed on the front page of the Sunday book-review section of the *New York Herald Tribune,* the *New York Times,* and the *Chicago Tribune. Life* magazine placed MacArthur's photograph on its front cover and serialized parts of the book. *Reader's Digest* carried six pages of excerpts from it. Raymond Moley (*Newsweek*), Roscoe Drummond (*New York Herald Tribune*), Hanson W. Baldwin (*New York Times*), Walter Trohan (*Chicago Tribune*), Gerry Robichaud (*Chicago Sun-Times*), Bill Cunningham (*Boston Herald*), Gordon Walker (*Christian Science Monitor*), Howard Handleman (*Washington Post*), Sterling North (Scripps-Howard chain), and many others found much to criticize, but among them used the following adjectives to describe it: gripping, indispensable, moving, illuminating, meaty, fact-laden, valuable, provocative, readable, authoritative, well-prepared, comprehensive, absorbing, fascinating, convincing, soul-stirring, thrilling, hard hitting. Thinking of reviewers of the Gayn stripe who raked MacArthur fore and aft as the quintessence of reaction, Bill Cunningham asked: "What's a woodtick's opinion of the Washington monument?" Hanson W. Baldwin believed that the Whitney book added to the portrait of MacArthur. [3] As an authentic revelation of MacArthur's innermost feelings, suspicions, prejudices, amour propre, the drives of his life, and the fuel of his indomitable spirit, it adds greatly to an understanding of what he accomplished, and why. It presents an indispensable side of his character, which otherwise never would have come to light.

American viewers of the passing parade in Japan were less and less impressed by accounts charging MacArthur with pomposity, egotism, purple prose, showmanship, and arrogance. They shrugged off the mutterings of doctrinaire liberals about a conceited autocrat and a strutting peacock. What struck them was the image MacArthur projected of an extraordinary man sincerely bent on hacking out new paths for the good of all peoples. To some members of the Government Section staff his stock shot up when he decided in January 1946, as explained earlier, not to Americanize Japan's election law by SCAP fiat, because he believed the existing law, as amended in December 1945, to be basically sound and democratic. Decisions of this kind portrayed MacArthur as he was.

MacArthur is seen more clearly as the man for the job in Japan against the background of the postwar situation in Washington. At that time, as diplomat George F. Kennan wrote, there was "utter confusion in the public mind with respect to U.S. foreign policy. The President doesn't understand it; Congress doesn't understand it; nor does the public nor does the press. They all wander around in a labyrinth of ignorance and error and conjecture in which truth is intermingled with fiction at a hundred points."[4] Had it not been for MacArthur, Japan would have become a football in the burgeoning cold war between the United States and the Soviet Union. Who else in the chaos of those years would have felt equal to the task of fabricating an enlightened policy for that defeated country, and of laying the groundwork for a humane and nonpunitive treaty?

His performance in Japan was the true measure of his character and caliber. He appealed to the mass mind of Japan by employing a combination of ham acting—stepping from his plane at Atsugi Airfield in late August 1945 unarmed; humanitarianism—committing himself at the surrender ceremony to be guided by freedom, tolerance, and justice; bold moves—drafting a model constitution and proposing an early peace treaty; and acuteness of feeling—showing unfailing respect for Emperor Hirohito, the dignity of the people, and the people's elected representatives. He did not seek to appease American hard peace advocates by being unduly severe with the Japanese. Just what impact his course had on the thinking of the Japanese was impossible to measure, but no one doubted that a substantial change was taking place.

Of his contemporaries in public life, MacArthur had much in common with Winston Churchill. Like Churchill, he was flamboyant, elitist, proud, perceptive, daring, and oracular. Like Churchill, he was conservative when he could be, liberal when he had to be, and consistent in his attachment to time-honored virtues. Like Churchill, he was a household name. Just as Churchill was blamed for the setback of the Allies at Gallipoli in 1915, so was MacArthur blamed for the Chinese push across the Yalu River in 1950. Churchill attacked Prime Minister Neville Chamberlain's military strategy in World War II, and replaced him; MacArthur took issue with United States government strategy in the Korean War, which was his right, and was removed by the president, exercising the prerogative of the Commander-in-Chief. Both Churchill and MacArthur lent credence to Carlyle's theory that the history of the world is essentially the history of its great men. But where Churchill showed to best advantage in situations involving the very survival of his country, MacArthur cut his best figure as global statesman and civil administrator.

It was in the role of global statesman that he conferred with Prime Minister Shidehara Kijuro on 24 January 1946. At the conclusion of the meeting he was convinced that the veteran Japanese statesman favored renunciation of the use of military force by Japan in settling international differences.[5] Accordingly, a week or so later, MacArthur directed that the revolutionary Shidehara proposal be incorporated in the model democratic constitution about to be drafted in Government Section. His decision on this point, like his companion decisions on retention of the emperor and abolition of the peerage, was final. Over objections of some of the best legal minds on his staff, he had the crust to deny the right of belligerency to a great Oriental nation. But Japan now adamantly upholds Article 9, the no-war clause, of her democratic constitution, and the United States government, at last, supports her position.

MacArthur showed the stuff he was made of when he refrained from dissolving or otherwise punishing the National Diet for its outright rejection of the highly important occupation-sponsored local tax bill in 1950. This is not to imply that he was not uncommonly provoked by that serious blow to his prestige as Supreme Commander. So angry was he, in fact, that he called to account the chiefs of SCAP's two most important staff sections and flayed the presiding officers of the two Diet chambers. Nevertheless, his press release on that near disaster simply said that in a democracy it sometimes takes a little longer to get things done.

MacArthur did not cultivate his Japanese constituency by delivering "firesides," in the manner of the late Franklin D. Roosevelt, or by strolling with pressmen at daybreak, as Harry Truman did. Instead he captured their imagination by skillfully spacing occupation reforms, conducting a benevolent administration, issuing timely and high-minded public statements to explain his actions, maintaining proper relations with the emperor, showing a personal interest in representative government, and staying at his job seven days a week. Even his daily routine of commuting between the United States Embassy and the Dai Ichi Building seemed to give the people a feeling of safety and security.

His instincts about democracy, liberty, freedom, progress, patriotism, and religion may have been old-fashioned, but they did not detract from his devotion to the highest standards of public service, or from his concern for the welfare of the people he governed. Whether right or wrong, he was never without a refreshing and challenging approach to a wide range of problems. Orville Prescott in his *New York Times* book-review column (31 January 1951) characterized him as a "not uncommon phenomenon of remarkable abilities combined with remarkable egoism, but without the usual conventional pretense of polite humility."

Unlike Napoleon, who failed because he grew tired, MacArthur never lost his drive. He understood the difference between right and wrong. He appealed to the Japanese mind because he accorded each Japanese full dignity. His power was absolute, but he went out of his way to establish responsible government with the consent of the people. Deferring to Japanese public opinion, he supported the coalition of Socialists, Democrats, and People's Cooperatives in 1947–1948, and then backed the conservative Yoshida government from the fall of 1948. As a result, he was denounced by American conservatives for advancing the cause of socialism in Japan, and by American liberals for giving aid and comfort to the Japanese rightists. By the course he followed, he left his stamp on the Japanese bureaucracy, the Emperor institution, the feudal aristocracy, the Diet, the family, religion, freedom, disarmament, education, the legal system, farm tenancy, labor.

As a steadfast civil libertarian, MacArthur directed the Japanese government to guarantee the untrammeled rights of speech, press, assembly, and religion to the people. Yet he harassed foreign correspondents who found fault with him or with his handling of the occupation. At one time or another he sought, unsuccessfully, to ration the number of correspondents assigned to his command, to deny theater amenities to his worst newspaper critics, and to bar the return of those who left the area. He labeled as police court reporters those whose strictures he deemed trite, and as "pinks" or "reds" those whose writings he considered malignant. He ordered the expulsion from Japan of Malcolm Muggeridge, the eminent British correspondent, and Warren Hunsberger, a visiting

State Department economist, for having voiced the opinion in the presence of an Army captain that he, MacArthur, was "a showman who did not know everything."[6] To a War Department recommendation in late 1946 that a group of American newspaper editors and correspondents be permitted to tour Japan to "get a real picture of the occupation," MacArthur objected. He acceded to the Pentagon's follow-up request, but urged, again unsuccessfully, that the list not include representatives of the *Christian Science Monitor, New York Herald Tribune, Chicago Sun, San Francisco Chronicle, PM, Daily Worker,* "and others of this stamp whose articles and editorials . . . have approached downright quackery and dishonesty" (Drew Pearson column, *Philadelphia Record,* 3 December 1946). He objected to those papers for, in his opinion, appealing to the ignorant and the cynical by concentrating on the sensational headline and sacrificing the underlying cause and effect. Replying to a letter from a former American missionary in Japan, who had read that the Japanese press was censored by SCAP, he insisted that there was no censorship except of false and inflammatory statements against the occupation made by pressure groups of the extreme left and the extreme right along with would-be carpetbaggers and special pleaders, all of whom found common cause in subverting the truth and creating false impressions.

The question is not whether MacArthur had a low tolerance for adverse press criticism, but whether as a head of state he was in a class by himself. In the United States a powerful press, playing the role of a fourth branch of government, keeps a close check on the other three branches, often to their dismay. President Truman, it will be recalled, was infuriated at mention of the press. President Kennedy was so outraged by what the *New York Herald Tribune* said about him that he wrathfully canceled the White House subscription to that journal. President Johnson hated the press. President Nixon's antagonism toward the press became an obsession that influenced his aides in the White House. In the early days of the republic, Jefferson angrily assailed the calumnies of the press against himself and against the government. MacArthur's quarrel with critical newsmen did not mean that he opposed the First Amendment, which guarantees freedom of the press.

On the contrary, it should be noted that conservative newspaper publishers not only never found fault with his attitude toward the press but regarded him as a strong defender of press freedom. During the early months of the Korean War, for example, when MacArthur was criticized by some United States newspapers for a press censorship plan he proposed, Roy Howard, president of the Scripps-Howard chain of papers, wrote to one critic: "MacArthur . . . is to my personal knowledge allergic to press censorship . . . and . . . wished to avoid any unnecessary handicaps to the working newspaperman." [7] MacArthur himself cabled *Editor and Publisher:* "It is indeed a screwy world . . . when a soldier fighting to preserve freedom of the press finds himself opposed by the press itself." [8] He was enraged by unfair and inaccurate press stories, and he never hesitated to challenge those whom he thought wrong and misguided.

Unfriendly newspaper correspondents traced MacArthur's alleged failings to the sycophants and mediocrities with whom he supposedly surrounded himself. The implication was, of course, that able and free-thinking individuals were persona non grata to him, and that, as a consequence, only second-rate men filled the top spots in GHQ. Such sophistry has no place in any serious discussion of MacArthur. The top officers under him were exactly like the top officers in commands around the world, all bucking for favor, recognition, and promotion. In military circles everywhere, not just in Japan, disloyalty to "the old man" was a mortal sin. MacArthur required each of his assistants to deliver, or move on. General Crist, the first chief of Government Section, was ineffective, and bowed out. Ex-Brig. Gen. Frayne Baker could not hack it as public relations officer, and was replaced.

As a basis for judging MacArthur's lieutenants, it might be well to look at sycophancy in another quarter. President Truman's first order of business on taking office was to surround himself with men who were personally loyal to him. Every recent President has been served by sycophants anxious for position and power but afraid to argue, challenge, and disagree. White House staffs have become notoriously nondescript—and deeply resentful of the press.

This state of affairs did not exist in MacArthur's "court," as some have called his headquarters. He consistently picked the brains of his underlings and of visiting dignitaries. Many of his ideas originated with his section chiefs, like General Whitney (Government Section), Lt. Col. Hubert Schenck (Natural Resources Section), Brig. Gen. Crawford Sams (Public Health and Welfare Section), Ambassador William Sebald (Diplomatic Section), and others, all of whom briefed him regularly. Each section chief, it must be remembered, drew freely on the expertise of a carefully selected body of professionals. When there were serious differences between the experts, and satisfactory solutions could not be found in SCAP, MacArthur had the Pentagon send out a mission of knowledgeable people to advise him.

How he used his staff was shown in his resolution of the conflict over the right of the Japanese government monopoly employees to strike, as explained earlier. Government Section's Blaine Hoover, a recognized authority on public administration, and ESS's James Killen, a high official of an American Federation of Labor union, spent hours arguing the question before MacArthur. In the end MacArthur accepted Hoover's recommendation (about which more is said later in this chapter), based on a major principle incorporated in the New Deal's Wagner Labor Relations Act of 1935. These experts were not sycophants. They did not toady to MacArthur. On the contrary, each served notice that he would resign if not upheld. Both presented their cases with every resource at their command. Killen lost, and resigned.

On loan from the Agriculture Department in Washington, Wolf I. Ladejinsky was the kind of official MacArthur wanted on his staff. Ladejinsky masterminded the successful land reform program in Japan, and then returned to the United States. But at MacArthur's request he returned to Tokyo for further work on land reform.

Had he been a sycophant, Lt. Col. Donald Nugent, chief of CIE, would not have stood up to MacArthur in the ruckus over the legal status of Christianity in Japan. In 1947, MacArthur received a letter from a Christian missionary objecting that Nugent's staff had placed Christianity and Japanese Shinto on the same plane, thus equating the principal religion of the West with idolatry. Aware that the Supreme Commander strongly favored Christianizing Japan and hoped that thousands of missionaries would flock to the country, Nugent nevertheless reminded him that the occupation had sponsored a law making all religious groups equal in Japan. MacArthur conceded the point, not, however, without letting Nugent know that some American churchmen thought CIE's Religions Division showed too little enthusiasm for the propagation of Christianity. This left Nugent no choice but to tone down his Religions Division, which he did, but without yielding ground on the main point. He was not servile. Had he been, he would not have lasted long as a section chief.

Those who observed MacArthur closely did not believe that he sought the Republican party's nomination for president in 1948. Although he permitted his name to be entered in the Wisconsin primary election, he did not conduct himself like a presidential contender. He knew that no American after Washington was ever handed the nomination on a platter, that it took a lot of hard personal campaigning on the hustings to develop a platform and to win convention delegates. It is difficult to imagine MacArthur pushing through crowds, shaking hands, getting slapped on the back, and marching in local parades.

His main concern in entering the Wisconsin and Nebraska primaries was to remind the Truman administration not to take lightly his views on running the occupation of Japan. His capacity to prevent interference by top officials in Washington would increase in proportion as he fortified his backing by conservative newspaper chains and conservative United States senators with evidence of strong popular support in the friendly Middle West. Leverage, not elective office, was what he had in mind, according to Col. Laurence E. Bunker, his aide for many years.[9]

If MacArthur ever hoped to run for the presidency, it had to be in 1948. But he took none of the necessary steps to run. Instead of wooing press correspondents, as any serious candidate for the nomination would have done, he contrived to alienate them. He made no effort to enlist the support of potent Republican politicians, to form an organization, to put together a platform, to start a groundswell of popular support. Better than anyone else, he knew that the odds against him were overwhelming. He was getting along in years. He had not been in personal contact with the American scene for fourteen years. Older Americans identified him with the destructiveness of war, not with the pursuits of peace in a nuclear age. He was aloof and lacked the common touch. Veterans of both world wars tended to be hostile to him. Above all, he did not bend the knee to powerful commercial and financial interests in the Republican party. Let the family caretaker of long-standing, Col. Sid Huff, tell what price he paid for his independence:

In the months leading up to the 1948 presidential campaign, MacArthur was often mentioned as a possible Republican nominee. . . . Col. Robert McCormick, publisher of the Chicago Tribune, came out on what he described as merely a junket, but I felt that he probably was trying to decide whether to get behind MacArthur for the nomination. We rolled out the red carpet for him and he was the General's guest at the embassy and everybody enjoyed his visit, especially MacArthur, who had a chance to give him a good picture of the occupation. Apparently, politics didn't enter into their discussions in a very definite way, because when the publisher departed, MacArthur grinned in quizzical fashion and mused, "Now I wonder what he really came out here for?" Later, McCormick supported Sen. Robert A. Taft.[10]

Thus, it would appear that MacArthur's passionate belief in the political and social revolution he was directing caused his conservative backers in the United States to doubt not only his attachment to genuine conservative principles but also their ability to manage him should he be nominated and elected. By taking the higher ground of principle, he automatically eliminated himself from the presidential race.

It would serve no useful purpose to speculate on the kind of president he would have made, but the temptation to inject two thoughts is overpowering. First, fully aware of communism's dedication in principle and doctrine to our destruction, he might very well have prevented the Korean War, for he would not have permitted the notion to get around, as the Truman administration did, that South Korea was not essential to the security of the United States. Second, if he could have brought to the White House the statesmanship, the administrative skill, and the integrity of office that he demonstrated as proconsul of Japan, he would have been the outstanding president since Franklin D. Roosevelt.

MacArthur's stature is heightened in a scenario featuring a different five-star general or admiral as Supreme Commander. The first question that comes to mind is: how would a different Supreme Commander have approached constitutional revision, the essential step in Japan's democratization? The odds are that he would have thanked his lucky stars for having at his side a Political Adviser representing the State Department and primed to tackle the problem. Actually, in October 1945, two months before General Whitney became chief of Government Section, Ambassador George Atcheson, Jr., left MacArthur vulnerable to a blast from the *New York Times* by encouraging Prince Konoye Fumimaro, a prewar prime minister, to launch a constitutional revision project along lines recommended by the State Department.[11] There being no provisions in the State Department's plan for establishing popular sovereignty and renouncing the right of belligerency, the corner stones of the subsequent MacArthur constitution, it may be assumed that, had the State Department's revision plan been adopted, the old Japanese military clique might very well have regained full control of postoccupation Japan by adroitly exploiting Imperial sovereignty in connection with massive rearmament. Whether a rearmed Japan answering to the emperor would have had free access to world markets and resources, and how she might have jockeyed for a place in the sun, are not just academic questions.

But prospects for constitutional revision as contemplated by the State Department would have worsened conspicuously after Secretary Byrnes agreed at Moscow in December 1945 to entrust all policy decisions for occupied Japan, including constitutional revision, to the FEC, beginning 26 February 1946. With the United States, the USSR, the United Kingdom, and China exercising the veto power, any constitutional revision plan not based on a quid pro quo arrangement between the United States and the USSR would have stood no chance of being adopted. Inasmuch as the USSR would have submitted to the FEC proposals of the Japanese Communist party, echoing Moscow, the United States could have won approval for its proposals only by accepting those of the USSR. Just as the United States would have vetoed a Soviet proposal to abolish the throne, so would the

USSR have vetoed any United States proposal for a limited monarchy and parliamentary rule. A stalemate on these and other vital constitutional issues may very well have been what the Shidehara Cabinet had in mind when it instructed State Minister Matsumoto Joji to submit to SCAP at the end of January 1946 an insubstantial draft revision of the Meiji Constitution. The Matsumoto draft, in the scenario presented here, would no doubt have been referred by SCAP, on the advice of the Political Adviser, to Washington for a ruling, leaving the United States government no alternative but to place it before the FEC. In other respects, a dangerously muddled situation would have been created.

Coincident with the FEC deadlock envisioned in this scenario over constitutional revision was the actual determined drive in the winter of 1946–1947 of radical labor leaders, backed by marching thousands of recently organized government and private workers, to pull down the conservative Yoshida government and to seize power. Where MacArthur forestalled this scheme by threatening the use of military force, another Supreme Commander, following the advice of his Political Adviser to respect the injunction of the Washington directive to stand aside if the people tried to overthrow a reactionary regime by force, would, in effect, have aided and abetted the extremists of the left. Controlled by these extremists, the new revolutionary government, advised and encouraged by the Soviet member of the Allied Council in Tokyo, protected by the Soviet veto in the FEC, and supported by a duly cowed Japanese public, could have been expected to draft a people's constitution abolishing the emperor and socializing the economy, to force the Diet to legalize the large-sized election district and plural voting system (the next thing to proportional representation), and then to hold a general election for the 466 seats in the House of Representatives. Members of the Political Adviser's office in Tokyo and of the State Department's Office of Far Eastern Affairs in Washington, strongly sympathetic as they were to the thinking of Nozaka Sanzo in Tokyo and to the "agrarian reformers" led by Mao Tse-tung in China, would have thrown their weight behind the Moscow-supported movement of workers, tenant farmers, small shopkeepers, and intellectuals in Japan. At the end of the occupation, Japan would not have aligned herself with the free world, and the balance of power situation facing the United States in the Far East would have been ominous. It is in this context that the leadership of MacArthur should be judged.

History consists as much of correcting false impressions about a leader as of telling his story. Because MacArthur was usually right in Japan, the most his detractors could do was disparage his mode of expression and his air of self-confidence. They failed to point out that he was not afraid and could not be muzzled, that he was not devious and not scheming, not playing a deep game, and not given to deception. Writers who visited him in Tokyo were struck by the fact that the atmosphere around him, though charged on occasion, was pure and wholesome, as if cleansed by a current of fresh air; and that he always conveyed the same impression of dignity and concern, along with a calm manner and a serious purpose. Why no commentator ever drew attention to his profound commitment to the United States Constitution, parliamentary government, and democracy remains a mystery.

It was not MacArthur's style to beguile those whom he wished to influence, but to convince them, and he tailored his approach accordingly. His knowledge, imagination, personality, and integrity were enough to inspire his staff. To convince his conservative supporters in the United States Congress and among the voters, he sometimes resorted to sensationalism, knowing that what made newspaper headlines moved his backers to speak up for him. But it was by orderly presentation of the facts and sound reasoning, combined, if necessary, with an implied threat to carry his case to the president and to the public, that he consistently beat down attempts by the newly established National Security Council to make piecemeal and disruptive changes in occupation policy. How he successfully defended his enforcement of the purge against a National Security Council proposal in 1948 is related in Chapter 11 of this book. Three other examples will be cited here to demonstrate his technique for bringing official Washington around to his way of thinking.

The first of these had to do with the right of Japanese government employees to strike. It will be recalled that the Hoover-Killen debate on this issue was followed by MacArthur's 22 July 1948 letter to Prime Minister Ashida recommending that the National Public Service Law be amended to prohibit collective bargaining or strikes by government workers. On 31 July the Japanese cabinet issued an order implementing SCAP's instructions, to remain in effect until Diet action could be taken on the matter, and on 2 August SCAP reported these developments to the Department of the Army as routine information.[12]

Two weeks later the Department of the Army radioed MacArthur that the State Department, Labor Department, and United States organized labor were concerned over the prospect of democratic unionism being hampered by the terms of the cabinet order. Denial of collective bargaining rights to government workers outside the normal civil service category, such as employees of railways, communications (except postal), salt, tobacco, and camphor monopolies, it was felt, could be in conflict with United States and FEC labor policies. SCAP's views were requested on this question, and also on the circumstances surrounding Killen's resignation, which had received considerable notice in the United States press. In a supplementary message citing "the general tenor of the fears held here," Army Under Secretary William H. Draper, seconded by Army Secretary Kenneth Royall, requested that MacArthur take steps to avoid improper damage to workers' rights.[13]

General MacArthur responded at great length. He stressed that his 22 July letter to the prime minister reflected his concern over possible seizure of the nascent labor movement in Japan by self-appointed radical leaders, the imminence of a general strike, and refusal of the Communist-controlled government unions of transportation and communications workers to obey their superiors—conditions that had caused an unfavorable reaction in the United States House of Representatives Appropriations Committee to the Japanese labor situation. "I know of nothing more calculated to impede recovery and to destroy occupation gains already made through painstaking effort and heavy United States expense," he said, "than to permit this trend toward disaster to continue." The main source of trouble, he went on, was the FEC policy decision of 6 December 1946, encouraging trade unions "to take part in political activities and to support political parties." This provision, he declared, was approved by the United States without his knowledge or the knowledge and approval of any senior official of the Department of the Army. It focused attention on the government unions as the most fertile field in which the Communist party might find a shortcut to political power.[14]

Regarding Killen's separation from SCAP, MacArthur said that he would have been removed had he not resigned. Characterized as a single-minded professional labor leader whose moves were calculated to see established in Japan a labor oligarchy, Killen did little, MacArthur added, to enforce that part of the FEC labor policy which called for democratic election of union officials and public inspection of union finance. This failure, MacArthur believed, resulted in Communist domination of the two large unions of government employees.

To counter Killen's version of the labor controversey, which was accepted by Labor Department officials and United States labor leaders, MacArthur gave his estimate of Killen. Though not a Communist himself, he said, Killen permitted a broad advance in Communist leadership of the unions. That he lost control of Japanese labor was best evidenced by the fact that officials of the union of government communications workers kept Killen waiting outside while they deliberated in closed session for over an hour. When they did elect to permit his appearance, he was subjected to "most unseemly and disrespectful conduct," which was not merely a defiance of Killen but of the occupation, and gave "decisive and final warning of an alarming tendency under communistic influence directed against future occupation policy." [15]

Immediately following his 22 July letter, MacArthur continued, Killen, "in complete insubordination," publicly announced to the press his resignation without previous consultation with his chief of section or with other official authority. This was seen as an effort on Killen's part to arouse Japanese labor against the occupation. Shortly before the issue reached a climax, MacArthur said, Killen himself became increasingly apprehensive over the situation and over his ability to keep it under control. It was proposed, with Killen's full concurrence, that all strikes in Japan in private enterprise and in government be banned by SCAP order. This proposal, MacArthur declared, "I rejected as unthinkable." Furthermore, in a seven-hour conference held with Killen and other interested officials—Marquat, Whitney, Hoover, Kades—in MacArthur's office just before his decision in favor of Hoover, Killen fully accepted the need to ban strikes by government workers. The specific proposal for amending the National Public Service Law to which Killen referred as the crux of the whole issue read: "Personnel of the service shall not strike or engage in delaying tactics which reduce the efficiency of governmental operations." This proposal, MacArthur concluded, appeared to be in complete harmony with United States government policy and practice. [16]

Fifty-two days went by before Washington replied to MacArthur's message. [17] Washington's counterproposals, representing the composite views of the Departments of the Army, State, and Labor need not be summarized here, as their nature is made clear in MacArthur's rejoinder. As MacArthur saw it, Washington's principal objective was to appease those friendly powers, notably the United Kingdom and Australia where labor governments ruled, that interpreted FEC labor policy to embrace state employees as well as workers in private enterprise. As he saw it, the discussions on which the FEC decision was based "clearly refuted such an interpretation." Apart from this, he found it "fantastic to believe" that the highest officials in Washington would endorse policies so completely contrary to American law and precedent. Because the situation in Japan did not lend itself to experimentation with advanced labor concepts, MacArthur thought it prudent for the Japanese to follow the time-honored and successful American practice. Washington's position that government workers should be permitted to strike, "unless expressly forbidden by military fiat," would, in his view, constitute a complete repudiation of his 22 July letter to the prime minister, the essential purpose of which was to curb the strike threat by civil servants, "in the interest of the emergence of responsible government." [18]

Nor could MacArthur see the sense of Washington's referring to him a request by the United States delegation to the United Nations Assembly for background information on the Japanese labor situation, "in the event Soviet Russia raised the subject." Inasmuch as the United Nations had no authority whatever over Japan, which was administered under separate international controls and agreements, he said, the United States delegation "should merely be fully apprised of the international character of the occupation." [19]

MacArthur concluded his case for moderation in the handling of the Japanese labor situation with three points. First, he questioned whether the American taxpayer should be required to underwrite the damage that would result from giving Japanese government workers the right to strike, a right not enjoyed by United States civil servants. Second, in his 22 July letter on this subject, he had resorted to all the coercive pressure he could exert "without radically altering the character of the occupation and legislating by military fiat." Third, he did not believe it was possible for agencies as far away as Washington "to prescribe with wisdom details for the best course for government in Japan." [20] On the last day of November 1948, the National Diet enacted the National Public Service Law Amendment bill on MacArthur's original terms.

Equally instructive was the manner in which MacArthur dealt with a Washington proposal in 1949 to replace him with a high commissioner. In June of that year, Gen. Omar Bradley, Army Chief of Staff, wrote him, saying that the trend of thought in Washington was to have the State Department "take over the Military Government in Japan," once the German government was established and functioning. In his reply, MacArthur told General Bradley that the proposition appeared to reflect a misunderstanding within the Department of the Army as to the situation actually existing in Japan. No military government had ever been established in Japan, he said. The civil phase of the occupation was carried out mainly by civilians recruited in Washington. Of 2,798 persons on duty in SCAP, 2,443 were civilians. On the other hand, in the American Zone of Germany, where Mr. John J. McCloy was about to enter on his duties as High Commissioner, the American forces had actually ruled through military government, and the United States had maintained unilateral control over policy and administration. But in Japan such unilateral control was yielded at the Moscow Conference in late 1945, when an Allied setup was approved by the United States. That setup embodied the

FEC, the Allied Council for Japan, and SCAP. The United States could alter at will the regime of occupation control in the American Zone of Germany, but only the FEC could change the regime of occupation control in Japan. The FEC, he said, could not be expected to surrender its power by voting for a regime of control analagous to that being established in the American Zone of Germany.[21]

MacArthur went further to explain to General Bradley the political folly of making the kind of change proposed. Nothing could give greater impetus to the Communist drive to bring all of Asia under control, he said. A drastic readjustment in the regime of control in Japan "could not fail to be regarded as a decisive step toward yielding in the face of the Communist successes in China and as a tacit acknowledgment of our inability to maintain our position, support our responsibilities, and defend our rights and interest in the Far East."[22]

He also emphasized the immorality of such a change. It would require sacrificing the unique position the United States had attained in the hearts of the Japanese people, "a position of respect bordering on reverence and veneration." To most Japanese, "the benign qualities of the Occupation policy and administration, the bestowal and safeguard of human rights, and the social reformation to enhance individual dignity have made a penetrating and lasting impression." MacArthur placed great store on the "strong spiritual front which has been erected here in Japan against the Communist advance in Asia."[23]

Rather than risk "catastrophic consequences throughout Asia," MacArthur told General Bradley, in the event the proposed change was receiving serious consideration in Washington, he requested the right to present his views to Secretary Acheson and President Truman, before it was too late.[24] With that, General Bradley's project for having the State Department take over in Japan was pigeonholed.

MacArthur reacted similarly to a plan transmitted to him by the Department of the Army in 1950 for defending Japan. Prepared by a National Security Council working committee and concurred in by representatives of the Departments of State and Defense, the National Security Resources Board, and the Central Intelligence Agency, the plan was to be formally considered by the National Security Council just as soon as MacArthur's opinion on it was received. A thoroughly coordinated staff study, obviously put together by zealous middle-level officials, it recommended that Japan's police forces be augmented to supplement United States defensive strength in the Far East, and that MacArthur be directed by the United States government to render all possible assistance in the event of internal subversion or insurrection in Japan.[25] In his reply, MacArthur strongly urged the Department of the Army to oppose adoption of the proposal, which was "unrealistic and dangerous in light of factual and policy considerations." His responsibility to secure the country, he said, was made abundantly clear in the 6 September 1945 directive he had from the president. He had already directed Prime Minister Yoshida to augment the Japanese police forces. But formal centralization of those forces, as proposed, "would require a change in the law either by act of the Diet, which would give rise to . . . general unrest, or by Occupation edict which would be even more harmful." Besides being unnecessary, he said, such action could not be effected without gravely undermining the strength of our position in Japan, "which rests more firmly on the moral support of Japanese public opinion than on the existence or threat of military force." It would be widely interpreted as complete abandonment of the reform of the police system, which was intended to prevent the reemergence of a police state.[26]

MacArthur interpreted the NSC working committee's suggestion about increasing United States defensive strength to mean that Japan should be rearmed and brought into a military alliance with the United States. If that was the intent, he said, the committee failed to consider the political, economic, and other factors involved. Japan was under Allied military occupation, he pointed out, and under Allied policy Japan had been completely disarmed and demilitarized. The first steps taken to reverse this policy would provide a legal rationalization for an attempt at military occupation by the Soviet Union. More than that, the average Japanese citizen would not willingly see Japan remilitarized; "nothing could more quickly and completely alienate the Japanese people from American leadership." As for internal subversion or insurrection, MacArthur said simply that since he would take such action as the situation required, a new directive such as proposed would be superfluous. That ended the matter.[27]

Most of the resentment toward MacArthur was caused by his opposition to the Truman-Acheson policy on the Far East. He had, by default, virtually taken over direction of American Far East affairs, in consequence of which a few of the highest officials in Washington, rather than seeking ways to use his superior knowledge and his ideas, as Roosevelt had done, chose instead to go after his scalp. The Korean War gave them the opening they had been seeking. MacArthur's relief of his several commands by President Truman in April 1951 became a cause célèbre, with highly emotional overtones. To this day, the same emotions are still easily aroused. But what interests us here is the fact that the further we get from the date of his dismissal, the sounder his side of the policy argument seems to become.

When a foreign adventure, like the Bay of Pigs fiasco of 1961, is approved by the nation's civilian leaders, the responsible generals and admirals should feel free to speak up. It is easy to imagine what MacArthur would have done as, say, chairman of the Joint Chiefs of Staff had he attended the high-level discussions preceding that event. National security is too important to leave entirely to the judgment of civilians. The country needs respected public figures like MacArthur to speak out on important foreign policy issues, whether or not their views prove to be acceptable. In a June 1954 syndicated column, Joseph and Stewart Alsop, among the harshest of MacArthur's detractors, defended his position on the Korean War. The free world "would not now be menaced with a catastrophe" in Indochina, they wrote, "if MacArthur had won his fight against artificial limits on the Korean War." [28] Hanson W. Baldwin held with MacArthur that Korea was the right war in the right place and at the right time, "if we wished to stop the spread of Asiatic communism." The French defeat in Indochina and the corrosion of the anti-Communist front in Asia, Baldwin wrote, "stem in part from the equivocal 'peace' in Korea." [29] Richard H. Rovere, no MacArthur fan, thought that the general was fired less for insubordination than for taking his case to the public. "What was wrong," he said, "was the case itself." [30] On this basis, the question can be discussed without heat.

MacArthur believed that, had Truman called him to Washington, he could have convinced the man from Missouri of the logic of his views on Korea in fifteen minutes. Three years before he died, still mindful of his Korean experience, he advised President Kennedy not to put a single American soldier on the continent of Asia. "We would not win a fight in Southeast Asia," he said, warning that if the Chinese moved against us there, we might have to use nuclear weapons. [31]

The root of our troubles in Asia from the 1950s to the 1970s was not MacArthur's insistence on taking out the bridges across the Yalu River and destroying the enemy's supply bases in the privileged sanctuary of Manchuria, but, according to the revisionist view, the Truman Doctrine. According to that doctrine, "it must be the policy of the United States to support free peoples who are resisting attempted subjection by armed minorities or by outside pressures." [32] Its underlying purpose was to contain the USSR. In retrospect, it can be seen that it was based on two false assumptions, that the communist movement was a monolith and that the Kremlin was bent on world dominion. Created and implemented by the leaders of the Truman administration and carried forward by the top advisers of Presidents Eisenhower, Kennedy, Johnson, and Nixon, the policy led to the debacle in Vietnam. Herbert Feis, a Pulitzer prize-winning historian, called the language of the Truman Doctrine "a compound of evangelism, as propounded by extreme and excited internationalists, and of spreadeagle bluster . . . puffed up with the assumption that the United States had the power to make its wishes or its will effective anywhere in the world." [33] Feis also pointed out that the widely respected General Marshall, a principal architect of the doctrine, had "fumbled before Pearl Harbor . . . approved the unworkable setup for Germany, and . . . failed in China." [34] Ironically it was MacArthur, whom Marshall would have fired much earlier, who bluntly warned of a staggering defeat if American ground forces were committed a second time to the Asian mainland. Might Vietnam have been avoided if the Truman administration had let MacArthur fight the Korean War his way, or had the subsequent administrations followed MacArthur's advice, based on the Korean stalemate, not to fight another war on Asian soil?

The Japanese Diet's resolution of gratitude to General MacArthur, adopted within hours of his departure from the country, was not entirely perfunctory, as it afforded each political faction an opportunity to publicly appraise the MacArthur regime. For the record, the Communist party spokesman declared that it was idiotic to say that MacArthur had promoted democratization or set up a self-supporting economy. "What nonsense to say that all Japanese are moved with deep emotion over MacArthur's leaving. Most Japanese wish that the rest of the conquerors would go home." But the feelings of most Japanese were expressed by spokesmen for the other political parties. People's Democrat Miki Takeo remembered that MacArthur protected Japan "against the selfish designs of different Allied nations" and "never thought of inflicting punishment on the Japanese people." Socialist Asanuma Inejiro was thankful that under General MacArthur "we Japanese replaced a feudalistic, despotic, and militaristic system with a truly democratic and peace-loving one, a great revolutionary change brought about without bloodshed." Prime Minister Yoshida was thankful to MacArthur for "the special attention he always gave the Imperial family," and for creating "the present atmosphere for restoring Japan's independence."

MacArthur's dismissal had no substantial effect on Japan's progress toward democracy and independence. Except for a few finishing touches, he had completed his work. Within months a Japanese peace treaty as envisioned by him was signed at San Francisco, and shortly thereafter the occupation came to an end. His insight, obstinacy, and drive had paid off handsomely.

A final word about MacArthur. J. Frank Dobie, a well-known Texan who wrote about the American Southwest, participated briefly in the Department of the Army's post-World War II European Information and Education Program. He did not take kindly to the military way as he observed it. "No idea for emancipating the mind, for enlarging the conception of human rights, or for dignifying human life has ever come out of the military ranks," he grumbled.[35] Had he been sent to Japan, he might have modified his blanket statement somewhat. At the very least he would have been able to agree with Dr. Wilson Compton, then president of Washington State College, who said after visiting Japan early in the occupation: "General MacArthur is not orthodox. . . . His personality is not orthodox. . . . he is not merely a conqueror, but a leader—and it is leadership which Japan wants most."[36]

If MacArthur forged the strong bond of amity and understanding that now links the United States and Japan, does it matter much that he wrapped himself in thundering generalities, or sounded sometimes as though he had just received a special briefing from heavenly quarters? Is not the payoff that he gave the Japanese neither "the bitter bread of defeat nor the galling tutelage of colonial rule, but a new freedom and a new friendship," realizing that "nothing less would do—if history's door was not to slam shut in America's face" (*Time* magazine, 9 May 1949, p. 18)?

MacArthur was appreciated by true liberals. Norman Cousins said of him: "He was not a tub-thumping jingoist. . . . He may have been autocratic in manner but he was democratic in purpose. . . . he wanted ultimately to be remembered . . . as a man determined to create a genuine basis for justice and peace."[37] Samuel Eliot Morison wrote that MacArthur's efforts for peace and goodwill entitled him to a place among the immortals. No proconsul and no conqueror of ancient or modern times equaled him "in winning the hearts of a proud and warlike people who had suffered defeat." His victory was a dual one—"military, and in the highest sense, spiritual."[38]

Notes

In addition to the references cited, this study is based on the author's occupation notes and SCAP documents in his personal files.

Chapter 1

1. The brief and hectic existence of the Military Government Section is described in Richard Tregaskis, "Road to Tokyo," *Saturday Evening Post*, 29 September 1945; 6, 13, 20, 27 October 1945.

2. U.S., State-War-Navy Coordinating Committee (SWNCC). "United States Initial Post-Surrender Policy for Japan." Prepared jointly by officials of the Departments of State, War, and Navy, the document, in substance, was sent to General MacArthur by radio on 29 August 1945 and, after approval by the president, by messenger on 6 September. On 3 November 1945, the "Basic Directive for Post-Surrender Military Government in Japan Proper," approved by SWNCC and concurred in by the Joint Chiefs of Staff, was forwarded to SCAP. These documents are in SCAP, Government Section, *Political Reorientation of Japan, September 1945 to September 1948* (hereafter cited as *Political Reorientation*), 2 vols., 2:423–26, 429–39.

3. In a 1 September 1945 memorandum to the Chief of Staff, General Crist requested that a copy of each of the three proclamations be signed by the Commander-in-Chief. Penciled in the margin of the memorandum was this comment: "Ordered not published by C/G 3 September 1945. WEC."

4. Mamoru Shigemitsu, *Japan and Her Destiny*, pp. 375–77.

5. *The Chrysanthemum and the Sword*.

6. Dean Acheson, *Present at the Creation*, p. 126.

7. Shigeru Yoshida, *The Yoshida Memoirs*, p. 21.

8. Edwin O. Reischauer, *The United States and Japan*, 3d ed., p. 255.

9. Owen Lattimore, *Solution in Asia*, jacket; p. 189.

10. Andrew Roth, *Dilemma in Japan*, pp. 284–91.

11. U.S., SWNCC (approved by the president), "Authority of General MacArthur as Supreme Commander for the Allied Powers," 6 September 1945, *Political Reorientation*, 2:427.

12. Both statements are printed in ibid., pp. 470–71.

Chapter 2

1. See *Political Reorientation*, 2:796–806.

2. *Baltimore Sun* (20 December 1945).

3. SCAPIN 179, "Proceedings of the Diet," 22 October 1945, *Political Reorientation*, 2:695.

4. Ibid., 1:147–48.

5. Ibid., p. 148.

Chapter 3

1. George B. Sansom, review of *Political Reorientation* by SCAP, Government Section, *Pacific Affairs* 24 (September 1951):306–12.
2. *Political Reorientation*, 1:xxix.
3. Ibid., pp. xxvi–xxvii.
4. Hugh Borton, *American Presurrender Planning for Postwar Japan*, 37 pp., passim.
5. *Political Reorientation*, 1:xxvii.
6. Ibid., p. xxxi.
7. Courtney Whitney, *MacArthur: His Rendezvous with History*, p. 249; Douglas MacArthur, *Reminiscences*, pp. 314–15; Charles A. Willoughby, *MacArthur, 1941–1951*, p. 334; W. Macmahon Ball, *Japan . . . Enemy or Ally?*, p. 98; Mark Gayn, *Japan Diary*, pp. 127–28, 177, 338, 474; John Gunther, *The Riddle of MacArthur*, p. 128.
8. SCAPINS 548 and 550, *Political Reorientation*, 2:479–88.
9. Gayn, *Japan Diary*, pp. 42–43.
10. Ibid., pp. 241–42.
11. SCAP, Government Section, *A Brief Report on the Political Reorientation of Japan*, December 1949, p. 20; Hans H. Baerwald, *The Purge of Japanese Leaders under the Occupation*, p. 80.
12. Ball, *Japan . . . Enemy or Ally?*, pp. 190–91.
13. *Political Reorientation*, 1:44.
14. Shortly after General MacArthur died in 1964, General Whitney established residence in Washington, D.C., where I had frequent contacts with him. He answered frankly every question I asked him about the occupation—except one. To my question whether the decision to draft a model constitution was his or General MacArthur's, he replied: "I never accept credit for any decision it was General MacArthur's responsibility to make."
15. *Political Reorientation*, 2:622–23.
16. Kades, conversation, 1971.
17. *Political Reorientation*, 2:680.
18. Whitney, *MacArthur*, pp. 287–89; MacArthur, *Reminiscences*, p. 314; *Political Reorientation*, 1:291–304.
19. Yoshida, *Memoirs*, pp. 43–45.
20. *Political Reorientation*, 1:296.
21. Kazuo Kawai, *Japan's American Interlude*, p. 109.
22. *Political Reorientation*, 1:307–13.
23. Ibid.
24. Irie to Williams, 25 March 1960. Supreme Court Associate Justice Irie Toshio wrote: "Yesterday . . . Chief Justice Dr. Tanaka . . . told me he was given a good suggestion from you about the resolution of the Diet declaring the invalidity of the Imperial Decree concerning Education."
25. Miki Takeo, conversation, 1969.

Chapter 4

1. Sansom, review of *Political Reorientation*, *Pacific Affairs* 24 (September 1951):306–12.
2. Ibid.

3. Swope memorandum, 12 December 1947.
4. Swope to Williams, 21 May 1948; 13 September 1948.
5. Williams to JHU Operations Research Office, 22 April 1952.
6. Harry Emerson Wildes, *Typhoon in Tokyo*, pp. 110–11.
7. Roest memorandum, 23 January 1947.
8. "Road to Tokyo," 29 September 1945; 6, 13, 20, 27 October 1945.
9. Noel F. Busch, "A Report on Japan," *Life* 21 (2 December 1946):115.
10. Sansom, review of *Political Reorientation, Pacific Affairs* 24 (September 1951): 306–12.
11. Kazuo Kawai, *Japan's American Interlude*, p. 107. A full-length study of the local government effort is Kurt Steiner, *Local Government in Japan*, 1965.
12. John Gunther, *The Riddle of MacArthur*, p. 121.
13. Whitney, *MacArthur*, p. 249.
14. *Asahi Evening News*, 22 November 1973.
15. Japanese Ministry of Foreign Affairs to Rizzo, 20 November 1973.
16. Sansom, review of *Political Reorientation, Pacific Affairs* 24 (September 1951):306–12.
17. Oppler to Williams, 31 December 1973.
18. *Political Reorientation*, 2:662–66.
19. Princeton: Princeton University Press.
20. *Political Reorientation*, 2:578.
21. Blaine Hoover, "Address to Civil Service Assembly of the United States and Canada" (Ottawa, Canada, 6 October 1948), p. 2.
22. Ibid., p. 3.
23. Ibid., p. 4.
24. Ibid. pp. 5–6.
25. *Political Reorientation*, 1:258.
26. Representative Matsumoto Takizo telephoned me after midnight to say that the Diet leaders were ignoring the pleas of Baker and Hoover because they were outside Government Section channels.
27. *Yomiuri Shimbun*, 22 December 1948.
28. John M. Maki, *Government and Politics in Japan*, pp. 142–43.
29. Whitney, *MacArthur*, p. 249.
30. Yoshida, *Memoirs*, p. 154.
31. *Who's Who in America, 1948–1949*, s.v. "Bisson, Thomas Arthur."
32. T. A. Bisson, *Japan's War Economy*, pp. xi, 204–5.
33. Wildes, p. 71.
34. Theodore Cohen, interview with Takemae Eiji, 25 December 1971, Tokyo Metropolitan University *Journal of Law and Politics* 14 (1973):16–17.
35. Eleanor M. Hadley, *Antitrust in Japan*, jacket, pp. 9–10.
36. Darnell memorandum, 27 December 1946.

Chapter 5

1. George F. Kennan, *Memoirs, 1925–1950*, pp. 371–72.
2. *Political Reorientation*, 1:xix.
3. Whitney, *MacArthur*, p. 244.
4. Russell Brines, *MacArthur's Japan*, pp. 259–60.
5. Mark Gayn, *Japan Diary*, pp. 180–81.
6. W. Macmahon Ball, *Japan . . . Enemy or Ally?*, pp. 34–37.

7. Kennan, p. 359.

8. *Newsweek*, 27 January 1947, p. 40; 19 March 1947, p. 24; 23 June 1947, p. 24; 8 March 1948, p. 17.

9. Whitney, conversation, 1966.

10. Whitney, *MacArthur*, pp. 132–33.

11. Ibid., p. 146.

12. Ibid., p. 211.

13. Whitney to Osmena, 20 September 1945.

14. Whitney, conversation, 1966.

15. Ibid.

16. Hunsberger, conversation, 1971.

17. Kades, conversation, 1974.

18. MacArthur, *Reminiscences*, p. 205.

19. Liberal party members at 17 March 1948 meeting: Shidehara Kijuro, Uehara Etsujiro, Hitosumatsu Sadayoshi, Yamazaki Takeshi, Saito Takao, Yamaguchi Kikuichiro, Hoshijima Niro, Ono Bamboku, Kudo Tetsuo, Sudo Hideo, Masuda Kaneshichi, Harada Ken, Kuriyama Chojiro.

20. Whitney, *MacArthur*, p. 475.

21. Whitney, conversation, 1966.

22. Carl Darnell report, 2 October 1946.

Chapter 6

1. Toshikazu Kase, *Journey to the Missouri*, p. 243.

2. The Basic Initial Post-Surrender Directive of 3 November 1945 has this instruction: "You will not remove the Emperor or take any steps toward his removal without prior consultation with and advice issued to you through the Joint Chiefs of Staff."

3. Joseph C. Grew, *Turbulent Era*, chap. 36, passim.

4. Henry L. Stimson and McGeorge Bundy, *On Active Service in Peace and War*, p. 626.

5. Edwin O. Reischauer, *The United States and Japan*, 3d ed., p. 261.

6. SWNCC 228, "Reform of the Japanese Governmental System," Theodore McNelly, *Sources in Modern East Asian History and Politics*, pp. 177–86.

7. The State Department made available to the writer the SWNCC 228 folder, including SWNCC 228/1.

8. SCAP, Government Section, "Report to the Far Eastern Commission," 17 January 1946, in the writer's files.

9. George H. Blakeslee, *The Far Eastern Commission*, p. 44.

10. Ibid., p. 45.

11. Hugh Borton, *Japan's Modern Century*, p. 424, n. 7.

12. Theodore McNelly, "The Japanese Constitution: Child of the Cold War," *Political Science Quarterly* 74 (June 1959):179.

13. *Political Reorientation*, 1:98.

14. Ibid., p. 102.

15. Whitney, *MacArthur*, pp. 248–49, 257.

16. MacArthur, *Reminiscences*, p. 302. As of September 1946, "all members [of the FEC] with the exception of the Soviet representative expressed at least qualified approval of the draft Constitution." Blakeslee, p. 58.

17. The Terms of Reference of the Far Eastern Commission contained this statement: "any directives dealing with fundamental changes in the Japanese constitutional structure . . . will be issued only following consultation and following the attainment of agreement in the Far Eastern Commission." State Department, Publication 2888 (September 1947), *Activities of the Far Eastern Commission,* app. 2.

18. *Political Reorientation,* 2:622–23.

19. Blakeslee, pp. 43–45.

20. Four FEC policy decisions sent to SCAP as Joint Chiefs of Staff (JCS) directives between March and October are printed in *Political Reorientation,* 2:658, 659, 661, 667. Regarding the FEC policy decision of 20 March requiring that the Japanese people be given adequate opportunity to study the provisions of the constitution revision bill, SCAP informed the JCS of his compliance, but "most reluctantly, in view of the invalid premise upon which, in my view, it is based, the failure of the U.S. Government to exercise its right of veto at the appropriate time, and its potentially adverse consequences." Concerning the FEC's proposal to make public its 2 July decision to adopt the basic principles of SWNCC 228, SCAP expressed the opinion that such a move "at this time would be a grave, if not fatal, error. . . .[its] publication . . . would tend to provoke a revulsion of the Japanese against any such reform. . . . It would vitiate the requirement . . . that . . . constitutional reform . . . must be responsible to the free will of the Japanese people." The trouble was, according to Professor Blakeslee, that the FEC, thousands of miles away, "could not understand the complicated details of conditions in Japan, and General MacArthur could not appreciate the problems . . . within the Commission of 11 and later 13 different states without close, effective liaison." Blakeslee, pp. 49, 55, 238.

21. Whitney, *MacArthur,* p. 249.

22. Kenzo Takayanagi, "Making the Japanese Constitution: What Really Happened," *Japan Times,* 16 March 1959.

23. Whitney, *MacArthur,* p. 249.

24. Yoshida, *Memoirs,* pp. 132–33.

25. Ibid., p. 133.

26. Whitney, *MacArthur,* p. 251.

27. *Political Reorientation,* 1:105–6.

28. Ibid., 2:624.

29. Ibid., 1:106.

30. Tatsuo Sato, "The Origin and Development of the Draft Constitution of Japan," *Contemporary Japan* 24 (1957):13–15.

31. Ibid., pp. 16–18.

32. The SCAP draft is in ibid., pp. 31–42. The cabinet's 4 March draft is in *Political Reorientation,* 2:625–30.

33. Sato, pp. 17–19.

34. The carbons used by Kades in the conferences mentioned here are in the writer's files.

35. Sato, pp. 20–21. Messrs. Irie and Sato had distinguished postoccupation careers as associate justice of the Supreme Court and president of the National Personnel Authority, respectively.

36. Yoshida, *Memoirs,* p. 143.

37. Japan, Privy Council, Examination Committee on Revision Bill of the

Imperial Constitution, 1st sess., 22 April 1946, pp. 2–7. This is one of the dozen or so copies of the Privy Council hearings and Diet deliberations on the constitution revision bill, in English, made available to SCAP.

38. Ibid., pp. 8–10; 3d sess., 3 June 1946, p. 2.

39. Yoshida, *Memoirs,* pp. 140, 145.

40. *Political Reorientation,* 1:111.

41. SCAP, Government Section, "Diet Report" no. 60–A, 31 August 1946. Under the supervision of the writer, eighty-five such reports were prepared on the deliberations of the Ninetieth Diet.

42. Theodore McNelly, "The Renunciation of War in the Japanese Constitution," *Political Science Quarterly* 77 (September 1962):360, n.15.

43. Ibid., p. 370.

44. Ibid., p. 371, n. 42.

Chapter 7

1. H. Fukui, "Twenty Years of Revisionism," *Washington Law Review* 43 (June 1968):954.

2. John M. Maki, "The Japanese Constitutional Style," ibid., p. 903.

3. H. Fukui, ibid., p. 934.

4. Paul de Gyarmathy, *An Appeal to the Emperor of Japan,* printed as a manuscript (Tokyo, 1945), p. 7.

5. Ibid., p. 11.

6. Ibid., p. 18.

7. Ibid., pp. 18–21.

8. Ibid., pp. 34–35.

9. Ibid., pp. 34–92.

10. Gyarmathy to Williams, 15 March 1946.

11. Gyarmathy to Williams, 18 March 1946.

12. Hugh Borton, "Preparation for the Occupation of Japan," *Journal of Asian Studies* 25 (February 1966):206.

13. SCAPIN 448, 15 December 1945, in *Political Reorientation,* 2:467; William P. Woodward, *The Allied Occupation of Japan 1945–1952 and Japanese Religions,* chap. 27, passim.

14. *Political Reorientation,* 2:460–66.

15. Ibid., 1:101.

16. Ibid., 94.

17. SCAP, CIE, *Press Analysis,* 15, 17, 19, 20, 23, 25, 31 October 1945.

18. Ibid., 21 November 1945; 6, 18, 21–22, 29 December 1945; 1, 27–28 January 1946; 1 February 1946.

19. Ibid., 4, 7, 9 February 1946.

20. Government Section, "Memorandum for Record" (Government Section conferences on preparation of draft constitution), 16 December 1947.

21. Kenzo Takayanagi, "Some Reminiscences of Japan's Commission on the Constitution," *Washington Law Review* 43 (June 1968):970. See also *Political Reorientation,* 1:109–10.

22. CIE, *Press Analysis,* 7 March 1946.

23. Ibid., 8 March 1946.

24. Ibid.

25. Ibid., 9 March 1946.

26. Ibid., 10, 13, 14 March 1946.

27. Ibid., 8 May 1946; 25 June 1946.

28. Ibid., 20 June 1946; 1, 2, 7–8, 25, 26 July 1946; 1, 17, 18–19, 25–26, 27, 28 August 1946; 7 September 1946; 8, 9 October 1946.

29. Teramitsu to Williams, 6 February 1975.

30. CIE, *Publications Analysis*, 23 January 1947.

31. Ibid., 13 June 1947; 15 April 1948.

32. Ibid., 30 June 1948.

33. CIE, *Press Analysis*, 2–3 May 1948; 28 August 1948.

34. ATIS, *Press Translations and Summaries*, 3 May 1949.

Chapter 8

1. Japan, Imperial Diet, *Official Gazette Extra*, no. 12 (19 December 1946).

2. Japan, Imperial Diet, *Minutes of the House of Peers Subcommittee on the Draft Constitution*, 2 October 1946.

3. Ibid., *Minutes of the House of Peers Special Committee on the Diet Law Bill*, 18 March 1947.

4. Far Eastern Commission, Committee no. 3, *Minutes*, 20 January 1947; ibid., 23 January 1947.

5. FEC, "Request for Consultation with SCAP Relative to the Draft Diet Law" (FEC–107/1), 28 January 1947; ibid., Reply of SCAP, 7 February 1947.

6. Ibid., Reply of SCAP, 7 February 1947.

7. FEC, Committee no. 3, *Minutes*, 17 February 1947.

8. Hiroshi Itoh, trans. and ed., *Japanese Politics—An Inside View*, pp. 17–18.

9. Warren M. Tsuneishi, *Japanese Political Style*, p. 95.

Chapter 9

1. Floyd M. Riddick, *The United States Congress*, p. v.

2. ATIS, *Press Translations and Summaries—Japan*, was published daily except Sunday from October 1945 to August 1949. It carried articles selected from representative national and provincial newspapers, magazines, and special journals as well as analyses of current trends in Japanese thought and activity.

3. Alfred Stead, ed., *Japan by the Japanese*, p. 5.

4. Ibid., p. 72.

5. MacArthur to Prime Minister Katayama, 18 September 1947.

6. George B. Sansom, *The Western World and Japan*, p. 6.

7. George Etsujiro Uyehara, *Political Development of Japan, 1867–1909*, pp. 213–14.

8. George B. Galloway, *Congress at the Crossroads*, p. 10.

9. Ibid.

10. Ibid., p. 11.

Chapter 10

1. SCAP, *Summation of Non-Military Activities in Japan*, March 1947, p. 208. Effective with the May 1947 cocoon harvest, the price was upped from ¥98 to ¥154 per *kan*, a retroactive increase from ¥98 to ¥125 was granted for the summer-fall crop of 1946, and for each ten *kan* of cocoons delivered to official

collecting stations the producer would receive a bonus of one *tan* (about 3.9 square yards) of silk cloth.

2. U.S. Department of State, *Administrative Agreement between the United States and Japan,* 28 February 1952, *Bulletin* 26 (10 March 1952):382–90.

Chapter 11

1. Miriam Farley, "SCAP and Government Employees, 1948," *Postwar Japan: 1945 to the Present,* eds. Jon Livingston, Joe Moore, and Felicia Oldfather, p. 169.

2. Mei Ju-ao, "The Future of Japan," ibid., pp. 123–25.

3. W. Macmahon Ball, *Japan . . . Enemy or Ally?*, p. 194.

4. Theodore McNelly, *Politics and Government in Japan,* 2d ed., p. 41.

5. Charles A. Beard and Mary Beard, *America in Midpassage* (New York: Macmillan, 1939), p. 485.

6. Norfolk, Va., MacArthur Archives, Record Group 9, Blue Binder, "NSC," 28 October 1948.

7. Ibid., 8, 12 June 1948; 28 January 1949; 28 July 1949.

8. Ibid., 8, 12 June 1948.

9. Ibid., 2, 18 December 1948.

10. Ibid., 18 December 1948.

11. Ibid., 18, 25, 26 December 1948; 22, 23, 28 January 1949; 22 July 1949.

12. Ibid., 28 July 1949.

13. Marcel Grilli, "Political Reorientation of Japan, 1949–1952," chap. on control of antidemocratic elements, p. 18.

14. MacArthur Archives, Record Group 9, Blue Binder, "Economic Recovery," 5, 11 December 1948; "NSC," 22 January 1949.

15. U.S. Department of State, *Activities of the Far Eastern Commission,* no. 2888, p. 57.

16. MacArthur Archives, Record Group 9, Blue Binder, "NSC," 29 May 1949.

17. MacArthur, *Reminiscences,* p. 307.

18. Kennan, *Memoirs, 1925–1950,* pp. 392–93.

19. MacArthur Archives, Record Group 9, Blue Binder, "NSC," 28 July 1949.

20. Ibid., 28 January 1949.

21. Ibid., 16 April 1949, 28 July 1949.

22. *Political Reorientation,* 2:581–83.

23. MacArthur to Yoshida, 15 September 1949.

24. Yoshida to MacArthur, 18 March 1950.

25. MacArthur to Yoshida, 21 March 1950.

26. T. A. Bisson, *Prospects for Democracy in Japan,* pp. 56–57.

27. Grilli, chap. on popular elections, pp. 16–17.

28. Ibid.

Chapter 12

1. Before most audiences, Colonel Lynch and I were called on for an introductory statement. Colonel Lynch stressed DA's role in the cultural exchange project, and I emphasized SCAP's role. Before the Rotary Club in Columbia, South Carolina, as on other occasions during the tour, my extension of General MacArthur's personal greeting evoked loud and long applause.

2. Washington newspaper coverage of the delegation was skimpy. Stories of

their activities were carried on inside pages of the three big dailies, with few pictures; not a single photograph appeared during the first week. In his *Daily News* column for 17 February 1950, Peter Edson said that the visitors, trying so hard to please, "are under apparent instructions to create no incidents, make no remarks that would be considered out of turn." No member of the delegation ever raised the question of calling on President Truman.

3. George P. Lynch, "Report on Visit to the United States of the Japanese Diet Delegation," Department of the Army, 6 April 1950.

Chapter 13

1. Hoshijima to Williams, 19 August 1958.
2. U.S. War Department, Military Intelligence Division, *Friendly Japanese*, 21 August 1945.
3. Ibid.
4. Chamberlain, *Things Japanese*, 3d ed., rev., pp. 373–74; Benedict, *The Chrysanthemum and the Sword*, chaps. 7 and 8.
5. Robert Jungk, *Vivre à Hiroshima*, pp. 174–76.
6. Kennan, *Memoirs, 1925–1950*, pp. 375–76.
7. Paul F. Langer, *Communism in Japan*, pp. 72–77.
8. Masao Maruyama, *Thought and Behavior in Modern Japanese Politics*, ed. Ivan Morris, chap. 7.

Chapter 14

1. Mark Gayn, review of *MacArthur* by Whitney, *Nation*, 3 March 1956, pp. 181–82.
2. Published in 1965 under the title *The MacArthur Controversy and American Foreign Policy* (New York: Farrar, Strauss and Giroux, Noonday Press).
3. Courtney Whitney, "Summary of Reviews," 5 pp. (1956), Whitney's files.
4. Kennan, *Memoirs: 1925–1950*, p. 500.
5. MacArthur, *Reminiscences*, pp. 302–3.
6. Warren Hunsberger, conversation, 1971.
7. Howard to Robert U. Brown, *Editor and Publisher*, 22 January 1951, Whitney's files.
8. *Editor and Publisher*, 20 January 1951, Whitney's files.
9. Bunker, conversation, 1975.
10. Sid Huff with Joe Alex Morris, *My Fifteen Years with General MacArthur*, pp. 125–26.
11. Nathaniel Peffer's letter in the *New York Times* on 26 October 1945 said: "To allow someone like Prince Konoye to preside at the drafting of Japan's new constitution . . . is grotesque. It is like restoring the Hohenzollerns in Germany—perhaps worse."
12. MacArthur Archives, Record Group 9, Blue Binder, "National Public Service Law Revision Bill," 2 August 1948.
13. Ibid., 14, 17 August 1948.
14. Ibid., 18 August 1948.
15. Ibid.
16. Ibid.
17. Ibid., 9 October 1948.

18. Ibid., 12 October 1948.

19. Ibid.

20. Ibid.

21. MacArthur to Bradley, 16 June 1949, copy in author's files.

22. Ibid.

23. Ibid.

24. Ibid.

25. MacArthur Archives, Record Group 9, Blue Binder, "Japanese National Police Reserve," 1 August 1950.

26. Ibid., 2 August 1950.

27. Ibid.

28. *Washington Post and Times Herald*, 13 June 1954.

29. Hanson W. Baldwin, review of *MacArthur* by Whitney, *New York Times Book Review*, 22 January 1956.

30. Richard H. Rovere, review of *MacArthur* by Whitney, *New Republic*, 9 April 1956, pp. 26–28.

31. Arthur M. Schlesinger, Jr., *A Thousand Days: John F. Kennedy in the White House* (Boston: Houghton Mifflin, 1965), p. 339.

32. Herbert Feis, *From Trust to Terror*, p. 194.

33. Ibid., p. 197.

34. Ibid., p. 171.

35. J. Frank Dobie, "Samples of the Army Mind," *Harper's Magazine*, December 1946, p. 18.

36. Wilson Compton, Honors Convocation Address, University of Washington, Seattle, 15 May 1946.

37. *Saturday Review*, 2 May 1964, pp. 18–19.

38. Samuel Eliot Morison, *Oxford History of the American People* (New York: Oxford University Press, 1965), p. 1065.

Bibliography

Acheson, Dean. *Present at the Creation: My Years in the State Department.* New York: W. W. Norton, 1969.

Baerwald, Hans H. *The Purge of Japanese Leaders under the Occupation.* Berkeley and Los Angeles: University of California Press, 1959.

Ball, W. Macmahon. *Japan . . . Enemy or Ally?* Melbourne, Australia: Cassell, 1948.

Benedict, Ruth. *The Chrysanthemum and the Sword: Patterns of Japanese Culture.* Cambridge, Mass.: Houghton Mifflin, 1946.

Bisson, T. A. *Japan's War Economy.* New York: Macmillan, 1945.

———. *Prospects for Democracy in Japan.* New York: Macmillan, 1949.

Blakeslee, George H. *The Far Eastern Commission: A Study in International Cooperation, 1945–1952.* Washington, D.C.: Government Printing Office, 1953.

Borton, Hugh. *Japan's Modern Century.* New York: Ronald Press, 1955.

———. "Preparation for the Occupation of Japan." *Journal of Asian Studies* 25 (February 1966):203–12.

———. *American Presurrender Planning for Postwar Japan.* New York: East Asian Institute, Columbia University, 1967.

Brines, Russell. *MacArthur's Japan.* Philadelphia and New York: J. B. Lippincott, 1948.

Busch, Noel F. "A Report on Japan." *Life,* 2 December 1946, p. 115.

Byrnes, James F. *Speaking Frankly.* New York: Harper and Bros., 1947.

Chamberlain, Basil Hall. *Things Japanese.* 3d rev. ed. London: John Murray, 1898.

Cohen, Theodore. Interview with Takemae Eiji, 25 December 1971. Tokyo Metropolitan University *Journal of Law and Politics,* Vol. 14, no. 1 (1973).

Cousins, Norman. "Douglas MacArthur." *Saturday Review,* 2 May 1964, pp. 18–19.

Craig, William. *The Fall of Japan.* New York: Dial Press, 1967.

Deverall, Richard L-G. *Red Star Over Japan.* Calcutta: Temple Press, 1952.

Dunn, Frederick S. *Peacemaking and the Settlement with Japan.* Princeton: Princeton University Press, 1963.

Far Eastern Commission. Committee no. 3. *Minutes,* 1946–1947.

Feary, Robert A. *The Occupation of Japan, Second Phase: 1948–1950.* New York: Macmillan, 1950.

Feis, Herbert. *Contest Over Japan.* New York: W. W. Norton, 1967.

———. *From Trust to Terror: The Onset of the Cold War, 1945–1950.* New York: W. W. Norton, 1970.

Fleisher, Wilfrid. *What to Do with Japan.* New York: Doubleday, Doran, 1945.

Fukui, H. "Twenty Years of Revisionism." *Washington Law Review* 43 (June 1968):931–60.

Galloway, George B. *Congress at the Crossroads.* New York: Thomas Y. Crowell, 1946.

Gayn, Mark. *Japan Diary*. New York: William Sloane Associates, 1948.
———. Review of *MacArthur: His Rendezvous with History* by Whitney. *Nation*, 3 March 1956, pp. 181–82.
Grew, Joseph C. *Turbulent Era: A Diplomatic Record of Forty Years*, 2 vols. Boston: Houghton Mifflin, 1952.
Grilli, Marcel. "Political Reorientation of Japan, 1949–1952." Typescript. SCAP, Government Section, 1952.
Gunther, John. *The Riddle of MacArthur*. New York: Harper and Bros., 1950.
Gyarmathy, Paul de. *An Appeal to the Emperor of Japan*. Tokyo: privately printed, 1945.
Hadley, Eleanor M. *Antitrust in Japan*. Princeton: Princeton University Press, 1970.
Hearn, Lafcadio. *Japan: An Attempt at Interpretation*. New York: Macmillan, 1910.
Huff, Sid, with Morris, Joe Alex. *My Fifteen Years with General MacArthur*. New York: Paperback Library, 1964.
Hunt, Frazier. *The Untold Story of Douglas MacArthur*. New York: Devin-Adair, 1954.
Ike, Nobutaka. *Japanese Politics*. 2d ed. New York: Alfred A. Knopf, 1972.
Ito, Hirobumi. *Commentaries on the Constitution of the Empire of Japan*. 3d ed. Translated by Miyoji Ito. Tokyo: Chuo Daigaku, 1931.
Itoh, Hiroshi, trans. and ed. *Japanese Politics—An Inside View: Readings from Japan*. Ithaca: Cornell University Press, 1973.
James, D. Clayton. *The Years of MacArthur*, 2 vols. to date. Boston: Houghton Mifflin, 1970–.
Japan, Imperial Diet. *Hearings on the Constitution of Japan*. House of Representatives and House of Peers plenary, committee, and subcommittee sessions, Ninetieth Diet, 8 vols. (in English and Japanese), 1946.
Japan, Imperial Diet. *Official Gazette Extra. Minutes of the Proceedings of the House of Representatives*, Ninetieth, Ninety-first, and Ninety-second sessions, 1946–1947.
Japan, National Diet. *Official Gazette Extra. Minutes of the Proceedings of the House of Representatives*, sessions 1–13, 1947–1952.
Japan, Privy Council. *Hearings on the Constitution of Japan* (in English and Japanese), 1946.
Johnstone, William C. *The Future of Japan*. New York: Oxford University Press, 1945.
Jungk, Robert. *Vivre à Hiroshima*. Paris: Arthaud, 1960.
Kase, Toshikazu. *Journey to the Missouri*. New Haven: Yale University Press, 1950.
Kawai, Kazuo. *Japan's American Interlude*. Chicago: University of Chicago Press, 1960.
Kennan, George F. *Memoirs, 1925–1950*. Boston: Little, Brown, 1967.
Langer, Paul F. *Communism in Japan*. Stanford: Hoover Institution Press, 1972.
Lattimore, Owen. *Solution in Asia*. Boston: Little, Brown, 1945.
Lee, Clark, and Henschel, Richard. *Douglas MacArthur*. New York: Henry Holt, 1952.
Livingston, John; Moore, Joe; and Oldfather, Felicia, eds. *Postwar Japan: 1945 to the Present*. New York: Pantheon Books, 1973.

Lohbeck, Don. *Patrick J. Hurley.* Chicago: Henry Regnery, 1956.

Lynch, George P. "Report on Visit to the United States of the Japanese Diet Delegation." Mimeographed. Washington, D.C.: Department of the Army, 6 April 1950.

MacArthur, Douglas. *Reminiscences.* New York: McGraw-Hill, 1964.

McNelly, Theodore. "The Japanese Constitution: Child of the Cold War." *Political Science Quarterly* 74 (June 1958):176–95.

———. "The Renunciation of War in the Japanese Constitution." *Political Science Quarterly* 77 (September 1962):350–78.

———. ed. *Sources in Modern East Asian History and Politics.* New York: Appleton-Century-Crofts, 1967.

———. *Politics and Government in Japan,* 2d ed. Boston: Houghton Mifflin, 1972.

Maki, John. *Government and Politics in Japan: The Road to Democracy.* New York: Frederick A. Praeger, 1962.

———. "The Japanese Constitutional Style." *Washington Law Review* 43 (June 1968):893–929.

Maruyama, Masao. *Thought and Behavior in Modern Japanese Politics.* Expanded. Edited by Ivan Morris. New York: Oxford University Press, 1969.

Meller, Norman. *Institutional Adaptability: Legislative Reference in Japan and the United States.* Beverly Hills, Cal.: Sage Publications, 1974.

Nippon Times, 1945–1952.

Norfolk, Va. MacArthur Archives. Record Group 9, Blue Binder. *Messages, 1945–1951.* Boxes labeled "NSC," "Economic Recovery," "National Public Service Law Revision Bill," and "Japanese National Police Reserve."

Oppler, Alfred C. *Legal Reform in Occupied Japan: A Participant Looks Back.* Princeton: Princeton University Press, 1976.

Pacific Stars and Stripes, 1945–1952.

Quigley, Harold S., and Turner, John E. *The New Japan: Government and Politics.* Minneapolis: University of Minnesota Press, 1956.

Reischauer, Edwin O. *The United States and Japan.* 3d ed. New York: Viking Press, 1965.

———. *The Japanese.* Cambridge: Belknap-Harvard Press, 1977.

Riddick, Floyd M. *The United States Congress: Organization and Procedure.* Washington, D.C.: National Capitol Publishers, 1949.

Roth, Andrew. *Dilemma in Japan.* Boston: Little, Brown, 1945.

Sansom, George B. *The Western World and Japan.* New York: Alfred A. Knopf, 1950.

———. Review of *Political Reorientation of Japan* by SCAP, Government Section. *Pacific Affairs* 24 (September 1951):306–12.

Sato, Tatsuo. "The Origin and Development of the Draft Constitution of Japan." *Contemporary Japan,* vol. 24, nos. 4–6, 7–9 (1957).

Scalapino, Robert A., and Masumi, Junnosuke. *Parties and Politics in Contemporary Japan.* Berkeley and Los Angeles: University of California Press, 1962.

SCAP. Civil Information and Education Section. *Publications Analysis; Press Analysis; Prefectural Press Analysis.* 1945–1948.

———. G–2. Allied Translator and Interpreter Section. *Press Translations and Summaries.* September 1945 to August 1949.

———. Government Section. "Report to the Far East Commission." 17 January 1946.

————. Government Section. "Memorandum for Record" (Government Section conferences on preparation of draft constitution, 5–12 February 1946), 16 December 1947, 18 pp.

————. Government Section. *Political Reorientation of Japan, September 1945 to September 1948*, 2 vols. Washington, D.C.: Government Printing Office, 1949.

————. Government Section. *A Brief Progress Report on the Political Reorientation of Japan.* December 1949.

————, Public Information Office. *Selected Data on the Occupation of Japan.* 1950.

————. *Summation of Non-Military Activities in Japan.* 35 vols. September–October 1945 through August 1948.

Sebald, William, with Brines, Russell. *With MacArthur in Japan: A Personal History of the Occupation.* New York: W. W. Norton, 1965.

Shigemitsu, Mamoru. *Japan and Her Destiny: My Struggle for Peace.* New York: E. P. Dutton, 1958.

Stead, Alfred, ed. *Japan by the Japanese.* London: William Heinemann, 1904.

Steiner, Kurt. *Local Government in Japan.* Stanford: Stanford University Press, 1965.

Stimson, Henry L., and Bundy, McGeorge. *On Active Service in Peace and War.* New York: Harper and Bros., 1947.

Takayanagi, Kenzo. "Making the Japanese Constitution: What Really Happened." *Nippon Times,* 16 March 1959.

————. "Some Reminiscences of Japan's Commission on the Constitution." *Washington Law Review* 43 (June 1968):961–78.

Tregaskis, Richard. "Road to Tokyo." *Saturday Evening Post,* 29 September 1945; 6, 13, 20, 27 October 1945.

Truman, Harry S. *Memoirs,* vol. 1, *Year of Decisions.* New York: Doubleday, 1955.

Tsuneishi, Warren M. *Japanese Political Style.* New York: Harper and Row, 1966.

Tuchman, Barbara W. *Stilwell and the American Experience in China, 1911–45.* New York: Bantam Books, 1971.

U.S. Department of the Army, Public Information Division. *Civil Affairs in Occupied and Liberated Territory: Weekly Digest of Press Opinion.* 1945–1948.

U.S. Department of State. *Occupation of Japan: Policy and Progress.* Far East Series, vol. 17, no. 2671 (1946).

————. *Activities of the Far Eastern Commission.* Far East Series, vol. 24, no. 2888 (1947).

————. *Foreign Relations of the United States 1948,* vol. 6. *The Far East and Australia.* Washington, D.C.: Government Printing Office, 1974.

Uyehara, George Etsujiro. *Political Development of Japan, 1867–1909.* London: Constable, 1910.

Ward, Robert E. *Japan's Political System.* Englewood Cliffs, N.J.: Prentice-Hall, 1967.

Whitney, Courtney. *MacArthur: His Rendezvous with History.* New York: Alfred A. Knopf, 1955.

Wildes, Harry Emerson. *Typhoon in Tokyo.* New York: Macmillan, 1954.

Williams, Justin. "The Japanese Diet under the New Constitution." *American Political Science Review* 42 (October 1948):927–39.

————. "Party Politics in the New Japanese Diet." *American Political Science Review* 42 (December 1948):1163–80.

————. "Making the Japanese Constitution: A Further Look." *American Political Science Review* 59 (September 1965):665–79.

————. "Completing Japan's Political Reorientation, 1947–1952: Crucial Phase of the Allied Occupation." *American Historical Review* 73 (June 1968):1454–69.

Willoughby, Charles A. *MacArthur, 1941–1951.* New York: McGraw-Hill, 1954.

Woodward, William P. *The Allied Occupation of Japan 1945–1952 and Japanese Religions.* Leiden, The Netherlands: E. J. Brill, 1972.

Yanaga, Chitoshi. *Japanese People and Politics.* New York: John Wiley and Sons, 1956.

Yoshida, Shigeru. *The Yoshida Memoirs: The Story of Japan in Crisis.* Translated by Kenichi Yoshida. Boston: Houghton Mifflin, 1962.

Index

Index